A
HISTORY OF GREEK
LITERATURE

CW01496673

A
HISTORY OF GREEK
LITERATURE

From Homer to the Hellenistic Period

Albrecht Dihle

translated by
Clare Krojzl

Routledge
Taylor & Francis Group

LONDON AND NEW YORK

First published by C.H. Beck'sche
Verlagsbuchhandlung 1991

First published in English 1994
by Routledge
2 Park Square, Milton Park, Abingdon, Oxfordshire OX14 4RN

Simultaneously published in the USA and Canada
by Routledge
711 Third Avenue, New York, NY 10017

Routledge is an imprint of the Taylor & Francis Group, an informa business

First issued in paperback 2013

© 1991 C.H. Beck'sche Verlagsbuchhandlung, Munich

Translation © 1994 Routledge

Typeset in Garamond by
Ponting–Green Publishing Services, Chesham, Bucks

All rights reserved. No part of this book may be
reprinted or reproduced or utilized in any form or by
any electronic, mechanical, or other means, now
known or hereafter invented, including photocopying
and recording, or in any storage or information
retrieval system, without permission in writing
from the publishers.

British Library Cataloguing in Publication Data
A catalogue record for this book is available from
the British Library

Library of Congress Cataloging in Publication Data
Dihle, Albrecht.
[Griechische Literaturgeschichte. English]
History of Greek literature: from Homer to the Hellenistic
Period / Albrecht Dihle.
p.   cm.
Includes bibliographical references and index.
1. Greek literature–History and criticism.   I. Title.
PA3057.D513   1994
880.9–dc20   93–45284

ISBN 978-0-415-08620-2 hardcover
ISBN 978-0-415-64291-0 paperback

CONTENTS

CONTENTS

Part IV   Hellenistic literature

PREFACE

An attempt will be made in the pages that follow to give an account of the most important events in Greek literature from its beginnings up to the age of Augustus. The reasons for this time-span will hopefully become clear from the account itself, and will be further discussed in the Epilogue.

This book is concerned with literary history in the conventional sense, i.e. with both the historical circumstances in which specific opportunities for linguistic and literary communication were discovered and implemented, and the emergence, development and repercussions of literary forms. These objectives should explain the endeavour to examine linguistic works of art as far as possible in terms of their wider historical background.

So far the most concerted efforts to come to terms with Greek literature date from the humanist tradition. This way of thinking about and looking at literature first manifested itself in the intellectual life of the Imperial Roman period, in the attention paid to Classical Greek and Roman works. Later it also became the established approach in fifteenth- and sixteenth-century Renaissance Europe. It is characterised by a tendency to deal with individual literary works of art to some degree in isolation, viewing them primarily as documents of specific moral and aesthetic values which are acknowledged as indispensable by the observer. For this approach, the historical background to a work may be interesting, but is not important for evaluating the work itself.

The fact that our own civilisation – and by no means solely the literary and philosophical spheres – has largely been shaped by the values of this humanist tradition makes it more than legitimate to seek a deeper understanding of its Greek foundations as part of our inquiry into the nature of humanism. Every generation in the last century has supplied examples of how such inquiry can bring forth fresh insights into the nature of Greek literature, thus demonstrating most forcibly the enduring fruitfulness of this tradition. Scholars and amateurs alike can still gain as many aesthetic and moral insights by examining a Sophoclean tragedy today as they could a hundred or two hundred years ago. These insights are valuable inasmuch as they enrich the discernment of readers and audiences with new perspectives or heightened intensity, thus increasing their capacity to face intellectual challenges.

PREFACE

It has none the less been generally apparent since the nineteenth century at least that while the constructive insights gained in the manner described above – and the notions about the nature of Greek tragedy that derive from them – are valid in the sense indicated, they have little to do either with what Greek tragedy was about in the fifth century BC, or with the intentions of their poets. It therefore behoves scholars concerned with examining the great works of Greek literature as a fountainhead of our own humanist-oriented civilisation – while on the other hand remaining cognisant of the potential inherent in investigating historical facts – to test their convictions continuously against the results of historical inquiry. The failure to do so, for fear of jeopardising one's own convictions, leads scholars to a perpetual *sacrificium intellectus*, as no few exponents of neo-humanism of various shades have indeed shown, and continue to show. Alternatively, where scholars attempt to dispense with the values upheld by tradition, with the aim of focusing on ancient texts in an unhampered way, their inquiry is left devoid of direction, since this approach removes all incentive to broach the question posed by the ancient text, insofar as the scholar is correlating its newly interpreted message with his or her own values and those laid down by tradition.

Fresh access to the foundations of our own civilisation is thus nowadays only available to scholars prepared to meet two conditions: firstly, to take seriously the tradition relating to the objects of inquiry, and take it into account when formulating questions; secondly, the willingness, based on newly acquired insights, to correct or modify the traditional values underpinning inquiries – in other words not to be cavalier with the capacity of the intellect to free itself from traditional criteria, or modify their validity.

Scholars have admittedly long been aware that a cherished misinterpretation of ancient achievements, derived from the perceptions and exigencies of a subsequent epoch, has proved a thousand times over in human history to be a catalyst for intellectual growth. The history of literary genres across the boundaries between ages, languages and peoples, for example, is a string of such productive misunderstandings. In reality, however, only naive misunderstandings of this kind are productive – those whose emergence has not entailed a deliberate neglect of existing possibilities for verification in the epoch concerned. Since the nineteenth century, when history was truly discovered, and the dramatic increase in opportunities for interpreting documents in terms of their specific historical context, this naivety displayed when dealing with ancient literary documents has become a matter for concern.

Taking seriously the humanist tradition and its values, and examining the documents on which it is based in terms of those values, while at the same time not skirting the issue of the historical background to particular works of art, is no easy task. It places severe demands principally on intellectual integrity, and grows no easier as research advances. On the other hand, a rich panorama of all ancient culture has gradually been opened up, and concomitantly, an ever more complicated background of historical – which implies unique in each case – causes, effects and conditions has been uncovered against which specific documents need to be looked at. While this process debunks the naive notion of the absolutely timeless, normative validity of the great classics, it nevertheless also highlights with far greater clarity and subtlety their relevance for human civilisation – a relevance that far transcends the respective epochs in which they were written – as well as facilitating an understanding of the traditions to which they gave rise. As historical scholarship advances, the spectrum of what is seen as important or potentially important in ancient culture is constantly being expanded and enriched. It is sufficient to recall the literature of the Archaic epoch, for example, which has only recently come to be appreciated as a testimony to human civilisation in its own right, rather than merely an incomplete preparatory stage preceding the Classical.

This book makes no attempt to offer a synthesis of the historical and humanist perspectives. It limits itself to the historical viewpoint, since the modern reader, shaped by the prevalent forces in modern intellectual life, is more accustomed to seeking a descriptive and normative accommodation of material, therefore being particularly in need of aids to understanding that derive from a historical treatment of it. The fact that such a study is based on a humanist preconception, i.e. a positive presupposition about the value of the subject-matter, should not be concealed, any more than the hope that as it proceeds the account will confirm the correctness of that presupposition.

A book such as this is intended to facilitate rather than take the place of reading Greek poetry and prose works – either in the original or in translation. For this reason the number of specimen texts has been kept to a minimum, although these cannot be dispensed with entirely where the mode of thought and expression of the author in question is particularly far removed from our own, as is the case notably with Archaic literature. Greek literature of the Classical and post-Classical periods is marked by such a degree of continuity with the literary and philosophical conventions of Europe – via the Romans, Christianity and the humanist tradition – that it is relatively rare for the modern reader to encounter barriers to understanding that can only be overcome exclusively by means of historical research. In the reading of Archaic texts, however, such barriers are commonplace. Since the major foundations of modern intellectual life were still being laid during the Archaic epoch, whereas they were already in place by the Classical and post-Classical periods, communication with Thucydides or Plato in the modern era poses fewer obstacles than one might expect, given the time gap involved. To put it another way, the obstacles we encounter to our understanding reside in the subject-matter being discussed or the subtlety of speculation about it, rather than in the idiosyncrasies of their historical context.

The Bibliography at the end of the book has been kept as brief as possible, having been compiled solely with the aim of assisting interested non-specialists or students in rapid orientation or finding more detailed information in one or other specialist area.

PREFACE TO THE REVISED EDITION

For the new edition of this short history of literature additions and modifications have been made to the text at certain points, while the Bibliography has been thoroughly revised to bring it in line with advances made in Classical studies during the last decade. The author would like to thank the editors of the first edition for correcting numerous errors and oversights. It only remains for me to express my indebtedness to Albin Lesky for his valuable comments, communicated by letter, over and above his editing suggestions.

Part I

ARCHAIC LITERATURE

1

THE BEGINNINGS AND
THE EARLY EPIC POEM

There has been a need felt since the very earliest times to stylise verbal utterances containing a meaning that transcends the specifically everyday context. This is accomplished by employing rhythmic and tonal counterparts, and by distinguishing such utterances from everyday speech with the aid of a specially selected vocabulary. In this way, the invocation of gods, magic spells, accounts of memorable events and the formulation of a personal experience or of craftsmanship skills are all made easier to memorise, as well as being endowed through their very outward form with greater force than the casual utterances of everyday life. Virtually every nation can be shown to possess the above-mentioned dispositions towards a literature, arising as they do out of the aspiration to clothe significant utterances that are worth being handed down in a form that is appropriate to circumstances.

We tend to associate the word 'literature' with the notion of a written form, but the art of verbal stylisation connected with significant utterances can clearly attain a high standard of accomplishment without the society in question necessarily having a written language at its disposal. Conversely, it has also been shown that the writing systems of ancient or exotic peoples were by no means always used, or even devised, for literary purposes. In many cases they were developed in the first instance to facilitate trade and administration in such tasks as drawing up inventories and similar documents.

Where, however, a writing system is indeed used to record literary texts, this has major repercussions for the art of language. Fresh potential arises for handing down texts, for literary reference to earlier works, for the arrangement of subject-matter and for imparting language skills. One of the unique attributes of Greek literature, indeed, is the fact that the two earliest known extant works, which for various reasons exerted an influence on subsequent developments that can scarcely be overestimated, both date from the transition period between oral and written poetry. This holds good not merely in the mechanical sense that they represent the first written records of works both composed and handed down in oral form. They in fact document the use of stylistic devices that were originally invented for oral purposes, in poetry composed in written form, but intended for oral performance.

These documents thus form an inseparable compositional unity with purely oral poetry.

In this very specific sense, therefore, the two major extant epic poems, the *Iliad* and the *Odyssey*, document the emergence of literature in a way unmatched by any other extant work in world literature. More than this, they represent the earliest and perhaps most impressive records depicting the Greek world and its people, as well as the threshold to a long literary tradition in which authors were to have recourse to them again and again as admired models.

The historical preconditions that led up to the emergence of Greek epic poetry are briefly as follows: the first Greek-speaking tribes to migrate into the Balkan peninsula in the period around 2000 BC were very soon influenced in their new homeland by an advanced pre-Greek civilisation centred on the wealthy palaces of Crete. This highly distinctive culture, which was in communication with both the Greek mainland and Egypt by virtue of its vigorous maritime commercial traffic, was to live on in later Greek tradition in the legends about King Minos of Knossos. It is for this reason that archaeologists, excavating Cretan palaces since the beginning of the twentieth century, tend to refer to it as the Minoan civilisation. Under this influence, the Greeks had developed an advanced culture by the middle of the second millennium BC. Despite adopting countless details from Crete in terms of mores, dress, technology and religion, among other spheres, it differed in a number of substantial respects from its Cretan archetype. The palaces of Crete, for example, are open edifices, evincing a sophisticated capacity for the enjoyment of life. The seats of the rising early Greek state, on the other hand, are defiant, massive strongholds.

By the middle of the second millennium BC, the Greeks seem to have gained hegemony over previous cultural centres. They continued the commercial activity of their Minoan predecessors, cultivating links with Syria, Egypt, Sicily and Spain, founding colonies on the Aegean islands, as well as on the mainland of Asia Minor.

Greek acquisitions from the Cretans included a writing system that they adapted to suit their language. This system has been successfully deciphered: the texts – clay tablets documenting lists of tribute and similar material – provide insight into the make-up of the state and society. Theirs was a state system and society rigidly structured along hierarchical lines, with an extensive bureaucracy and highly advanced military organisation – a fitting counterpart to the monarchies in power in the Near East and Egypt at that time. This culture was highly homogeneous throughout Greece, and has left palpable archaeological relics in the form of strongholds, sewage systems, ostentatious tombs and other such monuments. Its main centres were in the fertile plains of Messenia and Laconia, on Aegina and in Athens, Boeotia and Thessaly, as well as on the Ionian islands. The most impressive of all its cultural centres, however, was located in the Argolis where, to this day, the

4

massive walls of Tiryns and Mycenae bear witness to the glory of the age. It is not known whether the dynasty resident in Mycenae exercised hegemony over the remainder of Greece, but Mycenae has rightly lent its name to the whole culture in the language of scholarship.

This culture suffered complete disintegration during the last quarter of the second millennium, the Mycenaean strongholds being destroyed and abandoned. This occurred against the background of a huge wave of migration that shook the entire eastern Mediterranean region, also putting an end to the great Hittite Empire in Anatolia. Around this time, a new, as yet uncivilised Greek tribe migrated into Hellas. It is difficult to ascertain whether these Dorians drove out or wiped out the ruling class of Mycenaean culture everywhere. Social upheavals may also have been taking place apart from any action by the Dorians. At all events, the Greek population was in a state of flux, so that by the onset of the historical age, some time around the tenth century BC, a distinct division of dialects had taken place that sheds light on the outcome of those upheavals.

Extending over wide areas of the Peloponnese, northern and central Greece, and the southern islands of the Aegean, was the region of the Doric, north-western Greek language, dominated by the idiom of the most recent immigrants. Major local differences in the degree of persistence of certain earlier dialect features were nevertheless retained. In the heart of the Peloponnese, in the inaccessible mountain country of Arcadia, as well as on remote Cyprus, a dialect persisted that may be regarded as a direct descendant of Mycenaean Greek. Numerous inhabitants from Mycenaean cultural areas seem to have migrated *en masse* at the end of the second millennium BC to Attica, where the Dorians were never able to penetrate. Refugees such as these then settled both on the central Aegean islands and along the coast of Asia Minor immediately opposite them – an ancient outlet for Mycenaean commerce. Similarly, the Ionic linguistic region extended from Attica across Euboea, Chios, Naxos and other islands, as far as Ephesus and Miletus in Anatolia. Migrants from northern Greece ultimately settled the islands of the northern Aegean and the north-west coast of Asia Minor. Like Ionic, their dialect, known as Aeolic, also derives from Mycenaean, although remaining more akin to it than the former.

The differentiation process of Greek dialects, documented by inscriptions, persisted until the final centuries of the pre-Christian era, and was to become a major factor in Greek literature. The fact that these differences could develop to such a marked degree (Spanish and Italian are probably more closely related than Lesbian and Laconian) relates to social and economic developments following the demise of the Mycenaean culture. The ensuing, so-called 'dark centuries' witnessed throughout Greece a simple, robust peasant culture associated with a feudal social structure. They are also known as the geometric period on account of the exclusively geometrically stylised ornamentation (circles, curves, angles, etc.) used to decorate the austerely structured clay vessels of that time. Unlike the various districts during the Mycenaean era, in this period there was considerable divergence among material cultures, which may be attributed to their distinctly separate ways of life. Similarly, links with the non-Greek world were far more limited than in the Mycenaean period. It was the Phoenicians who carried on the heritage of the Mycenaeans as the leading trading nation of the eastern Mediterranean, and it was from them that the Greeks took their script, adapting it to their own language, at the end of this 'dark age', some time in the mid-eighth century BC. The writing skill utilised by the Mycenaean authorities, and possibly mastered by no more than a handful of professional scribes, had disappeared with the destruction of their strongholds.

The Greeks of this 'dark age' none the less continued to recall the glorious Mycenaean age: the massive walls of the abandoned strongholds were there for all to see. The cult of the dead persisted for centuries at a number of royal burial places, while many a noble dynasty rightly or wrongly traced its origins back to those who had once reigned in the great strongholds. Such recollection of the magnificent past was particularly active among Greeks who had found a new home in Asia Minor. Precisely because the land in which they had settled was devoid of all traces of Mycenaean history, they felt the need for this cultivation of a verbal tradition. A typical colonial people in this regard, they were able to deal with that tradition with greater intellectual agility than the Greeks of the mother country.

None the less, it was through the medium of oral epic poetry that information about this long-lost glory was formed into a garland of myths, which even today has lost none of its attractive force, and which continues to supply European literature with motifs, metaphors and symbols.

Oral heroic poetry exists or has existed among many peoples. Our understanding of Homeric poetry has been greatly enhanced by the Austrian scholar Murko and the American scholar Milman Parry, who have made detailed studies of the oral poetry of south Slavonic Muslims, which was still a living tradition until very recently. The preconditions and structural elements of oral epic poetry may be described roughly as follows.

In a society of largely aristocratic make-up, and above all among its leading families, there is a need to keep alive the memory of forefathers and their deeds. This helps to bolster both their own privileged position and the system of values associated with it. In other forms of society, a sense of history of this kind is linked more with such social institutions as the believing community, the nation or class. Leisure time is thus pleasurably taken up with listening again and again to accounts of the deeds of forefathers, already highly familiar in outline. The more often they are repeated, the better it is to hear them from people who are outstanding for their powers of recollection, their creative genius and their elegance of speech. This earliest class of 'intellectuals' thus found itself responsible for the technical perfection of these accounts. Over the course of generations, this work produced a poetry, often accompanied by music. During this process, oral epic poetry was able to draw in full measure on the specific technical achievements of other forms of early poetry, prayer and magic formulas, and working and marching songs.

For technical reasons of memorability and educational psychology, the verse form, recited or sung in a continuous rhythm, recommended itself for such accounts, having been adapted more and more to the requirements of narrative within the craftsmanship tradition. It was this form that lent oral performance its memorable quality. Accounts composed in verse form, however, cannot simply be repeated word for word every time. The audience hopes each time to hear the well-known episode about the combat between two famous heroes performed more beautifully than ever before by the wandering bard. The latter is only able to meet this demand for a freshly formulated, improvised account, firstly by possessing a perfect command of every single detail of the handed-down version, and secondly by having at his disposal a readily accessible storehouse of expressions adapted to the verse form.

The development of a storehouse of formulas is indeed the main prerequisite for oral epic poetry. Traditionally, every hero is associated with a particularly remarkable weapon; in other cases the name of his father is important; a famous horse is distinguished by its colour, or a town by its seven gates, etc. Each and every hero and theme is in this way endowed with at least one epithet that triggers the familiar association in the listener. However, such a combination of a noun and its characteristic adjective cannot, for reasons of rhythm, simply be inserted at any point in the verse, particularly if it is structured in a regular sequence of long and short syllables. This situation is further complicated by the fact that the rhythmic value of the combination can change as soon as it is placed in a different number or case. All this called for a large number of parallel forms, to enable the characters and themes of a narrative to appear if possible at any point in the verse and in any grammatical context, and still be properly recognised as such. In the case of simple appellatives such as cow, town, sea or sword, performers could obviously bring in as many synonyms as possible.

On the other hand, the use of differently worded formulas having the same meaning and rhythmical value was avoided, simply in order not to overtax the memory. It goes without saying that this stereotyped language, refined and consolidated by centuries of constantly renewed accounts of the same events, came to describe in a virtually mechanical way an abundance of long-forgotten themes and circumstances, involving many words and names whose meaning was no longer understood by anyone, including the poet. It was these very words, firmly embedded in verse, however, which lent poetry its ceremonial, momentous tone.

Nevertheless, the use of formulas went further than this. Memorable incidents from the heroic past include typical features. The taking of arms, combat, injury, councils of war, meals, burial and other scenes are mostly

7

described by the improvising poet using set formulas, which may comprise one or several verses. Overall, therefore, it may be asserted that such a poet composes his or her work of art from formulas rather than words as such. All this applies to extant Homeric poetry, whose total of 28,000 verses contain at least 25,000 formulas, and which by comparison display few features suggesting a written conception of the relevant passages.

It may be stated with some certainty that oral epic poetry of the kind described above already existed in the Mycenaean period. Book 10 of the *Iliad*, for example, describes through the devices of epic language a helmet which according to current (archaeological) knowledge of the era had already fallen into disuse by the end of the Mycenaean period, hence prior to the final catastrophe. The Greeks – or the Achaeans, as they are called in the *Iliad*, written before the name Hellenes became a generic term – are denoted by the epithet 'those with the good greaves'. This relates to the fact that throughout the Mediterranean world of the second millennium BC greaves were an item of armour known solely in Greece, whereas by the first millennium they had become indispensable for heavily armed men everywhere. Similarly, a number of locations mentioned in the *Iliad* and the *Odyssey*, verifiable from the descriptions given, bear names which were unknown to the Greeks of the historical age, and which must, therefore, derive from Mycenaean names.

A study of Homeric language is similarly instructive. Scholars have long been aware that this poetry was written in a synthetic language that had never been spoken, combining elements which never appeared side by side in any historically demonstrable dialect. Homeric Greek is closest, if anything, to the Ionic dialect; to this may be added the fact that diverse traditions tell of a particularly active cultivation of epic poetry in the Ionian colonial lands in Asia Minor and its offshore islands.

Nevertheless, so deeply embedded in the Ionic fund of poetry that its various layers are impossible to separate, are elements that were formerly termed Aeolic, denoting a stage in the development of epic poetry that can be located in the north-west Anatolian colonial region. Nowadays, however, there is an increasing tendency to regard these elements as archaisms, components from Mycenaean Greek which preceded the process of dialect differentiation after the great wave of migration.

The picture that emerges from all this is of a history of oral epic poetry in which a shift took place from the princely courts of the Mycenaean period to the noble courts and rising towns of Ionian and Aeolian emigrants to Asia Minor, culminating in the first written records of oral compositions some time after the adoption of the Phoenician alphabet.

The history of oral epic poetry may also be traced on the basis of other details. Poets were very fond of illustrating the mood of key scenes in their accounts by means of extensive similes. Thus, whereas the heroes themselves lived and moved in a world in which, as in the Mycenaean culture, only bronze was known, these similes contain references to iron, which did not come into use until after the demise of the Mycenaean culture. Likewise, heroes never eat fish, and yet fishing plays a considerable role in similes. These and other aspects of daily life in the context of epic narrative thus derive from the post-Mycenaean period, as probably does most of the outlook on the world and its people to be found in these epics, whereas the names and main events must date from an earlier period. Not surprisingly, therefore, all epic sagas, those extant and lost epic poems that can be reconstructed from adaptations in later tragedies, prose and the visual arts, relate to the archaeologically demonstrable focal points of Mycenaean culture: Agamemnon comes from Mycenae, Achilles from Thessaly, Nestor from Pylos, and so on. Precisely the same blend of 'contemporary' and archaic elements is to be found in the fairy tales of the Brothers Grimm, which were written down from tales told by old women in the early nineteenth century. The details of everyday life, such as the appearance of discharged musketeers or schoolmasters, indicate the eighteenth century, but the plots themselves and their morals date back to a much earlier era.

During the period between the beginning of high Mycenaean culture and the end of the geometric epoch, the fund of epic language formulae was developed into such a fine and highly differentiated instrument of poetic utterance that it raised ancient Greek oral poetry far above all kindred forms so far known among the Slavs, the Malayans and other peoples. Similarly, the hexameter verse form developed for this oral poetry transcends in its length, variability and its capacity for articulation all other known verse forms of oral poetry, and continued to play a dominant role in the following, written epoch of Greek literature. The potential inherent in being able, in four out of six metrical feet, to replace with a long syllable the two short syllables alternating with a long syllable, afforded a wealth of graphic effects:

$$-\overline{\cup\cup}-\overline{\cup\cup}-\overline{\cup\cup}-\overline{\cup\cup}-\cup\cup-\overline{\cup}$$

(– signifies long syllable, ∪ short, ⎵⎵ or ⊽ alternatives). Each verse is moreover arranged into shorter sections by means of two or three caesuras, inserted at precisely regulated points. This both avoids monotony in oral performance, and allows the formulaic character of epic language to be displayed to full effect in the metre, since the caesura and the end of the formula invariably coincide. Significantly, early inscriptions, composed in hexameters, frequently use punctuation not at the ends of verses or in accordance with syntactic requirements, but to mark caesuras or formulaic elements. The *Odyssey* gives a favourable impression of the work of wandering bards or poets, two of whom, Phemius and Demodocus, feature in it. In contrast, the *Iliad* was still familiar with the gallant hero who sings of the 'glorious deeds of men' to the accompaniment of the phorminx, the lyre. Later popular tradition also gives accounts of singing contests and similar events. In one particular developmental phase a transition took place from musically accompanied to purely oral performances of improvised works, the staff becoming the professional symbol of the wandering poet or reciter, the rhapsode.

The *Iliad* and the *Odyssey* form but one part of a cycle or series of epic poems giving accounts of the war between the allied princes of Hellas and Troy on the north-west coast of Anatolia. Excavations by Schliemann and Blegen at Hissarlik have confirmed conclusively that a heavily fortified, wealthy town was destroyed by force there towards the end of the thirteenth century BC, shortly before the demise of the Mycenaean culture in Greece. This does not mean, however, that the Trojan War described by Homer can be taken as fact. The titles of these epic poems (e.g. *The Cypria, The Destruction of Ilion*) were handed down by ancient grammarians. The adventures of the Achaean heroes on their return voyage are also sung in this cycle. Another cycle of epic poems gave an account of events connected with Thebes, the fortunes of Oedipus, his forefathers and his descendants.

Of all these epic poems which can be reconstructed on the basis of summaries, and of texts and accounts which use them as source material, only the extant ones, the *Iliad* and the *Odyssey*, have been unanimously attributed to a blind poet by the name of Homeros, of whom tradition tentatively holds that he lived in the eighth century BC in the region inhabited by the Ionian tribe. Much later, there was a singers' guild in Chios that traced itself back to Homer.

Of the remaining epic poems, some continue to be anonymous, while others are attributed to poets of a possibly later period, often from the same above-mentioned geographical area (including Stasinos and Arctinos). The name of Homer, however, also occurs as a collective author for the entire body of earlier epic poetry.

The fact that the *Iliad* and the *Odyssey* are extant, however, is not the sole factor that distinguishes them within their cycle. Both are over twice as long as the third longest known today. This length is appropriate to their content. Although, strictly speaking, the *Iliad* describes the events of only a few days in the tenth year of the Trojan War, it contains so many references to preceding and subsequent events, and so many scenes that one might expect in a different context, that the poem *de facto* provides a complete account of the whole Trojan War. This also applies to the *Odyssey*, which contains not only an account by Odysseus of his fantastic travels and a description of his homecoming, including his revenge on the suitors, but also of the journey of his son Telemachus, in which the poet collates a considerable quantity of information about the fortunes of other homeward voyagers. This complexity of content, which can hardly be credited to the other much shorter epic poems in the cycle, assured these two extant works a special status even in ancient times, and one which renders their attribution to Homer appropriate.

For many reasons, however, it would be wrong to see these two extant poems as the first major epics to have been composed from pieces intended for oral recitation, but conceived in written form. They both contain too many discrepancies of plot for this, and too many inconsistencies with regard to language and poetic quality. This makes it quite impossible to describe them as two homogeneous works each attributable to a single author, as the *Divina Commedia* is.

On the other hand, both epic poems evince unmistakable signs of a large-scale plan of composition, even if this plan is not always consistently carried out in the relevant extant text. The proem to the *Iliad* declares that the poem deals with the wrath Achilles nurtures on account of a dispute with Agamemnon the commander-in-chief, and with the fateful consequences of this wrath for the interests of the Achaeans at Troy. In fact, however, the final third of the epic poem is no longer concerned with the theme of wrath and reconciliation as the focal point of events. Instead, attention shifts to the character of Achilles' companion Patroclus, his death at the hands of Hector, Achilles' revenge on Hector, and a look ahead to Achilles' own ultimate fate.

Over and above this shift in theme, the main storyline is interrupted by numerous, sometimes very lengthy episodes which do not always permit conscientious application of the term intentional retardation – aside from innumerable short verse groups which constitute nothing short of a distraction.

The same applies to the *Odyssey*: the account given of the return voyage of Odysseus and the punishment of the suitors is scarcely organically linked with the narrative dealing with the voyage of Telemachus. Here, too, we find a compositional plan for the major proportion of the epic poem which is not consistently carried out. The *Odyssey* similarly contains a doubling up of motifs, contradictory passages and substantial inconsistencies in literary quality.

The brief elucidation of these points places us right at the centre of a complex of problems known in philological terminology as the 'Homeric question'. Based on observations made about Homer's text in the eighteenth century, as well as ancient accounts of a collation of Homeric songs made in Athens in the sixth century BC, the extant texts were declared to be more or less random collections of separate songs, originally conceived orally. This view immediately raised objections from scholars pointing to the homogeneity of the epic style and compositional plan of both epic poems, and seeking to offer these arguments to support the idea of the literary unity of the *Iliad* and the *Odyssey*. This idea had always been an unquestioned assumption both for ancient Homeric criticism, and for imitation of Homer in European literature.

This dispute between the unitarians and the analysts persisted for over a century and a half, both parties using the rapid advances being made in the fields of historical philology to rearm themselves with fresh arguments from the fields of philology, history, archaeology and the history of literature. This protracted debate led to a highly subtle study of Homeric poetry, bringing to light numerous peculiarities that might otherwise have remained undiscovered. Over the decades, the results of Homeric research, presented in the form of hypotheses of origin, shifted constantly, but remained captive to this controversy. Nowadays, not even the most stringent analyst still believes in a mechanical collection of separate, mutually unconnected songs, but assumes instead a series of epic poems, subjected to fresh adaptations and contaminations, resulting in the texts now at our disposal. By the same token, no unitarian would now deny the subsequent insertion of certain passages or verse groups into an overall context which can nevertheless be interpreted as homogeneous.

Since the discovery of the essential characteristics of oral poetry, the overall focus of this problem has in fact shifted, its traditional formulation having been shown to be inadequate. The processes involved between the living practice of oral poetry and the writing down of those texts which are available to us are far too complex to be completely clarified using traditional methods of interpretation, developed for use with texts conceived in written form. The profound differences in style demonstrated by W. H. Friedrich (1956) on the smallest scale within epic narrative are sufficient proof that further study will be required before scholars learn to distinguish with any certainty between, for example, the written form of oral poetry, written conception in oral form, and oral form adapted for a written version. This will be necessary, however, before analysis of the narrative context produces any fresh insights. The incomparable sophistication of the storehouse of formulas in Greek compared to other oral poetry traditions makes it highly likely that even before the use of the written form the composition of verse narratives was subject to rigorous standards, and that the orally composed 'original' *Iliad* was even then a lengthy and complex piece of narrative.

It may be added that there is most unlikely to have been a prolonged period of written epic poetry retaining the strict rules of oral formulation, such as is evinced by lengthy passages of the *Iliad*. Poets with writing at their disposal for the conception of their poems would be more inclined to proceed by composing poetry from words rather than formulas, no longer adhering to the mnemotechnical convention of using a single expression for a specific point in the verse, likewise avoiding all metrical and semantic parallel expressions. For poets composing with the aid of writing, the form of the oral epic poem provides no more than a model, not the binding rules of their diction.

With regard to the documented use of writing among the Greeks from the late eighth century BC onwards, however, it is difficult to reconcile our knowledge of the earliest writing techniques with the idea of lengthy texts being written down in one piece before the sixth century BC, or even being composed in written form. It is possible, therefore, that the earliest written poetry consisted solely of short poems, with major epic works still for a long time being preserved in oral form.

In view of this vast new field of research, which has scarcely mastered the idiosyncrasies of oral poetry, it would be presumptuous to designate the number of allegedly reconstructible written versions of the *Iliad* or to divide the *Odyssey* up among three poets. Certain more or less discrete parts of the *Iliad* may be separated out as probable later additions, originally independent short epic poems originally conceived in the written form – on account of their singular vocabulary, their sharp deviations from the oral storehouse of formulas, and not least on account of their less than convincing insertion into the overall plot. This would apply both to the story of the duping of Zeus in book 14 and the duel between Achilles and Aeneas in book 20.

The true complexity of the situation, however, is revealed by a glance at book 10, undoubtedly one of these later insertions. Its plot, a reconnaissance by a group of Achaean heroes to the camp of the Trojan allies, falls entirely outside the context of the *Iliad* narrative, so much so that its deletion from the overall composition of the *Iliad* would be more of a help than a hindrance. The book also evinces many remarkable features. Its language shows a particular abundance of deviations from the storehouse of epic formulas; the entire action takes place at night, which is unknown elsewhere in epic poetry; as well as the charioteer warriors of the epic age, Phrygians and riders appear who can otherwise be named nowhere and who did not in fact exist in the Aegean world until after the first Dorian migration – and so on. And yet in the self-same narrative we find, deeply and inextricably embedded in ancient epic formulas, the description of a helmet which was demonstrably no longer worn by the late Mycenaean period. This shows how complex were the conditions whereby poems were handed down, ultimately leading to the emergence of the present extant versions of the epic poems.

In what follows below, epic texts will be viewed without further differentiation, and the world depicted in them and the literary achievements they represent as homogeneous phenomena. This will be done from the viewpoint of the literary and indeed national tradition of the Greeks that followed on from Homeric poetry.

The first, and perhaps most significant observation usually made when reading epic texts is that the poet is able, using the stylistic devices at his disposal, to evoke an entirely distinct, discrete world before the inner eye of his listener. These devices include the consistent use of reiterated epithets for virtually all characters and objects, the repetition of whole sections of narrative – predictable even after brief reading, and functioning as it were as a message within the plot – as well as the regular reappearance of typical scenes, subject-matter and events. All this gives the listener or reader the feeling of being in another world, subject to strict laws of its own, which nevertheless soon becomes familiar. The alien nature of this world must have been even more striking to the Greek listener, since epic language corresponded to no dialect spoken at that time, and contained many words of quite unknown origin and meaning. The use of such stylistic devices meant that not every object was individually described in accordance with the given situation, but still had its fixed place in the epic scheme of things. This prevented listeners from making inappropriate associations drawn from their own realm of experience.

The prerequisites for this remarkable consistency of stylisation, whereby traditional elements from various epochs were fused to create a unity achieved only in verse, in the poem, are multifarious. For one thing, the essential outline of the external course of events was a given for poets. They were not free in their work to leave Troy unconquered, or to laud Hector's victory over Achilles. This fixed, predetermined course of external events required the poet to create a corresponding logic in the internal structure of the epic world. The people involved in the events being described, like the audiences who listened to early epic poetry, belonged to an aristocratic society whose thought, speech and actions unfolded according to fixed rules, bound by tradition. Listeners could therefore entirely predict the reactions of their heroes in specific situations.

The more consistent and discrete a system of communication is, the less detailed information is required to understand a set of circumstances: a few points of reference suffice to reconstruct the whole. The art of epic poetry used this 'law' to the utmost. The wholly individual characterisations of Achilles and Odysseus, Ajax and Hector, Paris and Agamemnon have never escaped the notice of any reader of Homer, nor has any of their individuality been lost over three millennia of literary and artistic tradition. Only in the course of explicit mythological criticism or re-evaluation has this changed. What makes this precision in the portrayal of the main characters possible is the fact that many of the typical features of the Homeric hero could be taken for granted within the society to which he belonged. Few additional traits were required, therefore, to create an individual out of the typical hero.

The same applies to the depiction of events themselves. Given the marked typification of numerous scenes and sequences of events, relatively few hints are needed to evoke the unusual aspects of a situation before the inner eye of the listener. A rhythm may, moreover, frequently be observed in epic narrative, whereby a weapon, a contingent of troops, a splendid house or other such feature is depicted with that famous epic breadth, and even ease, that was so highly prized in the eighteenth century, whereas the deeds of the hero or god, his decisions and ordeals, are described with the barest minimum of words. In addition, the listener is always led by the poet, through the direct speech of those involved, to the emotion intended. Occasionally, this art of omission or leaving things unsaid can condense into creative achievements of unsurpassed force, as in book 1 of the *Iliad*. Agamemnon has rudely rebuffed the old man Chryses, who is seeking the release of his daughter, captured by the Greeks, by impressing on him the sanctity of his office as priest of Apollo. The old man makes his way to the seashore and asks the god to punish this outrage against his servant. The god Apollo, who is able both to inflict and dispel pestilence, hears his plea (1, 43ff.):

> And so he said his prayer, and Phoebus Apollo heard him.
> He came down from the heights of Olympus with rage in his heart,
> Carrying on his shoulders the bow and the double-covered quiver.
> The arrows rattled against the shoulder of the enraged Apollo

As he strode down, and he came like the night.
Then he took up his position a short way from the ships
And fired his first arrow.
Terrible was the sound of the silver bow.
First he struck the mules and the grey dogs,
But then he aimed his barbed missiles at the Argives themselves,
Shooting again and again. And in rapid succession burned the
      funeral pyres for the dead.

The potential for condensed utterance of this kind can only arise where a poet, both sustained and constrained by the strict rules of the relevant tradition, must search with utmost concentration for that part of the overall picture which is best suited to the emotional content of his or her message, but whose strong colouring will not distort or alter the given setting. The enormous impact of Homeric poetry on Greek literature as a whole becomes clear through the realisation that it represents the first occasion on which this principle of literary stylisation was put into effect with such consummate skill. By virtue of the precise, fixed nature of the epic storehouse of formulas, it is possible even today to retrace how the tension between the liberties and constraints of the epic poet had to be constantly reaccommodated on the creative level.

To return to Homeric similes: the epic style also includes the way in which the atmosphere pertaining to an event is illustrated by means of similes. During one particular retreat by the Achaeans, Ajax, the most defiant and status-conscious of all the heroes, is particularly loath to go. This is depicted by the poet through a simile showing a stubborn ass that refuses to be moved by noise, tugging or beating. It has been observed that these similes, which naturally contain many relatively modern aspects of everyday life and few real features from the Mycenaean period, cannot be analysed or interpreted on the assumption that each aspect of the simile corresponds to a counterpart in the main narrative. The author was far more concerned simply to add colour to the overall situation. As a result, the simile often also becomes syntactically separate, compelling the author to return to the main plot by using a transitional formula. This adding of colour to the atmosphere through the use of similes, however, by no means implies the disclosure of a secret meaning below the surface. It is far more a matter of exterior illustration by means of a lively and realistic picture evoked from the listener's realm of experience. Astonishingly enough, the entirely artificial and extremely formalised language of the epic tradition retained its capacity for this often robust imagery precisely because it was never burdened with hidden meanings or deeper significances, being devoid of dual or multiple layers of meaning. Epic poets mean exactly what they say, even if this sometimes seems to entail a breach of conventional propriety, as when Odysseus, tossing and turning sleepless on his couch, is compared with a sausage sizzling and being turned in the pan. By and large, however, passages of this kind are rare. For the most part the vocabulary of epic poetry is scrupulously decent, albeit in an unforced way, making it a true reflection of the noble way of life of the society it seeks to depict.

Homer's people, as Hermann Fränkel has put it (1962), are thoroughly straightforward beings. Lacking the dimension of psychological depth, their speech and action embrace their whole being. Homeric language does in fact contain a rich psychological vocabulary for the purposes of clearly distinguishing and describing the rational and irrational aspects of human beings. The sum of these aspects, however, does not constitute a sphere of inner, spiritual life subject to laws of its own, and a counterpart to the physical sphere. Instead, all psychological notions are directly linked to the outer manifestations of the person, whose legs, for example, are gripped with fear as he flees from danger. Not only the diversity of psychological expressions, but also the convention in Homeric language of designating as 'knowledge' almost all the emotions deduced from human actions, bear witness to the careful way in which human doings were accounted for. This reflection, however, was aimed not at achieving a body of collective psychological concepts, but at shedding light on specific actions.

Homer's people acknowledged no life after death that was of any relevance to their moral criteria. The meaning of their lives was fully taken up by their earthly existence. With death, a person fell to the 'dogs and birds', the psyche – which is not the soul – leading a meaningless nonexistence that Achilles would gladly have exchanged for the existence of the poorest journeyman. This focus on the here and now is matched by the capacity of the Homeric personality for unalloyed joy over what is good, and unrestrained grief over what is bad. No suffering or deed is made relative by reference to a reality beyond this world. The task in hand is to do or suffer with dignity and decorum what custom and honour demand. This is how Achilles, for example, addresses the very young Trojan pleading for his life on the battlefield (21, 1044ff.):

> So you die too, dear boy. Why these vain complaints?
> For Patroclus also died who was so much better than you.
> Look at myself, how handsome and imposing I am,
> Son of a great father and a goddess for a mother;
> Yet death and stronger fate lurk behind me too.
> The hour will come, morning, even, or midday,
> When an adversary takes my life on the battlefield,
> With a lance, perhaps, or with an arrow from the bow.
> (transl. from the German tr. of H. Fränkel 1962, 90)

Since the Homeric hero recognises no inner authority such as conscience or anything of that kind with which to assess his actions independently of the judgement of those around him, his moral existence stands or falls with the recognition of the society in which he lives. Physical strength and beauty are just as much a part of the realisation of his personality as success, wealth and fame. The honour he enjoys is expressed largely through the material gifts bestowed on him by his peers. A reduction in the share of booty to be accepted by Achilles in fact triggers the entire story of the *Iliad*. The word that came in later Greek to mean friendly or kind affection can be used in Homer quite specifically to denote the act of entertainment. No sentiment occurs in the absence of its direct expression in action.

The rules adhered to by this aristocratic society in all situations in life are harsh, calling for a high degree of self-control, decorum and personal commitment. Gallantry, the most attractive virtue an aristocratic society can produce, is best revealed in the non-partisan way in which the shortcomings and strengths of friend and foe alike are depicted. The most moving character among all the heroes is the non-Greek, Hector.

In order to understand the role played in the events of the saga by Homer's heroes as described above, it is necessary to take into account the particular situation of the poet. He was faced with a predetermined storyline which, in anthropological terms, he was best able to interpret in terms of a strict determinism. We know, for example, from other epic poems, such as the *Oedipodia*, that the continuing curse, which persists quite irrespective of the personal responsibility of individuals born later, was the driving force behind events. The moral judgement of the poet, therefore, is restricted largely to the 'how' aspect of the plot and of suffering, the 'what' already being laid down by tradition. Nevertheless, wherever the poet has his hero do something unexpected, mostly in a plot of his own invention, this is attributed to the direct intervention of a deity, and perceived by those involved with no great surprise.

These gods who take direct part in human conflicts, who weep, laugh and indeed who 'steal, whore and cheat', as one scandalised sixth-century BC poet put it, are themselves no more than a glorified aristocratic society with a king and queen and their royal retinue, complete with more or less rebellious nobles, and their various proclivities, aversions, strengths and weaknesses. Of course, they are all larger than life, stronger, more powerful, hence more unpredictable than human beings. Capable of deeds that would be impossible for humans, they are still not sinister in their heightened humanity, and even less are they punishment-dealing arbiters of human behaviour. They are immortal and unageing, also having one advantage described in epic language as the 'easy life'. Human beings are obliged to live out their destinies, and each human action brings with it inexorable consequences to be borne by those involved. The gods, on the other hand, are free after a furious bout of combat to sit down together to a cheerful feast, as if nothing had happened. They are not bound by any doom arising out of their actions, and leave humans to their own devices in times of calamity.

The question is, however, do they also shape the events in which they participate so actively as the fancy takes them? On the battlefield at Troy,

Zeus, father of the gods and humans alike, is unable to save his beloved son Sarpedon from the death for which he is destined. This point seems to be hard to reconcile to the proclamation given in the proem to the *Iliad* that everything that occurred at Troy was by the decree of Zeus. The explanation of contradictions is again facilitated by recalling that the course of events was laid down for the poet by tradition, thus corresponding to 'the decree of Zeus'. Where, however, poetic inventiveness made specific modifications to the course of the plot, and this was placed in relation to the desire and will of particular gods, a divergence could arise between what was predetermined, *moira*, and the subsequent intention of a god.

The characters of the gods as portrayed by Homer, with their distinct, individual profiles, exerted enormous impact in subsequent centuries. Herodotus went so far as to declare that Homer and Hesiod had given the Greeks their gods. Certainly the three-dimensional quality of Homer's portrayal of the gods, which became known throughout Greece through the recitation of epic poetry, displaced notions of earlier origin and a vaguer nature connected with local cults and their legends. These gods, who lived unconfined by any human constraints, aiding or harming human beings on a whim, but neither rewarding their good deeds nor punishing their wickedness, and who themselves did anything but set a good moral example, were soon severely criticised in Greece for their 'immorality'.

It may be asserted that the glorified aristocratic society represented by the Homeric firmament of deities had an extraordinary aesthetic appeal, but was of no outstanding significance in terms of the history of religion. Homer's gods shed little light on the religious notions of a Greek landowner of the geometric age within the practice of his inherited cult. Indeed, the gods to whom simple folk prayed are only mentioned peripherally in Homer, if at all. Just how unsatisfactory the role of the gods, in their epic guise within the mythical tradition, was for religious feeling, even in earlier centuries, is already hinted at in the *Odyssey*, but most particularly in Hesiod.

The ancient world consistently held the *Odyssey* to be the work of Homer, the author of the *Iliad*. Closer examination, however, reveals substantial differences between these two works, not merely in language and style, but above all in their outlook on humanity and the world. It is difficult to ascertain whether this is owing to a considerably later period of origin for the *Odyssey*, or simply to its entirely different themes.

The poem about the return of Odysseus combines three motifs, each of which merits handling in a separate narrative: the unexpected return of a hero after a long voyage, bringing liberation from diverse calamities for his loyal and long-suffering wife, Penelope; the first expedition by the young hero of good family, Telemachus, in which he must prove his manhood; and the hair-raising adventures of the well-travelled seafarer, who has voyaged to the ends of the earth, to the very kingdom of the dead, and who has had to deal with giants and sorcerers. The third series of motifs in the extant text is closely linked with first through the account of Odysseus at the court of Alcinous, King of Phaeacia, while the spellbinding plot surrounding Telemachus, elaborated in the tenor of a high social culture, has retained a certain degree of autonomy. Despite its entirely peaceful character, this corresponds most closely to the lifestyle of the Iliadic hero, whereas the Odysseus of the two other series of motifs displays few of the traits associated with such a hero. The hero of the *Odyssey* is outstanding neither for his straightforward, gallant conduct, in line with the yardstick imposed by the honour of his rank, nor for his honest accomplishment of what has been ordained by Fate, but rather for his astute adroitness in all kinds of unexpected situations, his agility, and his inexhaustible resourcefulness. He is undeniably courageous and spirited, but the goals for which he strives are survival and success, not the realisation of gallant concepts of honour. This enables him even to humiliate himself and dispense with esteem and honour, so as later to triumph all the more conclusively over his adversary.

Odysseus, who bears a name of non-Greek origin, enjoys a special status even in the earlier *Iliad*. The esteem in which he is held by the Achaean army is based neither on his power (he comes from the poor island of Ithaca on the western periphery of the Greek world), nor even on his military prowess, in which he is far outstripped by Diomedes, Ajax or especially Achilles. It is based on his intelligence. It may very well be that Odysseus was not accorded a place in the Trojan cycle at all until the later addition of traditional seafaring tales, of which he was the hero, to the myths relating the return of the protagonists in the Trojan War. Seafaring tales are documented from as early as the ancient Egyptian tales of the second millennium, complete with all their traditional motifs – best known to western readers from the Oriental stories of Sinbad the Sailor. Admittedly, in the epic poetry of the Greeks such tales were also incorporated into the epic sagas elsewhere besides the *Nostoi* (*Returns*) poems relating stories not only of the return voyage of the heroes from the Trojan War, but even before them. Karl Meuli (1921) demonstrated that the extant account in the *Odyssey* of the wanderings of Odysseus already presupposes the epic, extended saga of the Argonauts, the story of a voyage by a group of Greek heroes to the ends of the earth. The prototypes of the narrative suggest that the journey to the underworld belongs in this story. In the *Odyssey*, the Phaeacian land of the dead, of the grey men, visited by Odysseus became a fairy-tale land of uninterrupted joy. Instead, a *descensus ad inferos* was incorporated into the series of adventures, in line with notions of the underworld present also in the *Iliad*.

The *Odyssey*, focused entirely on its main character, depicts both here and in the auxiliary characters a far broader spectrum of emotional motives than the *Iliad* does for its heroes. The relationships between Odysseus and his ageing parents, his loyal wife, his servants, even the old court dog, and his homesickness for hearth and home, are all present in the *Odyssey*, as are those idyllic scenes in which Odysseus meets the young Phaeacian princess

Nausicaa, or becomes immersed in conversation with the nymph Calypso. Odysseus enjoys a relationship of personal confidence with his patron goddess Athena such as is quite unknown among the heroes of the *Iliad*, even having scope for humour.

On the other hand, granted the fate of such a self-reliant man, the poet reflects far more extensively on human action than is the case in the *Iliad*. He is no longer satisfied by the notion of the predetermination of all events by the decree of Zeus. Instead, he explains the many unexpected vicissitudes of mortals by asserting that people, through their own folly and wickedness, bring on themselves events that transcend the bounds set by Fate. For the first time in Greek literature, we discern a new sense of real human responsibility in the making.

Both this and the above-mentioned social dimension encompassed in the *Odyssey* make it a quite different work from the *Iliad*. The return of Odysseus signifies a restoration of political order on Ithaca. The portrayal of the Phaeacians and the Cyclopes may be read as didactic pieces on political theory, illustrating both a perfectly functioning and an entirely absent social order. Odysseus shows a tireless concern for the welfare of his companions, whereas the heroes of the *Iliad* are solicitous exclusively for their own fame, their underlings being immaterial to their actions.

As has rightly been pointed out, the *Odyssey* contains out-and-out criticism of the epic world and its ideals (*Odyssey* 8, 521ff.). The as yet unrecognised Odysseus, a guest at the Phaeacian court, on hearing a singer lauding the fame of his own deeds at the defeat of Troy, sheds bitter tears. Using a simile, the poet compares these tears with those of the woman who clings distraught to the corpse of her husband, fallen in the defence of the city, and who is then beaten and led away to slavery. In this way, Odysseus the hero and conqueror is placed on the same plane as the defenceless victims of his epic deeds.

It has likewise correctly been pointed out that the *Odyssey* contains much more detailed reference to everyday life than the *Iliad*, where such information appears solely in similes. The latter occur much less frequently in the *Odyssey*. Similarly, Phoenicians and Egyptians appear in the *Odyssey*, and it has also been remarked that the island of the Cyclopes is described from the viewpoint of Greek colonists in search of land. As the unrecognised guest of his former swineherd, the returned Odysseus spins a long fabricated yarn about military and pirate life in which the Trojan War is depicted from the perspective of a freezing guard. All these are realistic touches betraying a feeling for life that is quite alien to the *Iliad*, although not necessarily one that came chronologically later. However tempting it is to interpret these details historically, this is a precarious enterprise, since the entire work is deeply embedded in a fairy-tale world embracing elements of widely diverse origins.

To return to the manner in which Homeric poetry was handed down: the art of epic poetry rapidly spread throughout the Greek-speaking region, making it the most important medium in preparing the ground for pan-

Hellenic national feeling. It is not known whether this dissemination was intensified by the shift to a written form. This is not a crucial point, however, since the first texts to become established in written form were not intended for reading, but appeared in a sparse number of copies for recitation purposes.

It is known that Homer's poetry was compiled in a set form in the mid-sixth century BC in connection with the creation of the Panathenaeic festival, a civic festival intended to replace the former cults of the aristocracy and leading families. Today's extant Homer text shows signs of editing that could only have been carried out in the Attic dialect region.

The popularity of Homer throughout antiquity, during which time he remained set reading in schools for centuries, is documented by hundreds of Homer quotations found among the most diverse authors, and by innumerable Homer papyri found in Egypt. From the third century BC onwards, philological scholars who had found a second home at the library of Ptolemaic Alexandria made efforts to compile an 'authentic' text from countless local traditional versions. It would appear that the Athenian text offered in the critical editions of the great philologists Zenodotus, Aristophanes and Aristarchus (third to second centuries BC) for the most part prevailed, to become the prototype for innumerable popular and school editions.

A wealth of literature on the interpretation of this poetry, in particular more difficult points of language and style, emerged parallel with these, continuing to expand well into the era of the Roman Empire. Commentaries dating from the Byzantine era, preserved in a number of medieval Homer manuscripts, have preserved substantial relics of this scholarly literature.

In its land of origin, epic poetry was already on the decline by the seventh century BC. In other Greek areas, however, especially in the more conservative mother country, it experienced another lengthy late flowering, by that time in written form. Epic poetry burgeoned in Corinth, for example, in the seventh and sixth centuries BC. This is known from sporadic accounts of a poet by the name of Eumelus, and from the high poetic standard of contemporary verse inscriptions in Corinth and its daughter town Corcyra (Corfu). Local myths from the mainland, such as those of Alcmaeon, Amphiaraus, Jason and Europa, were probably first conceived in epic form in this cycle, and also exerted their influence on fifth-century BC visual arts and Attic tragedy in this form. The Heraclean myths were probably first compiled into a single body in epic form around the sixth century BC, by Creophylus of Samos and Peisandrus of Rhodes. The fifth century saw the late proponents of the epic art who attempted to write on historical themes outside Greek myth. Such poets include Panyassis of Halicarnassus and Choerilus of Samos, who composed an epic poem on the Persian Wars, and the philosopher Xenophanes who turned the stories of the founding of Colophon in Asia Minor and Elea (Velia) in Italy into epic poems. One ancient epic poet, however, the Boeotian Hesiod, merits a more detailed account, since his poetry constituted a literary tradition in its own right.

Hesiod grew up in the poor peasant village of Ascra. He tells how as he grazed sheep on the mountain of Helicon, the Muses passed on to him the staff of the rhapsodes, bestowed on him the art of poetry, and consecrated him as their servant. It would scarcely be feasible to interpret this account psychologically as the result of a vision. It would nevertheless be acceptable to assert that at some time in his youth Hesiod had an opportunity to learn the language of poetry, and thus enter the ranks of the rhapsodes through whom the Muses spoke – this being an expression for the constant reformulation of the same traditional material. In Homeric poetry, numerous invocations of the Muses prior to a new section of narrative bear witness to the underlying notion of the inspired poet. But for Hesiod, his personal consecration by the Muses, who although they were the Olympian daughters of Zeus appeared to him on his home mountain of Helicon, has an additional significance. Following a disparaging reference to the shepherds and peasants among whom Hesiod lives, the Muses expressly declare that they are able to disclose both 'illusion, similar to truth', and truth itself. The only possible interpretation of this is that Hesiod intends to use his new-found ability to serve the language of poetry not in epic sagas, the usual subject-matter for this poetic language, but in something new.

The new phenomenon which the Muses seek to proclaim through the mouth of the poet differs from what went before in its greater truthfulness. There being no reason to ascribe to Hesiod an understanding of myth as 'mere writing', as fiction, this call for truthfulness in his new poetic utterance can only be understood in terms of a higher degree of meaning, and a greater proximity to the day-to-day reality of his listeners. Hesiod's work reveals hime as the first known theologian in the Greek language.

In a grandiose version of the Hesiodic text, highly fluid as a consequence of centuries of being handed down, certainly severely interrupted here and there by omissions and additions, Hesiod's *Theogony* describes both how the world came into being and unfolded, and all the beings and forces that permeate it. The model by which this comprehensive cosmology is delineated is obtained not through any process of thought that is subject to logic, but through the viewpoint of a genealogical interconnection. Out of the primeval chaos, the great void, emerges the earth, with Tartarus concealed below it, and able to sustain all beings on its 'wide breast', as well as Eros, the fairest of all the gods. After the appearance of Eros, all further unfolding of the cosmos takes place through a process of procreation and birth. The diversity of beings who come about one after the other in this process embraces more than such major cosmic phenomena as the ocean, the sun or night, and the gods and men as seen in cult and mythical tradition (Hesiod makes a point of creating a genealogical harmony out of the divergent notions of local cult legends). Much more important, Hesiod seeks to use his own genealogical, theological invention to present the entire sequence of forces governing nature and human life, even those that we are accustomed to describe solely in terms of invisible abstractions. He thus has Eris, discord, derive from night, and from Eris in turn

> forgetfulness, hunger and tearful suffering, combat, war, murder and slaying, discord, lies, deceitful speech, as well as lawlessness and injury, which are closely related to one another, like the oath, which is particularly injurious to men on Earth – namely when someone intentionally commits perjury.
>
> (Hesiod, *Theogony* 225ff.)

It would be incorrect to use the term personification to define this mode of thought and speech. The causal relationship between the basic phenomenon of disunity and all disagreeable occurrences in human society is not being conceptualised here and then illustrated using 'symbolic' figures through personification. Instead, the poet perceives this relationship directly as a filial one between active, and hence vital forces, which may be imagined as persons.

Hesiod's *Theogony* nevertheless goes further than postulating an automatic unfolding and proliferation of the world and its forces. Besides, or over and above this, as it were, is a historical aspect. In Hesiod's view, the world is not merely a cosmos unfolding according to discernible rules: it is also governed by a supreme deity, an ultimate will. Government of the world, however, has been held successively by three supreme deities with their clan. Cronus emasculates his father Uranus, the god of the heavens, in order to come to power. Cronus, who is in the habit of devouring his offspring, is, however, himself outwitted by means of the handing over of a stone after the birth of his son Zeus, and dethroned together with his entire family, the Titans, after a furious battle with the Olympian gods, who are to rule henceforth led by Zeus.

This clumsy, barbaric myth of succession is without parallel in the whole world of Greek myth, and cuts a particularly poor figure beside the Homeric Mount Olympus, with its aloof elegance. It has been known for some time that this myth originates in the Near East. It has exact parallels in texts deriving from the Hittite Empire of the second millennium, although there were comparable traditions in Ras Shamra, the ancient city of Ugarit, where traditions of the pre-Semitic inhabitants of Syria, the Hurrians, had persisted, as they did also among the Mesopotamian Sumerians. Obviously, the Ullikumi and Kumarbi myths known from Hittite sources could hardly have been Hesiod's primary source, but the Near Eastern origin of his borrowings is beyond doubt. It is less certain, however, whether Hesiod was the first to introduce these stories into the body of his cosmology, and hence to the Greek-speaking world, or whether these were earlier borrowings already present in the Mycenaean period.

What is new in Hesiod's theology is the meaning ascribed to succession in the dynasties of the gods. His cosmogony becomes complete only with victory over the unbridled chaos of previous dynasties. Only does Zeus, with his various consorts, create those forces of order, moderation, justice and beauty which distinguish his rule of the world. Only then, under the sceptre of Zeus, is the world truly a cosmos, the gods becoming the champions of law and order among humans. It is now that the Muses are born, the daughters of Zeus and Mnemosyne, memory. They give men not only dance and song, but also the gift of being able to resolve disputes and discord without violence. The gloomy myth adopted by Hesiod from the Orient thus serves to demonstrate law and order as hard-won achievements, only possible through the defeat of the unbridled chaos out of which the world nevertheless arose.

This impressive conception, which could only have been achieved through perspicacious reflection on both experienced and inherited knowledge, reveals Hesiod to be a particularly venerable figure in Greek history. He was not a great poet: his wording is clumsy and provincial, and far removed from the elegant fluency of the Homeric narrative style. However, it may simply have been too mammoth a task to adapt the epic formulas, intended for utterances of quite a different kind, to these profound speculations.

Another epic poem has come down to us from the pen of Hesiod that is even more original and engaging than the *Theogony*, and even less convincing as a literary composition. Like the *Theogony*, however, it has been marred by diverse errors in the process of being handed down. Hesiod had a brother by the name of Perses, who cheated him in the partition of their estate, finding patronage among bribable 'kings', as Hesiod, in epic style, calls the members of local noble families in whose hands rested all cult and other traditions of importance for the community, hence also control of the judicial system. A bad manager, however, Perses soon squandered his dishonestly acquired property. Using the same means as the first time, he then set about acquiring other portions of his brother's assets.

It was while in this predicament that Hesiod wrote the epic poem known in later antiquity as *Works and Days* (there were no book titles in Hesiod's own time). It has been suggested that Hesiod's dispute with Perses was a mere poetic fiction used to clothe his didactic content. Other undoubtedly biographical details in the work make this most unlikely, however.

The second, more substantial part of the work contains the rules, arranged according to the calendar, for rural life and work, including both technical instructions for the farmer, and a wealth of information on the customs and taboos of rural folk religion. Although the composition may be regarded as loose and amateurish, the poet manages some vivid depiction of scenes from rural life. The second part additionally contains seafaring rules, of which Hesiod, a Boeotian farmer who travelled but once as a rhapsode to a festival in Euboea, undoubtedly had no personal experience. He must have obtained this information from his father, who came from Cyme in Asia Minor and who, Hesiod tells us, only settled as a farmer in the impoverished backwater of Ascra out of financial necessity.

More interesting is the first part of the epic poem, from which may be deduced the reasons for Hesiod's composition of this utterly unheroic, rural didactic poem. It comprises what at first glance seems to be an endless collection of quite short verse groups containing diverse fables, both adopted myths and some invented by Hesiod himself, and some direct admonitory speeches addressed to his brother and the judges. The keynote of these original observations is the idea that the present state of humanity on earth is poor and deplorable. People are subject to disease, poverty, misery and death without really being able to help themselves. Only two things make life tolerable. The first is the presence among people of Aidos and Nemesis, i.e. shame at committing evil acts and indignation at the commission of evil acts. Whereas animals eat one another without a qualm, Zeus rules the world with the aid of Dike, justice, seeing and sooner or later punishing all wickedness among men, which, through the presence of Aidos and Nemesis, they themselves condemn using the self-same criteria as the highest deity and judge.

The other gift which makes life worth living is work, through which man is able to overcome the sheer indigence of his existence. It is in this context that we find in Hesiod for the first time the famous metaphor of the two paths, of which only one, stony, steep and arduous, leads to Arete. Arete signifies not moral virtue, but proficiency in life and the success that springs from it. Naturally enough, Hesiod's observations on justice are directed for the most part at judges, and his admonition to work at the idle brother seeking to extricate himself from his self-inflicted penury by legal chicanery.

Hesiod has clothed his insights into the course and order of human life in highly diverse tales. For his description of the present lamentable state of the world, he adopts the idea, undoubtedly of Oriental origin, of a sequence of ages or human generations, each one worse than the last. The first generation, the golden, lived in a state of perpetual youth, without poverty, disease, work or dispute. When this generation disappeared from the earth, its members became the protecting spirits for subsequent mortal generations. Hesiod's adopted scheme proceeds via silver and bronze ages to the present iron generation, in which wickedness and destitution continue to spread. Between the previous and present iron generation, however, he places a respite in the continuous decline: here he locates the heroic generation who fought at Thebes and Troy, the source of the heroic tradition of the Hellenes.

In describing the present iron generation, however, he also outlines the future: corruption will so increase among men that Aidos and Nemesis will be forced to flee from the earth back to Zeus. Then, of course, there will be nothing left with which to combat evil.

This scheme of decadence in narrative, where for the first time in the Greek-speaking world justice is put forward as a prerequisite for the continued survival of human society, stands in striking contrast with another, in which Hesiod takes up again a passage from the *Theogony*. Here men are depicted as initially wretched and helpless, chiefly because Zeus withholds fire from them. Prometheus, member of a family of gods who are hostile to the Olympians, steals fire and brings it to men, thereby becoming the originator of culture. To balance out this advantage, unforeseen in his plan for mankind,

Zeus sends them something evil in the form of Pandora, a woman equipped by the gods with seductive attraction. To introduce her among men, who have so far followed the clever advice of Prometheus ('forethought'), Zeus sends her, accompanied by Hermes, to Epimetheus ('afterthought') – a figure undoubtedly invented by Hesiod for this very purpose – who accepts her. The question is why is woman the great evil intended to spoil again what, through fire, had become a more tolerable life for men. Without doubt, Hesiod's position here is first and foremost that of a long line of rural misogynists, demonstrable with numerous examples, by whom women were accused of idleness, extravagance and so on.

Hesiod takes this speculation on a vulgar folk tradition a stage further, however: Pandora removes the lid from the box in which Zeus keeps all diseases and all that is evil. These are now free to roam the earth at will, and no man can predict when they will strike or defend himself against them. In this, Hesiod has adapted an earlier notion, documented in the *Iliad*, in which Zeus possessed one storage receptacle containing good things, and another containing evil things from which he bestowed to men accordingly. In line with Hesiod's thoughts on the origin of evil, the latter is now inflicted on men by themselves, without any particular intervention by Zeus. Nevertheless, Hesiod adds one more detail which at first seems startling. Hope alone remains in the box, as Pandora replaces the lid before it can fly out. Does this mean that hope is an evil? Hermann Fränkel was the first scholar to shed light on this enigmatic point (Fränkel, 1962, 128ff.). The meaning is undoubtedly that in the face of all the evil that befalls men in the natural course of things, without specific cause, and of the task of coming to terms with it, the anticipation of unpredictable events is a crucial element in the structure of human existence. This hope or anticipation, however, is distinguished by the fact that, despite its power in human life, it never makes an actual appearance – it is never fulfilled. This perseverance in potentiality, as it might be defined in later philosophical terminology, is expressed through hope remaining in the box. The Prometheus–Pandora saga, therefore, presumes not a perpetual process whereby mankind distances itself from some primeval golden age, but rather a process of liberation from a miserable primeval condition, which must nevertheless be paid for with hitherto unknown evils. This makes the Prometheus saga more consistent with the world view of the *Theogony* than is the theory of the ages, since in the *Theogony* it is Zeus, with the final generation of gods, who ultimately brings about a positive, ordered state of affairs.

A dual aspect in the dawn of human history, depicted alternately as golden and blessed, or miserable and poverty-stricken and improved by civilisation, has endured since Hesiod in every theory of the origin of culture, and every description of primitive peoples. In *Works and Days*, the theory of the ages seems to be used to justify Hesiod's principle of justice, and the Prometheus myth his notion of work. It emerges that he is more concerned with an elucidation of his own views than with coherence in his narration of myth.

26

We thus frequently find Hesiod correcting himself. We saw above (p. 23) the role he ascribed to discord, Eris, in the earthly scheme of things. In *Works and Days*, however, he expressly declares that there are not one but two Erises, a good and a bad. The bad Eris is already familiar from the *Theogony*. The good Eris, however, is what we would call competitiveness, a quality recommended to the attention of the idle Perses.

Hesiod similarly recruits animal fables to support his line of argument. With reference to the 'kings', he explains what human society would be like if there were no justice, by means of a dialogue between a nightingale and a goshawk who preys on her. Karl Meuli (1954) has shown that the fable relates to a quite specific social situation, in which one who is powerless tenders a request to one who is powerful, albeit not a modest or otherwise obvious one. In this sense, the humorous story about the freezing guard at Troy mentioned above (p. 20) is also a fable, since Odysseus uses it to ask for a blanket. In Hesiod's case, however, animal fable is but one means employed to point out to judges the road to that justice about which he pondered so long.

The idea of Zeus as champion of strangers and petitioners, people whose special status meant that they could not rely on the protection of the clan or community, had been a familiar and general one since the time of early epic poetry. Hesiod, however, portrays Zeus and the gods under his tutelage as defenders of law and order among humanity in general. This, as well as his ethical appreciation of the hard work of peasants, something which scarcely entered the field of vision of the early epic poet, distinguishes his thought from the aristocratic realm of ideas in epic poetry.

In subsequent times, the Greeks accorded great esteem to Hesiod, despite the formal shortcomings of his provincial style. He was regarded as the originator of didactic poetry, a genre cultivated chiefly in the Hellenistic era. His speculations on the essence of law found direct continuation in the ideas of Solon, Greek tragedy and Classical philosophy. His moral admiration for physical work, however, was not taken up again until the quite altered conditions of the late Hellenistic period, and even then not with unanimous approval. As everyday Greek usage reflects, the aristocratic tendency of early epic poetry prevailed in Greek thought over the rural tendency of Hesiod in this and other respects. The word denoting the person laden with toil and compelled to physical labour soon acquired the meaning of scoundrel, and even in modern Greek work in general is still denoted by the ancient Greek word for slavery.

Although Hesiod still comes over today as a more definite personality than many other figures in the history of Greek literature, it is impossible to ascertain the exact time in which he lived. The period either shortly before or around 700 BC seems most likely. A popular tradition first given literary form by the Sophist Prodicus in the late fifth century BC gives an account of a rhapsodic contest between Homer and Hesiod. This is by no means misleading, since some parts of the modern extant versions of the *Iliad* and the

27

Odyssey were undoubtedly not composed until after Hesiod's poetry. Like the latter, they also bear witness to a written poetry, as is evident here and there from numerous breaches in the rules of oral epic formula. Similarly, a correct rendition of Hesiod's complicated genealogical accounts, most of which are based not on tradition, but on the invention of the poet himself, is hardly conceivable without the aid of a written text.

In antiquity a large number of epic texts were attributed to Hesiod which offer a genealogical description of heroic clans deriving from the union of a god with a mortal. This form, known as catalogue poetry, is assumed to be very ancient, being linked with the interest of great noble families in their own family trees. One such piece is included in the *Odyssey* at the point where the hero visits the underworld. The need for catalogue poetry of this kind must have increased proportionately with the desire to correlate the baffling profusion of local traditions with major epic works of pan-Hellenic significance. Extant relics of this poetry have latterly increased substantially with finds of papyri. These reveal huge differences with regard to the minuteness of detail given, over and above simple genealogical enumeration, in the stories of heroines, and the heroes descended from them and divine fathers. Since such poems of highly variable quality were probably produced over many centuries, these fragments can hardly ever be dated, and if at all only on the strength of unequivocally late forms of language and style. An example which includes the mention of a Greek colony in Cyrene founded in 630 BC, thus providing a *terminus post quem*, is an exception.

Hesiod is held to be the author of a relatively late short epic poem, not particularly significant in quality, from the Heraclean cycle of myths. It deals with the combat between Heracles and the monster Cycnus, the main section consisting of a description of Heracles' shield inspired by the famous description of Achilles' shield in the *Iliad*.

As the epic technique continued to spread, and the sense of inner detachment from the epic world, already discernible in the *Odyssey*, likewise increased, so too did the tendency both to apply the epic style to fresh subject-matter, and even to use it to satirise the world of epic poetry. This is the case with a poem entitled *Margites*, now known only from quotations of some of its passages. It sings of a country bumpkin who does everything wrong, and does not even know what to do with his young wife. This parody, composed using various verse forms, was attributed to Homer by Aristotle, although it probably dates from the sixth century BC. An extant comic epic poem, *Batrachomyomachia*, which relates in high epic style the war waged by mice against frogs, and which is likewise attributed to Homer, was not composed until the third century.

Another innovation was the use of epic technique in a poem dating from the late seventh or early sixth century BC, in which one Aristeas of the island of Proconnesus in the Sea of Marmara recounts his knowledge of the peoples of southern Russia and Siberia, probably obtained on travels connected with the

28

Greek colonisation of the Black Sea coast. Aristeas provides the first evidence of the influence of shamanistic motifs from the steppes of Asia on the religious life of the Greeks. He is one of a number of miracle-workers repeatedly mentioned during the seventh and sixth centuries BC, a period of newly-emerging religious movements.

In contrast, one literary form of the epic style, known from a collection probably compiled in the Hellenistic era, and containing pieces covering a broad time-span, goes back to very early times. This collection is known today as the *Homeric Hymns*. These are invocations of various gods from the Olympian pantheon, containing narratives of deeds of the various gods comprising sometimes up to several hundred verses. The style is fully-fledged epic.

The longest of these hymns, made up of two originally separate parts to Apollo at Delphi and Delos, and probably dating from the sixth century BC, is styled as a prelude for a recitation of epic poems, and even contains a personal testimony by the reciting poet, the 'blind poet of Chios'.

It is by no means certain, however, whether the origins of this hymn form are to be sought in a request for the blessing of a god at the beginning of an epic recitation, occasionally extended to include a narrated story. One may just as reasonably assume that it occurred to someone at some point to formulate prayer and the account of a great deed of the god, part of the cult act, using the devices of the epic art, thereby shifting the recited epic hymn into the category of the sung work. Some of the extant pieces in this collection are prayers to deities who were more remote from epic poetry. One of the finest is a hymn to Demeter of Eleusis, probably dating from as early as the seventh century BC. In a way unparalleled by virtually any other document, this detailed account of the cult legend provides information about the Eleusinian Mysteries and the hopes of the mystics for the world to come – matters of which epic poetry took almost no notice at all. A number of hymns of various dates are dedicated to the god Dionysus, who was likewise peripheral to the epic world of deities, being more a god of the rural peasant population.

The form of hymnic poetry in the epic style is one we shall be encountering frequently in our account as it unfolds.

2

THE EARLIEST
NON-EPIC
POETRY

Greek epic poetry evolved in an agrarian society ruled by noble families with a strong sense of tradition. It was a society fragmented into numerous politically independent and geographically distinct clans, each with its own separate identity – and one not enjoying particularly close ties with the non-Greek world. (In the latter respect, the Ionians on the mainland of Asia Minor may perhaps be regarded as an exception.)

From the eighth century BC onwards, Greek society was gripped by profound upheavals. Part of the body of extant epic texts, all of which date from the latter phase of the epic tradition, documents these upheavals quite clearly. In their aftermath, the productive energies of epic poetry waned in Greek society.

The most important of these changes may be described as a replacement of the institutions of the aristocratic federation by the city-state – the emergence of the Greek *polis*. Initially, however, this did not entail a concentration of the population in urban settlements. The institutions of commerce were still too weak for this. Nevertheless, those who were economically self-sufficient probably increasingly saw themselves less as members of a clan association dependent on a noble estate, and more as members of a community.

This manifested itself most clearly in military organisation. In the society described by Homer, except in a handful of verses, only the aristocratic lone combatant mattered. All other participants in war were mere retainers. Now, however, came the advent of the phalanx of heavily armed foot soldiers, whose military superiority depended on numbers and the disciplined solidarity of an egalitarian fighting body. Since arms were costly, only relatively well-off warriors could afford to fight in the phalanx, but the numbers of men risking life and property for the common weal, and who consequently also expected to have a say in government in peace time, increased substantially compared with earlier times.

Clearly the social and above all cultic privileges of ancient noble families were not to be swept aside overnight, but the city-state grew steadily in strength, especially in Ionia. In many instances the family cults of the nobility were adopted as municipal institutions, thereby ensuring the favour of the gods. Similarly, new associations of fully-fledged citizens were created, centred on the cult, as the former aristocratic federations had been.

These developments were both encouraged and led in some dangerous directions by economic factors. As trade began to flourish, the formerly natural privileged status of the landowner tended to be undermined in most areas, though with varying degrees of rapidity. Another factor was the introduction from Asia Minor in the seventh century BC of the use of coinage, a measure which permitted the propertied classes a certain degree of mobility and new opportunities for socio-economic advancement, but which also brought new, hitherto unknown forms of expropriation and enslavement, resulting from harsh debt laws. In the seventh and sixth centuries, the social tensions brought about in this way led in many *poleis* to conditions of so-called tyranny, in which a member of the ruling class of full citizens, composed at that time of both the old nobility and nouveaux riches, would take control of a discontented lower class that was not further involved in affairs of state, and establish a monarchy legitimated by personal influence rather than law or descent. There were also sporadic attempts from time to time to curb social unrest by means of piecemeal reforms such as debt remission, or the written codification of laws hitherto handed down orally in family traditions – in other words by improving the unequivocal administration of law. Despite a range of typical features common to all Greek city-states, socio-political developments were so heterogeneous that by the fifth century BC, the Classical period, a profusion of diverging constitutional systems was in place, ranging from radical democracy to monarchy.

The unrest that seized the Greeks from the end of the eighth century BC onwards propelled them equally forcibly in an outward direction. Aside from a few tribes with a strong inland orientation, the Greeks once again became a seafaring nation, trading with all the Mediterranean countries from Syria to Spain, and from the Nile to the Don estuary. In addition to this, there was a great wave of colonisation, beginning with a movement of western Ionians in Euboea, and then involving all Greek tribes, including the Dorians. The coasts of Sicily and southern Italy were soon garlanded with burgeoning Greek towns, to be followed by the coasts of the northern Aegean and the Black Sea as far as the Crimea and the Caucasus. Other colonial cities sprang up in Libya, Egypt, Syria, southern France and Spain, even though the western Mediterranean was actually the domain of the Carthaginian Phoenicians and the Etruscans of northern Italy.

In this way, the Greeks came into close contact with the great cultures of the east. There are seventh-century accounts of Greek mercenaries serving in the Egyptian and Babylonian armies, and a sixth-century reference to a Greek personal physician to the Persian king. Particularly close and to some extent friendly ties emerged between the Greeks of Asia Minor and the Lydian Empire, which rose to become a great power in the seventh century BC.

Given all this, it is not surprising that from the eighth century onwards we find evidence all over Greece of the impact of advanced Oriental cultures. This is perhaps most clearly discernible in pottery, where the austere ornamentation of the geometric period gave way to the full gamut of Oriental pictorial sense, unleashing an immense flowering of figurative vase decoration. Inspired by Oriental models, the seventh century BC saw the first achievements in major sculptures and temples. Musical instruments, melodies and compositional techniques – and the use of coinage – came from Asia Minor. Advances in shipbuilding, systems of measurement, and above all a script, were adopted from Phoenicia, medical knowledge from Egypt, and other advances from other Oriental countries. Most important of all, perhaps, were the religious notions and conceptions that swept into Greece, chiefly from Egypt but also from the Near East.

The Greeks were avid for knowledge, opening themselves unreservedly up to outside influences in the centuries between the demise of the epic-geometric epoch and the Persian Wars. In this period nothing could have been further from their minds than a preoccupation with their own national character. Because of this openness, probably no other epoch in the history of the human mind witnessed the discovery of so much that was new, or so much fresh potential in thought, speech and creativity as those two centuries of Archaic Greek culture.

The first post-Hesiodic poet who is even tolerably accessible to us is the Ephesian Callinus, who probably lived in the early or mid-seventh century BC. Ephesus, one of the foremost towns in the Ionian colonial land, where cultural and social developments had progressed the furthest, was at that time having to wage a number of arduous wars against other Greek cities and against the Lydians. In addition to this, the whole of Anatolia was being disrupted by raids carried out by Iranian or Thracian–Phrygian nomadic tribes, the Cimmerians and the Trerians. The sole extant elegy by Callinus elucidates this situation for us. In forceful language that is nevertheless so restrained in general that it gives us no historical clues, he calls on his fellow citizens to face the enemy manfully, to fight for their land, wives and children, and not to shrink from the death that is none the less to be their universal lot. All that counts is the incomparably greater esteem enjoyed by the courageous man, both alive and dead, among his people.

A new tone may be discerned here compared to epic war poetry. It is one's fellow citizens, the *demos*, who are to be protected, and the land which is to be defended. Fame rests not on the tradition of a noble dynasty, but on the judgement of fellow citizens concerning the living and the dead. The combatant whom Callinus has in mind is not the lone aristocratic combatant, but the hoplite (heavily armed foot soldier) in the phalanx.

The style used by the poet, however, differs from the epic only in its new Ionisms, although the tone is sterner. The metre has been developed out of epic metre, and consists of a sequence of verse pairs, in which the first verse is a normal epic hexameter, the second a slightly adapted dactylic verse:

$$-\overline{\cup\cup}-\overline{\cup\cup}-\overline{\cup\cup}-\overline{\cup\cup}-\cup\cup-\overline{\cup}$$
$$-\overline{\cup\cup}--\cup\cup-\cup\cup-\cup$$

A poem of this type has by its very sequence of verses a more emphatically articulated effect than a purely hexametric epic narrative. This makes the elegy a highly suitable form in which to couch an admonitory speech that is to deal as clearly and forcefully as possible – and hence not too extensively – with a number of diverging but at the same time equally topical points. The poet's choice of the Homeric stylistic idiom – one that differed from the idiom spoken by everyone, and was only comprehensible to those with a Homeric education – arises quite simply from the absence of any other alternative for stylisation capable of raising utterance above the everyday level. Dactylic metre (– UU) was moreover closely linked with the epic stylistic tradition and its formulas.

The term elegy is of non-Greek origin. As late as the Classical period, etymologically related words were still part of the vocabulary of the dirge. It may be, therefore, that the elegy started out as a form of ritual dirge. The poem by Archilochus to be dealt with below (p. 38) at any rate demonstrates that a dirge could quite easily be the subject of an elegy in the seventh century BC.

The majority of examples of early elegiac art may nevertheless safely be classed as 'journalism'. This 'journalism' naturally reached its audience, the members of a class of full citizens continuing the aristocratic tradition in the oldest *poleis*, by means of oral rendition, most frequently at an all-male banquet. In the society of that time, this was an exceptionally important institution, subject to strict ritual. It is understood that both elegy and epic poetry were recited, but to a flute accompaniment. A developed art form of flute music was unknown to the Homeric noble society, being an import from Asia Minor that did not reach the Greek world until the eighth or seventh century BC. Flute music never attained the same degree of social esteem as music played on stringed instruments, already indigenous to Greece in earlier times and under the special patronage of the god Apollo. It was also regarded as uninhibited and provocative, an idea which may derive from the use of the flute in orgiastic cults in Asia Minor. Nevertheless, by the seventh century the names of famous virtuoso flautists and flute composers began to appear, some from Asia Minor, but some from the Peloponnese. At the same time, the flute solo asserted itself as an event in the programme of some of the great pan-Hellenic musical and athletic contests. It may be that the close connection between the elegy and flute music contributed to the speedy recognition of this instrument. The combination of elegist and flute composer in one and the same person, as, for example, in the poet Mimnermus of Colophon (see below, p. 52) was certainly not rare.

A glance at the very similar elegiac poetry of the Greek homeland is provided by relics of a collection attributed to a poet by the name of Tyrtaeus, of which the earliest parts date back to the late seventh century BC. (Later pieces in the collection, identifiable partly by their different compositional technique and partly by their use of late linguistic morphology, date from the sixth and fifth centuries BC.).

Tyrtaeus, author of the earliest pieces, wrote in a highly specific historical context for the upper class of the Spartan state, becoming the originator of the genre of Spartan war poetry. A brief look at the Spartan state will therefore be necessary for an understanding of these elegies.

That proportion of Dorian immigrants who pressed down as far as the south-eastern Peloponnese occupied the fertile plain of Eurotas. The local population were forced into serfdom as helots, and sent into harsh forced labour working the estates appropriated by the invaders. Inhabitants of less fertile tracts of land became politically dependent, but their small communities did at least retain a degree of autonomy. Known as *perioikoi*, these people plied trades and crafts.

The upper class of Spartans lived on the income generated by the landed property divided up among their families. Aside from two royal families, who supplied the two commanders-in-chief in time of war, there were no social distinctions among them, or only slight ones arising out of unequal property holdings. There was, however, a strict subordination of all private interests to that of maintaining the defensive capacity of the state. The Spartans were educated in institutions envisaged for this purpose, living out their lives as soldiers under an administration that wielded extensive powers. Not surprisingly, therefore, the Spartan hoplite phalanx appeared undefeatable for centuries, while Spartan names found their way into the winners' lists of the Olympic games with unusual frequency.

The characteristic state system that began to take shape some time around the early sixth century BC, and to which the Spartans continued to adhere despite severe difficulties until the Hellenistic age, was attributed to a lawmaker by the name of Lycurgus, a figure shrouded in legend. In the first centuries of its existence, the Spartan state did not yet harbour that formidable hostility to all things intellectual, but participated fully in the blossoming of music, poetry and the visual arts that was so characteristic of the age. In the seventh and sixth centuries BC, this particular form of social organisation represented no more than a coupling of aristocratic traditions and the new middle-class spirit that typified the times.

Not surprisingly, therefore, sixth-century Sparta came to be the undisputed leading power in Greece, despite the fact that this state never had the kind of urban focus that fostered the civic sense among other Greek tribes. In the early seventh century BC Sparta launched a bloody war so as to provide the swelling ranks of its citizens with estates, and thus enable all of them to live a military lifestyle. They conquered the fertile plain of Messenia, enslaving the indigenous population just as they had the helots of the Eurotas valley. Towards the end of the same century, however, the Messenians rebelled, and since the courageous rebels were able to make considerable headway at first, the entire social system of the Spartan state, based as it was on an adequate income from landed property for every Spartan, threatened to disintegrate.

It was at this critical point that Tyrtaeus composed his war elegies, specially commissioned, as it were, by the Spartans to rekindle the fighting spirit of a nation at war. These poems are thus war propaganda. He sets out the aims of the war with great precision: the unconditional subjugation of the Messenians, who should once again hand over half their harvest to the Spartan landowner and attend the prescribed mourning ceremony at his funeral. Tyrtaeus recalls the twenty-year-long war of conquest waged in the time of 'our fathers' fathers', urging his listeners to recall that the Spartan constitution was sanctioned by the Delphic Apollo himself through an oracle. He probably does this as a riposte to those seeking to give up Messenia and change the social and land tenure system for the benefit of those Spartans who had been driven out. Elsewhere he depicts with merciless realism the plight of the dispossessed, expelled Spartan suffering hunger with his wife and family, whose destitution brings disgrace on his dynasty. For Tyrtaeus, as for Homer, human dignity is unthinkable without property or social esteem. Tyrtaeus uses this bleak picture of hopelessly lost prestige as the basis for his call for all-out war. In other poems, the poet directs separate appeals to older and younger Spartans, whose functions in the Spartan fighting body differed. He describes with horrific accuracy the hideous sight of an old man left in the lurch in the front line by the young men, lying slain on the ground, 'holding his bloody member of shame in his dear hands'. The word 'hideous' at that time still denoted both an ugly sight, and moral condemnation of the conduct that led to such a pass.

Elsewhere, Tyrtaeus depicts the Greek phalanx in detail: foot placed against foot, shield held against shield, crest beside crest, helmet beside helmet, and breast against breast. Almost every detail in the tumult of war is deliberately mentioned – the lightly armed men seeking shelter behind the shields of the hoplites, the division into three aristocratic associations, or the teeth of the combatants as they bite into their lips.

These tough, stirring poems have certainly lost none of their impact even today, particularly if the reader is mindful of the context in which they were composed. Nevertheless, however famous the war elegies of Tyrtaeus may have been, this does not justify ranking them among the finest poetry. Set beside the masterpieces of Homeric scene depiction, their composition is primitive and wooden. Descriptions and admonition are placed side by side in blocks, the sole discernible principle of composition being that of contrast. The horrendous depiction of the slain old warrior mentioned above, for example, linking up with the realisation that the young man will have to take his place in the front line, is followed by a reference to the beauty of such a youthful warrior. He is 'an impressive sight to men, desirable to women as long as he lives, and beautiful if he falls in the front line'. Here, therefore, the image of the hideousness of the dead old man, which is essentially concerned with the moral shame that such a sight should inspire, at the same time automatically evokes the counter-image of the beauty of youth.

Apart from fragments by Callinus and Tyrtaeus, little worth mentioning has been preserved of what was undoubtedly a rich body of elegiac poetry in the seventh century BC. The spread of proficiency in elegiac composition is none the less apparent from surviving shrine and tomb inscriptions in verse form, which from the sixth century BC onwards consisted in the main of one or more elegiac verse pairs (distichs), although prior to that often only of epic hexameters. Although the literary merit of these inscriptions is not always high, they do include some examples of fine poetic invention. Another remarkable feature is the way they manage to combine epic style, which in literature was firmly associated with the use of hexameters and pentameters, with elements of local dialect.

The elegiac form was likewise employed in numerous poems by the one and only poetic genius of the early Archaic period, Archilochus of Paros. Of the prolific body of work by this poet, only a handful of scant snatches have survived, mostly in the form of citations by later authors, although the number of these has increased somewhat since the 1950s as a result of papyrus and inscription finds. Not one single complete poem is extant, however, and even fragments of six or eight lines are an exception.

Despite this lamentable fact, it is still possible to appreciate the unique talent of this poet. His work, all of which was composed entirely for the needs of the moment, contains such a wealth of biographical allusion that a rich body of legend grew up around him in later times that now enables us to glean some useful clues for the interpretation of one of his mutilated texts. This may be seen, for example, in a lengthy inscription dating from the third or second century BC pertaining to a *heroon*, a cult edifice in honour of the poet, on his native island of Paros. The inscription includes an account of his consecration as a poet following an encounter with the Muses. Archilochus, whose life has been dated roughly on the strength of a reference to an eclipse of the sun in the year 648 BC, seems to have been the illegitimate son of a nobleman of Paros and a Thracian slave. As was customary in semi-feudal societies, however, he was undoubtedly brought up as if he had been legitimate, apart from his rights of inheritance. In this way he became a mercenary, involved in many escapades of those turbulent times, such as the attempt to colonise the island of Thasos in which there was fierce fighting with Thracians of the adjacent coast. Life among his war comrades, the various incidents of a precarious existence, as well as sensual love, hatred, derision, grief over bereavement, disgust at the faithlessness of a friend, and lastly, perhaps the most moving of all, his reflections on the nature of man and his fate, all inspired by a life lived to the utmost, are the themes of Archilochus' poetry.

In one distich whose context is unknown, Archilochus presents himself as the servant of Ares and the Muses; in another he describes himself drinking fine Ismarian wine, leaning on his spear. He is no warrior in the accepted sense, however, committed to the code of honour of a Homeric hero or a Spartan.

> Some Thracian is now parading my shield. I was forced to leave it behind near a bush – a fine specimen. But I myself came away in one piece: what is the shield to me? What's gone is gone – I'll buy myself a new one that's no worse.
>
> (Archilochus fr. 5 West)

According to traditional notions of honour, loss of a shield was regarded as the worst possible disgrace. Similarly, Archilochus has no time for the aristocratic ideal of the equally handsome and courageous warrior:

> I do not like the imposing officer who wears his raiment in elegant folds, proud of his attractive hairstyle, and who struts along cleanshaven. My kind of man may be small in stature and bow-legged, but he should stand bravely with his feet firmly on the ground.
>
> (Archilocus fr. 114 West)

In antiquity, Archilochus was particularly famous, or notorious, for his rancour and derision, and a number of fragments do indeed bear witness to the vitriol of his invective. One poem, most of which has survived in a papyrus under the name of Hipponax, depicts with relish the punishment that should befall a faithless friend:

> ... be driven off course by the waves. And may the Thracians with topknots give a warm reception in Salmydessus – and he will experience unspeakable suffering, dining on the bread of slavery – naked and stiff with cold. May seaweed cover him in the billows, his teeth chattering, and lie on his muzzle like a dog in infinite helplessness on the beach ... I would like to see that. He wounded me deeply when he trod our oath underfoot – and yet he was once my friend.
>
> (Archilochus fr. 131 West)

The daughters of Lycambes, hounded with scorn by Archilochus, are said to have hanged themselves as a consequence. A fragment of an erotic poem, which came to light some years ago with the discovery of a papyrus, may be connected with this.

Numerous fragments reveal Archilochus' direct response to any given situation, flouting convention and governed solely by love, hate or other such basic emotions. He nevertheless goes further, reflecting on this subject-matter, thereby breaking entirely new ground in the assessment of his own life and deeds. In one well-known fragment he emphatically assures his readers that men are 'ephemeral' beings. As Rudolf Pfeiffer and Hermann Fränkel (Fränkel 1975, 149f.) have shown, the word 'ephemeral' here denotes not the short-lived nature of man, but his helplessness in the face of the vicissitudes of life, which he is powerless to influence. Constantly confronted with the new and unexpected, he is unable on his own to carry through his own actions and intentions, or even his own feelings and thoughts. The task in hand is to come to terms with this fact of life, which Archilochus never tires of describing. Given the transience of all human experience, it behoves us to rejoice with moderation in our good fortune, and not to grieve excessively over misfortune. Humans lack the ability of the gods to carry out what is worth striving for. They are, however, equipped with the gift of manfully enduring what they are obliged to go through for the short span of their life, without losing their own identity in the process.

Archilochus' credo arose out of an eventful life lived to the full, a strong sense of his own identity, and an ability to reflect on the circumstances of his own existence that was unhampered by the conventional value-judgements of his society. Perhaps the most moving expression of these qualities is found in a poem written after a group of men dear to him, including his brother-in-law, were drowned in a shipwreck. Although unfortunately only a few groups of lines have survived, it is still possible to piece together something of the surrounding circumstances:

> None of the citizens, Pericles, nor anyone in the town, will reprove our loud lament, even if they have now given vent to festive mood, for fine men have been snatched from us by the ocean swell. Our very lungs are sore with lamentation. But the gods, my friend, have bestowed perseverance on us to soften irrevocable misfortune. It strikes first one, then another; here and now misfortune has struck ourselves, and we groan, wounded and bleeding. Soon, however, it will strike others down. Therefore collect yourselves and bear it, and do away with this womanly lamentation.
>
> (Archilochus fr. 13 West)

Later in the poem, Archilochus gives voice to his distress at not being able to give his brother-in-law a proper burial. The verse is worded with great tenderness: 'if Hephaestus had clothed and cared for his head and graceful limbs in pure linen' (these lines have only survived because Plutarch wanted to illustrate the metaphorical use of the name of Hephaestus, god of fire, with a citation). Whether the beautiful line 'and so we wish to recover the distressing gifts of Poseidon, lord of the seas' also formed part of this poem is uncertain. Tracing the line of thought back to its starting-point, like many literary compositions of the Archaic period, it probably concluded with the couplet: 'I am unable to assuage my grief with anything, but can make matters no worse by taking part in the feasting and the festive mood.' Three motifs are combined here: complete immersion in pain and grief, overcoming it with deliberate patience and endurance – the sole safeguard of the individual against the vicissitudes of life – and an equally deliberate return to the company of the living (rendered particularly graphic here as misfortune coincided with a festival in the town).

Archilochus' poems are more than a testimony to a new approach to life and a hitherto unknown self-assurance. They are also among the most consummately formed works of Greek poetry. Aside from a few insignificant relics of various hymns attributed to Archilochus, written in lyric song metre, his extant pieces may be divided into three groups, according to metrical type: elegies, iambic-trochaic verse, and composite verse types. Concerning the elegies, there has been a tendency in recent times to place unilateral emphasis on Archilochus' independence from the epic tradition, undoubtedly failing to do him justice in the process. Archilochus was assuredly one in a long line of poets who made use of the epic-dactylic verse technique and the stylistic form that went with it. The number of demonstrably traditional formulas to be found in his work is strikingly small, and the number of formulations that strike the reader as innovative and surprising, despite their skilful inclusion in the flow of dactylic verse, is unusually high. It is none the less his use of traditional formulations that achieves a fresh tone, often through slight semantic shifts.

It is a different matter with iambic verse. The original meaning of this verse name, of non-Greek origin, is unclear. In earlier Greek usage, however, there is a verb derived from this word denoting the jocular or derisory speech expressly permitted and envisaged in the context of certain cults. This equal alternating rhythm of short and long syllables came closest to the sequence of colloquial speech, and alternating verse was subsequently therefore perceived as spoken verse par excellence. It would be appropriate, therefore, to give some thought to the development of specific alternating metrical forms for the needs of impromptu satirical or humorous speech, even in the pre-literary era. (In primitive societies, people were wont to use the cult and its exceptional context as an outlet for open accusation or derision which under normal circumstances would jeopardise social harmony.)

The metrical forms obviously already available to Archilochus were the iambic trimeter and the trochaic tetrameter, indicated by the following schemata:

$$\bar{u}-u-\bar{u}-u-\bar{u}-u\underset{\smile}{u}$$

$$-u-\bar{u}-u-\bar{u}-u-\bar{u}-u\underset{\smile}{u}$$

Both these forms have the same conclusion, both allowing at the same point in the line some latitude for choosing between a long and a short syllable. The tetrameter has only a three-syllable extension at the beginning, transforming the rising rhythm (short/long) of the trimeter into a falling rhythm (long/short). The terms trimeter and tetrameter (three- and four-measure line) derive from the fact that the latitudes available for choosing quantity within the line allow groups of four syllables to be distinguished. In the trimeter these are repeated three times, in the tetrameter four times – in this case, however, shortening the final group (metron) by one syllable.

Archilochus employed this metre in accordance with tradition by using it to clothe his invective. The thematic scope of Archilochus' poetry undoubtedly went far beyond anything so far dealt with in pre-literary popular iambic poetry. More than this, however, he furnished this verse type, hereafter the most widely used spoken verse type in Greek poetry, with a formal perfection not encountered again until the highly sophisticated Hellenistic poetry, which was intended for an exclusive public of connoisseurs. The formal elegance of Archilochus' poetry is a marvel of literary history defying all explanation. He observed rules of euphony, for example, which were not consistently adhered to by any fifth-century BC author of Greek tragedy. In addition, he managed with absolutely unfailing good taste to devise what in terms of choice of words and word order was the most unpretentious possible mode of expression to suit this typical spoken verse form. A 'poetic' word alien to everyday speech is quite a rare occurrence in his iambic and trochaic verse. The effect of his verse thus derives not from ornamentation of speech, or from a character that contrasts with everyday speech, as in the case of epic-elegiac poetry, but from a hitherto unknown degree of expressive concentration, and a rhythmic form that never flags.

The third category of Archilochus' poetry consists of composite verse types. It is not possible to ascertain whether or not these existed before he used them. They comprise both epodes composed of couplets with conflicting rhythms, such as

$$\bar{\cup}-\cup-\bar{\cup}-\cup-\bar{\cup}-\cup\underline{\cup}$$
$$-\cup\cup-\cup\cup-$$

in which an iambic trimeter alternates with a semi-dactylic pentameter, and asynartic ('unbound') verse, such as

$$\cup-\cup\cup-\cup\cup-\bar{\cup}-\cup-\cup-\bar{\cup}$$

in which two metrical components with conflicting rhythms are joined to form one long line. In these composite verse poems, the correlation between choice of words and word order on the one hand and the metre on the other is the same as in iambic and trochaic verse.

Archilochus' work marks a peak in Greek poetry that went unmatched for centuries. This makes it all the more lamentable that little more than snatches of his works are extant today. The unique status of Archilochus in his own time is most clearly revealed by an examination of iambography in the subsequent era. Several lengthy pieces by a poet named Semonides from the Ionian island of Amorgos have survived from the early sixth century BC. One of the two most important pieces deals with an ancient theme already broached in the *Odyssey*: the frailty of humanity. The other, a more amusing piece, seeks to expose woman as the greatest evil of mankind by means of a detailed comparison of various female types with a wide range of animals and objects, in order to illustrate their chief vices. This theme is already familiar from Hesiod. However, this inventory offers one type of woman in which there is nothing to criticise. Semonides likens her to the bee. The point of this, however, seems to be that the few 'bee women' who exist are no match for the overwhelming majority of other types, thus allowing Hesiod's overall position to be sustained. Like Hesiod and Archilochus, Semonides also wrote animal fables, popularising them in the form of iambic poetry.

Another iambographer, Hipponax of Ephesus, dates from the middle or even late sixth century BC. Judging from his name, he must have been of noble family, although in some extant fragments he presents himself as a starving, freezing beggar. No more is known today about the biography lying behind these verses than the little known in late antiquity, which fabricated a rich web of biographical legend on the strength of his uninhibited, often obscene invective.

Hipponax was the first Greek poet to avail himself of a deliberately vulgar idiom, which is given an added dimension of local colour by his frequent use of Lydian loan words and names such as were undoubtedly current among all Ephesians or Colophonians. He equals Archilochus in pungency of invective against all and sundry, but not in force of expression, and all trace of profound reflection is lacking entirely in surviving texts.

His verse structure is remarkably pure and meticulous, making a strange contrast with his vulgarity of expression. Hipponax may have been the first poet to make use of a playful variant of the trimeter, creating a light burlesque effect with abrupt changes of rhythm at the ends of lines, the most conspicuous place for the ear to pick them up:

$$\text{instead of} \quad \bar{\cup}-\cup-\bar{\cup}-\cup-\bar{\cup}-\cup\cup$$
$$\bar{\cup}-\cup-\bar{\cup}-\cup-\bar{\cup}--\bar{\cup}$$

Another Ionian poet of the same period, by the name of Ananius, a few of whose lines have survived, also used these 'limping' tetrameters.

In the terminology of modern literary history, Archilochus, Tyrtaeus and Hipponax are all designated without distinction as lyric poets. This is because all non-dramatic and non-epic poetry is nowadays classified under this term, which for the most part assumes the use of poetry to express the thoughts and feelings of an individual. In antiquity, however, lyric poetry was a term denoting poetry either recited by an individual, or sung by a chorus to an instrumental accompaniment – song poetry.

Our understanding of ancient lyric texts in the above-described sense is gravely impaired by our ignorance of the melodies that accompanied them: present-day knowledge of ancient Greek music is scant, to say the least. The few surviving scores of such music are of late origin, and their interpretation a matter of controversy. Surviving documents on music theory date without exception from a period far-removed from early lyric poetry by profound changes in compositional technique and musical taste. This may be illustrated by the example of the divergence between Baroque–classical theory of harmony and twelve-tone music. Where choral lyric poetry is concerned, there is an additional complicating factor: *choros* denoted both 'chorus' and 'dance', 'dancing-ground'. The words of poetry were thus not only sung and accompanied by musical instruments, but also illustrated choreographically. Owing to the sparsity of literary references and the few surviving pictorial accounts, present-day knowledge of Greek dance is likewise at best sketchy.

Music underwent a major flowering in the seventh century BC. Flute music as an art form had recently been adopted from Asia Minor, and music for stringed instruments was considerably enriched both by technical advances in instrument-making, and by the adoption of new instrumental forms, recognisable from their foreign names. Flute and kithara solos (aulody and kitharody) were included in the programmes of major musical contests such as those held at Delphi (Pythian) and Sparta (Carnaea) – regularly held competitions which accelerated the growth of the art. Even by the seventh century BC techniques of composition and playing had grown so complex that only professional musicians could compete. All that can be stated today about the character of this music is that, like Oriental music, it was strictly monophonic, and hence could only be further refined in terms of a constant enrichment of the formal fund of rhythm and melody. This resulted in a highly developed sense for the effects of certain rhythms and musical modes on ethics and educational psychology.

Some mention has already been made of flute music as an accompaniment to elegies. The first among the great innovators, composers and virtuosos of kitharody still known of today, Terpander of Lesbos, accompanied his musical performances with verses, a few of which have survived. His native soil was in very close contact with the Lydian hinterland. None the less, the musical triumph that caused his name to be handed down as inventor of the 'kitharodic nomos', the canonic compositional form for the kithara, was due to the fact that his success at the Carnaea in Sparta in 676 or 673 BC was placed first in the written list of winners.

It was now a question of applying the achievements of the flowering musical art to the many opportunities for singing and dancing available in early Greek society, as in other similar forms of society. Aside from work songs and children's songs, which the Greeks of course also had and of which there are even a few extant examples, the many existing cults provided the most noteworthy occasions for musical performance, most of these being enriched with dancing and song, as also was the ritual character of weddings and funerals. Responsibility for cults lay either with family associations or, as in a *polis* that had already evolved into a definite community, with the groups modelled on them (or so-called *thiasoi*). Cult associations originated from a horizontal division of the population into such groups as girls' and youths' sets, which were entrusted with quite specific social functions such as education, the fostering of tradition, and defence. They were encountered both in early Greek society, and in virtually all early cultures. (The institution of the *gymnasium*, for example, which was of infinite importance in Greek civilisation as a locus of continued athletic and musical education, undoubtedly derived from the male set.)

All such associations, however, controlled their particular cult with all its appurtenant festivals, being almost predestined by the nature of cult organisation to be responsible for an increasingly demanding musical and choreographic performance practice. Cults and rites naturally had from ancient times both fixed formulas and set, often incomprehensible texts which remained unchanging on account of the magical and legal quality of the sacred acts attached to them. To the extent that cults were furnished with musical and literary components, these words and formulas degenerated into refrains by which the appropriate songs could be identified and classified.

From the very beginnings of the lyric poetry that came about in this way, therefore, there was an abundance of song forms: paeans (hymns of thanksgiving) with the cult name of *ië paian* from the Apollo cult; dithyrambs (impassioned choric hymns) with the cult name *io dithyrambe*, sung to Dionysus; the hymeneal, named after the ritual wedding song; and the *ailinos* song, whose name derived from a formula used in the dirge. In addition to these were names such as the *partheneion*, a song for a *thiasos* of virgins, or *prosodion*, a song for a procession. For cognoscenti, such names also indicated the rhythmic and musical character, accompaniment (flute and/or kithara), mode of performance (solo or chorus) and choreographic arrangements (be this in the form of circular chorus, i.e. dance, procession, or standing chorus, which also stipulated the number of choral singers).

The sole extensive experiments among the rich production of 'total works of art' still dating from the seventh century BC are almost all attributable to the poet-composer, choreographer and musician Alcman, who hailed from the Aeolian east, like Terpander, an 'expatriate Greek' who boasted of origins in Sardis in Lydia. He did most of his important work in Sparta, however. This is no coincidence, since the unusually intense social life of the Spartan upper class made that city the main centre for this kind of lyric poetry. Other musicians and poets who worked mainly in Sparta are also known by name.

Alcman's most extensive extant fragment, comprising over a hundred lines, formed part of a *parthenaion* preserved on one of the first few papyri to be rediscovered. The first part gives an unfortunately mutilated account of a local Spartan myth, with emphasis less on depicting the battle scene it contains than on a complete enumeration of the persons involved. Following an abrupt transition, the second half deals with female singers from the chorus, in other words members of the Spartan girls' *thiasos*. All are named, and offered compliments in the distinctive, if somewhat rustic convention of the Spartan style.

This and other brief fragments give us a glimpse of the social conditions of which this lyric poetry is an expression. The poet allows the male and female singers to speak unabashedly about their preferences and rivalries, albeit using references whose topical nature does not always permit us to understand them now.

The poet is equally fond of speaking about himself at some length, sometimes with humour, sometimes with great self-assurance. He once refers to himself as the 'omnivorous Alcman', referring not to the fine cuisine but to the quantity of food he consumes, looking forward with gusto to a huge pot of peeled barley.

Among this body of predominantly somewhat dry, although stylistically pregnant and occasionally humorous texts, a small number of passages excel in which Alcman succeeds in creating poetic metaphors of astounding grace. The ageing poet, for example, finding it difficult to keep up with dance movements among the girls' chorus, expresses a wish to be turned into a kingfisher. Legend has it that the kingfisher is borne on the wings of the faithful female above the crests of the waves. These and other passages may encourage us to confirm, along with the majority of philologists, Alcman's authorship of a well-known fragment which he is traditionally held to have written:

> The mountain peaks and ravines are sleeping,
> The crags and valleys,
> And the forests and all that is
> Nourished by the black earth.
> The beasts who inhabit the mountains are sleeping,
> And the race of bees
> And the monsters in the depths of the purple sea.
> Hosts of wing-spreading birds are sleeping.
>
> (Alcman fr. 89 Page)

As may be discerned from the lengthy fragment of the *partheneion*, Alcman's poetry consists of long, rhythmically corresponding strophes arranged in pairs, evincing a variety of verse types. His poetry antedated the widespread prevalence of a triadic arrangement in later choral lyric poetry, in which such strophe pairs were combined with a third separate one to form a unit within the song, and where a triad thus arranged could take quite a different rhythmic form from its neighbour. Since the music to these songs has been irrevocably lost, scholars are utterly dependent on an examination of the language in order to recreate the rhythm. Such examination reveals certain recurring sequences of syllables that are generally classified as song verse types. This system is corroborated when specific poems are found to consist entirely or predominantly of such lines, showing that it was evidently usual to use only a limited number of combinations of different verse types. Some of the names used to denote these verse types have been coined by modern scholarship, while others derive from Hellenistic philology, whose position vis à vis ancient lyric metre was identical to our own.

Alcman's use of language is a true reflection of how this early lyric poetry came about. A major proportion of the words that give his texts their poetic character derive from epic vocabulary, that inexhaustible reservoir of all poetic word usage in Greek. Besides these, he also uses a number of Aeolic forms, pointing to the birthplace of this new art form. Finally, he overlays the whole with a thick blanket of Doric forms and words, reminding us that his songs were composed for Spartan choruses. The significance of Dorian communities commissioning such works lies in the fact that this particular mixed, but strongly Doricised, synthetic dialect became the hallmark of the choral lyric genre.

Naturally, the wide choice of word and form available in such a mixed dialect also afforded a certain metric ease. For all its splendid vocabulary, Alcman's style is syntactically straightforward. Objects are described, not reflected upon, or if so only sparingly. In this respect, however, choral lyric still had a long way to go.

This creative choral lyric genre soon also found itself being fostered in the up-and-coming Greek cities of the Sicilian and southern Italian colonial regions, which outstripped the homeland in terms of wealth. Among the first names to appear in the extant body of this western Greek choral lyric poetry is that of Stesichorus of Himera (some kilometres from present-day Palermo), which is associated with innumerable fragments, and not a few highly contradictory accounts. In order to make sense of these, two or even three poets of this name have been assumed, spread over a good century. This is not so absurd an approach as might at first appear, since the word *stesichoros* is more a professional designation (meaning something like a choirmaster) than an individual name. At all events it may safely be assumed that some time around or shortly after 600 BC a major Sicilian choral lyricist was composing, to whom the overwhelming majority of extant fragments under the name of Stesichorus may be attributed, although practically nothing is known about the poet's life.

The songs themselves treat mythical episodes, some drawn from major epic works, some from local traditions. The latter applies, for example, to the saga of Daphnis, who was later to become a central figure in so-called Bucolic poetry (see below, p. 274).

As far as may be judged from these relics, Stesichorus' great strength was his narrative technique – his ability to discover in a given myth an episode or scene able to arouse a sense of personal involvement in his listeners. Stesichorus shares his delight in narration, and his gift for the impressive re-creation of scenes, with the visual arts of the same period (metope reliefs – in the space between two triglyphs on a Doric frieze – and vase decoration). Next to epic works, therefore, his mythical narratives remained the most important mythographical sources for posterity. His *Palinode*, for example, was made famous through a reference by Plato. In an ode subsequently known by this title, also associated with the biographical legend about the poet going blind and then recovering his sight, Stesichorus retracts his previously narrated story of the abduction of Helen, asserting instead that she was in fact never taken off to Troy at all. This version of the myth, according to which the Trojan War was fought not over Helen, but over an illusion or something of that kind, is known from Herodotus and Euripides. It may have come about so that Helen, a revered goddess in Sparta in historical times, would not play the somewhat ambivalent role ascribed to her in the epic version of the myth.

Modern knowledge about poetry of the kind written by Stesichorus has recently been substantially enriched by papyrus finds. It remains an open question, however, whether all of these fragments may be ascribed to the Sicilian poet. They do nevertheless all evince the same narrative style, discernible from linguistic borrowings showing his reference to epic works. The most interesting piece is on a papyrus preserved in Lille, forming part of a poem dealing with an episode from the saga about Oedipus and his sons. Like later choral lyric poetry, it is divided into three verse groups, each with a different metre and consisting of two strophes which correspond to each other both rhythmically and musically, and a concluding epode with no corresponding anti-strophe.

The period around 600 BC witnessed the great flowering of the Lesbian lyric, which has left us with some of the finest pearls of Greek poetry. No preliminary phases are known, nor does there seem to have been any significant poetic tradition following the death of its two great exponents.

One frequently reads that Lesbian lyric poetry was 'melic' poetry which, unlike the choral lyric poetry examined so far, produced only songs (melos = song) for individual performance. This is making a distinction that misses the real point. It is indeed the case that most extant texts by Sappho and Alcaeus were undoubtedly intended for solo performance (the performer accompanying him or herself on a small stringed instrument, not the loud kithara). Nevertheless, both poets likewise wrote no small number of works that were clearly intended to be choral, but were no different from the others in formal terms – e.g. Sappho's famous wedding songs. The essential distinction between the Lesbian poets and the choral lyricists concerns the rhythmic and musical form of their respective poetry, and is all the more crucial in view of the fact that whereas the compositional technique of choral lyric had its master exponents throughout Greece from the seventh century BC onwards, Lesbian lyric remained confined to the island of Lesbos.

Even in the earliest extant texts, the strophic structure of choral lyric poetry was already massive. It is made up of lines which are entirely quantitative, acquiring their rhythm from a regular sequence of long and short syllables. The convention that applied here was that two short syllables were equivalent to one long one, thereby establishing a criterion for the overall quantity of lines, despite the latitude permitted in the number of syllables. The lines of the Lesbian poets are likewise quantitative in all extant texts, but with the additional regular licence of allowing the two first syllables to be either long or short. In this way the overall sum of quantities is not fixed. In contrast with this, they show a complete absence of the replacement of one long with two short syllables, which means that here, unlike choral lyric metres, the number of syllables was laid down. The verse technique of the Lesbian poets, in other words, operates with metres in which it would seem that originally only the number of syllables was laid down, but with a subsequent trend to regulate quantities as well, although this was not yet being consistently practised by the seventh to sixth centuries BC.

The credibility of this developmental hypothesis is enhanced by two things. Firstly, Lesbian verse types were adopted with a fixed number of syllables both by fifth-century BC Attic drama, and by late choral lyric. Secondly, in the Hellenistic period, when Lesbian metres were adopted and refined as forms of sophisticated recited verse, quantity regulation was extended to include the beginnings of lines. It was in this form that Horace introduced this metre to Roman poetry, from where it spread to a number of European literatures.

In the Lesbian poets, song strophes comprise only two to four lines, either similar or dissimilar (e.g. aab, aabc, aa). It is no longer possible to state how distinctions between purely quantitative metre and quantitative plus syllable-counting metre, deduced from a linguistic examination of these texts, were expressed musically. (Besides these two verse types in sung verse, there were also others whose extremely broad potential for variation, both in the number of syllables and in the sum of quantities, presupposes a previous form in which only the number of stresses was laid down, and where surrounding 'bad beats' were left unregulated in terms both of the number of syllables and quantity. Such verse types and their derivatives are to be found both in choral lyric poetry, which incorporated them into its own strictly quantitative verse system, and in some relics of popular poetry.)

Some details are known about the life of Sappho. She came from a prominent family in the town of Mytilene; she was small and dark-skinned; she was forced by political troubles in her home town to spend some time in exile, had a much-loved daughter, and a brother who spent all his money on several trips with a Greek hetaira to the Greek colony of Naucratis in the Nile Delta.

Sappho became a poet through her ability to reflect in an unusual way on human relationships in the context of her particular social status. On Lesbos, where the culture was rapidly becoming urbanised, not least under the influence of the much-admired Lydians, the former girls' sets of primitive society took on a new form. Under the auspices and roof of a prominent lady (this term is entirely appropriate here), girls of good family spent several years before their marriage being instructed in the traditions and arts of their society. There were a number of *thiasoi* of this kind, all of course united around a common cult, which were rivals among themselves, as tends to be the case in educational institutions in all intact societies. Within these *thiasoi*, which were entirely devoted to the beautification and stylisation of living, and in which everyday economic life played as peripheral a role as in any exclusive modern boarding-school, a close network of affection and friendship naturally formed between the girls and the lady of the house. Relationships of this kind, however, were more powerful emotionally than the marital bond between husband and wife, which in the social conditions of that time largely had the character of a contract between two families. Where emotion itself became a subject of reflection, however, this more powerful emotional bond also fostered the potential for sublimation and spiritualisation.

The Greeks were quick to realise that mutual, considerate affection between young people and their elders was the most important prerequisite for success in educational endeavour. In all parts of Archaic Greece where strong aristocratic tradition removed the education of young men from the institution of the family to institutions of the male association type (including Sparta and Crete) we thus also find the social sanctioning of homosexual love among men, which was regarded as a token of good breeding. This kind of love was very soon sublimated into literature. It is not known whether a similar situation pertained among the female *thiasoi* of Lesbos. The affection for her charges that radiates from Sappho's verse may very well have been accompanied by physical relationships which were devoid of lasciviousness and moral stain as long as society approved of them. To reiterate, however, nothing is known of this, and in any case it is irrelevant for an understanding of the poetry itself. The body of biographical legend that later attached itself to the poet's name, giving the word 'lesbian' its subsequent connotations, issued from the pens of literati whose imagination was only capable of being fired by what was forbidden in their own times.

In their critical edition, Alexandrian scholars classified Sappho's poetry by metrical criteria. This arrangement can still be discerned today from some papyri, which were readers based on these scholarly editions. More recent exegetes incline towards a classification based on occasion (farewell poems, wedding songs, cult songs), but even this is not entirely satisfactory. Only a few poetry fragments are known to derive from wedding songs, because of references made to wedding customs – in a quite conventional manner, incidentally. A delightful fragment that came to light with one papyrus find narrates in long dactylic lines, akin to the hexameter, and in language permeated by many Homerisms, the escorting of Andromache prior to her marriage: an enchanting example of the humanisation of the heroic world. H. Fränkel (1975, 164f.) has ventured to suggest that this poem was a song sung in a wedding procession; formulated in such a way that the end leads back to the beginning, it could be repeated indefinitely. There is no lack of other examples in archaic aristocratic society of major landmarks in life being likened to events from mythology, thereby lending them significance.

However, more impressive than any other group that could be distinguished within Sappho's poetry on the basis of the above-mentioned criteria are those numerous both shorter and longer fragments in which Sappho speaks of herself and her feelings, in a manner previously encountered perhaps only in Archilochus. One of these, originally a song comprising seven strophes, of which one papyrus gives us four in complete form, and another gives relics, may be examined more closely here:

Some say that the loveliest thing of all on the black Earth is an army of horsemen, others an army of foot soldiers, or a war fleet. But I say it is what one loves.

This is easy to explain to anyone, for did not Helen, loveliest of all mortals, abandon her excellent husband to voyage to Troy, with no thought for her child or her loving parents, for Aphrodite carried her away . . . (and thus does longing grip me also) to distant Anactoria. The sight of her graceful step and the radiant enchantment of her countenance would be dearer to me than all the host of Lydian chariots.

(Sappho fr. 16 Lobel and Page)

Sappho opens with a figure of speech, traditional since the time of Homer, used to emphasise the particular merit of one's own theme: others may praise this or that, but I . . . . Nevertheless Sappho, evoking the splendour of the fighting world of men with her counter-examples, does not follow this convention by stating: 'But I find Anactoria the loveliest.' Her reflection on the fact that for her at that moment this girl means more to her and seems lovelier to her than all else leads her to the insight that for human beings it is love that sets the criteria for what is beautiful and good – spheres which are inseparable in Sappho's mind. Sappho herself perceives this insight as on the one hand new, but on the other hand as so self-evident and obvious that she introduces her further elaboration of the theme with surprisingly uncon- ventional, almost prosaic words: it is, after all, quite simple, for even Helen, astonishingly, left behind a life that could not possibly have been finer (and whose advantages Sappho calls to mind with the typical Archaic delight in enumeration), to follow Paris, driven by love. The use of an example from mythology to elucidate the present was a standard form of thought and expression at that time.

What was innovative in Sappho's use of this device, however, is the fact that it is not highlighting a specifically envisaged person, object or event, but shedding light on a universal aspect of experience, realised by her for the first time. The most beautiful and worthwhile aspect of any situation for anyone is what he or she loves. Sappho's 'discovery' goes still further than this, however: Anactoria is far away. (She must have been one of the girls belonging to the poetess's *thiasos* prior to her marriage.) The yearning of love makes her likeness, 'her delightful step and her radiant countenance', appear with such intensity before the inner eye of the poet that it becomes the most beautiful thing there is. It is difficult for us, who are accustomed to dealing with abstractions, to gauge the power of reflection behind Sappho's utter- ances. The subjective experience of a profound love transcending all spatial and temporal boundaries leads Sappho to a clear understanding of the origin of human values.

In this process, however, her thought remains entirely confined within the bounds of the visible. No distinction is made between exterior and interior, between the impressions left by objects and people, and the spiritual reactions which respond to them. All this is contained within the intuitive, and yet at the same time precise description of the visible.

The same applies to a poem that was famous in antiquity, whose first part was translated by Catullus, and which is extant in the form of a citation. Here Sappho describes with immense force what happens to her whenever she catches sight of or recalls (it is no longer possible to say which of these two was meant) the beloved girl. This familiar 'pathology' of love is not enumerating the outward symptoms of an inner state. In Sappho's mode of thought, bodily trembling or turning pale are integral to the state being described. In another poem, the only one that has survived in its entirety, thanks to an ancient citation, the constantly recurring experience of an abrupt change of mind, the suddenly returned love of the beloved, crystallises into an image of the goddess Aphrodite descending from the heavens in a chariot drawn by sparrows at the entreaty of the poetess, to bring love to the girl and put an end to the anguish of unrequited courtship.

The intense and sublime quality of her love opens up for Sappho a wholly new sphere of mental and spiritual reality. In one farewell poem, she comforts the departing girl with the thought that recollections of their hours spent together playing and dancing are an enduring possession. Elsewhere, she appeals to a girl in the *thiasos* who is greatly missing a companion, now married in distant Sardis, by reminding her that at that very moment her companion's thoughts are turned to Lesbos and her circle of friends.

Innumerable particular formulations of the poet imprint themselves on the memory. One fragment describes the grove of Aphrodite's shrine, where the goddess is invoked to take part in cult celebrations. Sappho speaks of the fragrance of the incense, the cool water dripping through the branches of the apple trees, the roses casting a shadow over everything, and of the 'somnolence that glides down off the leaves shimmering (in the sunlight)'. (This fragment survived on a clay potsherd dating from the third century BC, and may have been noted down as an exercise by a schoolchild on what in those days was probably the cheapest available material.)

Sappho's language is the Lesbian (Aeolic) dialect of her homeland, interspersed to a greater extent in narrative poems, and in personal poems to a lesser extent, with epic words or words coined within the conventions of epic language. Her diction is exceptionally straightforward, allowing less traditional and poetic words to stand out all the more as decorative elements in her language. She shows admirable ease in managing, without the need for neologisms or conspicuous interference in the word order of everyday speech, to adapt her utterances to a demanding metre in a seamless way. This gives her mode of expression an incomparable grace and poise, invariably making her poetry seem more like a document of feeling than an expression of emotional excitement.

Whereas the picture we have from relics of Sappho's poetry is uncommonly multi-faceted, enabling us to discover new and surprising formulations again and again, the tenor and style evinced by the poetry of Alcaeus seem much more homogeneous by comparison. They were contemporaries, belonged to the same social class, and from time to time even referred to each other in their songs.

Around the end of the seventh and beginning of the sixth centuries BC, Lesbos and its most important town, Mytilene, were in the grip of bitter civil wars. The leading statesman Pittacus was finally able to bring these to an end by means of a wise policy of social equality, as well as military successes against external enemies. Alcaeus and his brother were involved in these conflicts, and their partisan shifts. They belonged to a *hetairia*, a sworn fraternity within the aristocracy, which was sometimes on the side of Pittacus and sometimes against him in the struggle against 'tyrants' (i.e. pretenders to exclusive hegemony) and which did not shrink from calling the Lydians to intervene from time to time. At least twice, Alcaeus found himself forced into exile, but towards the end of his life he seems to have made his peace with Pittacus. His songs, the *Stasiotika*, are direct accounts of his political commitment, entirely related to the situation he was in at the time, and formed the basis of his fame in antiquity. By far the majority have survived in the form of ancient citations, as extant fragments from the ten books of lyric poetry compiled by the Alexandrians from his complete works. They originally formed part of sympotic rites: in those days it was the festive *symposion* at which members of a hetairia assured one another of their loyalty and their common political objectives. It was already known that Alcaeus wrote other kinds of poetry as well, including hymns to the gods, love poems, and adaptations of mythical themes. Only the most recent papyrus finds published since 1941, however, have shed light on these parts of his overall work and given us an idea of the true breadth of his poetic vision. And yet even nowadays his verse is never more thrilling than where he gives vent to his hatred and derision, disgust and despair at the ups and downs of civil discord. These poems speak of treachery and loyalty, triumph and intrigue, the arming for war and of peril – in other words states of mind and events in which Alcaeus himself was involved. In one moving poem written at the time of his exile, he describes his longing for the heraldic call to the people's assembly, in which he would like to take part like his father and grandfather before him, even though 'the citizens have nothing but evil designs against one another'. He likens his present life to that of the peasant bondsman, or even the wolf, who must live alone in the wilderness. This poem may be the key to understanding the *Stasiotika*. However we may now envisage their impact within the *hetairia* for which they were written, the perspicacity and precision with which events and the mood of the poet are described make them first and foremost personal accounts.

Alcaeus does not measure up to Sappho in terms of poetic imagination, not to mention her sensitivity or her capacity to reflect on her own condition.

Nevertheless, the rich poetic and musical tradition of the island of Lesbos, the classical fruits of which are available to the modern reader in the works of Sappho and Alcaeus, provides the latter with the capacity to describe his own impressions and feelings effortlessly, while also doing justice to his own forceful temperament. From time to time he even succeeds in creating a new tradition with a poetic metaphor – as in the poem where he describes with thrilling vividness, from the viewpoint of a passenger, a ship in trouble at sea, meaning the polity tossed by the storms of civil war.

When Horace was translating into Latin the poetic style of the Lesbians, which experienced only a limited revival in the Hellenistic era, he adhered to Alcaeus rather than Sappho. This indicates his unfailing judgement: although the two poets were equal in technical mastery, Alcaeus' poetry is less differentiated and stylistically more homogeneous, despite dealing with a wider range of themes. The infinite sensitivity that marks the poetry of the Tenth Muse, as a later epigram styles her, was an obstacle to literary imitation.

For us, the lyric poets of the turn of the century must be taken as the originators of the contemporary literary genre, even though their art presupposes quite a long tradition. Everything prior to them is now irrevocably lost. The elegists of that time, on the other hand, bear witness to further growth within their sphere of poetry.

The first such poet to be mentioned in this regard is Mimnermus of Colophon or Smyrna (this variation in tradition has little significance, since in the seventh century BC what was originally Aeolian Smyrna was occupied by the Ionian Colophonians and turned into a colony). He was regarded by Hellenistic scholars as the true classic poet of old elegy, probably because he established new themes for the genre. A number of fragments reveal Mimnermus to be quite of the old school – parts of war poems relating examples of valour from previous generations for the encouragement of fellow citizens. What is new, however, is that certain deeds of the forefathers, in this case the conquest of Smyrna, are exposed to moral judgement. This shows that the poet is no longer able to separate affirmation and justification of his own conduct from the tradition of the family or the polity with the former degree of consistency.

In later times, Mimnermus became famous as a writer of love poetry. The Alexandrian anthology of his poetry, or part of his poetry, bore the title *Nanno*, the name of a hetaera. All we learn from these fragments, however, is that Mimnermus proclaims love, that is sensual love between men and women, as the sole beautiful and delightful experience, simply because on the other hand he laments the helplessness of humanity, its defencelessness and frailty, to a degree hardly matched by any other Archaic poet. He is especially horrified by old age and its infirmities, which he views as worse than death; he therefore hopes to die at the age of 60 after a life free of major afflictions.

Aside from one fragment, the surviving relics of Mimnermus' poetry tell us little about the formal qualities of his work, which was held in high esteem by no less than Callimachus. This fragment describes the route of the sun god as he climbs one evening with his chariot onto a golden bowl made by Hephaestus so as to travel on the northern ocean with all possible haste to the place of his rising near eastern Ethiopia. This bold piece of mythical invention is narrated in such a way as to arouse the sympathy of the listener for the poor sun god with his constant bustling activity, attributing to him human characteristics that go beyond the traditional anthropomorphism of epic notions of the gods into the realm of the idyllic.

The Athenian poet Solon was of quite a different mettle from Mimnermus, being one of the towering figures of Attic history. Like Pittacus in Mytilene, he managed, thanks to the moral authority he wielded, to restore social order to his native city. The troubles in Athens, however, were not so concerned with disputes among factions of the nobility. The Athenian economy, more developed than that on Lesbos, had given rise to insupportable differences in property ownership, and the catastrophic indebtedness of large sections of the population. The possibility of tyrannical rule establishing itself, in conjunction with a revolutionary transformation of the system of property ownership, was perilously close when the disputing parties called on Solon to act as their arbitrator, giving him unlimited powers. By means of shrewd and judicious measures – representing a happy medium between radical demands and traditional privileges – he succeeded not only in restoring social order, but also in initiating a series of legislative measures for which his name went down in history as the founder of Attic democracy. This accolade was certainly not justified, for his constitution not only retained all the higher offices of the propertied voting class, but even excluded the mass of unpropertied people, the *thetes*, from suffrage, a right which remained tied to hoplite service under one's own arms. Solon may, however, be said to have laid the foundation stone for Athenian greatness. The self-assurance of the Athenian citizen and his pride in the city of Athens were from now on closely bound up with the Solonic constitution. Having re-established both the domestic order and military prestige of his native city (by bringing a war over possession of the island of Salamis to a successful conclusion), Solon turned his back on Athens for the next ten years, so as to allow the new constitution to be tried out in the absence of his personal authority. He thus set out on a series of lengthy journeys in pursuit of his thirst for knowledge, a trait which was to persist into advanced old age. He was obliged at a great age to witness Peisistratus establish a tyranny, and yet the latter clearly in many respects followed the guidelines for domestic policy laid down by Solon, enhancing the reputation of Athens by means of successful external enterprises and a brilliant cultural policy.

It is a fortunate coincidence for our knowledge about the early periods of ancient history that Solon's elegies provide us with the quintessence of what a modern statesman would leave in manifestos, parliamentary speeches and memoirs. Solon was no major poet, but the diction of elegiac and iambic poetry was already so differentiated by that time, and with a lengthy tradition that made it so easy to learn, that he had no difficulty using it to give an account of his intentions and actions for contemporaries and posterity alike. But his fame also meant that poems of similar content to his own were attributed to his name, and that some of his were tampered with or expanded.

Part of this body of poetry is directly concerned with the measures whereby he restored peace to Athens. He tells, for example, of how he brought countless Athenians back from debt slavery abroad, and liberated the earth, the greatest mother of the Olympian gods – a reference to the removal of debt stones from arable fields. He also speaks with pride of having resisted the temptation to establish his own tyrannical rule, describing his position as one of arbitrator between the parties, 'like a boundary-stone'.

> I gave the people as much as was necessary, neither too many rights, nor too few. I adjured the rich and powerful, however, to keep nothing unlawful in their possession. Thus I stood, holding a great shield between them, and allowing none to gain the upper hand in the teeth of the law.

> (Solon fr. 37 West)

Compared to this, the poem in which he encourages his fellow citizens to join the campaign against Salamis has quite a feel of Tyrtaeus about it. Solon is the true father of Athenian patriotism. He is filled with sorrow to see the fall of 'the most ancient city of the Ionians' – probably a reference to the role of Attica as the territorial starting point for the settlement of central Asia Minor after the disintegration of the Mycenaean culture.

Nevertheless, these poems contain much more profound thoughts than these topical remarks suggest. Solon was the first poet to take up the torch of Hesiod's ideas about justice, that order among men established and guaranteed by the Olympian gods. However, whereas Hesiod views the penalising intervention of Zeus or the other gods in human events more in terms of something deliberate and personally motivated, for Solon divine retribution has, to use a modern expression, more of a quality of natural law about it. Punishment by Zeus strikes as suddenly and inexorably as the spring winds disperse the clouds. Sometimes it is delayed, striking the child or grandchild of the evildoer, although they themselves are innocent, as Solon emphatically asserts with an already keen sense of individual responsibility. Here we see incipient notions suggesting the imminent dethroning of the gods as moral authorities, in favour of morally autonomous individuals answerable solely to themselves.

Whereas Hesiod's theory of the ages presents the progressive deterioration of humanity as an inevitable given, Solon stresses their ever-renewed responsibility for the state of their world.

> By the will of Zeus and the other gods, our city will never be destroyed, for Pallas Athena has her shielding arm stretched over it. None the less,

the unreason of citizens and the injustice of the nobility will lead the great city to ruin.

(Solon fr. 5 West)

Again: 'Do not attribute the misfortune that befalls you to the gods, but to your own injustice' (Solon fr. 4 West).

This 'metaphysics of law' is the cornerstone of Solon's patriotism. His poetry is intended for a polity which he is trying to preserve from harm. The good of the individual, as he argues in one apt metaphor, is utterly dependent on the good of the community. Any harm that comes to the polity finds its way into the home of every individual. The order that Solon the statesman sought to establish, however, consisted essentially of finding a happy medium – a balance between the particular interests of specific groups.

Numerous passages in Solon's poetry, as in Archilochus or Mimnermus, speak of the fickleness, frailty and shortcomings of humanity. Here too, therefore, we find that characteristic pessimism of the early Archaic period which Archilochus sought to counterbalance by appealing for steadfastness, and Mimnermus by immersing himself in the joys of love.

In Solon, however, this pessimism takes on quite a different form. His conviction that the effort to establish justice within the polity is worthwhile springs from what is basically an optimistic view of life, compared to which the pessimism arising from his insight into the 'ephemeral' character of human existence almost fades into literary cliché. This is particularly clear from the relics of an elegy intended for Mimnermus: I would like to die at the age of 80, not 60. It is not known whether two fragments which appear to support this modification of Mimnermus' melancholy statement actually derive from the same elegy. At all events, when Solon expresses a wish to be lamented by friends on his death, it breathes the same spirit. Most apt in this regard is that famous verse of his which more than any other praises the blessing of an active old age: 'I grow old, and continue to learn day by day.'

The elegy, trimeter and tetrameter were not the sole available forms in which to couch significant insights and experiences for the benefit of society. The early Archaic period was doubtless also familiar with simple, single-strophe songs sung at feasts, although the earliest extant examples of such scholia date from as late as around 500 BC. Besides these, there was also an ancient tradition of hexametric aphoristic poetry. The large number of poetic texts ascribed to Hesiod included a collection of aphorisms entitled *The Precepts of Chiron*, the wise sayings of the centaur Chiron, held by myth to have tutored Achilles and other heroes. Epigrammatic poetry of this kind, which also makes up a good proportion of Hesiod's *Works and Days*, was probably a widespread form in all early literatures – a way of passing on generally valid insights in an easily memorable form. Collections of such sayings most often appear under the name of famous viziers, priests or kings, just as the epigrammatic poetry of the Old Testament bears the name of King

Solomon. (The same is also to be found in Egypt and Mesopotamia.) The collection ascribed to Chiron corresponds to this stage of literary development. Nevertheless, a number of well-known hexametric gnomes dating from the early Archaic period bear the name of an individual rather than an archetypal author. The first hexameter of these gnomes generally opens with the words: 'This too is the word of Phocylides.' Sayings, therefore, which more than any other type of literary document would seem made for handing down either anonymously, or under more or less mythical names, are presented here as the intellectual property of a quite specific author, albeit one unknown today. It was of course possible to falsify at some later date the *sphragis* (seal), as the endorsement of authorship set into the verse was known, so that not all the extant sayings of Phocylides are necessarily genuine. (Indeed, a Hellenic Jew subsequently published a moral didactic poem under the name of Phocylides.) Nevertheless, the use of the *sphragis* denotes an entirely new mark of esteem for individual achievement that was unknown to the Orient in this form.

The exact period in which the Milesian Phocylides lived is difficult to pinpoint. The date 544 BC assumed by ancient philology to have been his *floruit* (i.e. his fortieth year) is probably too late. His most delightful saying, which breathes the spirit of Solon, suggests another period: 'This too does Phocylides say: The small town on barren rock that lives in lawful order is mightier than foolish Nineveh.' The conquest of Nineveh that sealed the downfall of the overreached Assyrian Empire took place in 612 BC, and was an event of massive impact. For a Greek living in Asia Minor, however, this impact was eclipsed by the disintegration of the Lydian Empire – for him a byword for wealth and power. Since this latter event occurred in 547 BC, Phocylides' sayings can only have been written between 600 and 550 BC. It is moreover a Solonic, or perhaps universal Greek approach to denote lack of justice and lawful order, a negative moral and political phenomenon, using a word whose meaning is tantamount to 'foolishness' or 'unreason'. Socrates was not the first to view morality as knowledge.

3

EARLY PROSE

The first Greek prose texts in stylised form, i.e. above the level of everyday speech, were undoubtedly laws. From the late seventh century BC the precepts governing legal transactions, previously handed down in the oral tradition of noble families, were recorded in written form to meet the demands of the lower social classes for greater legal safeguards. From this time on, new legislation, inter-state treaties and the like were also recorded in writing. In Athens around 620 BC, for example, Draco recorded the penal code of that time, of which a few clauses are extant. Solon's legislation, which contains many amendments, ensued around 595 BC. We may assume that something similar occurred in 604 BC when 'democracy was introduced to Chios'. Some inscriptions of an ancient date, e.g. from Olympia, also testify to early legal texts of this kind.

Naturally, these developments took place at varying rates in the culturally and economically very different states of Greece. Similarly, there was a long way to go before all legal transactions were recorded in written form, a stage reached in Athens in the fourth century BC. Clearly, however, the process of growing accustomed to written records in legal life was a major factor in the continuing process of language education.

Ancient tradition has it that the earliest prose book is a cosmology compiled by Pherecydes of the small island of Syros some time around the mid-sixth century BC. As far as may be discerned from extant fragments, Pherecydes offered a theory of the origin of the world in which many details are reminiscent of Hesiod, albeit without the latter's consistency, clarity or vividness. There are also lengthy prose narratives of many local sagas. Pherecydes was first in a line of logographers (prose historians) lasting until the end of the fifth century BC, including Acusilaus of Argos, Hecataeus of Miletus, Hellanicus of Lesbos, Pherecydes of Athens, Herodorus of Heraclion, and Charon of Lampsacus.

This writing developed out of the need to record local myths, only a fraction of which had been compiled into epic poetry, and relate them by means of a process of precise genealogical classification to the pan-Hellenic myths – the body of epic works. The logographers enumerated above, however, comprise the full range who resulted from this need.

Initially, there was no awareness of a distinction between myth and history: epic myths, in their various local guises, constituted the picture the Greeks made of their own past. Their substance by no means dated solely from the Mycenaean period, or even earlier prehistory, but reached down well into the first millennium in the case of the foundation myths of cities in Asia Minor and Ionia, for example. The genealogical ordering of highly differentiated local material, however, soon diverted interest to questions of chronology. By that time every Greek *polis* had its own calendar and its own method of numbering years after eponymous officials or priests. There was thus soon a perceived need for a chronological system with which to correlate these many local traditions.

The above-mentioned logographer Hellanicus sought to meet this need in two ways: firstly by compiling a book on the Hera priestesses of Argos, whose succession had begun particularly early, and secondly by publishing a list of winners of the Carnaea in Sparta. (The list of Olympic winners, beginning in 776 BC, was first compiled by one of the Sophists into book form.)

During the fifth century BC logography developed into the chronicling of local history proper (horography). Apart from local myths handed down in noble families, the scope of these accounts also embraced popular narrative, and descriptions of cults, state institutions, etc. The local chronicle of Lampsacus by the above-mentioned Charon, for example, provided a delightful novella. The antique chronicling of local history was not subjected to scholarly methods until the fourth century BC, however, although its literary style was already fully developed by the early fifth century.

Regarding the language and style of the earliest logography (Pherecydes, Acusilaus), the reader is initially taken aback by the striking primitiveness of the syntax (an observation that is equally applicable to the earliest legal texts). It is dominated by short main clauses joined by 'and' or 'then'. The few hypotactic constructions to be found are frequently faulty. And yet this ineptitude dates from a time when an ability to make effortless use of a rich storehouse of complex sentence morphology within poetic diction had been manifest for centuries. It is difficult for us, who happen to be accustomed to complex sentence constructions in prose, but on the contrary have difficulty incorporating them into a predetermined metre, to grasp that the opposite was the case in the early Archaic period. The wealth of poetic vocabulary and compounds built up and tried and tested in Greek over many centuries had revealed many of the syntactic possibilities of the language by the time the pioneers of prose style found themselves having, as it were, to start from scratch and create a syntax.

From the outset, logography availed itself of the Ionic dialect, irrespective of the origins of particular authors. This, along with another even more significant development that began in Ionia, demonstrates both the cultural and economic pre-eminence of that region. It was in Miletus, the centre of Ionia in Asia Minor, that the first work of Greek philosophy was written,

Anaximander's prose work *On the World*. When examining the history of Greek literature – unlike, say, Spanish or German – it is essential to take a broad range of works into account, including philosophical works, scholarly and technical textbooks, although in the more recent view these do not constitute 'literature' in the sense that ballads or novels do. There are various reasons for this. One is that the philosophical and other specialist literature of the Greeks includes works of the highest literary merit. One only needs to think of such authors as Heraclitus or Plato. Another reason is that until the fourth century BC it was in the writing of 'specialist' literature that the Greeks discovered and used the first opportunities for writing literary prose. After the fourth century, which marks the zenith in prose style development, this was no longer the case. At this point specialist literature writing began to diverge from literary prose, and the man of letters no longer had anything to learn stylistically from the scholar or technical expert. However, it is not possible to understand early prose by regarding it solely as a literary phenomenon in the sense meant by ancient or modern theory.

Philosophy in Ionia, unlike India or China of that time, arose out of questions about the nature of the cosmos, the world around us. This question had already found one answer in Hesiod's *Theogony* with the aid of a comprehensive mythical construction comprising an original blend of traditional and invented elements. Learning today how Thales of Miletus declared in the first half of the sixth century BC that water was the origin of all things does not give us grounds to presume the advent of natural scientific or philosophical theory in the modern sense of the term. It is highly probable that Thales, like Anaximander and Anaximenes, the two Milesian philosophers of the next generation, were first and foremost applying cosmological models from Oriental (Babylonian and Persian) mythology, thereby making water, the 'boundless', or air, the primeval force (arché), origin and basic building material of the world.

What is innovative about this and indicative of future trends, is the way these writers remove such theories from the traditional context that gave them their unalterable quality in the Orient – thereby opening them up for discussion. Here, therefore, began that long sequence of hypotheses explaining nature, one referring to another, modifying it either in detail or overall conception, and evaluating constantly new, additional observations in the natural world. The alacrity with which Greek natural science went on to forge, on the basis of very limited observation, sweeping hypotheses which were in turn bound to be refuted by means of a few fresh observations, was thus established with these first beginnings.

Thales has left no extant written works, but in his own age enjoyed high esteem as an astronomer, geometrician and man of genius generally. Presumably on the basis of material gathered over centuries in Babylonian observatories, for example, he predicted the eclipse of the sun in 585 BC. Something is known today from accounts of how Anaximander and

Anaximenes later elaborated in book form fairly detailed hypotheses taking physical phenomena increasingly into account. Clearly, a written discussion of cosmological questions extending over generations, and in which phenomena were described and discussed, along with the views of others, was bound substantially to further the growth of the prose argument mode of expression.

What was to become a highly sophisticated technical literature likewise seems to have had its first beginnings in the sixth century BC, again in the Ionian tribal region. One entirely trustworthy tradition describes how Chersiphron and Metagenes, two of the architects involved in construction of the massive Artemis temple in Ephesus, wrote a book about their work. The fact that this project, made possible in part by donations from King Croesus of Lydia, proved to be a much-admired technical achievement, may well have sparked off technical literature as a new genre.

The early sixth century BC seems to have witnessed the first written records of popular prose tales and animal fables. Tradition attributed later fable anthologies to the hunchbacked slave Aesop, whose lifetime is placed by one detailed story, connected with some anthologies, in the time of the Lydian King Croesus. The true age of these texts is almost impossible to determine, since folk literature of this kind was never recorded in one definitive version, but passed down in countless variations.

In the art of coining prose aphorisms, which also first appeared in the sixth century BC, however, everything hinges on a definitive version. It is undoubtedly no coincidence that the earliest examples of a gnomic literature that sought to word generally significant insights without the aid of metre and poetic vocabulary, but in as memorable a form as possible, attached themselves to the names of historically very well-attested personalities of the sixth century. There is little enough proof that sayings such as 'Give security – and calamity is upon us' or: 'Nothing in excess' really derive from Thales or Pittacus. It is none the less significant that by the early sixth century BC people were sufficiently well-disposed towards the individual character of certain leading statesmen and 'wise men' to attribute to them wise sayings that lacked the conventional garb of poetic tradition.

The number of seven 'wise men' dates from a relatively late crystallisation of the canon. In a process observable from the fourth-century BC onwards, this number was arrived at from a constantly shifting selection of some dozen and a half or so names. None of them, however, were legendary figures – all historically thoroughly attested personalities such as Solon or Periander of Corinth and Pittacus of Mytilene.

The aphorisms themselves bear witness to a growing need to comprehend the inherent laws of social life independently of mythical trappings and traditional taboos. Later doxography thus quite rightly saw in the seven 'wise men' the first moral philosophers.

The degree of popularity of these sayings is evident from the fact that some of them were inscribed towards the end of the sixth century BC on the newly constructed temple to Apollo at Delphi. This allowed them to bask in the moral authority wielded by this god above all others throughout the whole Archaic period. The historical works of Herodotus provide us with a number of anecdotes dating from the sixth century which illustrate the work of moral education carried out by the Delphic priesthood throughout Greece through the medium of the oracle. The wording of these anecdotes, which elucidate through the oracle such matters as the moral significance of mental disposition in relation to a deed, the observance of the boundaries laid down for humanity and similar themes, also bears witness to an increasing adroitness, even in the sixth century, in the compilation of prose narratives.

The high Archaic period was marked by fervent religious life. Never again were so many temples built in Greece, nor at any other time did oracles, particularly the one at Delphi, command such immense influence over all social and political issues. Some features of this intense religious life proved to be of particular significance for literature. One of these was the adoption by up-and-coming city-states of those cults of the rural lower classes whose gods had played no part in the family traditions of the aristocracy, and hence in epic poetry. The rise of these cults, some of which were ecstatic (Dionysus), some secret (Demeter), created fresh tasks for all branches of the arts. This external refurbishment was nevertheless also accompanied by a renewed expansion of those cults and cult legends which in turn had been influenced in no small measure by the Oriental ideas permeating Greece since the end of the eighth century BC.

This process becomes clear in the new conceptions associated with the word *psyche*. As we have seen, in Homer's time this word denoted simply the dead soul of a human being after death, which continued to exist in the underworld after its separation from the body. The self of the deceased, however, had no part in this shadowy existence, and hence could not be involved in reward or punishment for the deeds of earthly life. This latter idea was acquired by the Greeks from Egypt, where there was a very ancient belief in the judgement of the dead, albeit over the entire person and not only over the soul. The Greeks now consistently began to apply the doctrine of reward and punishment in the afterlife to their idea of the psyche, which now came to be seen as the most essential, death-surviving aspect of the human being's moral person – the soul.

In the light of this it now also became possible to attribute a moral, eschatological significance to the ancient mystery cults of the Greek homeland, which had originally sought to impart such thoroughly palpable benefits as blessing, fertility or even immortality. This new complex of ideas crystallised in its most sophisticated form in the doctrine of the transmigration of souls, or reincarnation, which demonstrably existed in Greece from the sixth century BC, although it is not possible to name direct models for this in the Near East.

(A historical relationship between the Indian and Greek doctrines of the transmigration of souls is highly improbable.)

The transmigration of souls is central to the doctrines of one religio-political sect established by Pythagoras of Samos in the last third of the sixth century BC under the auspices of the nobility of the southern Italian Greek city of Croton, which rapidly gained decisive political influence in most southern Italian communities. Pythagorean communities, probably out of concern for the future of the individual soul, submitted to a strictly regulated lifestyle, observing numerous taboos, some quite ancient, which they interpreted in the light of their arcane doctrine. Some part was also played by speculation on cosmological numbers derived from the proportions between string length and tonal pitch on a musical instrument, also taking into account the pedagogical effects of music. However, the contribution made by the Pythagoreans to the disciplines of mathematics and music theory belongs to a later era.

Pythagorism as a religio-speculative doctrine arose in the context of similar sect groupings collectively known as Orphism, after Orpheus, the legendary Thracian musician and poet. Although these sects were highly diverse, the central themes of their mostly mysterious doctrines were the soul, its fate after death, and the genesis of the cosmos. Motifs from indigenous mysteries, Oriental mythology and speculation on cosmology and psychology all combined here to produce unusual new inventions or reinterpretations of existing myths. Complete extant examples of Orphic literature, chiefly hymns and epic poetry expounding on the above themes, in fact all date from the late period, such as an Orphic retelling of the Argonaut myth in epic form. However, occasional fragment finds, such as the papyrus of Derveni containing a cosmological text of this provenance, but above all parodies and references from the fifth century BC, give some idea of the rich early Orphic literature. The western part of the Greek-speaking world in Sicily and southern Italy seems to have been particularly open in this respect, as may be judged from small gold plaques inscribed with texts, or symbolic objects buried with the dead. And yet there are also fifth century BC inscriptions from the Greek colonial town of Olbia on the northern shore of the Black Sea which reveal Orphic concepts.

Closely linked with Orphism are the oracle collections compiled in the sixth century BC by Onomacritus and others. These arose out of the activities of wandering male and female prophets, beginning in the seventh century BC. The prophets, who may have originated in Asia Minor, bore the generic name of Bakis or Sibyl, and exerted a long-standing influence on divination as an institution of time-honoured Greek cults. The young Roman state also adopted a collection of Sybilline oracles as part of the accoutrements of its cult.

There was a huge number of prophets and miracle-workers in the sixth century BC, including Pythagoras and Epimenides of Crete. Some even seem to have imported to Greece practices and doctrines deriving from Eurasian shamanism, such as Aristeas, already mentioned in connection with his Arismaspean epic poem (see p. 28–9). The importance of this influx of new metaphors, concepts and speculations for the future growth of Greek spiritual and intellectual life is self evident.

4

LATE ARCHAIC POETRY

The second third of the sixth century BC was strikingly sparse in poetic talents, who did not begin to appear in numbers equalling the period around and shortly after 600 until the second half of the century. Craftsmanship within the various branches of lyric poetry naturally continued, but the surge in the second half of the century was in no small measure the result of a politically motivated, lavish promotion of poetry, music and the visual arts. This policy was initiated by some of the tyrants in Samos, Corinth and Athens, and carried on into the fifth century BC by the dynasties of the Greek west, and not least the wealthy aristocratic families of other Greek states such as Thessaly, Aegina and Rhodes.

The outstanding exponent of love poetry in the late Archaic period was Anacreon of Teos, who is traditionally held to have left his home on the Ionian coast of Asia Minor when it was incorporated into the Persian Empire in 546 BC. He moved first to the court of the tyrant Polycrates of Samos, and after the latter's overthrow to that of Peisistratus in Athens. He is said to have died at a great age in Abdera on the Thracian coast, where many of his compatriots had already fled in 546 BC.

Some of Anacreon's poetry is known from citations, some from subsequent papyrus finds. Aside from relics of a number of cult songs, most of his poetry was intended for recitation in highly sophisticated court circles, and sings of the joys of drinking and love. His diction, in the Ionic dialect, is of fascinating elegance, his tone light and full of irony. He is able to speak without the slightest tragic undertone of the power of Eros, who 'throws his ball of purple at him', leading him to seek the love of a young girl. 'But she, who comes from proud Lesbos – dislikes my hair, for it is already white' (Anacreon fr. 358 and 417 Page). Elsewhere he likens a young Thracian girl to a filly in a meadow which eyes him with mistrust, but which he is still able to bridle skilfully and cleverly.

Other extant verses by Anacreon derive from poetry of a different, non-sympotic or erotic character, such as a catalogue of sordid events from the earlier life of a wealthy parvenu, or a wonderful couple of lines from a poem lamenting the death of a young friend who has fallen in one of the wars waged by Abdera against the Thracians of the hinterland.

Nevertheless, Anacreon has gone down in the minds of posterity as a tipsy old man, and indeed drinking and love songs as such continued into the Byzantine age to be understood as spoken verse, but composed according to rhythmic principles deriving from Anacreon's metres, hence known as Anacreontic. Anacreon made use of various metres, but preferred the Ionic ($\cup\cup - -$), usually with two forming a verse that could be modified by means of shifts and omissions (e.g. $\cup \cup - - - \cup \cup -$, or $\cup \cup - \cup - \cup - \underline{\cup}$). Anacreon was as consummate as Archilochus at adapting words and clauses to his metre.

Some idea of the potential publicity import of short songs called scholia which were sung at feasts is conveyed by the verses of Timocreon of Rhodes. He gives vent to his anger with Themistocles for not having used his influence to help the poet return to his homeland, which he was forced to leave on account of his pro-Persian views. Other extant scholia by unknown poets take us to aristocratic Athenian circles in the period immediately following the fall of the Peisistratids. With the continuing process of democratisation of political life, at least in Athens, however, scholion poetry fell into disuse during the fifth century BC.

Splendid choral lyric poetry experienced a last great flowering in the late sixth and early fifth century BC, predominantly in states whose aristocracies were still intact. Here, young men and girls of the upper classes had sufficient leisure at their disposal, and enough sense of tradition, to be prepared to submit to the extreme demands placed on them by the choreographic and musical performances that accompanied this poetry. (It is no coincidence that the sung scores composed for citizens' choirs in Attic drama were considerably simpler.)

The great western tradition of choral lyric poetry was carried on at the end of the sixth century BC by Ibycus of Rhegium (modern Reggio di Calabria) who, like Anacreon, lived and worked mainly in the cultivated atmosphere of the tyrant courts on Samos and in Athens. The few surviving fragments of his work bear witness to an outstanding force of expression, affirming the high reputation Ibycus enjoyed in ancient tradition. One fairly long papyrus fragment published only quite recently may also be attributable to Ibycus, and at all events dates from the sixth century BC, being composed according to the triadic scheme used in later works, including dramatic choral lyric poetry (see above, p. 46). The fragment gives a lengthy enumeration of heroes at and in Troy, concluding by mentioning Troilus, the fairest among them, thereby moving on to praise the handsome Polycrates, who was to enjoy lasting fame as a result of this song by the poet. The compliment is thus glorified through the use of mythical example to lend it timeless validity.

Unfortunately, almost nothing is known about Lasus of Hermione, in the Peloponnese, who is said to have tutored Pindar and, like Ibycus, to have lived at the court of Peisistratus. He seems above all to have been a major musical innovator. Simonides, born in 557 BC on the small Ionian island of Ceos, was likewise active initially at the court of Peisistratus, and later at the residences of the Thessalian landed nobility, returning after the Persian Wars at the end of his long life to Athens, by then a democratic city. Simonides is said to have been the first poet to compose Epinician odes – festive songs in honour of particular winners of the pan-Hellenic contests, while his *threnoi*, his funeral songs, were especially famous. He did of course also write cult songs, but the fact that his choral songs in honour of people stood in particularly high esteem is symptomatic. Simonides was able to liberate from traditional perspectives his thoughts on the nature and value of humankind in a way previously achieved only by Archilochus, albeit under quite different conditions. In one scholion to which Plato dedicated a detailed interpretation in his *Protagoras*, he concludes from the now seasoned insight into the 'ephemeral' nature of humans that it is not merely difficult but impossible to achieve noble distinction. The poet is hence content to praise the man who does nothing intentionally reprehensible. This poem is addressed to a Scopad, a member of the leading Thessalian noble family, who, like Pindar, would have taken for granted the notion, prevalent among all hereditary nobility, of an inherited distinction to be constantly revealed anew by individual nobles. Simonides, however, does not see the merit of a human being in what he is, possesses or achieves, since all achievement is ultimately in the lap of the gods, hence outside his sphere of responsibility. He sees merit in the individual's way of thinking, in his view the sole ground for praise, i.e. social esteem.

Simonides propounds these ideas in lucid, almost dispassionate language, although at times achieving vivid expressions of exceptionally memorable quality. In one famous *threnos*, for example, written on the occasion of an accident that resulted in the deaths of several members of the Scopad house, he likens the erratic nature of human fortune to the abrupt manner in which a fly changes location.

Simonides' astute mind was fully cognisant of the implications behind the events of 480 BC, which distinguished him favourably from his younger contemporary, Pindar. The historian Diodorus records a lengthy passage from a eulogy (*enkomion*) of his to the fallen of Thermopylae, in which he describes in highly unusual, almost paradoxical fashion the unique fate of these victims of war in the great struggle for Hellenic liberation.

He nevertheless excels in more than what was for his time the quite extraordinary perspicaciousness and clarity of his reflections. Perhaps the finest extant piece of his poetry comes from a mythical tale dealing with the voyage of Danae, put out to sea in a wooden chest with her son (fr. 543 Page):

> When in the ornate chest
> The howling wind
> And swelling seas
> Filled them with fright,
> And their cheeks grew wet,

She put her loving arm around Perseus and said:
My child, what anguish I suffer.
But you sleep and slumber
In untroubled infant peace,
In joyless wood
Riveted with bronze . . .
Lying in leaden darkness.
The salty flood over your thick hair
As the waves crash over us
Troubles you not,
Nor the roaring of the storm
While you rest there on the purple blanket,
You lovely child.
If you were afeared of that which is fearful
Your keen ear
Would heed my words too.
But I say: sleep, my child,
And may the seas and immeasurable anguish sleep also.
May rescue, in whatever form, be forthcoming,
Father Zeus, sent by you.
But if my prayer was presumptuous,
Or beseeched more than is rightful,
Forgive me.

The depiction of a mythical event from the perspective of an innocent victim was something hitherto unknown. Simonides portrays the despair of the distraught mother with the utmost compassion. Even when her distraction unleashes a cry to the father of the child and initiator of her misfortune, she still immediately finds her way back to that submissive humility befitting her station as the chosen one of Zeus.

Long before Euripides, therefore, we have here the poetic reshaping of a scene from mythical tradition, depicted from the female perspective – an approach that as far as we know today remains without parallel in that epoch.

Biographical tradition captured chiefly those traits of Simonides that showed him to be a man of superior and practical intelligence. This was not entirely unjustified, since the moral reflections surviving in his fragments reveal him to be virtually a forerunner of the Sophists. The Danae fragment none the less demonstrates that the objectivity and astuteness of his rational judgement was combined with a sense of compassion rarely manifested before him.

As with Anacreon and Archilochus, antiquity attributed to Simonides a major body of fine epigrams, which often in fact date from his time. These include the famous epigram about the warriors at Thermopylae, a translation of which was included by Schiller in his *Der Spaziergang (The Walk)*:

'Wanderer, should you come to Sparta, tell them you saw/ Us lying here, as the law commanded.'

Pindar of Thebes was born over thirty years after Simonides in 522 BC, and died in 442, almost forty years after Salamis. Nevertheless this most outstanding poet of early choral lyric poetry was a complete devotee of Archaic aristocratic culture, even though by the time of the events of 480 BC this was no longer representative of most of the Greek-speaking world.

Alexandrian scholars classified Pindar's literary legacy according to genre or occasion. The four volumes comprising his victory odes to athletic winners at the pan-Hellenic contests of Olympia, Delphi, the Isthmus of Corinth, and Nemea have all survived. (However, the extant collection also includes numerous odes where athletic victories are merely mentioned in passing, not as the inspiration for the ode itself). Papyrus finds have also recovered substantial relics of paeans (hymns of thanksgiving to Apollo), dithyrambs (songs to Dionysus), *partheneia* (dance songs for virgin choruses), scholia (short symposium songs) and other poems.

The texts themselves contain numerous hints regarding performance practice. It is clear from these, for example, that a 'festival song' could be sent for performance in the form of a score, and did not necessarily need to be rehearsed by the poet-composer personally. The accompaniment sometimes consisted of flute and strings. What is most apparent, however, is that these were musical and choreographic performances calling for a considerable degree of skill on the part of all those involved in their rehearsal, led either by the poet himself or a choir master appointed by him.

Pindar occasionally refers to his profession, to literary feuds, or to personal matters. Since, moreover, most of the Epinician odes are precisely dated, Pindar is the first author in Greek literary history whose extant works and stylistic development can be correlated with his life story. Although the significance of biographical hints for an understanding of his poetry should not be overestimated, they do occasionally offer welcome assistance in the exegesis of a poetry that was difficult to understand even for philologists of the Hellenistic-Roman period.

Across a literary tradition stretching from Horace to Goethe, notions may be found linked with the name of Pindar that have little or nothing to do with the true character of his poetry. The history of Pindar imitation is a history of productive misunderstanding. Grammarians of the Hellenistic-Roman period studied and interpreted Pindar's difficult texts avidly. One scholion commentary on the Epinician odes, dating from the Byzantine era, has preserved for posterity a good proportion of the erudition accumulated over the generations. The dating of poems with the aid of winners' lists still available in the Hellenistic-Roman era is also possible thanks to these early grammarians.

Regardless of dissimilarities in detail and substantial differences in length, Pindar's Epinician odes tend to deal with three themes. The poet alludes to the athletic victory of the person being honoured (on occasion even those of his forefathers); he narrates, refers to or elucidates a myth that may not necessarily be related to the athletic victory, but is related to the person being addressed; lastly, partly following on from the myth and partly using free invention, he offers moral and theological instruction in the form of meticulously coined gnomes. Frequent direct transitions from one theme to another are as often as not marked by statements in the first person, mostly referring to the poet as a representative of his profession (not as an individual), and occasionally also to the chorus or its leader as the mouthpiece of the poet. In terms of the criteria with which we are familiar today, such as emerged in traditional literary criticism based on Aristotle, there is no substantial, representative piece of Pindaric poetry that blends these elements into an aesthetic unity. (Clearly, this problem takes a different form in complete extant examples of Pindar's short poems.) The modern reader is thus capable of appreciating the festive quality and dignity of Pindar's diction, and his religious feeling or ethos, but is only able to form an impression of the aesthetic nature of his overall compositions by taking the historical background into account. This is achieved by seeking to understand the social function of his poetry.

Pindar's uniquely seamless utterances acquire their artistic unity through the fact that all their various components relate directly to the sphere of ideas pertaining to an already waning aristocratic culture. Even the most fleeting allusion to a mythical episode or the moral maxims of those people who performed and enjoyed these works could thus be furnished with the required number of complementary ideas. The noble families of Rhodes or Aegina, the royal and tyrannical houses of Cyrene, Syracuse or Acragas – even if only by way of subsequent fiction – traced their descent from that heroic age, sung in the great epic works, when the gods took lovers from among the mortals and founded heroic dynasties.

The social pre-eminence of the Greek aristocracy, who in some communities maintained their position of political privilege for centuries, a claim obviously also made by the new tyrannical houses, was justified in terms of this ethos derived from the mythical heroic tradition. Every member of such a house had at his potential disposal the hereditary distinction that had to be made manifest through achievement. In this way he both affirmed his pre-eminent position, and took his place in the line of his forefathers, whose own deeds provided both the criteria and meaning for his own.

The excellent feats of noble families in the athletic events of the pan-Hellenic contests, in which only well-to-do athletes could afford to participate and pay the high cost of training, were interpreted and sublimated in this way. (The wins of professional jockeys from the stables of Sicilian tyrants, who were then personally proclaimed as the winners, reveal the overall questionable nature of such sublimation.)

Obviously, however, this system of generating moral values can only function when each new achievement is appropriately celebrated and publicised. A position of pre-eminence based on achievement is bound up with fame and recognition by others. The maxim: 'Be more than you appear', first coined by Pindar's contemporary Aeschylus is thus as alien to Pindar's way of thinking as Simonides' admonition that people should be judged more by their way of thinking than by their success, since success is in the hands of higher powers. Pindar asserts that the achievement of which no one speaks 'dies'. In another poem, he argues that when establishing the world Zeus created new deities, who were intended to enhance and praise his handiwork in words and music. In this way, Pindar anchored in the very natural order of things the two morally complementary concepts of achievement and fame, which in his conceptual world could not exist independently of each other.

This conviction also underpinned Pindar's self-confidence towards the nobility who commissioned his works, and from whose patronage he made his living. In his view, the poet was the sole informed source able to give meaning and lasting fame to aristocratic achievements, by placing them in the right traditional context and establishing the criteria by which they could be assessed for all time.

By Pindar's time, aspects of aristocratic culture, ranging from the nurturing of mythical tradition to athletics, music and poetry, had been made increasingly accessible to any citizen of the Greek *polis*. In the process, however, these pursuits had forfeited their high moral claims. And yet as late as the Hellenistic era Greeks living in the Orient were known as 'those of the *gymnasium*' – meaning people who practised athletics and read Homer. The vehement polemic unleashed by the early Church against Greek mythology, which by that time had long since lost all religious significance, derives from the fact that myth-oriented poetry continued to be the linchpin of a system of education perceived by Christians as both alien and opposed to biblical revelation.

The importance of Pindar, therefore, lies in the fact that at the last possible historical juncture he still sublimated and expounded in his literary works of art the myth-oriented conceptual world of a disappearing lifestyle with which he himself unreservedly identified. It is this self-same circumstance, of course, which gives rise to the difficulty alluded to above in attempting to assess his work from the literary and aesthetic point of view. The homogeneity of each of his creative achievements is only accessible to one capable of comprehending each detail in its expressive function within the context of that aristocratic culture. Only this approach to his work makes it possible to draw together the heterogeneous elements of these poems.

This outline of Pindar's poetry is obviously primarily concerned with the four extant volumes of his Epinician odes, which comprise but a small part of his complete works. Surviving relics of paeans, *partheneia*, etc. complement this outline by bearing out the religious feeling and ethos of the poet, but pose for the exegete fewer obstacles, on account of what is generally a more unified body of themes and simpler language.

In Pindar's earliest datable poem, the Tenth Pythian Ode of 498 BC, the stark juxtaposition of contrasting elements in his poetry is particularly striking, this being a document revealing the poet before his craft was fully mature. It is a song text in honour of the Thessalian Hippocles, winner in the boys' race over a distance of twice round the track. Verses 1–22, 55–9 and 64–72 are devoted to the athletic victory itself, while verses 30–48 contain a mythical narrative whose content scarcely relates to the other subject-matter, simply placing the person and achievement of the boy within a context of mythical tradition. The other seventy-two verses of the ode comprise aphorisms of a religious and moral nature, again bearing no logically discernible relation to the neighbouring themes. These shifts will have appeared less abrupt to contemporary listeners, members of an aristocratic class with highly distinct traditions, in whose context references and allusions would call forth so many associations that they would produce an entirely inevitable whole that is no longer possible for us to reproduce today.

This thematic division is not articulated further in formal terms. The skilfully composed strophes, grouped in threes according to a scheme first documented in the work of Stesichorus and Ibycus, open and conclude without regard to internal divisions of theme. Not even in this respect, therefore, can an answer as to the poetic unity of the whole be hoped for. In this poem Pindar uses verse types familiar from Aeolic lyric poetry, but without the latter's customary regulation of the number of syllables, so that specific metres appear in diverse variations. The strophic structure is likewise much more complex than in Sappho and Alcaeus. Even though the music is lost to us, it is still possible to ascertain from an examination of metre that the performance of such an ode would place high demands both on the musical erudition of the chorus, and on the artistic sophistication of the audience.

This brings us back to the social circle for whom these works were written, people who had sufficient leisure at their disposal to be able to cultivate their sacral, moral and social traditions through the medium of a highly refined practice of the arts. It is this prerequisite that needs to be borne in mind when assessing Pindar's language. Its artificial nature and deliberate distinctness from all spoken Greek dialects, and its rich potential for 'exhaustive allusion', make it a true reflection of this exclusive aristocratic class, which formed a unity despite all the local disparities between Aegina and Thessaly.

Pindar of course already had available to him a ready-made artificial, choral lyric language combining Homeric, Aeolic and Doric elements, and he made ample use of the potential this gave him for synonyms of different metrical and poetic value. This tradition had furthermore overlaid many words with quite specific affective qualities going beyond their conceptual meanings, by correlating individual or typical scenes from mythology that were central to the self-confidence of aristocratic society with certain themes of moral exhortation and theological reflection. In this way, such words acquired an unequivocal stylistic value within this social and poetic tradition that was

71

often far more important than their lexical meaning. This enabled a poet to maintain a highly distinctive level of diction throughout a lengthy text without undue difficulty.

An easily understandable example of this stylistic principle is available in the word group 'gold, golden', which was used by Pindar solely to designate the illustrious, the magnificent and the exquisite, independent of its 'real' meaning, when applied to many objects, ideas and events. Similarly, the ancient convention in epic language of using set epithets, regardless of the situation being narrated, to lend persons and things a fixed stylistic value, thereby transporting the listener into a separate world fundamentally different from the everyday one, was also further developed in choral lyric poetry. This possibility arose out of the fact that a poet such as Pindar only needed to mention a complex mythical context in order to evoke it for his public, and attach his didactic utterances to it. When he spoke, for example, of 'mangers dripping with blood', everyone knew he was referring to the bloodthirstiness of the Thracian King Diomedes, who used to throw his guests to his flesh-eating steeds until he was punished by Heracles.

Innumerable, often newly coined epithets of this type are to be found in Pindar, who often stretched Greek linguistic potential to the very limits of inventiveness. The occasional extravagance of such constructions brings an element into his style that one can safely call baroque. The fact that they often consign rich and lively mythical events to a nominal, static mode of expression only adds to the hieratic rigour of Pindar's style. This latter trait is also evident from his scrupulous avoidance of all forms of vulgarism, everyday idiom, indecency or colloquial licence. And yet for all this, his rigour is not dry and puritanical, but rather ceremonial and festive. This is because Pindar has an overwhelming abundance of dazzling expressions at his command, by means of which he is able to create images of rare beauty and immense evocative power. The scene he sets, for example, at the beginning of the First Pythian Ode is particularly fine, and directly accessible to the modern reader. It is intended to illustrate the ordering and peacemaking power of the song. The eagle of Zeus, sunk by the song into a pleasant slumber, sits with shining plumage and wings in repose, on the sceptre of his master. (We then learn that Zeus uses his power to direct and order forces in the natural world that are positive, albeit in need of guidance, whereas those forces that are evil and oppose him he tames by force.)

Equally accessible in their beauty are the pearls of Pindar's wise sayings to be found everywhere in his odes, such as the famous 'man is but a shadow's dream'. Gnomes of this kind have often come down to us in the form of citations by later authors, from poems of Pindar's which are now lost. Nevertheless, Pindar's compositions as a whole, in which these glorious images and valuable documents of his theological and moral reflection are embedded, can only be deciphered, if at all, by a painstaking process of detailed interpretation. This needs to take into account all the associations evoked in his listeners by his individual utterances, which from the modern viewpoint often seem to be juxtaposed in an unrelated way, without logical or aesthetic justification.

For decades, Pindar remained a much-admired and employed poet-composer, able to enhance his craft in the most diverse directions through the abundance of his commissions. In many cases the dating of his poems even makes it possible to speak of the growth of his craftsmanship. His increasingly virtuoso command of the dactyloepitrite, a verse form not invented but nevertheless preferred and enhanced by him, is a good example of this.

It might be inferred from the above that the language, style and content of Pindar's poetry constituted stereotypes, but this is not the case. A *partheneion*, for example, a cult song for a virgin chorus, tends to be expressively far more straightforward and undemanding than an Epinician ode. Other differences also exist, depending on genre. Aside from these, however, substantial contrasts of form and content may be discerned, prompted by the person commissioning the work and the particular situation surrounding it. Pindar was closely acquainted with the noble families of Aegina and Thessaly, the great tyrants of Sicily, and the kings of Cyrene in North Africa, not infrequently directing highly personal remarks to his patrons. This may be judged, for example, from two late poems, the Fifth and Fourth Pythian Odes, which may be dated 462 and 461 BC respectively on the basis of a Delphic chariot win of the royal stables of Cyrene. Neither of these poems is a true Epinician ode, although included in the Epinician anthology. The earlier of the two was intended as a processional song for the Carnaea, an Apollo festival brought by Greek settlers in Africa from their native city of Sparta. The poem gives a detailed account of the mythical tradition surrounding the settlement of Thera and Cyrene, without going into any detail about the personal ties between the poet and the Battiad royal household. The other, somewhat later poem seems to have been intended for solo recitation at court, not for a sacral occasion. Besides a fine lyrical adaptation of the Argonaut myth, it also contains a veritable code for princely conduct for the young king, culminating in an admonition to bring back home from exile a kinsman of the dynasty by the name of Damophilus, who is a friend of Pindar. This makes the poem a political epistle, although couched in personal terms.

An early example of variation on a theme occasioned by topical events is the sixth paean dating from 490 BC, together with the Seventh Nemean Ode. The paean was composed for a major annual festival of the Delphic Apollo cult. It contains, quite in the spirit of the Apollonine religion, a moral interpretation of the myth about the death of Neoptolemus. The latter, familiar as a son of Achilles, and as a member of the house of the Aeacides, one of the heroic forefathers of the Aeginetan nobility, was said to have been slain in Delphi. Pindar interprets this event as retribution for the misdeed committed by Neoptolemus at the conquest of Troy. This interpretation deviates from tradition, but may be offered as a typical example of Pindar's theological adaptation of mythology. The paean, which can be pieced together in almost complete form from a series of citations by later authors and papyrus fragments, does not conclude with the customary refrain of Apollo songs, an *ië paian*, but has an appendix containing a eulogy to the island of Aegina, 'mistress of the Dorian sea'. The only explanation for this is that Aeginetan singers performed the song in Delphi.

Some five years later, Pindar composed the song celebrating an athletic victory by an Aeginetan noble – the Seventh Nemean Ode, in which he solemnly retracted this earlier mythical exposition. Evidently it had provoked displeasure among the Aeginetan nobility, with whom he enjoyed friendly ties.

The personal character of Pindar's utterances is most pronounced in major odes written in honour of the Sicilian tyrants, at whose courts in Acragas and Syracuse he spent some two years. The rise of these tyrant states in Sicily, each of which comprised many towns, was a major event in early fifth-century BC history, since it enabled the Greeks on the island to assert themselves against the Carthaginians and the Etruscans. This concentration of power was effected using highly innovative and unconventional means, but it was for this very reason that Theron of Acragas and Hieron of Syracuse sought to establish cultural and social links with the old aristocracy of the Greek homeland. Their stables took part with particularly brilliant success in the pan-Hellenic contests, and they also invited poets, musicians and sculptors to their courts – among them Pindar, who established his first links with Sicily around 490 BC. He developed a friendship with Theron of Acragas, continuing to maintain contact with members of dynastic families even after the collapse of tyrannical rule in Sicily. Pindar likewise came and went at the far more splendid court of Hieron, until Bacchylides, nephew of Simonides, supplanted him in the ruler's favour.

Pindar's poetry from the time of his sojourn in Sicily (476–474 BC) and his close ties with the island (474–469 BC) was among his most brilliant work. However, the relevant pieces are not all true Epinician odes, as are the First Olympian Ode, which celebrates Hieron's victory in the horseback race, and the Third Olympian Ode, which celebrates Theron's victory in the quadriga, or four-in-hand chariot race – both in 476 BC. The Second Olympian Ode is styled as an epistle to Theron, and was only included in the collection on account of a passing reference to his win of 476. It may be assumed to have been intended for solo performance. It seeks to offer encouragement and comfort to the ruler, who, we know from other extant relics of ancient Pindaric interpretation, was faced with major political difficulties at that time. It does this using mythical examples of tests and adversity in human life, presenting them as necessary prerequisites for blessings bestowed by the gods. This idea of divine rewards for successfully withstood tests is then expanded upon with a description of the Island of the Blessed, to which good people were taken after their death. This is the first time in Greek literature that a belief in the afterlife, probably propounded at that time by Orphic sects, is explicitly elaborated. It unleashed a protracted dispute, still unresolved to this day, as to whether Pindar was adopting a conviction of Theron, or whether, as a related statement in another fragment seems to suggest, he shared this belief himself.

The First Pythian Ode, composed around 470 BC, refers to the founding of the new city of Etna, a process eagerly set in motion by Hieron, who then appointed his son Deinomenes as governor of the city. It is perhaps the most consummate extant poem by Pindar. Its opening verses have already been referred to above (p. 72), being followed by a grandiose description of Etna the volcano, using the mythical metaphor of a monster held captive under the mountain. This is a pregnant allusion to the hard-won state system that has materialised in the newly established city lying at the foot of the mountain. The third strophe triad – in the First Pythian Ode the relationship between verse and idea is more strictly regulated than is usually the case with Pindar – pleads for the blessing of the gods for the new city, also lauding Hieron's achievements in the Greek interest, chiefly his victory over the Etruscans (474 BC) and the victory at Himera which marked the final defeat of the Carthaginian threat, and which Pindar does not hesitate to set beside the victory at Salamis achieved in the same year (480 BC). The final triad contains a princely code addressed to the young Deinomenes, enumerating the virtues befitting a ruler – justice, benevolence, respect for civil liberty, and love of truth – using the positive example of Croesus, the negative of Phalaris. This is expanded, however, by a typically Pindaric, Archaic concept: the ideal of the ruler is only brought to fulfilment where the achievements of the ruler are willingly acknowledged by the ruled. Even here, therefore, there is no deed, and even less a way of thinking, that carried a moral value in its own right, independently of recognition by the world at large.

These magnificent Sicilian poems are outstanding for the ceremonial quality and grandiosity of their diction, which exceeds even those of his later odes to the king of Cyrene. The technique whereby quite general concepts, such as power, fame or glory, are transformed by ceremonially poetic and skilfully paraphrasing diction into vivid imagery particularly merits the highest admiration. A good example of this is provided by the opening to the First Olympian Ode:

> Surely water is the best; gold
> As blazing fire,
> Bright in the night shines
> Brighter than all haughty wealth.
> Yet when, my trusted heart,
> It presses thee to praise a contest,
> Then to the sun alone the gaze!
> For no star passes through the empty ether

75

By day that lights or warms more;
Thus too shines Olympia, nothing
Lovelier blooms to your song.
From thence the renowned fire song
Is enveloped by the poet's deep meditation, and he lauds
The son of Cronus when he comes to the fortunate,
To the blessed hearth of Hieron,
Who rules as judge, by right,
The meads of Sicily, governing
Those wealthy in sheep.

(after F. Wolde)

Pindar's invitation to Sicily, which led him to the highest achievements of his art, was by no means a self-evident step forward in his life history. Along with the nobles of his own native city (Thebes) and the priesthood of Apollo at Delphi, which set the moral standards for all Greece more than any other institution at that time, he had advised against resisting the Persian army. The subjection of Greece to the Persian Empire would undoubtedly have helped preserve the aristocratic culture that Pindar himself stood for. In Athens, on the other hand, which led the vanguard against the enemy from the Orient, new, powerful forces of democracy were already astir, finding their first historical affirmation in the victories at Marathon and Salamis. Following the victory of Plataeae (479 BC), Pindar's native city of Thebes only escaped heavy chastisement for its pro-Persian stance because some members of the city's nobility gave themselves up for execution.

Pindar was deeply affected by this dishonour to his home country, as he expresses without reserve in a victory song for an Aeginetan (Eighth Isthmian Ode), written in 478 BC. For him, unlike the Spartans, Athenians and eastern Greeks, the immense victory over the Persian Colossus, and the preservation of Greek liberty, meant virtually nothing. He thus sings in this ode of the military feats of Aegina, and yet utters not a word about the fact that these same Aeginetans, despite their traditional enmity towards Athens, added their own ships to the Greek fleet at the last moment, thereby sealing the outcome of the Battle of Salamis. Other passages in this fine poem also reveal how the national pride that prevailed in Greece after Salamis was alien to Pindar. For him, it was not the exploits of Marathon, Salamis and Plataeae which offered examples of human distinction, but those of the mythical ancestors of the Greek aristocracy, whose historical supremacy was brought irrevocably to an end by the Persian Wars. His invitation to Sicily thus meant release from a milieu with which he was now out of step, as well as an opportunity for fresh impressions and challenges.

Following his return from Sicily, Pindar was to remain a widely acclaimed and extremely active poet for another thirty years, despite the fact that his conceptual world was by now so far behind the times. He even established some fresh links, such as with Cyrene. But the fact that the post-460 BC period witnessed repeated military confrontations between his native city and the rising power of Athens did not hinder him from giving honourable mention to Athenian personalities.

None the less, there is no trace of the 'modern' in his late works. In the Ninth Paean, a hymn to Apollo, Pindar inquires, horror-struck and astonished, as to the significance of the solar eclipse of 30 April 463 BC. The natural explanation discovered by Thales of Miletus in 585 BC was foreign to Pindar. The Sixth Nemean Ode dates from the 450s BC; its opening lines contain what are perhaps Pindar's most profound statements about the nature of man. The manifest conviction of the Greek nobility that man was of divine origin is combined here with an awareness, heightened by Delphic piety, of the limitations that separate him from the gods. Nothing asserted by later Greek poetry or philosophy about the dignity or limitations of man adds anything substantial to the view expressed in this poem.

The last datable poem by Pindar was written in 446 BC. By 468, however, one of the rivals frequently mentioned in the major Sicilian poems had supplanted him in Hieron's favour. Bacchylides of Ceus, nephew of the great Simonides, had the honour of singing of Hieron's first Olympic chariot victory in 468 BC in a poem among those restored to posterity in 1896 as a result of a papyrus find.

Bacchylides' Epinician odes show exactly the same components as Pindar's: praise of the victory, mythical narrative, gnomes and occasional declarations about his own art. Whereas Pindar produced his best work when reflecting on present and mythical events, rightly conceiving his profession chiefly as that of interpreter and admonisher, the gnomic and encomiastic utterances of Bacchylides never transcend the dullest convention. Pindar, on the other hand, who was preoccupied with the meaning of myth, showed only the most perfunctory interest in narrative detail, whereas Bacchylides was a born storyteller, able to carry off the most charming depictions. Although no innovator in language or style, his diction was more pleasing, his compositional method smoother, and the structure of his rhythms richer than Pindar's.

Unlike his uncle Simonides, whose moral observations not infrequently led him to open criticism of the traditional notions of his noble patrons, Bacchylides avoided all confrontation with the conceptual world associated with mythical tradition. This very side-stepping into the straightforward elaboration of mythical narrative in itself indicates that the intellectual foundations of great choral lyric poetry had by then evaporated, despite the prolific work that can be documented for this period. (Epinician odes, for example, were occasionally composed by several poets for the same victory: Bacchylides' Thirteenth Ode, dated 485 BC, celebrates the pancratist (wrestler and boxer) Pytheas of Aegina, for whom Pindar had written the Fifth Nemean Ode.)

Among Bacchylides' extant poems, his dithyrambs or songs to Dionysus deserve special mention, even though they do not differ substantially in language or verse structure from other types of major lyric poetry. The Seventeenth Ode contains an enchanting account of some length of the visit of the young Theseus to his divine ancestor Poseidon, god of the sea, at his palace on the seabed, where he is given a warm welcome by Poseidon's wife Amphitrite. The Eighteenth Ode is stylised as a dialogue between King Aegeus and a chorus of Athenian citizens conversing excitedly about the exploits of an attractive young hero, again Theseus, the son of Aegeus, who grew up in distant Troezen. This poem corresponds precisely to the description of pre-tragedy given by Aristotle. In dithyrambic poetry, therefore, this ancient type was still being practised, long after drama proper was fully developed.

Other lyric poets of that time are known today only by name. However, the scope of works documented by these names, and the extant works of Pindar and Bacchylides, cannot alter the fact that the social and intellectual prerequisites for major prestigious choral lyric works were visibly on the decline after the Persian Wars. More than any other lyric poet, Pindar expounded the moral and religious standards of this aristocratic world in its final days, thereby earning a place for himself in the Greek literary heritage.

Naturally, throughout the late fifth and subsequent centuries, songs and hymns continued to be composed for local cults. Little of this work made any impact on later literary tradition, however. This was largely shaped by a selection of ten lyric poets made by philologists of the museum of Alexandria in the late third or second century BC which established the guidelines for editions of the classics disseminated by the book trade in the Hellenistic-Roman era. A few relics of provincial cult poetry did none the less survive, either because they were recorded in written form for some reason, or because anecdotal or historical traditions were conducive to their preservation. A number of such cult hymns have been preserved, inscribed in the shrine at Epidaurus in the second century BC for example. Although a number of linguistic details fully bear out this late date, they may well be examples of older cult poetry handed down in liturgical practice before being recorded. They are simply structured poems with more stereotyped verse forms and primitively constructed strophes than Pindar's poetry. The language is that of lyrical artistic tradition with additional local idiosyncrasies.

It would certainly not be out of place to deduce from such documents some notion of the poetesses Praxilla of Sicyon and Telesilla of Argos, writers of cult songs whom historical tradition places in the fifth century BC. The fact that these documents manifest an extended use of a metre which Hellenistic grammarians named after Telesilla supports this view.

One rich biographical and anecdotal tradition prevalent among late historians and grammarians tells of the poetess Corinna, a contemporary of Pindar. Substantial fragments of her poetry, however, were not available until a recent papyrus find. The most easily accessible song narrates a naive provincial Boeotian saga in simply constructed strophes. This extant text was in a Boeotian orthography not documented until quite late, a fact which has led some exegetes to place Corinna in the Hellenistic era, a period in which the appeal of the provincial and archaic was first being discovered from the perspective of a refined civilisation. Disregarding its distinctive and un- doubtedly late orthography, the language of the text does betray elements of the Boeotian dialect, however. Its mode of expression and sphere of ideas, moreover, unmistakably evince a genuinely Archaic primitive quality, and not merely a would-be archaising style. This would seem to support defenders of its traditional dating. All the same, this controversy is symp- tomatic of our scholarship vis à vis poetry outside the mainstream of poetic tradition, where reliable categories for aesthetic and historical evaluation are not uncommonly lacking.

Elegiac poetry of the late Archaic period, which continued to be written for performance at the symposia of aristocratic clubs (*hetairia*), is particularly well-documented in a collection bearing the name of Theognis of Megara. In the manner of a students' song-book, it comprises some 1,500 lines, the poems varying in length from between two to three dozen lines, and manifesting great differences in both style and content, having been written by a variety of authors at different times and places. Their present order was arrived at by one or several successive editors on a rudimentary basis of associations arising out of key-words shared by a number of the poems.

The core of the collection comprises genuine elegies by Theognis which have as a sphragis or seal, albeit one imitated in some other pieces in the collection, the hallmark of the address to the young Cyrnus in the first line. They thus bear witness to the educational and homoerotic relationship between men and youths that was so widespread in Archaic aristocratic society.

Of the genuine and 'non-genuine' elegies, few are of great literary merit. Many provide some insight into the mood of an aristocratic class that had just been divested of its political power by a democratic opposition; some of the aristocrats had had their economic position weakened as well, and yet without forfeiting their social pre-eminence. These nobles were unable to assure themselves of their inherited rank with the same candour as their forefathers, having to do so with an envious sideways glance at the new rulers, the parvenus, in whose eyes a person's merit lay in his wealth, not in his noble birth or fulfilment of the demands of a noble way of life. Understandably, the demoted nobility also developed a heightened sense of the fragility of all social conditions, and consequently lived in anticipation of fresh feuds and civil wars. This lent many of the poems a particularly bitter tone.

Not all poems in the collection breathe this spirit, however. Some give fine and dignified expression to the values cherished by aristocratic ethics – loyalty in friendship, chivalry towards an adversary, or self-control – quite free of any resentment at being dispossessed. Others call for steadfastness in imminent conflict with domestic or foreign enemies, the Persians being specifically mentioned. Others again sing with cheerful lack of pretension of the delights of wine and love.

Surviving elegies by Solon (see pp. 53ff.) and Tyrtaeus (p. 35) also include pieces dating from the late Archaic period. On account of their themes and ethos, they were added to collections by these old poets compiled for practical use at symposia, and hence sometimes subject to editorial intervention. Hermann Fränkel (1975, 348ff.) has demonstrated this circumstance in exemplary fashion in the case of Tyrtaeus's Ninth Ode.

The elegies of Xenophanes, one of the most remarkable figures in the transitional period between the Archaic and Classical epochs, are of quite a different character. Born in 570 BC in Colophon in Asia Minor, he left his home town at the age of 25 or so when it was conquered by the Persians. After a lengthy period of wandering, probably as a rhapsode, he made his new home in Elea, an Ionian colonial town in Italy, where he died in 475 BC, around the age of 95.

His elegies give a vivid description of the milieu for which their performance may be envisaged. There is mention of the festively decorated and cleaned hall where everything has been prepared for the feast, and where the much-travelled poet is questioned as to his age and origins. What Xenophanes had to tell the assembled guests, however, ran contrary to all tradition. Myths of centaurs, Titans and giants are to no avail; it is foolish to shower with public honours and praise as a model of distinction the man who has achieved victory in Olympia as a runner or boxer. Only he who is able to improve humanity and the social order through his intelligence merits distinction.

With his severe criticism of time-honoured, universally cherished values, and in his praise of intelligence as the only significant factor in individual morality and political order, Xenophanes had much in common with the slightly younger Simonides. His theological speculation deviated even more sharply from all tradition, and was published in the form of short hexametric poems or *silloi* (satires), and in a Hesiod-style didactic epic poem later given the title *On Nature*. His arguments were based on moral criticism of the 'thieving, whoring and swindling' gods of Homer, and on the correct observation that the gods of Ethiopia were black, while those of the Thracians were blond, so that lions would probably have to believe in lion-like gods, and horses in horse-like ones. In this way, he arrived at a concept of divinity that left far behind all forms of anthropomorphism, and indeed all connection with sensory impressions.

> There is a god . . . who resembles nothing mortal [or no mortal] in form or thought. He sees, thinks and hears in his totality. From a distance, and effortlessly, he moves all things with his thought. He does not move, and resides always in the same place.
>
> (Xenophanes frr. 11, 16, 15, 23, Diels-Kranz)

In Xenophanes' time, the Greeks had no term for pure, disembodied spirituality. The word translated above as 'thought' denoted both sensory perception and reflection on a subject, ultimately also encompassing the impulse of will, or intention, that derives from insight. If, therefore, Xenophanes' god sees, hears and thinks in his totality, possessing no discernible bodily organs for these activities, what we have here is a description, derived from activity and function, of a purely spiritual being. This conception hence manifests a higher capacity for reflection than all other notions of spirit hitherto documented either in Greece or elsewhere, which were arrived at with the aid of materially discernible analogies such as air, breath or fire. This is matched by the manner in which Xenophanes' god acts on the visible world without moving or changing himself, and without making any contact between himself and objects in spatial terms. This conceptual product of Xenophanes' genius pre-empted the Aristotelian theory of the 'unmoved mover' as the ultimate basis of being, thereby also creating the clarity and sublimity of the philosophical concept of the godhead. Following Greek adoption of the Christian revelation, this was to become an integral part of Christian theology.

Still other logical expositions, some pertaining to physics, are contained in the few surviving fragments of Xenophanes' hexametric poetry. His confidence in the power of human reason, which made him capable of such unalloyed spirituality, is also expressed in his belief in the slow ascent of human beings as a consequence of their own insights and inventions, rather than in the revelations of the culture-bestowing gods spoken about in religio-mythical tradition.

Ancient doxography, i.e. the history of philosophical opinion, viewed Xenophanes as the tutor of his fellow citizen Parmenides, hence as the ancestor of Eleatic philosophy. This was certainly not the case, despite the markedly philosophical character of some of the ideas traditionally attributed to Xenophanes, since the Parmenidean theory of being was rooted, in more than one respect, in an entirely new approach to thought. Nevertheless, scepticism with regard to acceptance of a school of thought that can be traced back to Xenophanes should in no way detract from our admiration for the boldness and independence of his thought. No subsequent philosopher could afford to ignore his theology.

For the literary historian, Xenophanes is a highly original exponent of the late Archaic phase of epic–elegiac poetry. In the early third century BC, his *silloi* (satires) were used by the sceptic Timon (see below, p. 246) as a model for philosophical polemical poetry. Unfortunately, not a single line has survived of the two historical epic poems also attributed to him, one a local history of the city of Colophon, the other the history of the founding of Elea.

5

PHILOSOPHY AND
SCIENCE

The period around or shortly after 500 BC saw the first major burgeoning of philosophy, associated with the names of Heraclitus of Ephesus in Asia Minor, and Parmenides of Elea in south-west Italy. Heraclitus was the first great prose stylist of the Greek language. Not only did he add numerous new stylistic devices to creative prose in order to convey his philosophical insights, but he did so some two generations before the literary reading public was made aware of them through a comprehensive theory of style. A number of fragments quoting verbatim from his book give the impression that it was a collection of sayings or aphorisms. More recent research has shown, however, that it must also have contained lengthy passages of discourse. The latter's succinct diction, replete with metaphors, puns, poetic figures of speech, and tonal and rhythmic parallels or antitheses, was thus by no means restricted to the formulation of maxims.

It is still unclear whether Heraclitus' theory 'on nature' marked a continuation of the Milesian approach, intended, as later doxographies suggest, to be taken literally as an explanatory description of physical events. What we do find clearly expressed here for the first time, however, is the view that the progress of perception must correspond step by step to the structure of the perceived. This of necessity transforms the purely physical Milesian formulation of the problem into a philosophical one, in a new sense of the word. Heraclitus was the first philosopher to raise the word *logos* to the status of a philosophical term intended to denote this subject-matter. It means on the one hand 'intelligible speech', that is the formulation of a perception – organised in such a way that it is accessible to understanding – and on the other 'order, conformity with natural law', thus a term for the structure of the natural world, the object of perception.

In Heraclitus' view, the most significant feature that being and perception held in common was that they could both only be understood as a process characterised by a constant interchange between opposite forces. Life comes out of death, and leads to death, warmth comes from cold and leads to cold. As a result of this, it is impossible to make meaningful statements about anything without also taking into account its opposite. This permanent coexistence of

82

opposites in being and thinking, however, also determines the relativity of all statements about them. Man is beautiful in relation to an ape, but ugly in relation to the gods. The correctness of the statement 'beautiful' or 'ugly' thus depends on the standpoint of the observer. Only when the latter is taken outside the given structure of the world, delineated by the extremes of 'ape' and 'god', can one of the two statements acquire absolute validity. This constitutes the earliest known description of a 'transcendent act'.

Heraclitus may have derived this principle of *coincidentia oppositorum*, the simultaneous existence of opposites in being and perception, from Pythagorean speculation about harmony. Doxographic tradition associates Heraclitus with the Pythagoreans, and the term 'harmony' also occurs in his work. In the Pythagorean view, however, 'harmony' consisted of the presence of a mean value between opposites. It was for this reason that they regarded uneven numbers with a mean as more perfect than those which were divisible into two halves. For Heraclitus, on the other hand, it was the permanent presence of the opposite value which at any particular moment gave a specific entity its meaning, and gave direction to its existence when understood as a process.

Further insights of significance for later philosophy are to be found in Heraclitus. These include the perception that only *logos* makes human communication possible, so that people become isolated beings in sleep. Another is that *logos* 'enlarges itself', enabling further perceptions to be inferred from articulated perception without the addition of new quantitative factors.

The literary articulation of these and other insights was given special emphasis, since Heraclitus was fully cognisant of the innovative nature of his theories, setting them with rigorous polemic against the opinions of such acclaimed authorities as Homer, Hesiod or Pythagoras. Besides this, we also encounter for the first time in Heraclitus the attribute of moral zeal that disqualifies the ignorant or the heterodox. His statements betray the self-certainty of the prophet. His finely honed use of words, giving every nuance of his thought processes the exact appropriate weight, is harnessed in the service of his passionate desire to convince. Such a convergence of philosophical insight and linguistic skill did not occur again in philosophical literature until the early and middle Dialogues of Plato.

For the history of philosophy, the achievements of Parmenides may be even more significant than those of Heraclitus. He also stood on the threshold of a rich school of thought, named the Eleatic school after his native city, that was to shape the development of logic and metaphysics in a number of ways. One of Parmenides' pupils was Zeno of Elea, who enjoyed huge fame for some considerable time. His logical masterpieces, some showing immense perspicacity, were derived from the ontological premisses of his master. Zeno's pupil Melissus of Samos, on the other hand, had links with Anaxagoras and Archelaus, tutor to Socrates, while other lines lead from Elea to the atomistic philosophy of northern Greece, to Leucippus and Democritus.

Parmenides inquired neither after the physical substratum of the world, like the Milesians, nor after its structure or *logos*, like Heraclitus. His discovery was that the thought of Being precluded the existence of non-existence, so that a clear distinction needed to be made between all human opinion and discourse about growth and decay, existence or non-existence on the one hand, and pure thought and its subject, that is truth, on the other. Here, therefore, the problem of transcendence is stated far more radically than in Heraclitus, and it is no coincidence that Plato's theory of ideas, which marked the first attempt to elaborate a comprehensive delineation of the transcendent and the true, of a reality independent of the world of the senses, is based on Parmenides in more than one respect. Parmenides was the first to suggest that it was thought, not sensory perception, that made Being possible, and hence that thought alone could result in indisputable truth. The significance of all this in relation to the second part of the didactic poem is still disputed. Accompanied by the comment that it is concerned with *doxa*, mere opinion, it sets forth a very solid cosmology, based wholly on sensory perception, and taking express account of the phenomena of growth and decay. It is thus out of step with Parmenides' theory of true, unalterable being.

It is remarkable that Parmenides chose the traditional, hexametric didactic poetry form in which to convey his ideas, despite the innovative nature of his philosophical approach. Epic language was far less suited to imparting such ideas than the Ionic of Heraclitus. The modern exegete frequently has difficulty distinguishing metaphors and images of traditional epic origin whose substance is not of great relevance, from those coined by the author himself. This applies equally to the famous proem to the work, in which the philosopher describes his consecration by the goddess Dike, to whose heavenly house he is carried up by a chariot and team. Among the surviving fragments of this fine poetic piece, it is difficult to discern the boundaries between the epic motif of consecration by the Muse, the theme of the shamanistic journey to heaven, documented in Greece since the sixth century BC, and metaphorical elements invented by the author himself by way of explanation for his philosophical approach. Particularly noteworthy, however, is that despite close parallels with prophetic and visionary accounts this magnificent metaphor clearly elucidates how his journey to heaven not only gave the poet-philosopher a revelation, but also pointed the way towards his own intellectual efforts and decisions.

Empedocles, another remarkable fifth-century philosopher, also made use of the hexametric didactic poem. Aristotle said that the latter's achievements would lead one to believe that he was older than Anaxagoras, born in 499 BC (see below, p. 143), although he was in fact younger. Empedocles of Agrigentum in Sicily lived as a wandering physician and miracle-worker, soon acquiring a rich body of legends. He seems to have had some connection with the Pythagorean conventicles of southern Italy, and like them to have been involved in political agitation against the monarchy. One of his two epic poems, known as *The Purifications*, is brimming with Pythagorean theories: the transmigration of souls, vegetarianism, the famous proscription on beans, punishment in the underworld, the gradation of reincarnations depending on culpability or merit, and so on. The other poem contains a natural philosophy made up of Milesian, Heraclitan and Parmenidean elements. The world consists of four eternal, non-created elements, which appear here for the first time in the familiar constellation. These are constantly divided and reunited by two cosmic forces, love and conflict, resulting in the course of cosmic events. This is clearly a retrograde philosophical step compared to Heraclitus and Parmenides, abolishing as it does their painstakingly elaborated distinction between substance and structure.

From the literary viewpoint, extensive fragments by Empedocles are of interest today for what they can teach us about the potential scope for variation and expansion still open to epic language in that period. He did not escape the pitfalls of baroque extravagances, often stretched to the limits of tenability, as for example when he calls the hospitable Acragantines 'honour-bestowing havens for foreigners', or bodily extremities 'branches of flesh'. Aristotle devoted some attention to this rhetorical character of Empedocles' style, while later theoreticians went so far as to construe a pupil–teacher relationship between Empedocles and Gorgias, originator of the theory of rhetoric.

Empedocles and his contemporary, Diogenes of Apollonia, who also drew on the vivid conceptual world of the Milesians, exerted enormous impact on their contemporaries precisely because of the non-progressive nature and limited abstraction of their explanations of nature. Their impact on medicinal physiology in particular is manifest at every turn. The Empedoclean version of one idea, not originally his, became widespread in philosophical and religious tradition. This was that man is a small-scale cosmos, a microcosm, whose make-up corresponds to that of the macrocosm in every detail, this being the reason why man is able to gain knowledge about the world.

Branches of scholarship other than philosophy also became accessible through literature from 500 BC onwards. In southern Italy, the physician Alcmaeon of Croton produced a major work on physiology, formulating both major discoveries such as the importance of the brain for perception and thought, and methodological insights such as the principle of inference from specific observation to natural law. Diogenes of Apollonia, already mentioned above, dealt in his treatise with the gill-breathing of fishes, while the Pythagorean Mnestor of Sybaris founded the science of botany. By the mid-fifth century BC, mathematics, astronomy, harmonics and optics were already making their presence felt in a substantial body of literature, whose authors came from all parts of the Greek-speaking world (including Hippocrates of Chios, Hippasus of Metapontum, and Bryson of Heraclea). However, only occasional descriptions of the contents of some passages by these authors are extant. Like the prose philosophical writings of that epoch, these works were also written in the Ionic dialect established by Anaximander and Hecataeus of Miletus as the language of literary prose, by then for over a century, whose role as a scholarly language is comparable with that of medieval Latin.

It would be a mistake to underestimate the literary importance of any of these very early scholarly disciplines, in which much of the potential for linguistic expression was being unfolded for the first time. Nevertheless, the significance of one of these stands head and shoulders above the rest in terms of its literary impact – namely geography, which in that early period was not yet distinguished from historiography.

The originator of this scholarly and literary tradition was the Milesian Hecataeus, already referred to above in his capacity as logographer – a prose chronicler of local mythical traditions who attempted to classify them into genealogical, chronological order. What survives of Hecataeus' *Genealogies* betrays the highly developed critical faculties of a man who made short shrift of venerable traditions wherever he was convinced he had found a rational explanation for extraordinary events. However, the tools for expanding this rational criticism from a subjective procedure into a teachable method were still lacking in his day.

Far more interesting than Hecataeus' logographic work, however, is his *Description of the Earth*, which was intended as a complementary text to the model of the world elaborated by his compatriot Anaximander. During work on this book, Hecataeus could already rely on literary sources, a number of *periploi* or coastal descriptions, compiled as the great venture of Greek seafaring progressed. Towards the end of the sixth century BC, for example, the Hellenised Carian Scylax had been commissioned by the Persian King Darius to chart the ocean route from the mouth of the Indus, round Arabia, to the northernmost corner of the Red Sea. He described this voyage in a *periplus* from which Hecataeus may have derived his information on India and Arabia. Such coastal descriptions, whose literary scheme provided exact details of coastal locations, and summary descriptions of the hinterland, were available for all parts of the world with which the Greeks had established maritime trade links, ranging as far afield as West Africa, whose coast had been explored and described by one Euthymenes of Massilia, modern Marseille.

A major part of Hecataeus' geography will probably have consisted of the simple enumeration of the names of peoples, countries and towns. Wherever detailed information was at his disposal, however, be it from literary sources or, as in the case of Egypt, from extensive voyages of his own, he gave detailed accounts of the manners and customs of the inhabitants, historical traditions, religion and governmental institutions of the distant country concerned.

The second book of Herodotus, which contains a well-known description of Egypt and its history, includes extensive passages evaluating Hecataeus' geography, and not infrequently taking issue with him. On the basis of information to this effect from a late ancient scholar, it is even known that some passages were adopted verbatim from Hecataeus, including a gripping account of a crocodile hunt. In this passage an astonishing vividness is extracted from the still somewhat awkward Ionic of that time.

Aside from fragments by Hecataeus, the rich geographical and ethnographic literature of the period is also accessible in a compilation dating from the fourth century BC. This takes the form of a coastal description of the three continents of Europe, Asia and Libya (Africa), and is traditionally attributed to Scylax. The geography is purely descriptive, and affirms the limitless interest of the Greeks, untarnished by prejudice, in the world outside their own. At that time the word 'barbarian' had no derogatory connotations, denoting simply those people who spoke a non-Greek, hence incomprehensible, language. The Greeks held the cultured nations of the east in particularly high esteem – not only on account of the technical and other achievements which they encountered there and learned from eagerly, but also because of the antiquity of living Oriental tradition. Herodotus relates, for example, how Hecataeus, a member of the oldest urban aristocracy of Miletus, was recounting his genealogical tree to an Egyptian, concluding with a divine ancestor in the eleventh generation. Smiling, the Egyptian then showed him proof of a genealogical tradition stemming back over several dozen generations, but which did not culminate in the gods. Some century and a half later, Plato either invented or used an anecdote in which an old priest tells Solon, travelling in Egypt, that the Greeks will always remain children. This is another nice illustration of how Archaic Greeks saw themselves in relation to the advanced cultures of the ancient Orient. From the very beginnings of their attempts to come to terms intellectually with the world outside their own, they always sought to grasp the historical dimension of a problem.

Understandably, the attitude of the Greeks towards the east changed with the impact of victorious Persian campaigns, as we shall be seeing later. Charon of Lampsacus, an older contemporary of Herodotus, may be regarded as the last representative of the old views. Although alive at the time of the Persian Wars, he had difficulty coming to terms with them. What remains of his extensive writings reveals his complete divergence from earlier logographers such as Acusilaus, since he was no longer interested in mythical tradition. Instead, he wrote a local history of his native town of Lampsacus that combines history and anecdote; a book about Spartan officialdom; one about the Minos tradition of Crete; a book about the Persians, another about the Ethiopians, a description of coasts outside the straits of Gibraltar, and more besides.

One Dionysius of Miletus wrote about Persian history after Darius I, while a Lydian by the name of Xanthus who wrote in Greek gave an account of the history of the ancient Lydian Empire. Various parts of his work survived by virtue of a historian of the Augustan era, Nicolaus of Damascus. Interest in foreign peoples was largely directed at their *nomoi*, traditions, customs and laws. There is evidence of many books on this theme in the fifth and fourth centuries BC, and a major part of the historical work of Herodotus (see below, pp. 158ff.) belongs to this tradition. It was in this sphere, rather than in that of physical characteristics, which were seldom touched on, that the features distinguishing non-Greeks, or barbarians (a word which at that time had no derogatory connotations), from Greeks were found.

Direct documentary evidence of the rich prose literature written in the Ionic dialect, by no means all of which was written by authors from the Ionic-speaking region, is available only in fragments. However, it is possible to draw inferences about the art of this earlier period, in which Ionic matured into a flexible medium for narrative and descriptive prose, from extant masterpieces of historiography and ethnology dating from the late fifth century BC, of which we shall be hearing more later.

Part II

CLASSICAL LITERATURE OF THE FIFTH CENTURY BC

6

AESCHYLUS AND THE BEGINNINGS OF TRAGEDY

Attic drama marks the undisputed high point of Classical literature. It was mainly from tragedy that Aristotle elaborated his theory of poetry, viewing it as the most differentiated of all poetic forms, uniting the achievements of all other genres. He devoted a great deal of thought to the growth of this unique literary form, and the more recent research examines early and primitive forms of mimetic drama, the more his laconic statements about the origins of tragedy are confirmed.

Dance and song, which are associated with the cult of the gods among virtually all peoples, invariably contain a mimetic element. As part of rites, they are devices for conveying events from the past – cosmic or historical – handed down in the form of myth, that were thought to have bestowed blessing or averted disaster. Their cult repetition is intended to reproduce these effects in the present. The mask, which transfigures the singer or dancer in the blessing-bestowing act of the gods, heroes or deities involved, or which at the very least protects and camouflages participants while they are in dangerous proximity to divine power, is likewise to be found among almost all peoples.

During our examination of choral lyric poetry it was shown how such dance songs can be expanded through progressive stylisation into literary, musical and choreographic works of art that leave their cult origins far behind. In the case of choral lyric poetry, this process occurred in an aristocratic milieu in which the more drastic features of primitive models were dispensed with to meet the demand for respectability and dignity. As a result, only a few stylised dance figures remained out of an entire mimetics. In contrast, an abundance of more drastic features may be envisaged in the dances and songs of rural community cults not associated with aristocratic family traditions. This assumption is confirmed by numerous pictorial accounts showing dancers in earthy, and for the modern taste often obscene positions, masks and costumes.

From the mid-sixth century BC onwards, however, these rural practices were fostered, expanded and adopted as the official cult in a number of Greek states, by tyrants seeking to establish broad-based support among the population, and to turn their states from aristocratic, noble associations into genuine polities. Accounts from several Greek states thus report how ruling tyrants called on poet-composers to provide songs for an obscure local cult and its legends.

The most important example of this kind of religious policy, and the one which had the greatest impact on literary history, comes from Athens, where the tyrant Peisistratus incorporated into its festival calendar the cult of Dionysus, the god of vegetation and wine, also instigating a programme for its artistic development. The fifth century saw the performance of the first tragedies, and later also comedies, at the Great (city) Dionysia festival (end of March), and of comedies, and later tragedies, at the Lenaea (beginning of February). Later, both were also performed at the Lesser (country) Dionysia (January).

These performances were financed by well-to-do citizens sponsoring by way of tax payment the rehearsal time (*choregia*) of the chorus for whom a poet had composed a piece. The performance of plays, always new at this stage, was in the form of a competition between three officially placed *choregoi* (producers), although in fact their three poet-composers were competing against one another. The first tragedy competition of this kind is traditionally said to have been held in 532 BC, the first comedy competition not until 486 BC, considerably later.

The third art form cultivated in a similar manner at the Dionysia was the dithyramb, a dance song that derived its name from a refrain used only in the Dionysiac cult, and which was elevated by Peisistratian reform into the style of great choral lyric. Clearly the fact that only amateur citizens' choruses were available placed certain constraints on the technical standard of performances: their training was no match for the *thiasoi* of the early Greek aristocracy. Professional singers and actors did not appear until the late fifth century BC, although sometimes poets themselves took roles in their own plays.

The complete rehearsed repertoire with which a *choregos* entered a tragedy *agon* (contest) in the fifth century comprised three tragedies – generally, although not necessarily, a trilogy with related subject-matter – and a satyr play, a burlesque adaptation of mythical themes, in which the chorus acted as a herd of satyrs (half-animal forest deities with horses' tails, from the retinue of Dionysus). Satyric drama seems to have been closely related to the original form of Dionysiac dance, which later developed into tragedy. Not even in the Classical period was it connected with comedy, even though this was also burlesque.

Since Aristotle characterised tragedy as the result of a process whereby earlier forms 'became serious', it is reasonable to see this process at work in the holding of public tragedy contests from 532 BC onwards – an event associated with the name of the first tragedy writer, Thespis. This view is not contradicted by assertions from other sources that the poet Pratinas of Phlius in the Peloponnese, who lived in Athens around 500 BC, was the 'originator' of satyric drama. A choral song of his survives in which a masked chorus, clearly acting in burlesque manner, protests against the use of the dancing area allotted to them for dance and music of other kinds. A likely explanation for this development is that Thespis' innovations led to the disappearance of the traditional burlesque satyric dance. Traditionalists raised objections to this, expounded in poetic form by Pratinas himself, with the result that the earlier burlesque satyr play, now formally brought into line with the more developed tragic form, became a fourth component added to the three mutually related tragedies.

However, the name 'tragedy', which literally means 'goat-song', remains unexplained, since neither the originally Peloponnesian satyrs, nor their Attic-Ionian cousins the Sileni, had the form of a goat. Already in antiquity another explanation was sought by interpreting the word as a 'song for the goat' (i.e. a winners' prize), a she-goat being the sacrificial animal at certain Dionysian festivals. On the other hand, it is equally possible that 'goat' was a traditional name for all animal mask dancers in the most diverse rural cults. The word might also be interpreted as 'song for the sacrificial goat'.

Whichever of the above applies, the roots of tragedy undoubtedly lie in these primitive cult dances. The process whereby these became 'serious', however, can only be guessed at by inference from more developed forms. The first factor to be taken into account is that in Classical Attic tragedy individual actors were clearly separate from the chorus – which at first consisted of twelve, later of more people – even though they participated in the same stage action. The chorus generally sang its comments, apart from occasional asides by the chorus leader, usually in traditional verse and strophe forms, and spoken in the artificial dialect of great choral lyric poetry. Actors, however, apart from occasional arias or antiphonic exchanges with the chorus, spoke their dialogues, making use both of the local Attic language, elevated by numerous Homerisms, and simple spoken lines in alternating rhythms of the iambic trimeter and trochaic tetrameter. The chorus acted, danced and sang in a circular arena known as the orchestra, with an altar at the centre marking the focal point of this cult act. Where possible, the audience stood or sat around three sides of this arena, which was therefore located by preference at the foot of a slope. Along the open edge of the circle and some distance from it an extended booth or *skene* (stage, tent) was erected, in which members of the chorus and actors could change. Its ends, situated opposite the open sides of the rows of spectators, also marked the passages (*parodoi*) through which the chorus entered the orchestra. The area between the long-side wall of the booth and the dancing area, known as the *proskenion*, was set aside for the performance of the actors. This made it appropriate to adapt this *skene* wall to the setting of the action by means of replaceable paintings, equipping it with doors through which actors could enter and exit from the stage, and using its roof for appearances by gods etc. All these elements are clearly discernible from the fourth century BC onwards in stone-built theatres, such as that of Epidaurus which was opened with great ceremony.

The distinction between chorus and actors was thus so sharply defined – in terms of language, scenic arrangements, choreography and music – that it can only be explained historically by a subsequent uniting of two originally quite different elements.

In connection with the review of iambography offered above, a tendency has already been pointed out, documented among many peoples, to tolerate open joking, abuse and derision in the context of relaxed and joyful festivals of the gods which under normal circumstances might threaten to disturb the peace. Its inclusion in ritual made it apt to become stylised in verse form. The form of verse and language in tragic dialogue corresponds to those of this ritual spoken verse. We do not, therefore, trace the rise of drama back to antiphony within a chorus, but explain it instead as a combination of two cult elements that were formerly merely justaposed but unrelated: improvised speech in verse, and dance-song. Verse speech will have contained an element of dialogue, specifically derision and response, from the very outset.

Further elucidation is provided by the traditional Greek term for actor: *hypokrites*. This does not mean 'respondent', as is sometimes asserted, but 'interpreter', and may thus contain some indication of the original connection between dance-song and verse speech. As we have seen, traditional verse speech originally had no functional connection with song, being used in the cult to expound, by means of a spoken proem, on the meaning of a highly stylised choral song. In the case of the Dionysiac cult, the audience was particularly heterogeneous. This would help to account for two other features of mature tragedy: firstly, for the often painstakingly composed prologue, irrespective of whether it was related to the action itself or not, and secondly for the fact that from the very beginning tragedy, although part of the Dionysiac cult, obviously drew its themes from the full range of myths about gods and heroes. This circumstance was so striking, even to the ancients, that the phrase, 'That has nothing to do with Dionysus', became proverbial. (Byzantine explanations of this proverb, incidentally, have preserved some of the post-Aristotelian erudition regarding the origins of tragedy.)

It is no longer possible to trace the details of the process whose beginnings have just been outlined. Nothing can be asserted with any certainty, for example, either about the form of the first tragedy contest held in 532 BC or about the significance of Thespis, regarded in antiquity as the originator of tragedy. All that can be said for certain is that the combination of spoken dialogue with mimetic elements of the dance-song, and the tapping of the entire mythical tradition as a storehouse of themes, constituted the most significant innovations paving the way for the great future of tragedy.

One remarkable feature is that despite both the rapidity with which this new art form developed, and numerous well-documented experiments with dramaturgy and stage technique, certain Archaic characteristics persisted. The number of actors was very slow to be increased, for example. It was only in his latter years, perhaps influenced by Sophocles, that Aeschylus used a third actor, while even Euripides only seems to have introduced a fourth in exceptional cases. Since the chosen themes called for a great many more roles, this restriction to two or three actors, each of whom consequently had to play several roles, placed great demands on the dramaturgical expertise of the poet, even if the custom of wearing masks did somewhat alleviate these role changes.

Equally little is known about tragic poetry prior to Aeschylus, although something can be deduced from surviving accounts as regards stylistic developments and changes in taste. Reference has already been made to Pratinas (see above, p. 92–3), who restored the burlesque element of the ancient cult dance to its former place of honour, and became a classic author of satyr plays. His work may perhaps be seen as the reaction to a rapid process of refinement within tragic writing that threatened to cut tragedy off from its roots entirely. This phenomenon is linked chiefly with the name of Phrynichus, who also wrote around 500 BC. Some vague notion at least of his style is conveyed by parodies and allusions in the comedies of Aristophanes. Of all tragedy authors, aside perhaps from the late Euripides, Phrynichus seems to have gone furthest towards bringing highly artificial stylistic features from great choral lyric poetry – at its most extreme phase of sophistication in the late sixth century – into the language and music of young tragedy. Resistance to this tendency was probably inspired by the correct view that a work of art performed by a citizens' chorus for a citizens' audience could only be of limited technical complexity. (Euripides' innovations in this regard at the end of the fifth century BC were preceded by the rise of a body of professional virtuosos, and were hence more prevalent in the increasingly popular arias than in the choruses.)

Phrynichus introduced yet another innovation. Two titles documented as being of his authorship show that he sometimes used events from contemporary history as themes for his tragedies. The *Conquest of Miletus* deals with an Ionian uprising against the Persians which took place in 499 BC, while the *Phoenissae*, in many respects a direct model for Aeschylus' *Persians*, deals with the impact of news of the Battle of Salamis at the Persian court in Susa.

This innovation by Phrynichus did not go unopposed, it seems. He was penalised, accounts tell us, for having moved his audience to tears with his depiction of the Milesian catastrophe, thereby desecrating the Dionysiac festival. The inclusion of contemporary historical themes was supported chiefly by the new-found confidence of Athens, where the first democratic institutions had been established immediately prior to the Persian Wars. Thus, whereas Greek aristocratic society had derived the criteria for its values from a mythology representing an utterly glorified past that was superior to the present, in those decisive first years of the fifth century BC the citizens of Athens ventured to attribute such exemplary characteristics to their own deeds and ordeals. This new attitude was of immense importance for the flowering of literature and the visual arts in the then incipient Classical period, which centred on Athens.

The transition from an Archaic to an unequivocally Classical literary form occurred first and in most exemplary fashion in Attic tragedy, where it was initiated specifically by Aeschylus. Born in 525 BC, he was a younger contemporary of Simonides, Phrynichus and Pratinas, and an exact contemporary of Pindar. Elements are discernible in the language, style and composition of all these writers, that is in the devices used for the intellectual accommodation of literary themes, which may be regarded as typical Classical fifth-century literature. Judging from their extant works, however, they were still firmly rooted in the traditions of the late Archaic mode of perception and expression. Stylistic elements from Archaic tradition may also be pinpointed in Aeschylus, and yet viewed overall his few extant tragedies, all of which date from between 472 and 458 BC, his latter years, belong to the world of early Classical form. Obviously, however, neither the development nor the character of the Classical period can be described or even explained in terms of purely formal categories. The literary forms taking shape in the fifth century, like the new plastic style, or the growth of the institutions of Attic democracy, were much more the expression of a whole new conception of the individual and the world.

There is no simple causal relationship between this change and the successfully withstood test of the Persian threat. It is particularly apparent in the visual arts that the essential features of this new human understanding – its increased seriousness, its move away from an abundance of colourful detail and towards a focus on essentials, and its innovative representation of the functional context of the human body – all manifest themselves for the first time soon after 500 BC. The reorganisation of the Athenian state system indeed began in the last decade of the sixth century. Athens thus embarked on the Persian Wars fully intellectually equipped, hence emerging from this acid test with increased vigour and self-confidence.

It is beyond the scope of this account to trace the historical chain of events leading to that burgeoning of Attic culture in the fifth century BC which was to prove so fundamental for Europe as a whole. The essential point is that writers such as Aeschylus and Sophocles were able to verbalise these new ideas in literary works of art of the highest possible quality and concentration. In this way, they established artistic standards whose importance far transcends the immediate historical significance of their works, however rare and remarkable they may have been in themselves as a consummate expression of the intellectual vigour of their age, particularly from the historical viewpoint.

The supreme mastery widely acknowledged in Classical writing despite all efforts to do justice to other epochs, a mastery which is more than the result of a merely emotional or pro-traditional assessment, may partly be explained in formal, artistic terms. It derived from the successful application of singularly appropriate, and not necessarily particularly complex rules of style and composition – in other words a normative poetics. More important than this, however, is the intensity and consistency with which the Classical work of art is able to expound intellectual processes and faculties – the extent to which it spiritualises the substance of language. This second defining characteristic of the Classical can only be verified through the interpretation of individual works of art. It manifested itself from constantly shifting perspectives, depending on the theme of the particular work. One simple example, however, may serve to illustrate the importance of this category of description and opinion.

The sixth century BC was marked by the discovery of the significance of human intention, expressed in free decision-making, and forming a basis for moral responsibility that was more powerful than the external course of events. The importance attached to intention in criminal procedure (i.e. the distinction between offence and responsibility that is foreign to primitive systems of justice), occasionally hinted at in the seventh, increasingly observed in the sixth, and generally recognised in the fifth centuries BC, is a particularly clear illustration of this change in legal and moral concepts. Simonides occasionally formulated the modern view of the paramount moral importance of good intention as a scholion or gnomic insertion in a choral lyric mythical narrative. The innovative nature of the idea is thus matched by the thoroughly traditional character of the form selected to express it. In the *Suppliants* by Aeschylus, however, a play with many passages of Archaic colourfulness and a still markedly undeveloped dramatic form, the structure of the central scene revolves entirely around this new view and its exposition in word and action. Despite its comparatively Archaic style, therefore, viewed as a whole this tragedy undoubtedly displays the second defining characteristic of the Classical described above.

Owing to various ways in which they were handed down, a couple of dozen plays at least out of the infinitely rich output of fifth-century tragedy writers can still be read today. Originally, at least three new tetralogies, not individual tragedies, were written and composed for every Dionysiac festival complete with its tragedy contest. Since this meant a yearly addition of several dozen plays, the massive scale of this output can be imagined. Likewise, there were initially no revivals of earlier plays, these first being permitted only after the death of Aeschylus, because of the impact of his masterpieces, and then provided for legislatively in the early fourth century for the plays of Aeschylus, Sophocles and Euripides. This step, which substantially checked the increase in new tragedy writing in the fourth century, documents the early date at which these three poets became part of the canon. This was already apparent from Aristophanes' *Frogs*, performed in 405 BC. These plays were understandably revised for a number of revivals during the fourth century – a practice still found in the modern theatrical world. Revisions could quite easily affect the scripts themselves, there being neither printing nor copyright law at that time. Nevertheless, in the fifth century a reading public began to show interest in dramatic poetry, giving rise to an expanding book trade.

Through tragedy, it seems, another innovation arose without which life would be unthinkable today. In earlier times, it was not customary to give titles to books (see below, p. 159). Since, however, the performance of tragedies and comedies as state cult events entailed the creation and archiving of files, this in turn necessitated a concise name for the plays that were to be filed and performed. As book trading and librarianship continued to develop, this practice proved to be extraordinarily expedient.

At the end of the fourth century BC, an attempt was made to impose some order on the prevailing chaos in the texts of tragedy, created by play revivals. The Athenian politician Lycurgus ordered that one copy be deposited in the archive – of the extant text then held to be authentic – of all tragedies written by the three 'Greats'. Extensive use was made of these copies by Alexandrian scholars, when from the third century BC onwards they came to collate and critically edit the texts of the entire Greek poetic legacy in the great research institute of their library.

Work on collating and editing was accompanied by a study of the language, style, metre and history of Attic drama. One of the major sources for these studies were *didascaliae* – official documents of performances stored in the Athenian archive. These had already been promulgated by Aristotle as a source for the history of poetics.

This wealth of scholarly literature continued to be written well into the Imperial age. Some of it has survived in scholia, commentaries dating from the Byzantine era, and in manuscripts of the same period containing the life stories of poets. The major critical 'complete editions' were understandably rarely reproduced, but they did serve as a basis for editions of selected works for school and home use. These enjoyed a wide distribution, especially in the Imperial age, when the general standard of education was astonishingly high. The clearest idea of the nature and distribution of such editions comes from papyrus fragments from Egypt dating from the third century BC to the sixth century AD. They also provide glimpses of texts that have been lost, or from which only occasional quotations from well-known plays are otherwise available. Euripides is naturally the best represented, as the linguistically simplest and most modern of the tragedians.

Here and there, an occasional copy of such editions of selected works survived in a private library through the so-called dark centuries of early Byzantine history. With the ninth-century revival of Classical studies in Byzantium, these became the basis for a series of copies and new editions that have continued to the present day, for work on Greek literature, the attempt to purify and interpret its texts, has never been fully interrupted since then. The high point of these studies was reached in the fourteenth century, which witnessed a flowering in Byzantine philology, and again in the early nineteenth century, when British and German philologists worked successfully on the texts of tragedies.

Seven dramas each by Aeschylus and Sophocles have survived in a famous codex written around AD 1000, today kept in the Biblioteca Laurenziana in Florence. They constitute a select edition dating from the height of the Imperial age. Euripides' eighteen plays, including *Rhesus*, which is traditionally attributed to him but is undoubtedly not authentic, are contained in a collection not made until the Middle Ages. Half of them are based on an ancient edition of selected works, accompanied by a valuable scholiastic commentary. The other half go back to a single volume, rescued from oblivion in the Middle Ages, of a complete edition arranged according to the opening letters of the plays, but with no scholia.

After this, the handing down of Greek tragedy was a purely literary matter, intended for a reading public. The performance of Classical, especially Euripidean, tragedies in the Hellenistic-Roman world, in which every town had a theatre and put on drama on certain days during its festival calendar, no longer exerted any influence on the handing down of texts. Thereafter, modifications mostly involved new musical adaptations of selected arias or specific scenes performed by wandering virtuosos.

Modern knowledge of this theatrical activity is derived mainly from the rolls of honour of successful actors. (This may be how the word 'tragedy' came to mean 'song' in vulgar Greek, retaining this meaning in modern Greek.) During this period, literature and theatrical practice lost all connection with each other. Even most of the tragedies written subsequently were intended solely for reading. Works by Classical authors were nevertheless read avidly to the very end of antiquity, as is documented by innumerable papyrus fragments from Egypt, as well as frequent quotations from tragedy authors by later writers.

Of the extant tragedies by Aeschylus, three are characterised by a relatively archaic dramatic structure: the *Persians* (472 BC), the *Seven Against Thebes* (467 BC) and the *Suppliants* (462 BC). Three show the most complete form: the *Oresteia*, a complete extant tragic trilogy (458 BC). One is so unlike Aeschylus' style that there are doubts as to its authenticity: *Prometheus Bound*, whose first year of performance is unknown.

Although the *Suppliants* is not the earliest extant play, its structure betrays so many Archaic features that it provides a particularly useful illustration of how dramatic form developed. The tragedy opens with the entrance of a chorus of twelve singers, representing the Danaids, the fifty daughters of Danaus. Together with their father they have fled from Egypt to escape the brutal courtship of their cousins, the sons of Aegyptus. Whereas the procession into the orchestra is accompanied by a typical marching song in anapaests ($\cup \cup -$), the ensuing choral song, in which the girls tell of their origins, is in grand choral lyric style, performed standing. This preliminary exposition of the situation is then followed by a spoken dialogue between

Danaus and the leader of the chorus. No more functional distinction is to be discerned here between the sung song and the spoken word. A hiatus is created by the entrance of Pelasgus, King of Argos, to whose land the fugitives have come. They now make their plea before him for protection from the sons of Aegyptus, who are in pursuit.

Pelasgus is faced with a dilemma: to refuse their request would be an offence against Zeus Hicesius, patron of the helpless petitioner. To take in the Danaids, on the other hand, will expose Argos to attack by the sons of Aegyptus. The debate between Pelasgus and the chorus, which began as a dialogue, is continued in the form of antiphony, culminating in a scene consisting mainly of monologue that is understood by Bruno Snell (1928) to be the true climax of the drama. Pelasgus eventually decides to propose to the Argive people's assembly that they take in the Danaids, and leaves with Danaus. The chorus, now alone, sings a song of prayer, during which time voting is to be imagined taking place at the people's assembly. Danaus then returns, giving an account of the favourable outcome of the vote, whereupon the chorus sings a song of thanksgiving.

Immediately thereafter, however, the horizon is clouded again: a dialogue between Danaus and the leader of the chorus, which again breaks into song, announces the arrival of an Egyptian herald. Danaus leaves the stage to fetch assistance from the city of Argos (and, since there are only two actors, to allow the herald to enter). The chorus sings a song expressing their anxiety, which proves justified on the arrival of the herald accompanied by a troop of soldiers. The Egyptians attempt to abduct the girls in a wild scene that is sung throughout. At this point Pelasgus enters, banishing the Egyptians from the land. They obey his order, but threaten to return with an army. The chorus strikes up a song of thanksgiving. Only now, after the herald has left the stage, does Danaus reappear to give a lengthy speech of thanks and admonition. The chorus then sets off for Argos, where the Danaids are from now on to enjoy citizens' rights.

Hopefully this brief outline will suffice to show that this was no drama in the modern sense of the term. The chorus plays a dominant role, never leaving the stage, the remaining characters appearing solely in temporary relationship to it. There is no entangled multilevel story of error, no process of arriving at a correct assessment of characters or situations, or of the dramatic effect arising from it. With one exception, no processes make it clear that a character behaves in one way rather than another, thereby influencing the course of events in the right way. For those familiar with the mythology, as was the case with the 462 BC audience, the course of events is entirely predictable.

The sole exception is the protracted decision of Pelasgus. The emphasis here is on the decision itself, rather than the ensuing course of the plot, and is in any case rendered provisional by the existence of an Argive people's assembly who have the final say. The decision of Pelasgus, whose moral significance is greatly exaggerated in the play, is not an act of will, but the result of a painfully exact analysis of the situation through argument and counter-argument, leaving an open choice between two equally perilous but morally defensible options. This marks the first encounter in Greek literature with such an exact description of the responsibility involved in a decision that is entirely distinct from the ensuing plot. It thus delimits the moral phenomenon to which tragedy owes its existence as a literary form in its own right.

The fact that the dilemma of Pelasgus is 'tragic' is clear to the audience, despite the positive outcome of the first extant play in the trilogy. The myth told of the return of the Egyptians, and how they involved Argos in a war that was to cost Pelasgus his life. This is depicted in the second play in Aeschylus' trilogy, the *Egyptians*. In fact, however, Pelasgus is not the main character, either in this play or in the extant version of the *Suppliants*. The central theme throughout is the fate of the Danaids, who at first recoil and take flight from the malevolent courtship of the sons of Aegyptus, but are then forced to marry their cousins after their campaign against Argos. This time they defend themselves against the loathsome union with a gruesome act: with the exception of Hypermestra, who spares Lynceus, they murder their suitors on the wedding night. (Obviously, it was beyond the scope of not only the Greek stage to depict this event, which will have been presented by Aeschylus in the form of a report by a messenger, like the outcome of the Battle of Salamis in the *Persians*.) The subsequent destiny of Hypermestra appears from later sources to have been central to the traditional version of the myth, whereas all that remains for her sisters is a place among the penitents in the underworld.

As Kurt von Fritz has suggested (1962, 251ff.), however, Aeschylus modifies or shifts the accent of the myth. The third play in the trilogy, the *Danaids*, recounts the exoneration of the daughters of Danaus through a restoration by the gods of the order disrupted first by the wickedness of the sons of Aegyptus, and then again by the Danaids' act of vengeance, which exceeded all bounds. The key to understanding both the form and the content of the extant tragedy lies in this initial modification of the myth. It is no longer a dispute between Aegyptus and Danaus that unleashes the chain of events, as in the ancient tradition, but the forcible courtship of Aegyptus' sons, which constitutes an infringement of moral law. Likewise at the end, the issue is no longer one of revenge and retribution, but of restoring a disrupted order.

The undramatic character of the *Suppliants* noted here may be explained by the fact that the various threads of the plot are laid out and disentangled throughout the entire trilogy. Deeds and their consequences, guilt and exoneration, are not dealt with in a single play, as we are accustomed to in later tragedy, and as Aristotle in his *Poetics* stated that they should be. The thematically close-knit trilogy seems to have been invented by Aeschylus, enabling him to use what were still simple technical and dramatic devices to reveal the theological and moral import he had discovered in myth. Trilogies of this kind do not seem to have existed before Aeschylus. His earliest extant play, the *Persians* (472 BC), was still only loosely connected to the rest of its trilogy. In the *Seven Against Thebes* (467 BC), on the other hand, the interpretation given for the fate that is to befall the Theban House of Labdacus, generation after generation until the death of the two enemy brothers Eteocles and Polynices, is clearly envisaged in the context of a trilogy.

Refinement of dramatic technique from the middle of the century onwards enabled poets to present mythical traditions in a more manageable, self-contained form, giving them dramatic shape as separate plays. This led to a corresponding loosening of the trilogy arrangement, even though this form, expanded into a tetralogy by the addition of a satyr play, still remained the official unit of performance at tragic contests throughout the Classical period. It may be viewed as singularly fortunate, therefore, that the sole complete trilogy extant today is a late work by Aeschylus. This enables us on the one hand to discern particularly clearly the nature and theological foundations of his trilogic art, while also uncovering in detail the attainments of his highly developed technique. Some of these are attributable to Aeschylus himself, and some to Sophocles, who had already been writing plays for ten years by 458 BC.

The number of actors, for example, had been increased to three, the chorus being ever more limited to a role of supporting the action on stage with reflections and maxims directed at the characters, or even the audience. Given the language, style, music and dance provided for the chorus by the tradition of choral lyric poetry, this dramatic function seems far more appropriate to it than direct and ongoing involvement in the plot.

One innovation in the *Oresteia* is the introduction of characters of low station, such as a sentry or an old wet-nurse. These characters do more than enliven the flow of the plot through their speech and action. They reveal the significance of mythical events – which are linked with the names of glorified heroes, but are intended to be meaningful in terms of timeless moral issues – from the perspective of those who are completely uninvolved in the intrigues of that heroic world. This gives a more human quality to the action without the main characters forfeiting any of their heroic dignity, as was the case later in Euripides.

Agamemnon, the first play in the *Oresteia* trilogy, relates the victorious return of the great king from the Trojan War, and how he is treacherously murdered in his royal stronghold by his faithless wife Clytemnestra and her lover Aegisthus, who then accedes to the throne as her husband. The second play, the *Choephori*, derives its name from the opening scene, in which Electra, the daughter of Agamemnon, offers a sacrifice for the dead (*choë*) at the grave of her slain father, finding clues suggesting the presence of her brother Orestes. A faithful retainer has saved the latter from persecution by Aegisthus, and he has grown up abroad. The two recognise each other, make plans for revenge, and Orestes slays the adulterous couple.

The act of vengeance perpetrated by Orestes is by the express orders of the god Apollo, but the deed draws the attention of other deities responsible for the sanctity of the bond between mother and child. These, the Erinyes or Furies (goddesses of curses), hound the matricide mercilessly from one town to the next. He finds only fleeting refuge with Apollo in the temple at Delphi. The third play in the trilogy, the *Eumenides*, resolves this apparently hopeless conflict. A legal battle is fought out at the Areopagus, the time-honoured murder court of the city of Athens, which convenes under the aegis of the goddess Athena. Apollo, representing the new order established by the Olympian gods, defends the deed of Orestes by pointing out the necessity of punishing the murder of a husband and king. The Erinyes, on the other hand, invoke the earlier order, calling for the expiation of matricide. The Areopagus dismisses the case against Orestes, at the same time mollifying the Erinyes by introducing their cult into Athens, where they are henceforth to dwell as *Eumenides*, the gracious bestowers of blessings.

Aeschylus' theological interpretation of myth is based on a firm belief in the essential justice of the divine order of the universe. The idea of this justice making the gods into defenders of law and order among humankind had already been put forward by Hesiod, and later with a heightened sense of political responsibility by Solon. The notion that the actions of gods and heroes related in myth ought to correspond to the moral standards of his own day had moreover been the most important motif in the mythical interpretations of Pindar. What was new about Aeschylus' conception is that the law established by Zeus was more than a body of fixed rules whose observance was watched over by the gods with a system of reward and punishment. Instead, it was seen as a vital force constantly proving itself in ever new manifestations, and even able to resolve conflict which seemed hopeless from the human viewpoint. Apollo's claim is as valid as that of the Erinyes, so that Orestes, who must satisfy both, seems bound to be destroyed by this dilemma, as two divine powers conduct a mutual conflict with each other through his action and suffering, without releasing him from his moral responsibility. The trial instigated by Athena, the motherless daughter of Zeus, allows the dynamic nature of his law to manifest itself clearly, thereby resolving a unique, unforeseeable conflict through a decision that is specific to the situation, but also creates a new order, while at the same time reconciling two equally valid claims that had seemed to be hopelessly at odds. Nevertheless, it is in human action, carried out with a consciousness of responsibility, that this conflict between divine powers is acted out and resolved. Were it not for human beings, as is demonstrated using the metaphor of the court of Athenian citizens, the law of Zeus would have no scope in which to unfold. Human dignity consists in becoming the necessary partner of the gods, and in the right order of human society matching the divine order as closely as possible.

The figure of Zeus is crucial to Aeschylus' conception of a universal order that is best learned by human beings through uncomprehended suffering, and in which they are led to carry out divine plans through their own, often involuntary co-operation in them. This becomes clear, for example, in a hymn to Zeus in *Agamemnon* that has proved quite a stumbling block to exegetes. The father of the gods known from traditional religion is glorified into a god of the world or universe, whose law directs all events, and in whose jurisdiction the ignorant person often sees only cruelty and injustice. This view does not contradict its association with the philosophical speculation documented in Xenophanes or Heraclitus in the generation preceding Aeschylus. Hellenised Jews of subsequent times had a particular fondness for Aeschylus, finding in his work the God of the Old Covenant. They liked to name their sons after the poet, while their literature (see below, p. 306) contains frequent references to his tragedies.

Aeschylus' reinterpretation of the ancient bloodthirsty saga of the House of Atreus in terms pertaining to theology and legal metaphysics undoubtedly predominates over the slight modification, which Aeschylus likewise gave to it, whereby he suppresses the tradition of the hereditary curse and divests the final exoneration of Orestes of its magical character. This reinterpretation and modification are nevertheless closely interlinked. The central idea of the allpervasive, dynamic justice of Zeus which must be carried out by and among humankind undoubtedly derives from the experience of the poet's own generation with the emergence and rise of the Athenian *polis*. For perhaps the first time in human history, Athens saw that governmental and social justice could be achieved neither by the might and arbitrary will of rulers, nor from its previously sanctioned source in cult and law, nor even from the immediate needs and demands of the population. Justice in the community was rather an order in constant need of renewal in a never-ending sequence of individual acts, whereby the authority of tradition needed to be brought to account just as much as new, previously unencountered needs arising out of the immediate situation.

Aeschylus' work, for all the limitations and distortions of its particular historical perspective, enshrined this experience of the constitutional state in human consciousness for all time. In his native city, at any rate, there were many who grasped his meaning correctly. In the *Frogs*, performed in 405 BC, Aristophanes has the poet declare with pride that he has improved the citizens with his tragedies. Despite the heroic milieu of the *Oresteia*, Aeschylus still manages to express his ideas about divine and human law in up-to-date language. This is clear from the fact that the trial scene in the *Eumenides* remains to this day a major source of information about Attic penal law.

Another aspect of Aeschylus' conception of justice is of major significance for the history of literature, however. Wherever law is understood to be an order that is constantly reaffirmed according to the divine will in the actions and sufferings of mankind, this is presented in the form of action and dialogue between human partners, the most appropriate means of conveying this view in a work of art. Despite the fact that only a tenth of his complete works are extant today, the development of tragedy into a dramatic art form in the modern sense can safely be attributed to Aeschylus, as ancient tradition indeed asserted. This fact is fundamentally linked with his metaphysics of justice. The necessity that associates form and content in the works of Aeschylus is one of the hallmarks of the Classical character generally acknowledged in his tragedies. This highlights the fact that the Greek Classical period cannot be summed up using purely formal criteria. This can be very aptly demonstrated using the contemporary contrast of Pindar's extremely refined lyric poetry, where the necessity for a newly conceived form was conspicuously lacking.

The political and moral foundation of Aeschylus' tragedies is most apparent in his two earliest plays, the *Seven Against Thebes* and the *Persians*. In the former, the character of Eteocles is most noteworthy. Fully aware of the destiny that awaits him, he none the less devotes all his energies to safeguarding the community that has been entrusted to him. The *Persians*, a highly archaic tragedy with an unresolved plot, loosely made up of isolated scenes and lacking any definite connection with the wider trilogy, may be described as one of the most astonishing ancient literary documents. It relates the impact at the Persian court of the news of the defeat at Salamis in 480 BC, culminating in a grand climax extending from the gloomy forebodings of the queen mother Atossa and a consultation which she instigates with the spirit of Darius the Great, to the devastating report of the catastrophe by a messenger and the entrance of the defeated King Xerxes.

The Battles of Marathon and Salamis, at which Aeschlyus himself fought, were soon placed by Athenians on the same plane as events in the mythical past, so great was the impact on Athenian civic pride of these unexpectedly glorious victories over the oppressive might of the Persian Empire. However, the lasting picture created by Aeschylus out of this historical experience contains no degradation of the defeated enemy, such as may be encountered in historical traditions related in the Old Testament. Nor does it involve any glorification of Athenian prowess, which, along with the degradation of the defeated enemy, to this day tend to make up the greater measure of national pride, based on military successes, in most European and non-European nations. Aeschylus is certainly not blind to the accomplishments of his compatriots, but he ascribes the triumphant success of the Persian Wars to the intervention of the gods, who wanted to ensure that Xerxes did not overstep the boundaries allotted to him as man and ruler. There is not one word of hostility or even rancour towards the defeated adversary in this play. On the contrary, in Atossa's dream Persia and Greece appear as sisters on an equal footing. The powerful position attained by Darius is expressly acknowledged to be the reward for Persian prowess, and the account of the Battle of Salamis depicts the downfall of a valiant and indeed much-admired adversary.

The naive and inquisitive predilection of Archaic Greeks for foreign and distant lands is still evident in some details of Aeschylus' tragedies (such as in the enumeration of foreign names, or references to ethnographic and geo-graphical curiosities). With the impact of the Persian Wars, which was as serious as it was uplifting, this predilection was sublimated into a concept of the equal status of different peoples. The fact that the *Persians* contains a clearly expressed awareness that Persians and Greeks alike are subject to the same divine order takes the sting out of the clearly perceived distinction between Hellenes and barbarians.

Prometheus Bound occupies a special place among extant plays that still awaits a satisfactory explanation. It combines Archaic features, such as the absence of a third actor, and a curious order of scenes, with modern features such as the withdrawal of the chorus, complex technical stage arrangements, and an extensive reference to a theory of how human culture came about that was much discussed in the second half of the fifth century BC. In terms of language and verse structure it differs markedly from all other tragedies by Aeschlyus, while the god Zeus who directs its action is far from being the founder and defender of a just universal order with whom we are familiar elsewhere in Aeschylus. The allocation of otherwise well-known themes to other extant titles of the *Prometheus* trilogy poses similar problems. As long as so little of the poet's work is known, however, it will be necessary to exercise caution regarding a verdict as to its authenticity, particularly since this qualitatively significant tragedy was always looked on as the work of Aeschylus in antiquity.

In Aeschylus' time, the tragic tetralogy generally concluded with a satyr play. Information concerning thematic links between tragedies and the burlesque play of half-animal deities is provided by such plays as *Amymone* – the satyr play attached to the *Danaid* trilogy that has been lost but reconstructed. The heroine of the title, one of the Danaids, is molested by a lascivious wood sprite while fetching water from the forest. She is rescued by the intervention of the god Poseidon, who then takes her as his lover after adopting the form of a handsome young man. This is thus a non-tragic variation of the fate of the Danaids: the satyr replaces the sons of Aegyptus, and Poseidon the suitors taken home by the Danaids following their exoneration.

The two most important papyri of Aeschylus found among those texts in Egypt contain extensive relics of two satyr plays, the tetralogical context of which is now lost, however. In one, the *Netfishers*, the chorus of satyrs discovers in a landed fishing-net the wooden case in which Danae was put out to sea with her young son Perseus and carried across the sea to Seriphus. The combined curiosity and fear of the satyrs is conveyed with delightful freshness as they approach this rare object with appropriately expressive gestures. In the other play, the *Isthmiasts*, old Silenus and his retinue of satyrs even engage in an athletics contest. The untroubled jollity of these satyr plays reveals the true scope of Aeschylean drama, which may justly be likened to that of Shakespeare.

The power of Aeschylus' language is also reminiscent of Shakespeare. Aristophanes said of Aeschylus that he 'built towers of lofty words' – an apt description of Aeschylus' choral songs. From the stylistic tradition of choral lyric poetry tragedy adopted not merely the artificial dialect, but also the excessive use of composite, and often newly coined epithets that lent utterance a quality of foreign, and often gloomy ceremoniality. Aeschlyus created and used words of this kind with particular skill, attaining a high degree of baroque splendour. What is innovative and impressive about his work, however, is that none of these words is used purely for the sake of decoration. Each component is entirely justified in terms of meaning. Two examples may serve to illustrate this. A choral song in the *Suppliants* refers to 'black-yoked Fate'. 'Black' in the sense of 'harmful' is an epithet common to poetic language of all hues, as is its replacement by 'blackish', 'black-coloured', etc. Here too, therefore, one is inclined to interpret the expression merely as a baroque variation of 'dark Fate'. There was a proclivity in poetic language, however, for using 'yoke' to designate all kinds of carpentry, including a ship or its deck. Since this passage refers to the pursuit of the Danaids by their Egyptian suitors, the word thus contains a very precise identification of the anticipated danger that is to arrive by sea. In a song of prayer in the same tragedy, the god is invoked with the words: 'become one who is much mindful', in a context in which the appropriate meaning is simply 'be mindful (of us)'. This paraphrase of the simple verb form certainly achieves a splendid and decorative effect. More than this, however, its substantive character suggests an enduring quality of the deity that is to be manifested in this specific situation. In this way the composite substantive preserves the full potential meaning of the verb to which it pertains.

Structures such as these demonstrate the density of Aeschylus' diction. Complete expressive fullness is retained, and there are no merely ornamental passages devoid of meaning, such as are to be found in Pindar, and which were to become commonplace in the lyric poetry of later tragedy. Aeschylus, moreover, loves to relate words by their meanings to two or even more words in the context, even though they ought only to relate to one from the strictly grammatical viewpoint. This overlays his lyric poetry with a dense network made up of various threads of meaning, knitting the text together far more closely than could ever be accomplished by customary grammatical relations.

Aeschylus' language in the dialogue passages is of great significance and plasticity. Key accounts by messengers especially, such as in the *Seven Against Thebes* and the *Persians*, are masterpieces of descriptive poetry. He uses largely the vocabulary of colloquial Attic, enriched with Homerisms. His syntax is distinguished from prose expression by his great originality.

In Aeschylus the strophic structure is generally simpler than in Pindar, a fact which may be explained principally by the less sophisticated musical training of Athenian citizens' choruses. For all that, the diversity of verse types used is astonishingly great. Modern understanding of this poetry is particularly sadly at a loss in that, as a result of the total disappearance of the music to these works, it is only possible in a few exceptional cases to guess at the ethos and atmosphere of particular verse forms. Verse translations into other, living languages can easily obscure this deficiency.

What can still be appreciated in Aeschylus's poetry relates firstly to the literary skill and dramatic technique manifest in the literary composition of his plays, and secondly to his theological and moral interpretation of myth. It is hardly possible nowadays to guess at the theatrical impact of performances in the Athenian theatre of Dionysus. We do still have some notion about the use of masks and stage machinery, and may imagine the high pathos, of a power that verged on the barbaric, of gestures and melodies in the most emotionally-charged scenes. What we are unable to do is connect this sparse knowledge and guesswork with our knowledge of extant texts, so as to form an impression of the work of art as a whole. We are thus compelled to limit ourselves to literary interpretation. Even in later antiquity, tragedies of the Classical era were handed down and evaluated as literature.

Aeschylus died in Sicily, where he had been invited by the tyrant Hieron, like Pindar. Nevertheless, he and Sophocles should be understood purely as poets of the classical Attic polis. The Athenian citizens' audience at Dionysiac festivals, and their historical experience, were the prerequisites of their poetry.

7

SOPHOCLES AND
EURIPIDES

Sophocles, the second great tragedy writer of the fifth century BC, achieved his first victory in 468 BC. His work thus ran parallel to that of Aeschylus for over ten years. Euripides' first victory took place in 456 BC, before the death of Aeschylus, the exact year of which is not known, and he died a year before Sophocles, in 406 BC. Ancient biographical legends illustrated this chronological concurrence, rather than succession, of the three 'Greats' with the aid of the Battle of Salamis – at which Aeschylus fought, and at the victory celebration of which Sophocles led the dance of youths, on the same day that Euripides was born.

In reality, the younger among the three did more than perpetuate the craft of their predecessors. Aeschlyus' *Oresteia* betrays the influence of Sophoclean stage technique, and Sophocles' *Trachiniae* that of the great women characters of Euripidean drama of the 430s. This network of mutual influence would appear even more close-knit than it does were we still able, like Alexandrian scholars, to read 75 tragedies by Aeschlyus, 125 by Sophocles and 90 by Euripides.

For us today, as for the late fifth century BC, Aeschylus epitomises the heroic era of the Persian Wars, just as his funeral epigram, which he allegedly composed himself, refers only to his participation in the Battle of Marathon, not to his poetry. Similarly, the name of Sophocles is inextricably linked with the glory of the Periclean age, in which the Parthenon was built on the Acropolis, Phidias carved his sculptures, and the Athenian Empire stretched across the entire Aegean.

Sophocles served his native city in high administrative and military offices. Even immediately after his death he seems to have been idealised, undoubtedly because of his personal charisma. Aristophanes praised his *eukolia* – his cheerful, balanced temperament. The memoirs of his contemporary, Ion of Chios, who also wrote tragedies, tell of his social poise, as we can read today from some extracts preserved in Plutarch (around AD 100). This biographical tradition is fully affirmed by a fourth-century BC statue of Sophocles, of which a copy made in the Roman era can still be seen in the Lateran Museum in Rome.

Of the seven extant tragedies by Sophocles, two, *Ajax* and *Antigone*, date from the 440s, written when the poet was around 50, while the performance dates of two, *Philoctetes* and *Oedipus Coloneus*, show them to be late works (409 and 405 BC respectively). For the three remaining tragedies there are some chronological points of reference arising from comparison with plays by Euripides. *Electra* is undoubtedly earlier than the work of the same name by Euripides, dated 412 BC. The *Trachiniae* betrays the influence of Euripidean dramas about women, despite several Archaic features. Even though *Oedipus Rex*, perhaps the most powerful of the extant tragedies, seems to indicate some familiarity with the achievements of Euripides' art, and may date from the period around 420 BC, other reasons suggest an earlier date.

In Sophocles' time, an incipient theory of art was manifesting itself in diverse spheres. He himself is said to have written a treatise on the chorus, accusing Aeschylus of 'writing superb poetry without knowing it'. The perfection that shines out of his arrangement of scenes and his command of linguistic devices, especially in his later tragedies, is indeed best understood in connection with debates about theories of art.

In the language of his dialogues, Sophocles shows less syntactic rigour, but more echoes of the epic than Aeschylus. The smoothness and lucidity of his diction also remove him further from everyday speech. In choral lyric poetry, Sophocles handled the traditional artificial language less tyrannically than his predecessor. His greater circumspection with regard to neologisms and composite forms, however, meant that he rarely achieved such evocative expressions, brimming with meaning to the very last syllable. On the other hand, his wording was more pleasing, and showed a particularly brilliant harmony between word and metre. It is for this reason that despite the loss of the accompanying music the modern reader has a less difficult task guessing at the ethos of the metre in Sophocles' sung lyric poetry. In his latter years, Sophocles developed his capacity for conveying moods in the lyric passages of his dramas to a supreme degree. *Oedipus Coloneus*, not performed until a year after his death, contains what is perhaps from this particular viewpoint the most consummate of all Greek lyric poetry, comparable only with some of Sappho's verses. His *Electra* offers a unique opportunity to elucidate the distinctive nature of his dramatic art, since the episode from the myth of the House of Atreus with which it deals also forms the basis of Aeschylus' *Choephori* and Euripides' *Electra*.

The play opens with the entrance of Orestes, accompanied by his friend Pylades and an old slave, in front of the royal palace in Mycenae. They are seeking vengeance on Aegisthus and Clytaemnestra, and must therefore at first hide, removing themselves on hearing a voice in the house. It is Electra, who appears immediately afterwards, singing of her distress in a monody. The chorus of Argive girls joins in, the antiphony changing to a dialogue giving an exposition of the drama. Next appears Electra's sister Chrysothemis, reporting a dream, prophesying doom, that Clytaemnestra had the previous night. Clytaemnestra has therefore sent her, Chrysothemis, to make sacrifices to the dead Agamemnon at his tomb. A long exchange between the sisters reveals their different characters. Despite Electra's powerlessness in the house of her hated mother, her thoughts still revolve around avenging the murder of Agamemnon. The gentle Chrysothemis, on the other hand, is willing to be reconciled to her mother and Aegisthus. Chrysothemis leaves to go to her father's grave, while a short choral song marks the hiatus between two acts. After this, Clytaemnestra appears out of the palace, becoming involved in a protracted exchange with her daughter that is filled with mutual and implacable hatred. This is brought to an end by the appearance of the old slave, disguised as a messenger, who has come to Mycenae with Orestes and Pylades. Elaborating his verse tale in sensational reportage style, he gives an account of the alleged death of Orestes as a result of an accident during a chariot race in Delphi. Clytaemnestra goes into the palace with the messenger, while Electra vents her grief in a monologue that develops into an antiphony with the chorus. At this point, an agitated Chrysothemis appears, having discovered at her father's grave evidence of the presence of Orestes – footprints and a lock of hair brought as a sacrifice for the dead. Her sister is sceptical, already having decided on the strength of the news of Orestes' death to avenge her father herself. After a vain attempt by Electra to win Chrysothemis over as an ally, the sisters are definitively estranged. A short choral song detached from the plot again marks the caesura between two acts. Then Orestes enters, also dressed as a messenger, bearing an urn of ashes allegedly containing the remains of the tragically killed Orestes. A heart-rending dialogue takes place between him and his sister Electra, during which they recognise each other. Electra's despair is transformed into ecstatic joy, expressed in an antiphony between her and the chorus. She and Orestes make plans for revenge. The old slave brings news from the palace that Aegisthus is out, and goes back into the palace with Orestes. The tension that reigns among those left behind is expressed in an antiphony, interrupted by the death scream of Clytaemnestra. Shortly thereafter Orestes appears, but must withdraw back into the palace immediately as Aegisthus is approaching. The latter inquires about the messenger from Phocis, of whose arrival he has heard, and is directed into the palace by Electra. At this moment the palace gate opens, and Orestes and Pylades appear beside the covered body of Clytaemnestra – probably on an *ekkyklema*, a stage machine constructed for rolling out large objects. Assuming this to be the body of Orestes, Aegisthus raises the cloth and steps back in shock. Orestes goes with him into the palace, intending to wreak revenge on him also. A final speech by the chorus concludes the drama.

Like epic poets, tragic authors were similarly unable to alter the basic events of mythical tradition. This highlights all the more strongly any new emphases in the course of the plot, or fresh moral evaluations of the characters and circumstances, evinced by each new adaptation of the material. Unlike Aeschylus' *Choephori*, Sophocles' drama is not part of a close-knit trilogy, but forms a complete unit in itself. The subject-matter of the play is not the sequence of deed and retribution, and the problems which arise out of it, but the retribution, presented as unique, of an equally unique misdeed preceding the present action. Even the fact that it is by command of Apollo himself that they slay their own mother to avenge their father is presented as entirely peripheral here, for it is not Orestes, the avenger stressed by tradition, who is the centre of interest, but Electra. It is her destiny, her suffering and her release from the oppression of her wicked mother, that constitute the real theme of the tragedy. Consequently, the act of vengeance is not the culmination of the action, but the moment when Electra's fortunes change, as she recognises the brother she had thought to be dead.

This shift of emphasis in the mythical plot is handled with immense skill by Sophocles, who avails himself of devices already used by his predecessors, as well as some dramaturgical inventions of his own. *Anagnorisis*, the motif of recognition, had already appeared in Aeschlyus. Sophocles, however, removes the traditional tokens of recognition – the sacrifices to the dead and footprints at the grave that were familiar to audiences – to the peripheral Chrysothemis' action, which does not achieve its objective. In this way he succeeds in shifting the key moment of recognition to a dialogue scene between Electra and Orestes. The central importance of this scene is abundantly stressed by the two entrances of an alleged messenger that pave the way for it. These are bound to convince Electra so fully of her brother's death that her recognition of the brother she had believed dead marks a true *peripeteia* – a complete transformation both of the dramatic situation and the state of mind of the main character. This is fully apparent in the motif invented by Sophocles: the urn containing the alleged ashes of Orestes.

The problem of a matricide ordered by Apollo, rooted in mythical tradition and stressed in Aeschylus' version, is suppressed by Sophocles by making the matricidal character subsidiary, and ultimately placing Clytaemnestra on the same plane as Electra alone. In this way, the distribution of moral weight cannot remain open to question. Moreover, while Orestes is not invested with any traits over and above those assigned to him by tradition, Sophocles goes to great pains to make the character of Electra psychologically comprehensible. He thus has her conduct a conversation with her mother in which the viewpoints of both sides are clearly formulated, and in the anagnorisis scene and its preparation takes her to every possible height and depth of emotion. Above all, he confronts her in two conversations with her very different-minded sister Chrysothemis, who is undoubtedly an invention purely for the sake of contrast and contributes nothing whatever to the course of events. Sophocles had already tried out his method of portraying a main character by means of comparing him or her to a subsidiary character largely uninvolved in the action, when he contrasted Antigone in the play of that name, with her gentle sister Ismene.

The dramaturgical devices discovered during analysis of the play are often invented *ad hoc*. Such a fundamental argument between Electra and

Clytaemnestra, for example, so crucial for our evaluation of the situation and characters, is highly improbable after so many years of living together. Similarly, when the old slave comes out of the palace with the news that Aegisthus is out at that time, thus immediately triggering the act of vengeance that follows, the audience is not intended to remember that Aegisthus' absence has been talked about since the very opening of the tragedy. Inconsistencies of this kind, pointed out, many years ago in a now famous book by Tycho von Wilamowitz-Moellendorf (1917), were nevertheless tolerated by Sophocles if they served to heighten the dramatic effect of a scene without disrupting the essential nature of the plot. It is in such details that Sophocles showed himself to be the most ingenious of the three 'Greats' at setting up scenes.

Another significant factor, with which we shall be having to deal even more in Euripides, is the way that certain formal dramatic elements take on a life of their own. Although, for example, the drawn-out arguments of Electra with Chrysothemis and Clytaemnestra serve a useful function in terms of plot exposition, and above all in characterisation, they also constitute virtually autonomous structures that might even be seen as model examples of the author's artistic prowess. This is even more clear in the case of the main messenger speech – the earliest extant sports report. In Aeschylus, messengers are only used to report incidents that are important to the plot but cannot be reproduced on stage. In terms of serving the plot of *Electra*, the simple news of Orestes' death would suffice. The ingenious and stirring account Sophocles gives of this fabricated occurrence adds colour to the scene, but is clearly rendered for its own sake.

Despite their sparse number, the extant dramas give some idea of the development of Sophocles' dramatic craft. They evince, for example, an increasing mastery of the technique of involving three characters simultaneously in conversation. *Antigone* and *Ajax* have hardly any of these; they are used cautiously in the *Trachiniae*, and in *Electra* with restraint. The three remaining dramas, however, contain highly artistic three-way conversations.

A similar process may be discerned in the internal structure of his dramas. Division into acts in the modern sense is not encountered until the Hellenistic art theory referred to by Horace (*Ars poetica*), albeit with the Classical number of five. This division derived in practice from the gradual elimination of the chorus from the plot, a process completed by the fourth century, having begun with Aeschylus and continued with some delays throughout the fifth century BC. This opened up the potential for experimenting with choral songs that were separate from the action as a means of dividing tragedies. The three 'Greats' experimented with the possibilities for dividing plays in the most diverse ways. Early Sophoclean tragedies, for example, even included two-act plays in which the destiny of the main figure was fulfilled in the first half, thereby making another central character, and even a different central problem, the subject of the second. Both the *Trachiniae* and *Ajax* fall into this category.

Sophocles rarely had his chorus intervene in the action, but it continued to have a close emotional bond with it in terms of its observations, advice and admonitions. The chorus rarely appeals to the audience, using words coming directly from the intentions of the poet. Nevertheless, however topical they may have seemed to his audiences, statements of this kind, such as the glorious tribute to Attica in *Oedipus Coloneus*, or the admonition against flouting divine law in *Oedipus Rex*, never lacked adequate motivation in terms of the action. This was to change with Euripides.

For reasons that do not need to be examined here, Aristotle designated Euripides the 'most tragic' of the three 'Greats' in his *Poetics*. If modern scholars are of the view that Sophocles marked the high point of tragic literature, this needs to be substantiated with a concept of the tragic that is applicable to Greek tragedy. In Greek, the word 'tragic' initially meant no more than 'pertaining to tragedy', or 'appropriate to tragedy', but by the fourth century BC the word is found to designate such moods as the pathetic, the gloomy, the devastatingly sad or the exalted. In modern language it has come to be a synonym for 'extremely sad'.

Greek tragedies were not mournful plays. The relevant tragic material, deriving from either myth or historical tradition, which were not distinguished in those days, could result in a positive outcome both for the main characters and in the emotional response of the audience. The essential line of the plot was of course as fixed for the tragic poet as it had been for the epic poet. In its mature form, however, epic poetry attributed this fixed determinative context to the decree of Zeus. The heroes involved were thus, for all their heroic valour, distinguished less by their deeds than by their suffering, that is by the consequences of their deeds, thereby acquiring unique destinies.

Tragic writers, on the other hand, invariably interpreted events in terms of the decisions and deeds of the protagonists, hence bestowing on them quite a different responsibility both for those events and for their own destinies. Their relationship to the gods was no longer simply one of carrying out their decrees unwittingly. Instead, human conduct, and most specifically of the kind which proved correct and effective in the human world, was measured against the demands placed by the gods. Not uncommonly, considerable divergences were to be found in these demands. Thus, although tragic writers were fond of referring to the totality of extra-human reality with terms such as 'the god', or 'the divine', in practice that reality manifested itself in a variety of divine personalities with unique characters and diverse inclinations.

For tragic authors, therefore, human action unfolded in two dimensions with one of which the protagonist was completely unfamiliar but which was either approved or condemned by the gods. Human dignity and human peril alike derived from this fact of belonging to two spheres. Within the constraints of human existence, the individual was obliged to make decisions and act, at the same time being liable at any time unknowingly to violate a divine precept – or alternatively be faced with a choice between two equally

114

catastrophic violations. Admittedly, the catastrophe did not always occur. Many myths work out positively, or allow the hero or heroine's actions to be approved by the gods after some period of tribulation. This does nothing to alter the fundamental view of the human condition put forward by dramatic poets in their depiction of mythical events, however. Aeschylus and Sophocles were in accord at least on this point. If it is admissible to make generalisations on the strength of their few extant tragedies, the difference between their approaches may be summed up as follows.

For Aeschylus, there was always a higher order to reconcile the diverging precepts that the tragic hero was expected to live up to in his or her actions. Sometimes this order only crystallised during the course of the drama itself, as in the *Oresteia*, or only became apparent through the failure of human action, as in the *Persians*. Whatever the case, however, the audience was given a glimpse of the objectively valid, overriding order that offered a meaningful explanation for even the most dire vicissitudes in the actions and sufferings of heroes.

In Sophocles' interpretation of myth, however, the entire conflict arising out of the overlapping of a number of precepts had to be worked out in the personality of the character involved. There was no overriding natural law to justify, even if only in retrospect, the irreconcilable conflicts to which people were subjected. Sophocles did not address the question of whether the precepts of the gods, and the gruelling human ordeals that arose out of them, were morally defensible or not. He accepted with all their incomprehensibility the events handed down by tradition as tokens of divine will and action, contenting himself with observing the inappropriateness of human moral criteria wherever the gods were involved. This gave him the freedom, however, to see human greatness and dignity in the very fact that the human arena was where these mighty conflicts were acted out, and indeed that the role of people in them was not merely that of puppets, but one of transforming the principles in conflict from a merely potential into a concrete form through their very decision-making and action. Whether the protagonist was physically and morally destroyed by this conflict, like Oedipus, or whether he emerged from it strengthened and vindicated, like Philoctetes and Neoptolemus, was immaterial to Sophocles. The crucial factor in the greatness and dignity of those involved was the greatness and momentousness of the conflict he or she endured.

These general remarks concerning the purely human aspects of tragedy in Sophoclean heroes, unsupported by any cosmological, theological or moral system, need to be clarified with a few specific comments. *Ajax*, probably the earliest extant play by Sophocles, is based on an episode from the Trojan cycle. On the death of Achilles, Ajax, the strongest of the Greek heroes, and Odysseus, pre-eminent on account of his shrewdness, both claim the armour of the great dead warrior. A court of arbitration decides in favour of Odysseus. His sense of honour deeply offended, the rejected Ajax is set on revenge. Athena, however, the special patron goddess of Odysseus, confuses Ajax's mind to such a degree that in a mad frenzy he attacks a flock of sheep in the belief that they are Greeks, first slaughtering three rams in his tent, taking them for Odysseus and the two sons of Atreus.

It is at this point in the story that the Sophoclean tragedy opens. Athena leads her protégé Odysseus to the tent of Ajax, triumphantly displaying his adversary in the intense humiliation of his deranged state. The downfall of Ajax is given a new motivation by Sophocles. His rage at the rejection of his case is shown to be justified in every respect, for the Atridae (the sons of Atreus) had helped Odysseus to win by manipulating the verdict. None the less, the punishment of madness inflicted by Athena is in fact for his earlier reliance on his own strength, and arrogant defiance of his father's advice on his departure for Troy always to entrust himself to her protection. Both details are inventions of Sophocles, intended to illustrate how an offended deity inflicts a punishment far heavier than any known among humans, precisely because that deity is infinitely greater, and able to select a moment for retribution in which the person concerned may even be fighting in a just cause among men. Human and divine justice are thus shown to be mutually incompatible.

Odysseus responds to the sight of his humiliated mortal enemy in the only appropriate manner: 'I pity him with all my heart, although he is my enemy, and my thoughts are no less for myself than for him. For I see that we men are all no more than illusions and empty shadows.' Ajax, on recovering his sanity, is unable to live with honour after the events which have occurred, and takes his own life. The greatest and most courageous of the Achaeans, Ajax's downfall occurs not because he fails to meet the criteria of human justice, but because he neglects for a single fleeting moment to pay deference to the gods.

Further developments in the plot, which involve the moving character of Tecmessa, the war captive who has remained faithful to Ajax, her husband, do not need to concern us here. They culminate in the final scene. A dangerous dispute arises between Teucer, the half-brother of Ajax, and the sons of Atreus that is hopeless for Teucer, since Agamemnon and Menelaus, in their implacable hatred, refuse to permit the burial of Ajax. The situation is saved by Odysseus who, following his insight at the opening of the play, restrains the sons of Atreus from committing such an offence against divine law, showing due honour to his defeated opponent and being formally reconciled to his brother. In this way the downfall of the hero serves to demonstrate the power of the gods. The correct insight into the power and dignity of the gods leads to right action among humans.

The power and arbitrariness of the gods on the one hand and the powerlessness of humankind on the other are revealed in even more terrible form in *Oedipus Rex*. The hero of the play, the king and deliverer of Thebes, has, unknowingly and because the gods so ordained, committed the most hideous of deeds in slaying his father and marrying his mother. The gods punish this horrific deed with a plague that breaks out in Thebes. The oracle of Delphi, when consulted by the king, reveals these circumstances in a general way. Being a dutiful and prudent king, Oedipus does everything in his power to clear the matter up and punish the guilty party. None the less, by the end of this responsible course of action, based on decisions guided by morality, all that remains is an insight into a bottomless abjectness which he had been powerless to foresee.

In *Oedipus Rex*, Sophocles refrains from justifying this divinely worked destruction of the hero in humanly comprehensible terms, either by incorporating the ancient motif of a curse effective across the generations, or by inventing any circumstance with which to establish the moral culpability of Oedipus. The tragic, morally undeserved ruin of the great and noble serves to reveal the sovereignty of the gods whom it behoves humankind to honour and hold in awe.

In his old age, Sophocles wrote another Oedipus tragedy. This shows us the aged hero seeking a place to die in Attica after a vagrant life as a blind beggar, driven from his native city by the curse that is upon him. The curse that once hung over his life is transformed into a blessing. The man in whose suffering the power of the gods was revealed becomes in death a bestower of blessings on the land that takes him in. His unique suffering, inflicted by the gods, and unjustified by any human guilt, does more than merely oppress him. It also raises him above his fellow men once he has lived through it and made his peace with the gods. This last word uttered by Sophocles as a dramatic poet thus speaks in a conciliatory tone of the nature and effects of tragic suffering, also bearing testimony to the poet's faith in the gods who reveal their strength in the frailty of humankind.

As has already been noted above (p. 115), Sophocles was evidently not generally concerned with depicting convincing characters. Yet his characters have had a lasting impact on the tradition of the western stage. The reason for this is that in Sophocles more than any other dramatic poet tragic conflicts are worked out solely and entirely in and through human beings. Their actions are not related to an abstract system of norms. The gods whose decrees shape events show their power in all the conduct and suffering of human beings, but not through their sporadic intervention in an otherwise human course of events. It is precisely because the dignity of human beings as the subjects and objects of divine processes is so great that their downfall can also be so complete. In this way, Sophocles' characters attain the highest potential of human existence, above which there are no more expressible norms or principles, merely the gods themselves.

What enabled Sophocles to achieve this conception of the tragic greatness of man was the fact that he never for a moment doubted the exemplary significance of the events handed down in mythology, nor did he seek to measure them against his own moral concepts. By the same token, however, the monumental events of mythology did not merely expose the shortcomings of moral standards. Their tragic interpretations also pointed to gods whose will extended further than anything that human beings had devised for one another.

Sophocles certainly added poetic adjuncts and shifts of emphasis to traditional storylines for a wide variety of reasons. In *Ajax*, for example, Agamemnon and Menelaus, the mythical representatives of the Dorian enemy of Athens, are made into spiteful, vindictive, tyrannical characters. In *Philoctetes*, Odysseus is likewise relegated to the role of a small-minded, cunning foil to the magnanimous Neoptolemus. None the less, these changes always affect only subsidiary or antagonistic roles. They do not impinge on the exemplary validity of the myth. If in *Philoctetes*, as in the considerably earlier play of the same name by Euripides, Odysseus appears as a politician willing to use any means to serve the interests of the Greeks, this signifies no more than the emphasis of a character trait already evident in the Odysseus of epic narratives.

This unbroken link with mythical tradition, which could provide an impetus for ethical and theological reflection, but could not itself form a subject for criticism, was one of the major reasons why Classical tragedy flourished as a part of religious festivals in public life. Sophocles was not averse to occasional references to themes that were modern in his time, such as those being discussed in ethnography or the rising Sophistic school, for example, but he invariably also upheld the authority of religious and mythical tradition.

Euripides, who directly carried on the artistic work of the other two 'Greats' in terms of its literary and dramaturgical aspects, was the first to take the step of seeking to evaluate myth. It was this that made it possible for Attic tragedy, a genre created purely for the citizens of Athens, to develop into European drama.

A single satyr play by Sophocles has been largely retrieved through a papyrus find. It is entitled *Trackers*, and deals with an episode from a divine myth known today also from the *Homeric Hymn to Hermes*. Soon after his birth, Hermes, the god of thieves, stole a herd of cattle from his brother Apollo, driving them backwards into an underground cave, thereby rendering all search for them fruitless. But the young god at the same time also invented the lyre by stretching strings over the shell of a dead tortoise. Sophocles joined these two episodes to create a satyr play. Apollo, the all-knowing god of the oracle, announced to the world a reward for anyone able to provide information about the whereabouts of his cattle. The satyrs respond, instigating an unruly search, until they are terrified by remarkable sounds never heard before coming out of the ground on the mountain of Cyllene in Arcadia. At this point the nymph of the mountain appears, reprimanding the boisterous troop for making a noise, and telling them how she has hidden a child of Zeus from the jealousy of Hera. This resolves the matter, and Apollo ultimately receives the lyre. This innocuous, burlesque play is acted out in a graceful text that is in no way vulgar in diction, its verses structured according to the more rigorous rules of tragedy, not those of comedy. The carefree manner in which such plays made fun of the very same gods whose inexplicable and terrible intervention was the subject of tragedies performed immediately prior to them is difficult to grasp in the light of the modern concept of piety, shaped by the Christian tradition. The gods of Classical drama were integral to this world, not from some other world, and could therefore freely be drawn into any aspect of life in the natural and human spheres. Once again, it was with Euripides that this notion of the gods disintegrated.

In his own lifetime, Euripides never enjoyed the kind of admiration accorded to the works of Sophocles and Aeschylus. In his career as a poet, stretching from 455–406 BC, only four times was he prizewinner of a tragedy contest. Evidently the Attic public did not entirely approve of either his dramaturgical innovations or his re-evaluation of mythical tradition. This is confirmed by the harsh criticism of his tragedies found in several comedies by Aristophanes. The fifth-century judgement of Euripides' dramas was linked, as is again confirmed by Aristophanes, with his being discredited as a person. The picture we have of his life story thus consists almost exclusively of slander, all too clearly bearing the stamp of malicious fabrications derived from motifs in his tragedies.

Nevertheless, from the fourth century BC onwards drama, both comedy and tragedy alike, developed entirely along the lines established by Euripides. Similarly, from then on, no other tragedy writer could match his popularity. His name is at the top of the list of revivals of earlier tragedies. From the Hellenistic period onwards, fifth-century tragedies were increasingly read rather than performed, and Euripides ousted all other authors vying for the favour of the public. The number of Euripides fragments surviving in the form of quotations by later writers similarly amounts to several times the quantity for all other tragic authors put together – both the two other 'Greats' and the dozens of other lesser tragic authors known by name. Fragments from papyrus finds, which taken together offer a cross-section of the bookshelves of Egyptian Greeks from the third century BC to the sixth century AD, reveal exactly the same ratio.

The reasons for this posthumous popularity lie firstly in Euripides' affinity with all later drama, secondly in what is, compared to Sophocles and Aeschylus, the far greater comprehensibility of his language, thirdly in his predilection for sententious sayings, which appealed to the rhetorically schooled taste of post-Classical antiquity, and finally in his consistent secularisation of myth, which made the dramatic action derived from it more accessible to those for whom traditional mythology had likewise lost all religious significance.

To illuminate the versatile artistry of Euripides, it would perhaps be advisable first to gain a clearer picture of the potential storehouse available to this relatively late exponent of an unusually rich drama tradition. Probably only less familiar myths were available for him to adapt to drama for the first time. In most cases he was obliged to relate both his literary and theatrical emphases, and his evaluation or interpretation of the mythical episode, to dramas by other tragic writers who had already chosen the same themes.

A clear illustration of this is his *Electra*, a theme for which extant versions by both Aeschylus and Sophocles are also available. (The task of comparison was undertaken with *Philoctetes* in 100 BC by Dion of Prusa, an orator trained in philosophy, and now forms the sole source of information about the tragedies of this name by Aeschylus and Euripides.) Following the example of Sophocles (and not the other way round, as was once believed), Euripides also created an Electra tragedy that was complete in itself – not a House of Atreus trilogy or an Orestes drama. The episode chosen is the same as in Sophocles' version, but is enriched with a number of extra features. Electra, for example, lives in the country, not at the royal palace of Mycenae. She has been married to an *Autourgos*, a simple country man, in order to avoid becoming the mother of a noble son who might seek to avenge Agamemnon. In a lengthy prologue, this *Autourgos* invented by Euripides clarifies the opening situation. Following a conversation between the married couple and a completely irrelevant song by the chorus of Argive maidens, Orestes and Pylades enter. The brother and sister do not yet recognise each other in the dialogue that ensues. Orestes leaves the stage, to be replaced by an old retainer, who reports with great agitation what he has seen at the grave of Agamemnon (a lock of hair and footprints), but Electra is still not convinced of the presence of her brother. Anagnorisis only occurs later, through the mediation of the old retainer when Orestes re-enters. The brother and sister lay their plans for revenge, the execution of which is partly acted out, and partly conveyed in a report by a messenger. The latter tells how Orestes has slain Aegisthus, the murderer of his father, at a festival for rural nymphs, while the other victim, Clytaemnestra, has been lured into the country by a fabricated report that Electra has been delivered of a child. Her entrance leads to a quarrel between mother and daughter. Clytaemnestra then enters the house, where she is slain by Orestes. Utterly oppressed by the burden of their gruesome deed, the brother and sister appear again. They are comforted by Castor and Polydeuces, the sons of Zeus, who appear immediately afterwards, recommending Orestes to seek purification at Delphi, and Electra to marry Pylades. The play concludes with an antiphony sung by all.

Let us examine first of all the technical dramatic details of the tragedy. The opening setting of the action, which is much more complex than in previous versions of the myth and must moreover be contained within a single tragedy, is expounded by Euripides in a long narrative prologue, spoken by someone involved in the plot yet completely detached from it. This dramatic device, later to become an indispensable feature of western drama, was used extensively by Euripides, enabling him to construct mythical plots that deviated substantially from the traditional course of events without having to expound them dramatically each time. In comparison, the exposition scenes opening

Aeschylus' and Sophocles' tragedies, be they in the form of dialogue (*Seven Against Thebes, Antigone, Philoctetes*), monologues (*Agamemnon, Trachiniae*), or in the most archaic form by means of a song by the entering chorus (the *Persians*, the *Suppliants*), invariably form part of the action itself.

Another detail that is a particularly good illustration of the maturing of dramatic technique through the variation of traditional motifs occurs in the recognition scene. In the *Choephori*, Aeschylus had the anagnorisis occur through the tokens of recognition given in the myth: the footprints and lock of hair at the grave of Agamemnon. Sophocles, by contrast, relegated this motif to a peripheral role by assigning it to Chrysothemis alone, Electra and Orestes recognising each other during a dialogue.

Euripides restored the ancient motif. He too had a subsidiary character, the old retainer, make the observation, but also had Electra persistently reject the conclusions to be drawn from it – with such persuasive arguments as the one that a brother and sister could hardly have the same shoe size, the footprint therefore not being a valid reason to assume a sibling relationship between the two. This discussion, conducted in straightforward rational arguments, has been explained as a later addition, on the grounds that such a prosaic piece of polemic against Aeschylus could not be attributed to Euripides. However, this explanation overlooks the dramatic effect linked with this refutation of the Archaic recognition motif. Electra's incredulity, however ostensibly reasonable, is false, as everyone in the audience, familiar with the myth, would have known. W. H. Friedrich (1953, 76ff.) was the first to grasp correctly this effect achieved using an Archaic motif by a late poet in the traditional succession. As in Sophocles' *Electra*, or in *Oedipus Rex*, here too the anagnorisis marks the climax of the play, in so far as it is the turning point in the action, or peripeteia. Euripides wrote particularly ingenious recognition scenes, such as in *Ion* or *Iphigenia in Tauris*.

Anagnorisis is followed by mechanema, intrigue, again as in Sophocles' version. Euripides' ingenious intrigue plots, which were to exert an enduring influence for centuries, particularly in the European comedy tradition, were famous – or rather notorious, at least among his contemporaries. The butt of huge derision by Aristophanes, they may be found in such plays as *Helen* or *Iphigenia in Aulis*. In *Electra* this aspect of the plot is given twice the weight it has in Sophocles, the revenge against the two guilty parties being both planned and executed in separate actions. Moreover, by having a messenger tell of the circumstances in which vengeance is wrought on Aegisthus, Euripides gives this traditional messenger's speech a superior dramatic function to the Sophoclean model. The thrilling account of the chariot race at Delphi described in Sophocles' *Electra* in fact marks a dramatic vacuum.

The quarrel or verbal contest between Electra and Clytaemnestra which eventually takes place as the intrigue unfolds is another typical tragic scene, such as is also to be found in both Aeschylus' and Sophocles' treatment of the theme. Here again, however, the carefully planned dramatic craft of the later

121

poet is revealed. A discussion between the quarrelling women, exposing all the fundamental differences between them, may serve to inform the audience but has no particular motivation if the two have been living under the same roof for years. As Albin Lesky has pointed out (1972, 392ff.), by having Electra banished to the countryside, Euripides makes this the first encounter between mother and daughter for many years, thereby rendering such a fundamental difference of opinion highly likely.

Euripides wrote many, sometimes highly contrived, battles of words, whose links with the then incipient theory of rhetoric are no longer discernible today. They are not always as well-motivated by the course of the action as they are in *Electra*. In *Heracles*, for example, the foster-father of the hero and the tyrant of Thebes have a well-composed dispute as to whether the bow or the sword and shield are the most seemly weapons for a warrior hero. Since Heracles enters as an archer, all available rhetorical devices have to be implemented in order to prove the bow to be the true weapon for chivalrous combat in the face of a time-honoured and persuasive prejudice. In the lost play *Antiope*, whose theme derives from the foundation myth of Thebes, the two sons of Zeus debate whether the contemplative or the active life is superior – a theme from the philosophy of the day.

At the end of *Electra*, the action is steered by the instructions of two gods who arrive unannounced. As a result of factual changes made by Euripides, and chiefly of his reassessment of key parts of the myth, the action veers considerably from the traditional path with which the audience would have been familiar from the usual version. This is the famous or notorious *deus ex machina* said to have been invented by Euripides, and indeed used by him in most of his extant tragedies. Given the prevailing tradition of dramatic technique, the use of this device is as understandable as the necessity for an explanatory prologue separate from the action – so that mythical plots, subject to ever greater modifications, could be staged without flouting the principles of that tradition. It tells us even more about Euripides' moral and theological evaluation of myth, however.

At the end of the play, the brother and sister appear in a state of total moral collapse. With the emphasis given by Euripides, the horrendous nature of the matricide is neither mitigated in their own eyes and those of the audience, as it is in Sophocles' version, nor balanced by the prospect of a new divine system of law, as in Aeschylus. On the contrary, in the quarrel scene Clytaemnestra is presented as gentle, maternal, and filled with remorse over her deed, making the cunning with which she is lured to her death through the ruse of Electra's confinement all the more repugnant. In this way, moral condemnation of matricide is if anything heightened compared with tradition. Nevertheless, Ulrich von Wilamowitz-Moellendorf (1883) was undoubtedly going too far in interpreting Electra at the end of the play as a 'self-confessed criminal'. Euripides leaves as little room for doubt that Clytaemnestra deserved her punishment, or that the brother and sister could not act otherwise, given the force of circumstance, as he does that the hatred that dominates Electra's passionate nature is justified. No one, however, is more guilty than Apollo for the fact that the whole course of events unfolds as one long sequence of evil deeds. Castor, spokesman for the Dioscuri, leaves the audience in no doubt on this point, saying to Orestes: 'She [Clytaemnestra] has received her just deserts, but you have not acted justly. And Phoebus, Phoebus – but he is my lord, and so I had better remain silent. And yet, though he is wise, he would give you no good oracle.' Against this background, the instructions then announced by the Dioscuri, leading to the conciliatory conclusion of the myth given by tradition, highlight the moral problem of such prophecies rather than resolving it, or suggesting to the audience that it should be endured out of a sense of awe for the power of the gods.

Euripides uses more than the horrors of traditional myths to demonstrate the inability of the Olympian gods to establish a moral order among humankind, however. His play *Ion* contains an invented myth, many details of which originated with Euripides himself, that traces the origins of the Athenians back to Apollo Patroios. Creusa has been raped by the god Apollo, and has exposed her child, as the daughter of an Athenian citizen would. Ignorant of his origins, the child grows up as a temple attendant at the shrine of Delphi. Later, Creusa marries King Xuthus of Athens. Since the marriage is childless, the couple seek advice from the Delphic Apollo, who informs Xuthus that he already has a son, whom he will meet on leaving the temple. Cheered by this news, the good-hearted Xuthus embraces his assumed son, Ion the temple slave, but Creusa feels cheated and, encouraged by an old servant, plots to murder this interloper into the dynasty. Catastrophe is averted when mother and son recognise each other. At this point, Athena appears on behalf of her brother Apollo, father of the child and the cause of the confusion, 'who is ashamed to show his face among you and have to listen to your remonstrances for his conduct'. Creusa is told to take Ion as crown prince (and eponym of the entire Ionian tribe) back to Athens, but not to reveal to Xuthos that Apollo is Ion's father. The whole affair is thus brushed under the carpet like a scandal in any citizens' family concerned with its respectability.

This dethroning of the Olympian gods, who still wielded power but were no longer sublime, was matched by a devaluation and re-evaluation of the heroes of mythical tradition, whose distinction in the eyes of earlier tragic authors lay in the very conviction that their deeds and ordeals revealed the greatness of the gods. For Euripides, the great heroes of the myths were at best human beings obliged to suffer heart-rending fates because of the unjust deeds of the gods, but without being raised above the common human lot by their suffering. This may be seen, for example, in the eponymous hero of *Heracles*, or the lost play *Bellerophon*, which can be reconstructed from fragments. Often, however, his heroes are no more than neurotic weaklings like Orestes in the tragedy of that name, first performed in 408 BC, plain cutthroats like

123

Menelaus in the same play, or unscrupulous dishonourable egoists such as Jason in *Medea*.

Contemporary critics arraigned Euripides for presenting heroes on stage as pitiful beggars, such as Telephus, King of the Mysians, in the lost tragedy of the same name. The modern reader is more likely to take offence at the moral shabbiness attributed by Euripides to so many traditional heroes. He does this not merely in specific instances so as to create powerful antagonists, as Sophocles does in the juxtaposition of Odysseus and the sons of Atreus in *Ajax*, but in a general way, with the express intention of throwing the entire heroic world open to question.

The characters provided by tradition in his *Electra* likewise do nothing to improve this unwholesome constellation of heroes. Salvation does not come from the action of heroes, and certainly not from the gods, but rather from a new kind of humanity that is alien and exceptional in the heroic world. Its representatives are either subsidiary characters of Euripides' own invention, or characters from the not particularly rich mythical tradition of his native land.

A typical example is the farmer in *Electra*, who treats the wife he has been forced to marry with the tenderest regard, and whose honesty and friendliness convince even Orestes that these traits, and not noble origin, are the guarantees of human worth. These and other passages have been interpreted as reproductions of philosophical doctrines that were gaining credence at that time. In these, the distinctions between Hellenes and barbarians, slaves and free, the well-to-do and the lowly were attributed to convention, to which no importance should be attached in view of the natural equality of human beings and the moral qualifications to be observed in each particular individual.

Euripides will undoubtedly have been familiar with and weighed up various theories of this kind. The fact remains, however, that he was not merely involving himself in a topical discussion of social and moral problems. These new ideas were rather the tools for subjecting both the form and content of tragedy, the greatest and proudest symbol of the art and piety of the people of Athens, to a thorough revision.

Like Ajax, the hero of *Heracles*, persecuted by the undeserved hatred of Hera, and deeply humiliated, wants to put an end to his life, having murdered his own children in a fit of madness induced by her. Theseus, embodiment at once of the old, glorious Athens and this new humanity, offers him the hand of help and friendship, encouraging him to face life again with all its trials and tribulations. In the *Heraclidae* representatives of the same old Athens offer their protection to the unjustly persecuted children of Heracles. Similarly, in the *Suppliants*, at the request of the defeated party, they force the victorious defenders of Thebes to permit the burial of fallen participants in the siege. In these and other episodes the poet presents actions of purely human instigation, thereby rendering more tolerable the mythical catastrophes that are engineered by the gods and acted out by human beings. This therefore marks the establishment of norms for moral and political conduct against a mythical background that is no more than a negative foil, in that the irreparable dilemmas it provides form the starting point for autonomous human moral action.

As Günther Zuntz (1963) has ably shown, the very up-to-date didactic intention of Euripides should not be overlooked here. It is particularly apparent in the Trojan trilogy, whose three scarcely interrelated plays are designed purely to illustrate the glaring injustices that even the most glorious history of pan-Hellenic mythology contains. Only the last play of the trilogy, the *Trojan Women*, is extant. Lacking a consistent plot, it depicts in moving separate scenes the unspeakable suffering of the captured women, the demoralisation of the victors, and the admission by the gods that the war they instigated was utterly pointless. Elsewhere, as in *Hecuba* and *Andromache*, Euripides also makes the suffering of the defeated rather than the heroism of the victors in the Trojan War a subject for a tragedy, but nowhere else does he so thoroughly discredit a myth as in the *Trojan Women*. The trilogy to which this play belongs, and in which no human deed mitigates the injustice and cruelty of war, was performed in 415 BC, when Athens was girding itself to the utmost in preparation for its most ambitious military campaign, the Sicilian expedition, whose failure in fact ushered in the collapse of the Athenian Empire.

Some accounts assert that the work of Euripides marked the transition from the 'tragedy of fate' to the 'tragedy of character or soul'. This highly misleading statement obscures the correct way of looking at the phenomenon of Euripides' art, which is best exemplified by a group of plays written around 430 BC. These were his great women's tragedies, whose impact, passed on by Seneca, continues even to this day. These plays are of a distinct character, deriving essentially from the passions of their heroines. Medea, the accursed barbarian woman, murders her own children to punish the baseness and faithlessness of the husband for whom she has given up everything. Phaedra falls hopelessly in love with her stepson Hippolytus, the eponymous hero of two Euripidean tragedies, engineering his downfall when her declaration of love meets with indignant rejection. Stheneboea, the heroine of a lost tragedy, burns with love for Bellerophon, her husband's guest. When he spurns all her advances, she seeks to destroy him with calumny, ultimately receiving her just deserts for all she has done.

In all these tragedies the outward course of events derives entirely from traditional myths, so that there can be no question of Euripides intending his drama to be acted out first and foremost in the human heart, or of attributing the cause of the action to unforeseeable emotional impulses. In *Hippolytus*, the second extant play, for example, the whole course of events is set in motion by Aphrodite to punish Hippolytus, hunter and chaste servant of Artemis, for his contempt for the power of love.

None the less, like no other writer before him, and even more markedly than in his own later tragedies, Euripides made the driving and accompanying passions of his heroines the subject of his portrayal as the dramatic action unfolded, thereby also creating a whole range of scenes and expressive forms for later psychological drama. Indeed, the dialogues and monologues of his main characters contain such exhaustive and heart-searching reflection on events that more recent scholars have sometimes sought to interpret these passages as an analysis of the psychological aspects of Socrates' theory of morality. The truth of this cannot be proved in this form, but Euripides did unquestionably show interest in a problem that remained a preoccupation of philosophy for centuries afterwards: how are we to understand the interplay between rational and irrational forces in the human soul that precedes a wrong action in the face of better judgement?

Euripides was not painting individual portraits in these female characters. His penetrating psychology operated more along typological lines, by presenting the effects and manifestations of a single great passion. The fact, however, that this potential for increasing the psychological depth of stage events was first attempted with female characters – a process that has parallels in comedy (see below, pp. 137–8) – was to make this achievement one of immense significance for the later dramatic tradition of Europe.

Strictly speaking, *Electra*, written considerably later, does not number among these women's dramas, and yet here too Euripides had all available devices at his disposal for portraying searing passions, so that it could hardly have been written without these earlier prototypes. Other psychological case studies may be encountered in further of his late works, such as *Orestes* (408 BC).

Euripides' contemporaries seem to have perceived him as amoral and atheistic – a view that has died hard. Many modern accounts present the poet as the intellectual companion of the Sophists, as Plato describes them, for teaching in his tragedies either the immorality or even non-existence of the gods, and the completely relative nature of moral norms. Aristophanes, for example, has Euripides swear by gods of his own invention – a perjury, of course – likewise denouncing the alleged disastrous effects of his plays on the education of Athenian citizens. Euripides does indeed make repeated references to the philosophical or Sophistic doctrines of his day, making his stage characters depict these through the devices of what was then modern rhetoric, which he was fond of using elsewhere too, for example in battles of words. For centuries, passages of this kind shaped the image people had of Euripides the man. Due to his phraseological skill, his statements found their way into popular collections of aphorisms under headings such as 'veneration of the gods', 'friendship' or 'education'. They were thus extracted from their dramatic context and handed down as the opinions of the poet himself, regardless of the simple rule that the utterances of characters in a drama should never be taken wholesale as the opinions of the playwright.

When radical statements of the kind mentioned above are placed in their dramatic context, a very different picture emerges. One lengthy fragment, often attributed to the Sophist Critias, and probably taken from a satyr play by Euripides, expounds a doctrine concerning the origin of belief in the gods attributed to the Sophist Prodicus, according to which this belief is said to have been invented by a shrewd man in order to restrain people from committing unjust deeds in secret. These lines are spoken by Sisyphus, the archswindler of Greek myth. In *Cyclops*, the barbarous giant refers to a theory about the origin of culture, also documented as Sophistic, which asserts the relativity of moral precepts in the face of the claims of nature. The Cyclops then uses this to justify his intention to eat his guests. Quite a similar theory on the origin of culture is used by Theseus, the utterly positive hero of the *Suppliants*, to justify the venture into war by his native city of Athens against neighbouring Thebes to uphold the unswerving nature of divine, time-honoured precepts.

Therefore, just as in *Electra* and *Heracles* the simple virtues of communal human life offer a way out of the insoluble dilemma posed by myth, so in the *Suppliants* the same goes for a return to a hallowed tradition of moral and religious conduct. Euripides' criticism of myth was thus not purely destructive, as ancient and modern exegetes have tended to assume. What Euripides sought to express in the contradictory utterances of his stage characters was his view, rooted in a long sequence of tragic versions of mythical themes, that fate-oriented constellations, explained solely in terms of supernatural divine activity, were irreconcilable with the necessity for steadfast precepts for communal human life.

Euripides was the great experimenter among the dramatic poets, ceaselessly attempting innovations, as well as drawing on earlier practices in language, style, dramaturgy, music and stage technique. These experiments were not all successful, nor were all well received by contemporary critics. Sometimes even the modern reader finds it hard to suppress the impression of a somewhat dubious proclivity of his for creating sensational effects. *Andromeda*, for example, a play now lost, opened with a monody by the eponymous heroine, chained to a rock overlooking the sea. The final words of the strophes are repeated by an echo to illustrate the loneliness of the poor exposed heroine.

The language of Euripides' dialogues is remarkably heterogeneous, but taken overall easier to understand than those of the two other 'Greats'. Occasionally, Euripides achieves evocative and ingenious phrasing of a kind sought after in rhetoric. In his latter years he increasingly took to using the trochaic tetrameter for spoken verse, in addition to the iambic trimeter, drawing here on early, perhaps even pre-Aeschylean practice. The device of stichomythia, for example – verse dialogue conducted by two speakers alternating line by line – had been used in earlier tragedy for scenes of great pathos, such as quarrel and recognition scenes. It was used extensively by Euripides, as was its enhanced version, antilabai, in which the speakers alternated once or even twice within a line.

In most Euripidean tragedies the chorus had little to do with the plot. Its songs comprise observations on the stage action, and occasionally statements by the playwright of such a basic nature that they hardly seem to have any direct bearing on the plot at all. In Euripides the artificial language of lyric perceptibly lapsed into mannerism, whereby the style-creating morphology and figures of this diction, always far removed from everyday speech, became detached from any meaningful relationship to what was being said. An example may serve to illustrate this. Aeschylus had been fond of making genitive nouns depend on adjectives. This usage was unknown in colloquial speech, lending an archaic effect, and may be rendered by the phrase 'with regard to'. Sophocles, for example, phrased the term 'unarmed' as 'unequipped with regard to shields and army'. Euripides takes this a step further, indicating the dark clothing of the bereaved by coining the expression 'unattired with regard to white raiment', in which only the word 'white' holds any specific meaning. His frequently used expression 'childless with regard to offspring' is an entirely stylistic usage, serving no semantic function at all. All this shows the ultimate consequences of following the laws of a completely autonomous artificial language.

The line and verse structure of choral passages in the late works of Euripides contain features unknown not only in previous tragedies, but in the entire choral lyric tradition. There suddenly appear long arias, sung not by the chorus but by individual actors, and either lacking the usual strophic arrangement or composed of extremely complex strophes involving a colourfully alternating succession of lines of the most diverse kinds and origins. Up to that time, songs and strophes had been constructed homogeneously using a single metrical type, or relatively few metrical combinations.

Ancient grammarians were already aware (also able to deduce from comic criticism) that this was a case of influence by the so-called 'new dithyramb'. This is a misleading term, since the dithyramb was no more than one form of great choral lyric poetry that grew out of the cult song in honour of the god Dionysus. Like comedies and tragedies, dithyrambs were performed every year by the Athenians in contests at Dionysiac festivals. It may be, therefore, that the word was used to denote the entire great choral lyric genre, in which the music was always held to be the most important part.

Music theory made huge strides during the fifth century BC. Attention was paid both to the rules of composition, and to the ethical and psycho-educational effects of specific rhythms and modes. Hardly any of the details of this process can now be traced, making it especially difficult to form a clear picture of the work of Damon, an older contemporary of Pericles to whom Plato occasionally refers.

Probably as a result of this theoretical penetration of musical practice, a New Music emerged towards the end of the fifth century whose distinction from the traditional form may be illustrated with the contrast between Classical-Romantic harmony theory and twelve-tone music. As late as the fourth century BC, philosophers such as Plato and Aristoxenus, a pupil of Aristotle, were vehemently opposed to it. In conservative Sparta, the extra strings over and above the customary number are said to have been cut from the kithara of Timotheus, one of its most famous exponents. Anecdotes such as these, and the derision of the 'new-tonists' to be found in comedies, have preserved for posterity the shocking impact of this New Music.

At all events, however, it continued to assert itself throughout the fourth century BC, so that by the Hellenistic period the earlier form had disappeared without trace, the choral songs of Classical tragedies from then on having to be performed with newly composed melodies.

The most significant innovation of the New Music was apparently a previously unknown diversity of rhythmic and melodic combinations. This placed very high demands on performers, thereby effectively precluding tragedy as a suitable testing-ground for it, since amateur choruses could only cope with relatively simple music scores. These obstacles were best overcome by professional virtuosos rather than choruses. At the song performances of lyrical contests, virtuosos tended to appear as soloists.

A half-dozen or so poet-composers from this last flowering of great ceremonial lyric, whose work was written between 420 and 330 BC, are known by name. There are even extant texts by the two best-known. A papyrus find has preserved the *Persians* by Timotheus of Miletus – a highly baroque song text describing the Battle of Salamis in colourful metrical combinations. From the works of two somewhat later poet-composers by the name of Philoxenus several extensive fragments have been preserved in the work of a grammarian who lived around 200 AD, including an equally stilted account of a feast.

Euripides made room for this new art in his tragedies, as may be seen from the increasing number of solo arias to be found in his late works, the most famous being one by a Phrygian slave in *Orestes*. The text is characterised throughout by a bizarre and pathetic diction that is stretched to the limits of endurance, while the kaleidoscopic use of metre in the play, which is composed without strophic arrangement, gives some idea of the highly modern music which must have baffled contemporary audiences. It is virtually certain that such arias could only be mastered by professional actors, comparable with modern opera singers. By the fourth century BC and the Hellenistic period, theatrical activity, then spreading throughout the entire Greek world, was exclusively in the hands of professionals, who were organised in inter-state associations, enjoying something akin to diplomatic status. The rise of the acting profession in the late fifth century BC was probably linked with the spread of New Music. Sophocles still occasionally appeared in his own plays.

The examination of Euripides' works undertaken so far has shown that in his hands tragedy grew from an institution deeply rooted in the religious and social life of Classical Athens into an art form that from then on could only be justly evaluated in terms of literary categories. Henceforth, it could be employed wherever there were playwrights, actors and an interested audience. This shift is not attributable particularly to the technical and artistic mastery that tragedy owes to him: the achievements of Aeschylus and Sophocles were at least as great. What is more important is that Euripides reflected with a hitherto unknown degree of objectivity on the content of mythical tradition that formed the material of tragedy. This reflection, and its illustration through drama, brought about a complete re-evaluation and devaluation of myth that shattered the ancient foundations of tragedy writing. At the same time, however, it also effected the emancipation of tragedy from Athenian religious life. Were it not for this, tragedy could never have developed from an Attic into a European art form, even though its structural elements remained Attic.

Certain branches of tragic writing were already dying out in Euripides' time. He wrote few satyr plays, of which only one has been preserved among his eighteen extant plays. This is not one of the familiar cheerful, untroubled plays about the gods, however, but the Cyclops episode from the Odyssey, dramatised with sardonic humour. The relaxed atmosphere of satyr plays familiar from Sophocles and Aeschylus offset the awesome seriousness of the preceding trilogy, which could only be digested by pious dispositions. Euripides, however, with the sound judgement of his own conception of the nature of tragedy, occasionally replaced the boisterous satyr play with an optimistic tragedy as the fourth component of the tetralogy. His earliest extant play, *Alcestis*, performed in 438 BC, was one such play.

The process of reduction to the human factor diminished the scope of drama both for the inexplicable and sublime, and the innocuous and burlesque. Fourth-century comedy marked a direct continuation of those tragedies by Euripides in which this reduction is particularly apparent, such as *Ion* or *Helen* – in terms of ethos as well as dramatic technique.

The above would suffice to conclude an account of Euripides, were it not for his last play, the *Bacchae*. This is arguably his most powerful play, and so different from all his others, particularly his late works, that it would probably not have been attributed to him at all if the posthumous date of performance (405 BC) and its authorship had not been reliably verified by external proof. (*Iphigenia in Aulis* was written even later but never completed, and has suffered so much through revisions that it is disregarded here.)

Even the technical details of the *Bacchae* are entirely unreminiscent of Euripidean style. The number of tetrameter scenes is small; the chorus is crucially involved in the action, there are no arias in the New Music style, and the prologue leads directly into the action. All this is more evocative of Aeschylean monumentality and directness. On his victorious advance through the world, Dionysus comes to Thebes, the native city of his mother. Everywhere he has instilled women with divine madness, luring them away from their children and looms and sweeping them off in droves into the virgin mountain forest to surrender themselves in blissful ecstasy to his divine presence. Pentheus, ruler of the city, seeks to put a stop to these events, but all his drastic measures fail in the face of the miraculous intervention of the god, who easily releases his adherents from prison. He also bewitches Pentheus, making him dress in maenad clothing and set off for the mountain forest himself to observe the Dionysiac rites of the women. There, however, the god exposes him to the fury of the frenzied women. His own mother, in the belief that she sees a lion before her, tears off his head, carrying it back to the city in triumph. Her awakening from this enchanted state is terrible. At a loss, all those involved acquiesce to the incomprehensible power of the new god.

This tragedy has been interpreted in the most contradictory ways. It has been seen as the last and most vehement protest by Euripides the 'educator' against the amorality of traditional religion. Two of the subsidiary roles in the play are invoked as an additional argument for this interpretation. Cadmus, the aged founder of the city, and the equally elderly seer Teiresias, seek with priestly, anxiety-ridden piety to come to terms with the appearance of the new god, making themselves utterly ridiculous by dressing up as maenads. They totally fail to grasp that this god is not even remotely interested in them.

Other exegetes, on the other hand, have seen the *Bacchae* as evidence of 'repentance' on the part of the old poet. They point chiefly to the unequivocally negative portrayal of Pentheus, who is presented as a ruthless and capricious tyrant who scents behind the Dionysiac cult merely clandestine promiscuity. It is to E. R. Dodds (1966) that scholarship owes an interpretation of the play in terms of religious history. He shows how Euripides depicted with extraordinary precision the typical manifestations of an ecstatic cult. Originally, the cult of Dionysus was an ecstatic religion that at certain times released its adherents from the constraints of their normal lives to disregard all the precepts of state and cult. Athens gradually domesticated this religion, incorporating it into its regular festival calendar, and sublimating its impulses into the magnificent creative achievements of tragedy, comedy and dithyramb. Nevertheless, the Greek world was seized again and again by epidemic waves of unfettered ecstatic piety. Most of these originated in Asia Minor, which was later to produce rather similar movements in the Montanism of the early Christian era and the dervishes of the Islamic era. Such cults also seem to have been indigenous, in a primeval, undomesticated form, to Macedon and Thrace in the northern Balkans, where the population was closely related to that of Anatolia. It was probably here that Euripides had an opportunity to observe them, spending the last two years of his life as a guest at Pella on the invitation of the King of Macedon. Here he may have come to know and understand the elemental power of Dionysiac ecstasy, of which the ancient myths and regulated cults of Classical Greece were mere pale reflections.

The story of Pentheus is a companion to others about the punished persecutors of the new god, such as that of the Thracian Lycurgus dealt with in a tetralogy by Aeschylus. In Euripides' version of the Pentheus tradition we thus find an ecstatic, orgiastic kind of piety that sweeps people to the very heights of proximity to the deity. After this glorious enthusiasm, however, they are left in a state of profound disenchantment that dissolves all the usual constraints of law and order, eclipsing the individual as a responsible person for a brief span. Euripides shows the impossibility of evaluating all this by means of the moral criteria used by the Greeks for centuries to derive ever purer and more sublime notions of the nature of the gods. The sheer power of Dionysus as revealed in the activities of his female adherents is not only mightier than that of the tyrant, but is contemptuous of attempts to organise it into the categories customarily used by people in their conduct towards one another and their gods.

At the end of a productive phase of tragedy writing, therefore, Euripides succeeded in illustrating the mysterious forces to which the Dionysiac cult, and hence tragedy itself, owed their origins. Whereas a major proportion of reflection on the content of myth found in Euripidean tragedies tended to demystify it and detach stage performance from its links with the cults and piety of the Attic *polis*, the *Bacchae* made clear once again the roots of the dramatic art in a level of elemental human piety that defies categorisation by any civilisation. It was not by chance that a poet as erudite as Euripides entirely dispensed in the conception of this drama with poetic, musical and dramaturgical innovations of any kind.

There is no need to go into detail here about the countless tragedy writers of the second half of the fifth century BC, known either by name or from occasional quotations and references. By the end of the fifth century BC it was quite clear, on the basis of Aristophanes' *Frogs*, that the three 'Greats' were completely representative of tragedy, constituting the sole reason for the legislation on revival performances that was passed in the early fourth century BC.

It may well be that there were more marked points of contact with other fifth-century poets in certain aspects of fourth-century tragedy, as expounded in Aristotle's *Poetics*. Agathon, for example, known as a participant in the dialogue in Plato's *Symposium*, wrote in the late fifth century, and seems to have used far more rhetorical devices in his tragedies than Euripides. This was to prove of some importance to later tragedy, when it had become a form intended solely for reading or oral performance.

However, the maturation process of drama as an art form for the stage leads directly from Euripides to the Attic comedy of the fourth and third centuries BC, from where it was adopted in the comedy and tragedy of the Romans, thus ultimately finding its way into western literatures. This makes Euripides more than any other playwright the forefather of European theatre.

8

OLD COMEDY

In 486 BC, two generations after the first state-organised tragic performance – associated with the name of Thespis – and again at the Lenaea, a Dionysiac festival, the first comedy contest was held, the winning play being written by one Chionides. On the strength of their inventory of extant texts, Alexandrian scholars of the third and second centuries BC compiled a classic canon of comedies similar to its counterpart for tragedies. Cratinus, who died at a great age in 410 BC, is credited with most of the technical achievements of comedy writing. Eupolis, killed in the prime of life in 405 in the Peloponnesian War, and Aristophanes, whose work continued into the second decade of the fourth century, are regarded as the culmination of 'old comedy', far surpassing contemporaries such as Crates, Hermippus or Plato. From a few fragments and anecdotes, it is still possible to form a picture of the genius and wit of Cratinus, but not of the way his plays were structured.

Eupolis is better known: the outline of his *Demes* is reconstructible from a papyrus find, revealing that his artistic approach did not differ substantially from that of his friend and later rival Aristophanes. Of the latter's forty-four comedies, aside from numerous fragments, eleven are extant in complete form. The last two of these, however, belong to a new developmental phase of comic stagecraft that will be dealt with later.

In late antiquity Aristophanes was avidly read and interpreted. The relics of ancient commentaries that have survived in the form of extensive marginal notes in Byzantine manuscripts continue to this day to offer valuable assistance in understanding this theatrical art. They show how it was deeply embedded in the social life of democratic Athens, and how it grew out of the songs and processions of the Dionysiac cult – a process described by Aristotle as on of 'growing serious'. What made this possible was a widespread drawing on myths quite separate from this cult, using episodes which provided the basic framework for complete stage performances. The burlesque elements of ancient tradition were preserved in satyr plays.

Comedy (*komos* means something akin to 'exuberant festival pageant') grew out of quite similar beginnings documentable in many parts of the Greek world, but unlike tragedy was never able to complete the process enabling it to become an art form that could be used again and again in other historical contexts. Its growth occurred under the oppressive influence of its elder sister, tragedy, whose metres, songs and dramaturgical rules it partly parodied, and partly adopted as a matter of course. However, even the incomparably larger-scale preparation and staging of tragic performances itself created an unbridgeable gulf between the two genres.

In comedy, the thread of a complete plot that is so essential for a homogeneous work of art was drawn not from myth, but from the social and political life of Athens. This provided no more than skeleton themes, however, such as an appearance by Socrates, the yearning for peace of Attic peasants in the Peloponnesian War, or conditions at law courts. These themes could only be made dramatically viable by creating a suitable setting for the plot – a process subject to strict constraints on account of numerous traditional elements that were either compulsory or alternatively forbidden in comedies, which formed part of cult ritual. All surviving 'old comedy' texts thus constitute examples of a still immature dramatic art form whose various components need to be explained individually in terms of tradition and the topical impetus for each particular play. Naturally enough, this is most apparent in the earliest of these plays, Aristophanes' *Acharnians*, which was performed before 424 BC, in the first phase of the Peloponnesian War.

The play opens with the worthy Dicaeopolis taking part in a people's assembly, which convenes late and proceeds laboriously (thus undoubtedly being quite realistically portrayed), and at which a Persian envoy is to be heard and consulted about peace. Much to Dicaeopolis' dismay, the eager advocate of a peace mission is roundly rejected. He thereupon sends this Amphitheus to Sparta to negotiate a separate peace for himself and his family, which is successfully obtained. Just as Dicaeopolis is about to celebrate this newly won peace with a procession and sacrifice, the chorus, comprising charcoal burners from the deme (a residential district) in Acharnai, rushes in with the aim of stoning the peacebroker. By means of a blackmail trick picked up from Euripides' *Telephus*, he is able to escape this fate, making his opponents listen to a speech in his defence. For this purpose Euripides himself appears, rolled out on the 'ekkyklema', a piece of stage paraphernalia borrowed from tragedy, to make some suitably heart-rending costumes available to his beggar heroes. Dressed as Euripides' Telephus, Dicaeopolis makes an extravagantly rhetorical speech against the unjust military policy of Athens, instigated by Pericles and pursued by his successors. The result is that half the chorus declare themselves in his favour, the remainder in favour of the general Lamachus, a famous Athenian of the day. The latter appears in comic military attire, and is obliged to remove his helmet so that Dicaeopolis can summon sufficient courage to vent his invective against the unfair distribution of war costs as a result of corruption. There is no battle of words: Lamachus declares his wish to return immediately to the battlefield and conquer the Spartans and their allies. Dicaeopolis declares the opening of a free market on his land, to be accessible to the hostile neighbours of Athens, the Megareans and Boeotians, but not to Lamachus. The chorus now declares itself to be unanimously behind Dicaeopolis.

The chorus then proceeds to step out of its role, addressing the audience directly on behalf of the poet in an interlude known as a parabasis, blending sung and spoken verse. He polemicises against Cleon, the leading figure of Athenian policy in those days – who had sued the poet for his attacks in an earlier comedy – as well as expressing candid views on various issues of public life. After the parabasis we are shown Dicaeopolis at his market. In the broad dialect of his native region, a man from famine-struck Megara offers his two daughters for sale, dressed up as piglets in a sack. A Boeotian offers eels from Lake Copais. A 'sycophant', as informants were known in Athens, is given the beating he deserves; a slave of Lamachus (instructed by his master to purchase genuine imported Boeotian eels for the banquet of the festival of *choes* (jugs)) is ejected from the market, since Lamachus is banned from it. Then Lamachus himself appears, but before an altercation can occur he is ordered with his troops to guard the frontier with Boeotia, in the middle of a blizzard. He is thus obliged to make preparations for a winter campaign, while Dicaeopolis gives instructions for the banquet of the festival of *choes*. They both leave the stage, reappearing shortly afterwards: Dicaeopolis having won a drinking contest, Lamachus like a wounded tragic hero on a litter, having sprained his foot jumping over a grave. The play concludes with a song by the chorus.

It will already be clear from the above synopsis of the play that only the first half evinces anything like a continuous plot, being constructed according to the dramatic rules of tragedy and containing detailed and extensive use of explicit allusions, verse quotations and parodies of scenes and text. The parabasis is entirely undramatic, and yet an integral part of the performance, whose traditional character is manifest from its complex but fixed structure. It is more than likely that the parabasis, which implies a separate appearance by the chorus, was originally an entirely separate event. The parabasis is followed by a sequence of isolated burlesque scenes for which the ground has been prepared in the first half, but which do nothing to further the plot and are only loosely connected. They involve a good deal of laughter, fisticuffs and ribaldry, and a great many opponents of the main heroes are dealt with. This clearly reveals the roots of this component of comedy in improvised 'clown and harlequin' performances, introduced as a secondary element within an overall dramatic plot.

Occasionally, these scenes included a contest – a prolonged battle of words between the main hero and an opponent – although it could be shifted into the first part and, as in the case of the *Acharnians*, reshaped to create a scene with a dramatic function. The original form of the contest may have been part of the tradition of dispute and derision that was common in certain cults, facilitating social criticism to a degree that would have endangered the fabric of society under everyday circumstances.

The above compositional analysis, which could be both modified and confirmed through an examination of other comedies, clearly shows that there is no question here of a mature form guaranteeing the unity of the work of art in the sense of a normative poetics. Despite this, however, the influence of these comedies, still evident today, is rooted in something more than the successful rendition of numerous details, such as situation comedy, witty puns and plays on words, or on the freshness and charm of the many lyrical passages. What draws everything together in these stage plays, albeit still in undeveloped form, is the direct connection of every detail to the social and political milieu in which they were performed. This is undoubtedly a highly 'inartistic' principle, and moreover one that in some cases cannot be properly explained, or only through precise historical and antiquarian interpretation. And yet even for the modern reader every detail in a comedy by Aristophanes is fired with a completely spontaneous commitment, unimpaired by any reduction of its themes to a timeless content, that must have been as much taken for granted by the poet as by his Athenian audience.

By modern standards, Athens was a small town, living at that time in a radical democracy in which citizens enjoyed substantial and direct control of the affairs of government through the medium of the people's assembly and the jury courts. Parliamentary representation was as alien to this state as the professional government official, despite the sometimes high and differentiated demands placed on the expertise of citizens by the Athenian *imperium* and its flourishing economy, and from 431 BC by the city's extensive military campaigns. Matters known about and discussed among the audience at a comedy performance thus ranged from themes such as a certain young man in the deme of Halimus who was a fop or leading a dissipated life, to the judiciousness of a recently passed decision to expand the fleet, or the options for diplomatic overtures at the Persian court. An appearance by Socrates could be as easily recognised by the audience as the salient features of a recently performed Euripidean tragedy, or the procedures of Gorgias, a teacher of rhetoric living in Athens. Since, moreover, the conventions of the Dionysiac cult expressly permitted and provided for words and scenes of open derision, giving the full name of its object, every line of such a play could make critical allusion to some matter of general interest without needing to restrict topical satire to the main theme.

Similarly, the playwright was not limited in his choice of the main subject-matter for a comedy by demands for a consistent, coherent plot, so that the entire social life of his city was available to his repertoire. Obviously, however, theatrical art of this kind was doomed as soon as open criticism of personalities and institutions could no longer be sustained by society, or as the character of social life became gradually less public. Furthermore, once the social and political prerequisites for it had changed, no literary tradition could draw on the existing stock of plays in the genre. The literary and dramatic forms that crystallised in fifth-century comedy, where they did not derive from tragedy, were untransferable to creative works intended for audiences living in different social conditions. The end of the Peloponnesian War thus in fact also spelled the demise of 'old comedy'.

The *Knights*, performed at the Lenaea in 424 BC, is chronologically closest to the *Acharnians*. This comedy ruthlessly lampoons Cleon, then the leading politician in Athens, depicting his replacement by a sausage trader, an even bigger scoundrel. This play was followed by the *Clouds*, which was a flop at the Great Dionysia of 423 BC and has only survived in a readaptation that was never performed. It depicts a worthy old Athenian who has married above his rank and been plunged into embarrassing debt by his son, one of the *jeunesse dorée*. He takes this promising progeny to the school of Socrates to have him taught the art of argument and thereby enable him to talk his way out of his obligations. The portrayal of Socrates it offers, as amusing as it is malicious, has led to various speculations which are somewhat at odds with fourth-century Socratic literature.

The *Wasps*, performed in 422 BC, parodies the Athenian mania for litigation. *Peace*, dated 421 BC, depicts the peasant Trygaeus flying to heaven on a dung beetle to plead with Zeus to bring the war to an end. (This motif of the ride to heaven is intended as a parody of Euripides' *Bellerophon*, in which the eponymous hero rides up to heaven on Pegasus to find out whether the gods who permit all the injustice on earth really live there).

The *Birds* (414 BC) is one of Aristophanes' most brilliant comedies, also being the first containing a smooth, consistently composed and dramatically almost coherent sequence of scenes. Two old Athenians, weary of the unrest, party bickering and litigation mania of their fellow citizens, emigrate to the bird kingdom, where, following various incidents involving their feathered friends, they found a state in the clouds. The latter, by virtue of its key position between heaven and earth, is able to make both humankind and the gods dependent on it. This fantastic synopsis is carried out in a series of scenes of the utmost charm, full of ingenious ideas involving people, birds and gods alike. The number of allusions and parodies is virtually limitless.

Quite apart from numerous references to individuals and public events, Aristophanes draws the motifs and particulars of his comic plot from contemporary theories of society and the state, and the cosmology of Orphic sects. He also makes use of elements from a then much-discussed mathematical and astronomical reform of the calendar, as well as offering an evocative parody of the breezy, vivacious style of modern choral lyric poetry.

Two comedies about women date from 411 BC: the *Thesmophoriazusae*, in which women involved in a Demeter cult resolve on severely punishing Euripides for having fuelled misogyny with the female characters in his tragedies, and *Lysistrata*, a peace play like the *Acharnians* and *Peace*. In *Lysistrata* the heroine of the title, like all women in the city sick to death of war, convinces her female companions to take matrimonial strike action, occupying the acropolis and establishing contact with the Spartan women in order to bring about peace. The play, whose comic side naturally derives largely from its extremely risqué humour, is one of the most delightful testimonies to the Athenian sense of humanity, Aristophanes showing profound empathy with the feelings that affect women suffering under the yoke of interminable war. Like a number of Euripidean tragedies, Aristophanes' *Lysistrata* should provide food for thought for those who are apt to accept too readily the timehonoured prejudice about the allegedly male-dominated ideas that governed Greek civilisation.

The *Frogs* (405 BC) is the last extant example of 'old comedy', and is perhaps Aristophanes' masterpiece. The god Dionysus, patron of the Attic stage, fears the demise of tragedy following the deaths of Euripides (406) and Sophocles (405), and therefore makes for the underworld to plead for the release of his favourite Euripides. Once there, however, he is witness to an argument in which the newly-arrived Euripides disputes Aeschylus' place of honour. (As Aristophanes knew, such claims would be quite uncharacterisic of Sophocles, who preserves his *bonhomie* or 'eukolia' even in the underworld.) Aeschylus wins the poetry contest, and Dionysus now wants to take him back with him to the world above to restore tragedy to its former dignity and use his poetry to make the Athenians as mighty as their forefathers were at Marathon.

Aristophanes was a lifelong critic of Euripides as a proponent of modern, 'de-heroised' tragedy, also voicing a number of his own ideas on the aims and meaning of tragedy in the process. The *Frogs*, which expounds the principles underlying this criticism, marks the epilogue to the most glorious of all epochs in Greek poetry. The remarkable aspect of this is how Aristophanes passes quite definitive judgement on the language, style, verse-making skill and dramatic technique of the great tragedians, while yet drawing all its individual threads together into an overall comparative assessment, all with the sole purpose of evaluating the moral and pedagogical significance of the poet for the life of the Athenian state. He is, in other words, opposed to Euripides on principle for the alleged corrupting influence of his dramas on the conduct of citizens. It is difficult to say whether this judgement on Euripides is justifiable, since the line of development then being taken by tragedy, not only in his but also in Sophocles' hands, was moving towards a literature emancipated from ties with quite specific social conditions. This line is affirmed by the unbroken literary tradition still alive today that goes back to Sophocles and Euripides, despite the fact that in their own time tragedy was still entirely an institution of the Attic state.

Old comedy, however, was and remained such an institution to a far greater degree, making Aristophanes' overall judgement as a political moralist a legitimate one. It is known that Aristophanes owed certain of his assertions to Gorgias, thus making use of the first ever writings on the theory of literature. The political commitment that motivated this literary criticism, however, and the unique combination of ingenious comic inventiveness, with the most searing political and moral exhortations, and the astounding perspicacity with which he predicts in this play the inevitable demise of the greatest epoch in the history of Greek poetry, are entirely his own.

Aristophanes' sympathies were conservative. He was equally opposed to modern poetry, rhetoric, Sophistic philosophy and anything else which in his view threatened the decency, morality, piety and valour that had made Athens great since the Persian Wars. He was thus also a lifelong advocate of the cause of the rural Attic population. They had suffered more severely from the war than the urban working classes, who on the contrary had gained materially from Imperial expansion and the radicalisation of democracy.

Aristophanes always had a thorough knowledge of whatever he was opposed to. Just as he showed consummate mastery in his parodies of theories of natural philosophy, Sophistic discourse and modern song composition, he also knew how best to bring out the comic aspects of the plans, objectives and measures of Athenian policy. His comic inventiveness, manifested in ever-fresh combinations and scenes, is inexhaustible. The versatility of his diction is also unusually great, capable of capturing the tone of ceremonial public choral lyric poetry or popular cult song, the style of the pathetic monologue from a tragedy or a street squabble. In the case of spoken verse this diversity was made easier by a certain licence in trimetrical structure, for which certain rules of the tragic trimeter did not apply. When composing choral songs, however, a comedy writer had to respect the constraints of the limited funds available for rehearsing the chorus parts. The lyric passages of comedy are thus relatively simply structured even when they are parodying modern choral lyric poetry or the ceremonial tone of Classical tragedies. The rich vocabulary of comedy blends poetic expressions of all shades with loan words from the vernacular, thus creating a virtually inexhaustible repertoire of witty and even startling phrases.

One particular insight to be gained by the modern reader of Aristophanes' comedies concerns the nature of the audiences for whom these dramas were written year after year. This was a society in the throes of a protracted and perilous war that was placing the utmost demands on its resources. We cannot fail to be amazed, therefore, that it was able to endure such extensive criticism of its entire public life, which spared no one and no event from the stigma of ridicule, without its stamina being sapped by the tensions created or heightened by it. The direct form of democracy in Athens furthermore entailed a degree of involvement of each and every citizen in both petty and state politics that can scarcely be conveyed with modern analogies. A law intended to curb the mockery of individuals in comedy is documented for 415 BC, but the comedies written by Aristophanes after that date show no sign whatsoever of abiding by it. Comprehension of all allusions to the details of public life may thus be sufficiently explained by the intensity of the social and political life of Athenian citizens.

Another astonishing feature of these dramas is the infinite number of jokes and witticisms in them which presume a detailed knowledge by the audience of philosophical or theological speculations, as well as of theories of rhetoric, poetry, music and literature. It may be that Aristophanes did not assume that the majority of his audiences would have understood some of his jests. The fact remains, however, that unless one is seeking to present him as an academic poet, which would certainly be quite false, one must presume the average spectator to have had an extraordinarily high level of literary and aesthetic education. Otherwise most of these jokes would have been lost on his audience. In the same way, the countless quoted and parodied verses and scenes from various tragedies would undoubtedly have been recognised by his audiences. The sheer breadth and depth of intellectual education that this compels us to postulate for fifth-century Athenians in fact matches the scarcely conceivable concentration of productive talent brought forth by a city with, by modern standards, a small population – moreover in virtually every sphere of art and literature, and parallel with political and economic expansion on a grand scale. This wealth of artistic creativity would have been absolutely unthinkable without a corresponding level of appreciation among a highly educated audience comprising most of the population – a wealth that admittedly came about through the institutions of a radical democratic state.

By the same token, however, the high level of creativity and appreciation that permeated fifth-century Athenian intellectual life probably also accounts for the intellectual turmoil that followed the catastrophic end of the Peloponnesian War in 404 BC. This turmoil arose despite the surprisingly rapid economic recovery of Athens, and the fact that state and social institutions remained largely intact, or were successfully restored after only a brief interim period.

Old comedy was doomed now that post-war Athenian society lacked the resilience to face systematic confrontation of its inherent inconsistencies through the burlesque work of art. This increased sensitivity to potential disruption of all kinds was also manifest in the condemnation of Socrates in 399 BC. In the aftermath of the Peloponnesian War harmony and decency became the prime movers of literary and moral taste. The risqué aspects of comedy as part of Dionysiac festivities were no longer tolerated. The link between the theatre and everyday politics became diffuse, even though the institutions underlying tragedy and comedy continued for some time to be identical to those of the fifth century. Comedy thus became an apolitical, domesticated comic form of entertainment, and tragedy an art form based on classic frequently revived texts, but increasingly classifiable according to inherently literary criteria.

Old comedy, however, that utterly Attic phenomenon that was not even to survive the key events of the fifth century, let alone be repeated or imitated in other societies, was not the only form of lighthearted mimetic play to develop out of the derisive verse, songs and dances of popular cults. A variety of such comic drama forms sprang up in the late sixth and early fifth centuries BC in the Greek colonial towns of Sicily and Lower Italy.

Epicharmus of Syracuse, whom Aristotle dates in the period before or around 500 BC, is the best-known exponent of this stage poetry, written in the local Doric dialect. It would seem from extant titles and fragments that these comic plays lacked a chorus (hence also dance and music), as well as the political commitment, personal polemic, name-dropping and parody of more serious dramatic poetry. The technique of dramatic exchanges, on the other hand, seems to have been at least as highly developed as that of early tragedies. Epicharmus was completely at ease in his command of verse, adopted from iambography – the tetrameter, trimeter and occasional anapaests. He seems to have derived his themes from myths about the gods and heroes, adapting them into episodes suitable for burlesque treatment. Heracles, for example, appears as the insatiable gourmand in *Hebe's Wedding*, and the cunning Odysseus as a malingerer in *Odysseus the Deserter*.

However, Epicharmus also wrote comic plays on more general human themes such as poverty and wealth, in which types such as the country bumpkin or allegorical figures such as a personification of the sea appear. This was matched by his fondness for moral aphorisms, to which many of his fragments owe their survival, and which was later to contribute to his reputation as a philosopher. Many pieces of anonymous epigrammatic poetry were attributed to him.

It is not known to what extent Epicharmus, admired by no less than Plato, was known in fifth-century BC Athens, and could therefore have influenced Attic comedy with the expertise of his dramatic technique. The appearance of allegorical figures such as The Just Speech and The Unjust Speech in Aristophanes' *Clouds* are reminiscent of Epicharmus, who invented the characters of Mr and Mrs Speech. In late comedies, no longer of the old comedy type but which are attributable to Aristophanes (see below, p. 224), the trend increased both towards artistic personification and the treatment of general moral questions.

In one early play, Aristophanes states that his work has no connection with 'Megaran burlesque', the popular comic play genre of Athens' Dorian neighbour. This could evidently not be taken for granted about the Attic comedy of that time. Furthermore, an additional, albeit somewhat doubtful tradition attributes the introduction of comedy into Attica to the Dorian Susarion. Some notion of the character of these burlesques may perhaps be derived from the *phlyakes*, the comedians of the Dorian Lower Italian city of Tarentum. Information about these comic plays is available from a few literary references, but mainly from a series of local vase paintings dating back to the third century BC. They were probably originally improvised stage plays, later in written form, featuring specific typical characters, as in later Italian *commedia dell'arte*: the cuckold, the parasite or the old procuress. The best-known of these *phlyax* poets was Rhinthon, who lived in the third century BC. Post-Aristophanic, 'middle' and 'New' Athenian comedy probably drew inspiration from such plays.

The literary and subliterary tradition that grew out of the burlesques of the Doric-speaking region is most clearly discernible from the *mimos* genre, the classic exponent of which was the Syracusan Sophron, whose works are said to have been avidly studied by Plato. This tradition suggests a literary theory attributing Plato's *Dialogues* to the mime genre.

Sophron wrote short prose dramatic scenes from everyday life. Nothing is now known about how they were performed. The few surviving fragments give no indication of the way in which scenes and dialogues were staged. In the early Hellenistic period, the early mime form came to expound the highest degree of linguistic and stylistic finesse, but without a hint of performance. On the other hand, throughout the Hellenistic-Roman period, prose mime was the customary form of light drama, on much the same level as modern light films. In those days, in thousands of theatres across the civilised world, the public attended predominantly mime performances of this kind, apart from concert performances of parts of tragedies.

9

PHILOSOPHY, RHETORIC
AND SCIENCE

The mid- and late fifth century BC was characterised by a rich proliferation of philosophy in a diversity of schools in greater or less contact with one another. Melissus, referred to on p. 83, for example, was associated with the Eleatic School of Lower Italy, although he worked in his home town in Samos, where he held high municipal offices and enjoyed close contact with Athens. Anaxagoras was born in 499 BC in Clazomenae in Asia Minor, but spent most of his life in Athens, where his pupil Archelaus of Miletus probably also studied with him. He in turn became one of Socrates' tutors. Cratylus, a pupil of Heraclitus of Ephesus, likewise seems to have lived mainly in Athens.

Shortly after the mid-fifth century BC, a movement of democratic opposition arose against the Pythagorean aristocratic association in Croton in Lower Italy, so that exiled Pythagoreans began to appear as tutors in the Peloponnese, in Thebes and Athens. Pythagoreanism had recently established close links with rapidly progressing mathematical research, thereby developing from an esoteric religious theory into a respectable philosophy.

This process was furthered by the work of Philolaus, of whom a few authentic and many inauthentic fragments are extant. Two of his pupils appear as conversation partners of Socrates in one of Plato's *Dialogues*. Philosophy teaching traditions and schools also sprang up in places including Abdera and Lampsacus, far in the north of the Greek-speaking world. The impetus for this may have derived as much from books as from the arrival of itinerant teachers. Similarly, men such as Ion of Chios, referred to above as the author of memoirs and tragedies (see above, p. 109), who were fond of travelling and interested in philosophy, could find willing conversation partners everywhere.

The leading philosophers in this period were Anaxagoras, who was numbered among the friends of the great Pericles, and who was obliged to leave Athens because of a court action brought against him by Pericles' opponents, and Democritus of Abdera, whose life extended into the fourth century BC. The achievement of Anaxagoras lay in the way he expanded what were then outdated Milesian theories of the nature and emergence of the universe to include such key questions as the distinction between substance and quality, and between the material components of the universe and their formation by a non-material spiritual force.

Democritus of Abdera, a generation younger than Anaxagoras, or perhaps even his tutor Leucippus, arrived at a concept that has lost none of its relevance even today. He explained the structure of the universe with the hypothesis of two factors: empty space and an enormous number of infinitely small, indivisible particles called atoms, whose integration and disintegration bring about the processes of growth and decay. How Democritus' hypothesis was applied to the various theoretical spheres concerning man and the universe is known only in outline from later accounts.

In later centuries, philosophy was dominated by the influence of the Athenian, Platonic–Aristotelian tradition, resulting in the loss of Democritus' original works. This is a particularly sad loss for literary historians, since erudite critics of the Hellenistic age unreservedly placed the stylistic qualities of Democritus on a par with those of Plato.

Surviving fragments are mostly not from the natural philosophy, scientific, medical, mathematical, linguistic, literary or music theory and logical works that comprised the bulk of his wide-ranging and prolific work, but from a number of treatises on ethics and philosophy. Most of them comprise aphorisms collected both for their content and their formal beauty. They bear witness to a profound preoccupation with the problems of living a moral life, which enabled the author to phrase his knowledge in a concise and memorable form. 'A good neighbour* is not one who thinks of recompense, but one who is resolved to do good.' 'Physical beauty without Reason is a bestial thing.' 'All moderation is excellent. I care neither for excess nor want.'

The moral ideal of Democritus was known as *euthymia*, a word denoting the cheerful ease of the reasoning person capable of insight. It seems to have been the fruit of a lifetime devoted to observation and research, during which Democritus travelled over large areas of the then known world in search of an understanding of the diversity of phenomena. He is reputed to have said that finding a single piece of real proof was worth more to him than to rule the entire Persian Empire.

The multifarious literary output of Democritus partly falls into the category of specialist literature, which was a rapidly expanding field in the second half of the century. This was partly owing to the rapid progress and burgeoning proliferation of the sciences. We shall be returning to medicine in more detail later. Besides Democritus, therefore, mathematics also found a leading exponent in Hippocrates of Chios, who made major discoveries in geometry. Similar strides were made in astronomy, the results being applied among other things to a reform of the Attic calendar at the end of the century

---

* The word thus translated here in fact denotes the correct way of giving and receiving, i.e. the person who does good while at the same time being grateful, these two concepts referring, however, not to mental disposition, but to practical proof in mutual relations.

by the scholar Meton. The persons who contributed to growth in specific branches cannot always be precisely dated. In mathematics, this development may already have been under way before the mid-fifth century (see above, p. 85).

Another development was the innovative practice of publishing almost all the business of public and private life, including specialist branches, in textbooks. Aristophanes derided proponents of this modern education as textbook-carriers, with a techne under their arm for everything. In Sicily, two orators by the names of Corax and Tisias wrote the first textbooks on the art of rhetoric and argument for use in the judicial system. Sophocles wrote a book on the proper use of the chorus in tragedy, and the great sculptor Polyclitus of Argos a work on the correct proportions for representing the human body. Hippodamus of Miletus, who drafted the plans for the newly founded central town on Rhodes and the port city of Athens, published a treatise on urban construction which also contained aspects of political theory, probably with a view to justifying his directions for urban architecture. Antiphon of Athens wrote the first book on psychotherapy, *On Harmony of Mind*, which expounded on meditation practices. Hippias of Elis wrote a work on memory technique, Damon a theory of music, and the turn of the century saw the first written works on painting, hunting, agriculture, horse-breeding, military tactics and many other specialist fields.

This boom in textbook-writing indicates in the first instance the progress that the Greeks had made in coming to rational terms with the world around them. This is quite apparent even to a modern observer of the fifth century BC in such spheres as administration, finance, commerce and construction. More significant than this, however, was the increasing endeavour evident in all these works towards emancipation from the authority of convention – evidently on the strength of the experience that rational understanding of a particular specialist sphere was better able to attain what was being aimed for, regardless of all tradition, than was any particular convention. Wherever it was possible to establish a system of learnable, rational, generally comprehensible sensible rules, this process of emancipation from the shackles of convention was effected, thereby enabling the skills involved to be handed on at will.

The leading proponents of this new-found belief in the power of human reason and the didactic optimism that it spawned were known as the Sophists. Their aim was to inculcate general competence through the written and spoken word, particularly in the public life of the *polis*. Socratic ethics grew out of the polemical debate surrounding this aspiration, for which reason Plato's *Dialogues* give a largely negative view of the Sophists. Indeed, on the strength of these accounts the words designating Sophists and sophistry acquired a negative connotation in modern times. In Greek, however, the word 'Sophist' originally merely denoted anyone who was an expert in a particular field. It was not until people began to assume the term as a form of

145

title that it acquired its precise meaning of specialist authority and teacher in the art of living. These Sophists made their living as peripatetic tutors.

The Sophistic vision was not quite as ambitious as it might appear. The means whereby a person became adept in the art of living had long been a subject for reflection. Pindar, for example, steeped as he was in the convictions of the Greek aristocracy, regarded this accomplishment as an inherent attribute that needed bringing out by practice and inurement, but which could never be inculcated through instruction alone. Another time-honoured tradition in the moral ideas of the Greeks held that right action marked by this accomplishment was to be understood as the result of sound judgement. In an age in which so much was being gained and experienced in terms of rational, systematic, learnable scholarship emancipated from traditional values there was good reason to place special stress on these intellectual aspects of the ancient concept of accomplishment or distinction. This made them the starting point for pedagogical efforts in general. It should also be borne in mind that whereas professional experts were becoming a category distinct from laymen in science, art, crafts, military science and other fields, political life still lacked such experts. The onus was still on every citizen to master the ability to evaluate situations, convince his fellow citizens of his views, and make responsible decisions for the community. Sophists' efforts towards achieving teachable proficiency were reflected in a copious literature covering moral philosophy, sociology, state theory, pedagogy and psychology. The extensive examination of all these fields by Plato and Aristotle would have been virtually unthinkable without all this preparatory groundwork.

One major complex of issues addressed by many Sophists concerned the relationship between nature and convention, a theme also reputed to have been treated by Socrates' tutor Archelaus. Reflection on the drives and inhibitions behind human behaviour in general, and an examination of conflicting notions of good and evil prevalent among different peoples – known to the reading public from ethnographic literature – led them to the conclusion that the values and objectives affecting human behaviour derived partly from nature (e.g. the instinct for self-preservation), and partly from convention. According to the account given in Plato's *Gorgias*, some Sophists held the view that natural givens, such as the tendency of stronger individuals to develop at the expense of weaker ones, had priority. Law and order, which imposed constraints on such modes of conduct, were thus merely devised by the weak for their own benefit, and did not therefore merit respect. This may constitute a radical theory that can be derived from Sophistic approaches, but which may never actually have been propounded by any Sophist.

The same polemical device is also to be found in Aristophanes. In the *Clouds* he has the pupil of Socrates, who is portrayed as a Sophist, stand up in both word and deed for the view that the generally accepted principle of retribution justifies a son beating his father as retribution for previously received chastisement. Theories such as these were frequently attributed to the Sophists, and of course resented, but were probably unjustified and merely an expression of outrage at their frank and open discussion of traditional ideas.

In the nature versus convention question, for instance, two surviving texts – a fragment by Antiphon of Athens and a lengthy quotation from an earlier work *On Laws* in a legal speech of the fourth century – reach quite different conclusions. In following natural urges, man is restrained by himself alone. The nature of man, the fact that he belongs to a species envisaged as part of the cosmic order, finds its confirmation principally in the individual. This conclusion was reached by Ionian science, chiefly in the field of medicine (see p. 157), where a distinct concept of nature was elaborated for the first time. It was the arrangements made among human beings and divergent from natural conditions which created society, in turn enabling the individual to develop to higher levels and raise him or herself above the naked struggle for survival. This required the individual to abide by 'unnatural' social precepts.

Similar theses had been propounded by Protagoras of Abdera, the oldest Sophist, in a work on the emergence of human culture. Some idea of its contents is provided in *Protagoras*, a dialogue of Plato, elaborating the process whereby only the gifts of mutual consideration and law had made it possible for the human race to survive. The idea of social life functioning according to laws of its own represents one of the major achievements of Sophistic speculation, although the opposing concept of nature tended to be invoked as an all too obvious way of explaining phenomena which seemed completely self-evident.

However, a further difficulty arose out of this conceptual separation of the social and natural orders, which had definitively replaced the cosmic order of the gods. Hitherto, the binding nature of moral norms had been rooted in human consciousness in the notion of their validity as part of a greater cosmic order presided over by the gods. This dovetailing of the divine order and political or moral norms was ensured by the cults of those deities responsible for community life. New speculation, however, now arrived at the conclusion that no such congruence existed between unalterable nature and the changing conventions of particular societies. It was thus not possible to name any authority to refer to in order to curb a possible relativisation and change in every single moral or political norm. The Sophists, who were anything but revolutionaries, and who were convinced of the indispensability of moral norms, seem to have advised people to rely in this regard on generally acknowledged principles. At all events Isocrates, in many respects a descendant of the Sophists, seems to have been emphatically in favour of this (see p. 206). Plato, on the other hand, was rigorously opposed to the 'opinion of the masses', and sought new ways of anchoring moral norms in the unalterable order of the cosmos and of existence.

The relativisation of convention similarly paved the way for comprehensive theories of the state and society. Some of these are known from fragments, and some from parodies by Aristophanes in which the customary distinctions between slave and frees or Greeks and barbarians, were questioned. For the first time, the basic forms of state organisation – democracy, aristocracy and monarchy – were divorced from their manifestations in political life, and organised conceptually (see p. 164).

The art and theory of argument were crucial to the Sophists. Here too Protagoras was a pioneer, publishing an instructive work entitled *Over-throwers*, a term borrowed from wrestling. At the root of this art of debating, eristic, lay a highly developed scepticism that precluded any possibility of familiarity with gods, and hence with any norms beyond those established by human beings themselves. The famous saying, 'Man is the measure of all things', formed part of this context. It was this scepticism that earned the Sophists in their own time their notoriety as godless deriders of all tradition, even though the conclusions they arrived at were largely quite laudable. They consequently obtained the norms for their theses from what we would nowadays call sound common sense. Their efforts were thus directed towards uncovering and expressing as clearly as possible those ideas and modes of evaluation which applied to all humankind, and which would hence be apparent to them – provided they were free of the chance encumbrances of social convention.

This aim explains the interest of many Sophists in popular sayings, the phrasing of which was perfectly suited to these requirements. Most Sophistic theses are similarly based on rational lines of thought and commonsense views, for which reason they often lack the logical stringency and differentiation of philosophical proof. Protagoras thus responded to the age-old question concerning the prerequisites for accomplishment or distinction by asserting that aptitude, instruction and practice needed to converge – a thoroughly home-spun conclusion that was applicable in pedagogical practice.

Nevertheless, one only needs to read Aristotle's penetrating analysis of the emergence of human modes of conduct to realise that the true nature of this whole question had never been grasped before. In one funeral oration, Gorgias, who had an intellectual affinity with the Sophists, praised people who preferred fairness over adhering to rigid legal stipulations. While this too is a convincing argument for sound common sense, it scarcely addresses the whole problem concerning the relationship between law and fairness.

Sophistic literary works covered a wide range of fields, and from time to time new themes arose out of their pedagogical and moral aims. It was thus via his art of argument that Protagoras arrived at his consideration of the use of language, thereby laying the foundations for modern traditional grammar by undertaking to distinguish word types (nouns, verbs, etc.). The same applies to the study of synonyms, documented for Prodicus of Ceos, a pupil of Protagoras. Both also attempted a moral interpretation of earlier writing that was parodied by Plato in the *Protagoras*. Prodicus was also the author of a moral allegorical tale about Heracles having to choose between Virtue and

Vice that has survived in a work by Xenophon. It formed part of a compilation, the *Horae*, intended to describe the evolution of humankind from primeval times.

Allegorical passages had already appeared in ancient poetry. The *Iliad* contains the story of swift-footed Ate, the inexplicable delusion that leads to wrong action, and the slow and laggardly solicitations that are only ever able to rectify damage after the event. Alcaeus likewise described imminent peril to the community using the image of a ship in distress.

Metrodorus of Lampsacus on the north Aegean coast was held to be the first to interpret myths related by poets as similes of cosmic natural processes or phenomena from moral life. In later centuries, this method of interpretation was to enjoy great popularity among philosophers, and Jews and Christians alike. Theagenes of Rhegium (Reggio di Calabria) in Lower Italy, the first exegete of Homer of whom we know and who was not a rhapsode (a professional performer of epic poetry), may also have used this method. Like Metrodorus, he lived around 400 BC, and was thus a contemporary of the Sophists.

Other works attributed to Sophistic authors indicate scholarly interests that were unconnected with Sophist concerns. Hippias of Elis, for example, satirised by Plato for his shrewdness as a moralist, made a name for himself as an able mathematician, his sure eye also perceiving the significance of the Olympian winners' lists for scholarly chronology. He was indeed responsible for the first publication of this document in book form.

Finally, some Sophists even clothed their theses in verse – such as Plato's uncle Critias, the key figure in the short-lived aristocratic regime of the 'Thirty Tyrants' after the Peloponnesian War. He composed elegies acclaiming the aristocratic ideals of old Sparta in the light of contemporary state theory, which was also central to his own political career.

One author is customarily numbered among the Sophists to whom this designation probably never applied, if one is to judge from the unanimous testimony of extant texts. Nevertheless, an inscription rediscovered on a statue erected in his honour in Olympia states that he invented a 'techne for training the soul for the struggle to be proficient'. Gorgias, who lived in the Sicilian town of Leontini, made his first public appearance in 427 BC as part of a legation from his native city to Athens, where he created a considerable stir. In the following three decades he travelled widely in the Greek-speaking world, teaching in several places and leaving behind pupils, among whom the Athenian Isocrates was the most outstanding.

The importance of Gorgias lies in the hitherto unknown intensity with which he focused on artificially created language as a means of influencing the mind, and in the conclusions he drew from his insights for the development of his prose style. The impact of this on the history of Greek prose literature can scarcely be overestimated (the few extant fragments indicating his acquaintance with western Greek philosophy are unimportant in comparison).

149

A debate had been under way for some considerable time in Greece concerning the pedagogical effects of various tone scales and rhythms in artistic music and the verses that pertained to it. This debate came to a head in the fifth century BC. The music theoretician Damon, a contemporary of Pericles, seems to have elaborated comprehensive theories on this subject. However, an anonymous treatise of a somewhat later date, retrieved through a papyrus find, disputes any lasting psychological effects through music.

Gorgias transferred the principle of rationally planned 'guidance of the mind' from music to prose speech, thereby elaborating generalised and vague notions concerning the power of the spoken word into a teachable technique. Compared to the earlier available theory of legal speeches (Corax, Tisias), Gorgias was less concerned with penetrating to the structures of proof whereby statements could be made plausible, although he did not disregard this aspect entirely. His main focus was on the formal aspects of the artistic spoken word.

Greek had particularly rich potential for drawing together contrasting and complementary statements. Gorgias accordingly worked on the assumption that a complete sentence should always consist of two mutually arranged parts, each containing a separate statement. He then sought to organise these parts in such a way that the length and division of their respective elements corresponded to each other precisely (*isocolia* and *parisosis*), further enhancing this rhythmic equivalence tonally by means of beginning and end rhyme. Clearly, this stylisation of speech exceeded the rigour even of poetic composition, since the dovetailing of the rhythm, tone, content and grammatical structuring of the text resulted in complete mutual harmony, whereas in poetry the metre and the statement do not necessarily coincide. Below is an example from a facetious address in defence of Helen:

> ei de biai härpasthä
> kai anomos ebiasthä
> kai adikos hybristhä

> dälon hoti ho men harpasas hos hybrisas ädikäsen
> hä de harpastheisa hos hybristheisa edystychäsen

> But if she was stolen by force
> And forced unlawfully
> And wickedly abused,

> Then clearly the robber is in the wrong as an evil-doer,
> Whereas she, being stolen, was unfortunate in suffering evil.
> (Gorgias §7)

The consistent application of this style of course only proved successful initially by being restricted to simple syntactic structures. It is difficult nowadays to grasp the near-intoxicating effects of this incipient style on the ears of audiences accustomed to highly sophisticated poetry. However, the full effects of Gorgias' aims with regard to setting stylistic trends did not make themselves fully felt until his pupils began to apply them unpedantically to complex syntactic structures, thereby ushering in the age of the Classical sentence. Credit for the further elaboration of prose technique with the aid of Gorgianic figures of speech goes largely to Isocrates. Then even the most complex subject-matter could be expressed not only in suitable grammar, but with aesthetic rhythmic and tonal accentuation of key points. Gorgianic theory also had other facets, such as a theory of 'the right moment' whose details are no longer fully available today, but which involved the adaptation of linguistic devices to suit the topic and the state of mind of the listener.

It is not certain whether Gorgias wrote a comprehensive textbook and handbook, or only certain chapters of his body of instruction. Specimens played a major part in the latter, however, and two of these, the Encomium of Helen and a defence of Palamedes, accused by Odysseus, have survived.

Gorgias' ongoing contest with high poetry is also amply manifest from his concentration on so-called epideictic eloquence rather than addresses for law courts and state. He thus cultivated the composition of speeches for major ceremonial occasions such as religious festivals, contests and banquets, intended to take the place of choral lyric songs, hymns, epic recitation, scholia and elegies. He made a very profound study of his rival, poetry. Unfortunately, only a few isolated observations have survived from his theory of poetry, and it is not possible to deduce from these whether they derive from a complete piece of discourse. Some are quoted by Aristophanes in the *Frogs*, and shown to be of his authorship on the basis of information from scholiastic commentaries.

Gorgias' remarks on the style of Aeschylus, or the nature of poetic illusion, which makes the 'deceived' listener wiser and more honest, rank among the most brilliant ever made on the subject, either before or after Aristotle, particularly with regard to tragedy. These remarks, as well as his principles of prose expression, would undoubtedly be far more accessible today if Democritus' prolific published works on rhythm, the harmony of certain sounds, the use of poetic vocabulary, linguistic beauty and poetic inspiration, etc. were still available in more than title form. It may at all events be assumed, however, that towards the end of the fifth century BC discussion of linguistic and literary theory had achieved a precise mastery of specific problem areas, as numerous statements in Aristophanes' comedies testify.

Gorgias made yet another highly progressive step. Himself from a Sicilian colonial town with a local Ionic dialect, and despite the existence of a ready-formed Ionic language for literary purposes that was current throughout Greece, he availed himself of the Attic language. There was a corpus of Attic prose by his time, but it was as yet only of local significance, being linguistically no match for the Ionic written language of the period.

Xenophon's extant works happen to include a pamphlet by an Athenian aristocrat polemicising against the domestic and foreign policy of the ruling

151

democrats. Although dating from the second third of the fifth century it provides clear evidence of the still crude level of the Attic written language.

In stylistic terms, the three extant legal speeches by Antiphon are highly sophisticated. He is probably not identical with the Sophist of the same name, and is known from an account by Thucydides to have been one of the main protagonists in the oligarchic coup of 411 BC whose failure cost him his life. The three speeches, a relic of sixty read in antiquity, were defence speeches in murder trials. They are masterly pleas made in markedly unpretentious language, their power lying in their skilful sequence of arguments rather than in their stylistic composition. The very fact that these addresses were published shows that the art of legal speeches was a subject for theoretical analysis and instruction in Athens at that time. This is supported by the information that Antiphon wrote a techne on rhetoric, a textbook on the use of argument in court. Twelve contemporary practice speeches are extant under his name, comprising two pleas each by the prosecution and the defence, in three fictitious murder cases, thus providing some insight into the training of lawyers in that period. As in the real speeches of the somewhat younger Andocides, linguistic polish was subordinated to refinement in the art of demonstrating probability. None the less, professional training in the complex sphere of the administration of justice and its terminology did entail an element of linguistic training that should not be underestimated. Andocides' speeches provide evidence not only about the degree of eloquence and the Attic judicial system generally in his day, but are also a valuable source of knowledge about historical events, since the author was involved in a scandal that proved crucial to the outcome of the campaign against Sicily in 415 BC.

Even by the end of the fifth century BC written Attic was still no match for Ionic in terms of flexibility and expressive power. Around the turn of the century, Stesimbrotus of Thasos wrote a pamphlet against Pericles and other pro-Imperial Attic politicians. It is largely a compilation of rumour and gossip – and of course in Ionic, although the author could unquestionably count on the hostility of readers in Athenian opposition circles to Athenian ambitions to be a great power.

Ion of Chios, already referred to several times above, is a similar case in point. In his later memoirs entitled *Epidemiae* ('Travels', or rather 'Sojourns'), he describes his impressions from contact with leading and interesting personalities in the Athenian sphere of influence, including Pericles, Sophocles and Socrates. For works of a would-be modern character, such as those of Stesimbrotus and Ion, extensive passages of which have survived in Plutarch (around AD 100), Ionic was preferable.

It was certainly not the available linguistic storehouse of the sparse Attic prose literature, therefore, that led Gorgias to switch from Ionic to Attic at the very juncture when he was seeking to supplant poetry with an entirely innovative prose style. The reason for his preference needs rather to be sought in the process whereby Attic had become a supra-regional language in trade, communications and credit transactions, as well as in administration and diplomacy in the wake of the economic and imperial expansion of the Athenian state. It was likewise widely used in the Greek-speaking world for the administration of justice, since Athens dealt with all cases between Athenians and its allies through its own courts. There is a substantial amount of evidence from documents and legislation that from the second half of the fifth century BC onwards Attic developed into an increasingly advanced medium for trade, administration and the judicial system.

Gorgias was completely successful in his choice of new literary idioms. Whereas his younger contemporary Thucydides continued to write in an Attic permeated with numerous Ionic elements, by the time of the generation that followed Gorgias Attic had ousted its former rival from nearly all branches of prose. Initially, Ionic still held its own in specialist medical literature and a few schools of philosophy, but Gorgias had helped to make written Attic an international lingua franca, and this at a time when the great-power status of Athens was waning, never to revive.

Aside from Isocrates, who will be dealt with in more detail later (pp. 153ff.), Gorgias' pupils included Polus, who wrote a handbook on rhetoric. The philosopher Antisthenes studied under Gorgias for a time, as did the Sophist Alcidamas, by whom a treatise survives on whether the orator should improvise or prepare his speeches in writing first.

Thrasymachus of Chalcedon on the Sea of Marmara was not among Gorgias' pupils, but also made quite a contribution to the development of artistic prose, for the first time laying down rules concerning the embellishment of the ends of sentences and clauses by means of regulating the sequence of their syllables. His main concern here was to accentuate through these metrical clauses different rhythms from those the listener was accustomed to hearing in verse. Here again, therefore, we find a sense of rivalry between verse and artistic prose.

The bulk of earlier extant texts written up to the beginning of the fourth century BC pertain to specialist medical literature. The major part of a great corpus of some seventy-two such papers, traditionally attributed to the great physician Hippocrates of Cos, has been preserved in medieval manuscripts. The fact that this compilation comprises a wide variety of authors and periods, including publications by rival schools of medicine, was already known to medical experts of the Hellenistic-Roman age, such as the famous Galen (second century AD) who eagerly used and commented on this literature. In all probability, this corpus of Hippocratic works made up the library of the medical school of Cos, of which Hippocrates the Asclepiad was the leading light.

It is known that Hippocrates was born around 460 BC and lived well into the fourth century. Something is also known of the circumstances of his life, as well as of his importance for the history of medicine, since the earliest and most valuable of the writings in the Hippocratic corpus were written in his lifetime. None of these has definitively been traced to the pen of the great Hippocrates himself, however.

The corpus embraces all types of medical literature. Seven books, some of which date from the fifth century BC, others from the third, contain quite unstylised precise case histories from the practice of wandering physicians. A good proportion consist of systematic handbooks or textbooks on specific medical fields, such as physiology, anatomy, gynaecology or surgery. Numerous works contain erudite discussions of a wide variety of problems, often polemically opposed to other schools of thought. Others deal with questions of method or the ethics of the medical profession, while others are compilations of diagnostic or therapeutic principles. Finally, for a wider readership and displaying more literary ambition, there are also treatises expounding on general issues of fundamental interest to medical science.

All these works were written in the Ionic dialect, even those dating from the first or second century AD, despite the fact that after the mid-fourth century BC many branches of the medical training tradition had gone over to the use of Attic (and later to the Hellenistic common language). From the third century BC, no productive contributions to medical research could be published in the old Ionic of the Cos school – located, incidentally, on an island in the Doric-speaking region.

The rise of medicine to the status of a science is linked with the name of Hippocrates. At the start of his working career, the Cnidos medical school on the mainland opposite, which was part of the Persian Empire from the mid-sixth century until the time of the Persian Wars, was undoubtedly more illustrious than the Cos school. It enjoyed close contact with Oriental medicine, and was famous for the precision of its symptoms catalogue, which classified all manifest ailments and assigned them a standardised, essentially dietary treatment. A number of Cnidos writings contained in the Hippocratic corpus, as well as polemical references to Cnidian theories, facilitate the reconstruction, at least in outline, of the practice of medicine at this school.

What was innovative about the early works of the Coan *Corpus Hippo-craticum*, and may with good reason be associated with the work of Hippocrates, whom Plato has speak for medical science in general, was the constantly readdressed question of the search for a complete explanation for each specific clinical picture. The onus on doctors was thus no longer solely on the minute observation of detail, the terminological classification of cases, and the subsequent administering of an empirically based therapy, but on an overall physiological and pathological explanation of all specifically observed symptoms, and a therapy based on this assessment. This can only be accomplished, of course, with the aid of natural science hypotheses capable of drawing those known and observable details of the human body and its functioning into a causal relationship. Medical scholars were able to derive the building blocks for such hypotheses from natural philosophy. Physicians of the southern Italian schools of Croton or Locri may already have done this

154

before Hippocrates, but without utilising a huge body of material from observation.

Given the outstanding gift of the Greeks for speculation, it is hardly surprising that hypotheses of this kind succeeded rapidly one upon another – partly since there were numerous trends in natural philosophy, and partly because a few fresh observations from medical practice sufficed to compel a revision of hypotheses that had been too hastily elaborated. However, this does nothing to alter the fact that the procedures used by this early medicine differed not at all in principle from those current in modern natural science.

In the Imperial Roman era, when medical research was on the wane, being replaced by the study of earlier medical works, the so-called theory of the four humours became the be-all and end-all of Hippocratic physiology, remaining so into the modern era. This thesis first appeared in a Hippocratic treatise entitled *On the Nature of Man*, attributed with good reason by second-century AD scholars to Hippocrates' son-in-law Polybus.

This thesis is based on the necessity of four fluids or humours – blood, phlegm, choler and black bile – being present in certain proportions in the human body in order to sustain its functioning. This did not mean, however, that they were to be understood as its basic components. All diseases were viewed as deriving from an imbalance in these humours. The task of the physician was to restore that balance, largely through dietary methods. (The derivation of temperament types, four basic mental constitutions, from the proportion of physical humours, was a later elaboration of this original thesis.)

This hypothesis, which by no means enjoyed widespread acceptance even throughout the prolonged productive phase of Greek medicine, is a typical example of early theoretical development, being linked via several inter-mediate components with Empedocles' theory of the elements, as well as the theory of four fundamental properties – cold, warmth, wetness and dryness – albeit more by way of inspiration than direct adoption.

A connection with natural philosophy theories is likewise discernible in hypotheses concerning the origins of epilepsy, expounded in one of the most impressive treatises in the Hippocratic corpus. Among the Greeks, as among other peoples, epilepsy was regarded as a disease inflicted by the gods, on account of its apparently sinister character. Its treatment thus entailed in-vocation and magic. The author of the paper *On the Sacred Disease*, however, was firmly convinced that epilepsy was no more 'sacred' than any other disease – or, as he puts it, all diseases are sacred inasmuch as they derive from nature. (This highlights the emphasis with which the concept of nature was at times used in the science of the time.) This scientific explanation of epilepsy is based on the assumption that not only blood but also air is transported in human veins. This insight derives from the theory of nature of Diogenes of Apollonia, who regarded air as the key sustaining element of all organic life. The argument continues that in the case of climatic effects (experiences with colds and chills are utilised) the otherwise invisible and regular drainage of phlegm from the area around the brain is impeded. This in turn could lead to a blockage of the veins supplying air to the brain, causing epileptic fits.

There is no need to comment here on the correctness or otherwise of this theory. Of far greater importance is the fact that here is an example of scientific thinking completely emancipated from magical and religious notions, and to the results of which the whole is subordinated.

The awe of nature evinced by the author of the treatise *On the Sacred Disease* is also manifest in another on the scientific nature of medicine – *On the Science*. It treats the question of insights into natural processes, which are seen as gained not so much from simple observation, as by exerting an influence on the organism under observation. In the process of prising a secret from nature, however, one should never inflict harm.

The overall causal explanations of these early physicians contained one factor deriving from medical experience, and not adopted along with natural philosophy theories. There is repeated investigation of how the physical and mental constitutions of people, and their susceptibility to quite specific ailments, depend on climatic and other environmental conditions. The importance attached to this factor derives from the fact that many physicians moved around from place to place, thus being unable to accumulate the modern lifelong experience of the family practitioner on which diagnostic and therapeutic efforts can be based. The issue, therefore, was one of finding generally valid diagnostic principles, so that the relationship between state of health, weather, climate, customary local foods and so on naturally suggested themselves as the main source of the physician's knowledge.

The corpus thus contains one extensive discussion by a widely travelled physician, who was also interested in ethnography, entitled *On Airs, Waters, Places*. On the basis of copious material gathered from observation in Greece, Asia Minor and southern Russia, he drew conclusions on the determination of physical and mental characteristics, as well as on the origins of certain diseases in climate and lifestyle. Even the experience of the Persian Wars, which proved the Greeks to be superior to their Oriental counterparts in terms of political and military accomplishments, is given an ecological explanation here. The anthropological and anthropo-geographical approaches devised for the first time in the second half of the fifth century BC have remained central to these disciplines to this day.

Since only sparse relics of fifth-century non-medical scientific literature have survived, it would be precipitate to make general comments about it which might pertain only to medical works. In one respect, however, medicine will have differed from the other incipient sciences: in its heightened sense of method. This specific feature helps to account for the profound influence exerted by medical concepts and modes of thought on fourth-century philosophy. In all other scholarly disciplines hypotheses could be debunked in rapid succession by fresh observations or by demonstrating their logical untenability, without throwing doubt on the hypothetical method itself. The physician, on the other hand, felt compelled to draw time and again on the storehouse of empirical knowledge of his profession, and apply it for the benefit of his patients, even if all theories were against it. In this way the elaboration of natural scientific hypotheses was subjected to constant criticism, particularly since many physicians practised their profession on a purely empirical basis, and yet were successful.

A treatise entitled *On Ancient Medicine*, probably written at the end of the fifth century BC, takes us to the nub of this problem of method. The author refuses to accept comprehensive hypotheses as the foundation of medicine, which could only ever rest on the rich and constantly expanding wealth of empirical knowledge accumulated by physicians over many generations. He is only prepared to accept hypotheses outright when they concern solely the explanation for individual phenomena. He none the less stresses the strictly limited validity of such theses, and the necessity for persistent ongoing research – an approach unfamiliar to natural philosophers. The question as to where to draw the line in medicine between empiricism and natural science remains just as relevant today as it was when it was first posed.

This particular work undoubtedly treats medicine in a manner intended for a wider readership, not solely for professionals. The author employs up-to-date Gorgianic stylistic devices, for example, unlike the author of a roughly contemporary treatise on the scientific character of medicine. At the same time, however, although avoiding all specialist detail in the strict sense of the term, he presumes quite an extensive knowledge of philosophical and Sophistic thought. This allows us to form quite an accurate picture of the educational level and intellectual aspirations of his readership. Unlike the present era, in antiquity medicine was one of the subjects included in general education. This is one of the reasons why its methodological formulation of questions came to acquire such enormous significance for philosophical thought in general.

Compared to obviously earlier writings in the corpus, the work *On the Ancient Art of Medicine* chiefly reveals the rapid and astounding momentum with which written information on scientific findings increased ability in terms of the appropriate structuring of prose texts, the logical presentation of arguments, and above all the ability to describe subject-matter concisely but exhaustively.

The *Prognosticon* is a compilation of diagnostic principles drawn from a rich body of case histories collated for school use into earlier books or *epidemiae*, which were the journals of peripatetic physicians. One famous passage in the book describes with no literary ornamentation but unsurpassable precision and conciseness the characteristics of a dying person known from this very description as the *facies Hippocratica*. The flowering of literary prose in the fourth century BC would have been unthinkable without the stylistic elegance achieved in scientific description and written discourse of the fifth century.

10

HERODOTUS AND
THUCYDIDES

The second half of the fifth century BC witnessed the appearance of two authors whose works have continued to shape historiographical tradition to this day. Something is known of the life of Herodotus from his works, and something from occasional information provided by late grammatical and antiquarian books which preserved specific results of Hellenistic literary research.

Herodotus was born in 485 BC in Halicarnassus, a Dorian colony in south-west Anatolia, into a family related by marriage to the indigenous Carian landed aristocracy, who lost their political influence during the first thirty years of his life in the course of bitter civil warfare. By 443 BC he was settled as a new citizen in the colony of Thurii in southern Italy, founded at the instigation of Pericles in place of Sybaris, which had been destroyed in 510 BC. By this point, Herodotus must already have spent some considerable time in Athens among prominent social circles. His friendship with Sophocles is well documented, and his involvement with the foundation of Thurii linked him with the Sophist Protagoras.

It is not known how long Herodotus lived in Italy, but he may have had to leave Thurii when anti-Athenian circles came to power there. At all events he seems to have spent his latter years back in Athens, where he lived to see the outbreak of the Peloponnesian War in 431 BC. He died in the mid-420s. There is likewise uncertainty as to when he undertook his major travels throughout the whole of Greece, Thrace, large parts of Asia Minor and southern Russia, Syria, Mesopotamia, Egypt and Cyrenaica. Most of his journeys were probably made before he first made Athens his home.

The opening sentence of Herodotus' opus, which was divided by Hellenistic philologists into nine books (papyrus scrolls), reads as follows:

> This is an account of the research of Herodotus of Thurii, being intended to ensure that events among men will not sink into oblivion with the passing of time – and that great and remarkable deeds, whether carried out by Hellenes or barbarians, might not remain without renown and may furthermore serve to show the reasons why they [i.e. the Hellenes and the barbarians] waged war on one another.

This sentence, which serves the function of a title, the giving of titles to books not being current practice in those days, describes the contents of this seminal work most aptly. Herodotus sought to collate and impart information available to him from the entire known world. In this process, the boundaries between ethnography, geography and history were as irrelevant to him as the distinctions between mythical, oral folk and documentary traditions.

The coherence and structure he managed to create out of his mass of material derive from his sound historical perception in viewing the war of 480/479 BC as a decisive confrontation between the Greeks, of whom only the Athenians and Spartans with a few of their allies actually took part in the fighting, and those peoples of the Orient encompassed by the Persian Empire. He arrived at this historical perspective as a result of the impressions he gathered in Athens, although himself a Greek from Asia Minor whose home town had only joined the Athenian maritime alliance in the 450s. He became an admiring witness to the outward expansion and domestic flowering of Periclean Athens, whose moral courage rested on the consciousness not only of having withstood an enormous test of its strength in the Marathon and Salamis years, but also of having won liberty for all Greece, going on to lead the whole nation against the enemy in the east. Herodotus identified with the claim of Athenians to live in 'the Hellas of Hellas'. It was thus from the Athenian perspective that he sought to give his account of all these events of immense temporal and geographical scope.

The structure of Herodotus' work is highly remarkable and has given rise to a variety of hypotheses, including one suggestion that it might in fact be a collation of a number of *logoi* – separate narratives on various subjects – intended to be read aloud at a ceremonial gathering, perhaps a great contest, and that the question concerning the literary composition of the whole could not be more meaningfully presented. In fact, however, few of the *logoi* in Herodotus' work are capable of standing alone. The entire second volume consists of an account of the geography and history of Egypt, some small part of which derives from his own observation, the majority, however, compiled from the geographical work of Hecataeus (see above, pp. 86–7ff.) Similar *logoi* deal with the Persians, Scythians, Ethiopians and Indians. Herodotus also refers occasionally to an 'Assyrian *logos*' which is not to be found in the extant work, however. Considerable space is also taken up by numerous myths, anecdotes, short stories and folk tales, most of which can easily be extracted from the context. Thanks to the form given them by Herodotus, some have been fortunate enough to find their way into the history of motifs in world literature, such as the story about the ring of Polycrates, tyrant of Samos, or of how Gyges came to ascend the Lydian throne.

None the less, closer examination reveals that all these descriptions and tales, created as they are with an archaic love of detail, do fit into a wider plan. The first striking feature is that some bodies of historical tradition are presented in *logos* form, i.e. separate narratives, for example the earlier story of

Cyrene relating the Persian conquest of the city (book four) or the account of the Ionian uprising of 499, the Datis campaign and the Battle of Marathon (books five and six). On the other hand, numerous items of information about the earlier history of Athens and Sparta are scattered throughout the whole work in the form of digressions, even though these could easily have been compiled into two separate and complete *logoi*. This in itself reveals the hand of an author seeking to create a broad coherence. This impression is confirmed by the fact that in the first three books a narrative thread is scarcely discernible at first glance; in the middle three volumes, however, even the artless reader cannot fail to notice such a thread, despite numerous digressions, while the final three books on the events of 480/479 BC constitute a completely single-theme narrative interspersed with only a few brief, lucid digressions. This overall structure, in drawing the account together step by step, is dictated by the theme. The respective characters of the Orient and the Greek world are revealed through traditions which are extraordinarily diverse and eclectic in both cases, even though the sheer vastness of the Orient poses problems. Ultimately, however, these two counterforces crystallise to clash in the major conflict described.

Prior to Herodotus, the Persian Wars had already been dealt with historio-graphically by Charon of Lampsacus. A history of Greece by Damastes of Sigeum should be dated as more or less contemporary with that of Herodotus. A study of the customs and history of a number of foreign nations was compiled by Hellanicus of Lesbos, a history of the Persians by Dionysius of Miletus (see above, p. 87), and Xanthus published a colourful adaptation of the story about the kings of the Lydians. Judging from what can be deduced from these fragments and accounts, however, none of these authors conceived his work in terms of an international history, and it is this quality which lends Herodotus' work its towering importance. The only other author who shows comparable insight into the events of 480 BC is Aeschylus, who fought both at Marathon and Salamis. He, however, was not a historian.

Herodotus opens his work with an interpretation of several Greek myths, for example the voyage of the Argonauts and the Trojan War, as evidence of an ancient and constantly recurring conflict between east and west. Through this he seeks an answer to the question of guilt and retribution. Without actually questioning the truth of these myths and hence drawing a distinct line between myth and history, he nevertheless makes clear the uncertainty of mythical tradition, thus opening the narrative itself with the nation that first incorporated Greeks into their sphere of hegemony – the Lydians under King Croesus. The Croesus heading opens a story of the Lydian kingdom comprising eighty-nine chapters, beginning with its emergence and extending to the fall of the last King Croesus and his subjugation by the Persian Cyrus, concluding with a brief description of the customs and mores of the Lydians. The story of the Lydians is thus presented in circular form, bringing readers back at the end to the point where the author made the first reference to Croesus. Albeit within the context of a broader plan, Herodotus makes extensive use of this narrative mode, which is documented in virtually all early forms of literary narrative and has hence been termed 'archaic ring composition'.

The Lydian kingdom was conquered by the Persians. Their advent thus appears at the end of the story of the Lydians, opening the second 'ring' which begins with the ancient history of the Medes and Persians and ends with the death of Cyrus, founder of the Empire. At the point where the expanding Persian Empire confronts Babylon and incorporates it, the historian opens a new ring of Babylonian history and national customs, then proceeding from the point of Persian history at which he had paused.

The second book opens with the ascent to the throne of Cambyses, conqueror of Egypt, going on to provide extensive information on national customs. The beginning of book three brings the conquest of Egypt, and so on. Naturally, the innumerable minor digressions are introduced in such a way that the thread of the main narrative can be resumed after them. If major ring compositions such as the story of the Lydians or the book on the Egyptians are of a scale and thematic wealth that tend to push the main narrative into the background, this was undoubtedly quite intentional on the part of an author seeking to give some idea of the sheer vastness, wealth and diverse historical tradition that characterised the Orient as it was gradually absorbed into the Persian Empire. As the latter gradually rose to become the sole ruling power in the Orient, so too the structure of the narrative likewise becomes more homogeneous. The study of Indian customs occasioned by the enumeration of satraps and tribute-paying regions of the Persian Empire, or the Scythian ethnography occasioned by an account of the campaign of Darius I in southern Russia, thus no longer interfere with the main course of the narrative.

Passages relating the earlier history of Greece mostly take the form of minor digressions within the overall narrative. Through the account of how Croesus, faced with the Persian threat, sends legations offering to form alliances with the Greek states, the reader at the same time learns something about the growth of Sparta to great-power status and the rise of the Athenian tyrant Peisistratus. We likewise learn something of the history of Greek cities in Asia Minor when the time comes to deal with their conflict with the Lydians. This is the procedure throughout the whole work, the task of structuring this immense body of material thus being resolved by Herodotus with great intelligence. Since in his day there were no such technical aids as chapter titles, sub-headings, footnotes or references, he was compelled to organise the entire work by compositional means alone.

Herodotus was a pious man who sought to discern the hand of the gods in the events he depicted, but his piety was not ancestral. Although oracles, dreams and similar motifs play no small part in his account, it should be borne in mind that most of his oracles derive from the Delphic tradition, and that since the sixth century BC the Delphic priesthood had used its immense influence to instruct people consulting the oracle in more progressive political and ethical views. In one anecdote, for example, Herodotus relates how the Delphic god instructed people to give priority to intention over deeds as a category of moral evaluation.

In his depiction of the Battle of Marathon, Herodotus is completely in the thrall of the Athenian tradition which immediately exalted this battle, unlike the Battle of Salamis in 480. Marathon was taken into the heroic sphere, since Athens had confronted the might of Persia single-handed. Precise descriptions were extant of paintings in the Stoa (colonnade) in the Athenian marketplace, dating from the 460s, twenty or thirty years before Herodotus' time, showing the direct intervention of heroes and gods in the battle, thus placing it on a par with mythical wars. Significantly, Herodotus refers to these supernatural circumstances pertaining to the official Athenian version in episodes before and after the battle itself, but accounts for the outcome of the battle by means of the objectives of the Persians, the decisions taken by the Athenian field marshal Miltiades, and the conduct of the combatants. His ideas about the nature of the gods and the human race are much clearer from those scenes in which he not uncommonly borrows from the formal structure and theological intentions of contemporary tragedy in order to explain major historical upheavals in terms of the plans of the powerful, and how they are endangered and deluded.

The significance behind the fall of the chivalrous Croesus is thus revealed to the reader in a conversation between the Lydian King and the wise Athenian Solon which precedes the catastrophe. The King, at the height of his success, views himself as the 'most fortunate' of men, convinced that he has transcended human imperfection. In so doing, however, he challenges the gods, who will not permit man to overstep his limits. The blows subsequently dealt by fate are thus not to be seen as the penalty for the shortcomings of the king, – there is not even a hint of moral culpability in his depiction – but as a demonstration by divine power of human limitations.

This view is presented perhaps even more radically in the account of the period leading up to the Xerxes campaign of 480 BC which led to catastrophe for the Persian Empire. Here too, Xerxes' defeat does not signify a just penalty by human standards for some misdeed of either the King or the Persians, but the triumph of a divine cosmic order whose defenders delude, humiliate and plunge into misfortune anyone who willingly or unwillingly jeopardises it.

Asked whom he regards as the most fortunate of men, Solon in Herodotus' story gives a most startling answer to his royal debating partner. He accords first place to Tellus the Athenian, a respected citizen who lived to see a large number of descendants, but fell in a war in defence of his native city; second place to the Argive youths Cleobis and Biton, whose mother, moved by a service rendered to her, prays for the best from the gods – to find on leaving the temple that they have died a peaceful death. The oft-pronounced conviction of the Archaic era that the individual was helpless in the face of the fate of the day and that no-one could therefore be regarded as fortunate before his or her death, is enriched here by another insight, already evident from Solon's poetry – namely that the sole positive attribute of a human life lies in the fulfilment of some service to the community at large.

Herodotus similarly derives the explanation for the resounding victory in the 480 BC Persian War from his reflection on the historical experience of the Greek city-state. Here too he demonstrated an ability to give narrative form to the results of his thought. As the Persian armed forces approach Thermopylae, where a handful of Spartan soldiers are blocking their path, the mighty King Xerxes inquires of the exiled Spartan King Demaratus who is in his entourage whether the Spartans would really dare to engage in battle against such an overwhelming force, since with all due respect to their military prowess one Spartan could scarcely take on ten men of the royal guard. Demaratus shows no interest in the question of whether the individual Spartan is superior to the individual Persian. Spartan prowess, exemplary here for the Greeks generally, was rooted in their free but equally disciplined fusion under law and justice, which made them a more powerful community than any group of even the most proficient individuals united solely by the will of a single ruler. Credit for Herodotus' clear description of the nature of communal strength un-doubtedly lies partly in his knowledge of contemporary Sophistic theories of the state.

Despite occasional errors brought to light by modern historical scholarship, and his one-sided pro-Athenian views, which incurred criticism even in antiquity, Herodotus was a highly conscientious historian with a painstaking desire for factual accuracy. He evaluated existing tradition with immense perspicacity, fully succeeding in devising viable criteria for the credibility of specific accounts. His rational criticism only goes as far as graduated distinc-tions in the value of his sources, however. The principal differences between chronicle and interpretative accounts, or between mythical and documentary traditions, were not apparent to him. He thus frequently confirmed the uncertainty and improbability of certain myths without drawing a line between myth and history *per se*.

Lastly, the narrative skill of Herodotus is remarkable. He unswervingly picks up on the essential, characteristic feature of an event or the matter under discussion. He never allows the attention of his readers to be distracted from the memorable part of a group of facts by introducing descriptive or other diverting passages into his account. Conversely, descriptions are never detached from their function by the insertion of comments on events. Admittedly, many of the stories of Periander and Polycrates, the treasure of Rameses or the murder of Candaules were already available to him. It is also known that some highly vivid detailed descriptions of Egyptian life were taken verbatim from Hecataeus. Other equally thrilling episodes and scenes, however, were of his own invention, showing that the reproduction of earlier short stories and myths was a deliberate narrative device in the overall context of the work whose formal potential could be used to support free invention.

Following on from the story of the murder of the false Smerdis, the Persian aristocracy, having liberated the throne from its usurper, gather to discuss the future of the Empire. In skilfully phrased speeches, three of them expound the advantages of the three basic forms of state organisation, democracy, aristocracy and monarchy, which appear here for the first time in their canonical order. This is undoubtedly a self-contained piece of what was then modern Sophistic state theory, introduced by Herodotus into his historical work in the guise of an Oriental short story. Quite rightly, the most famous of his invented episodes was the encounter between Croesus and Solon, which, as was already pointed out in antiquity, could not have taken place for chronological reasons.

Herodotus' work embraces the entire body of tradition and experience of the Archaic era, particularly in his innumerable anecdotes and short stories, as well as the lasting impressions accumulated by the Greeks in their contact with the civilised peoples of the Orient over many generations. Many passages thus strike the reader as archaic, while the vast abundance of the most diverse subject-matter indeed gives some idea of the Archaic delight in the direct portrayal of detail.

It should nevertheless not be forgotten that the historical perspective which Herodotus used to arrange all this detail derived entirely from the experience of the Classical period. Similarly, the literary devices used to organise this body of material far exceed the potential available for Archaic composition. Indeed, specifically Archaic narrative technique is utilised in the interest of a largely modern art of composition. Herodotus' historical work is both the final masterpiece of Ionic prose literature, and the gateway to European historiography.

Herodotus became a historian because the experience of the golden age of Athens opened up his vision to historical events of which the results were visible in his own day. Thucydides was to be the leading chronicler of the fatal battle for survival of his native city in which he himself was deeply involved. Where Herodotus had sought to classify an entire body of tradition, Thucydides strictly limited his attention to the political and military events of a period in which he himself was a protagonist, in the belief that in this way he would discover the key to understanding all phenomena arising from the traffic of human nature with power. Herodotus and Thucydides between them thereby uncovered two basic approaches to historiography that were to be put into practice again and again in the later course of history.

Something of Thucydides' life is known from his historical work and from a brief biography dating from around the fourth century AD that utilises the results of Hellenistic research. He belonged to a leading family related to Miltiades and Cimon by marriage and with property on the southern coast of Thrace. In 424 he commanded an Athenian fleet dispatched to defend the town of Amphipolis in the northern Aegean from attack by a Spartan expedition corps. When this failed he was condemned in absentia by the sovereign people, like many Athenian military leaders in similar situations. From then on he lived on the income from his property, and travelled widely. It was not until after the defeat of 404 BC that he was able to return to Athens, and he died shortly after 399 BC.

Thucydides sets out his aims and objectives in considerable detail at various points throughout his historical work (I.1, I.22, V.26). He aims for the utmost accuracy, dealing only with events he has experienced personally from various perspectives, or about which he has been able to gather eye-witness accounts. He does not share Herodotus' desire to rescue great deeds from historical oblivion, or even to make his accounts aesthetically pleasing. His writing is based on the conviction that the historical period selected is of supreme importance in the way it illustrates the struggle between two groups of states of hitherto unknown power. He sees this conflict as being of exemplary importance for future events, in view of unchanging human nature. By means of speeches inserted into his account, which of course make no claim to documentable authenticity, he seeks to illustrate the views and objectives of leading statesmen or military commanders prior to key decisions.

This agenda provides evidence of a concern with deep reflection about personal action, although Thucydides was not in fact able to complete his work. The extant parts were divided by Hellenistic grammarians into eight books. Book one comments on the early history of Greece, on historical method, on the history of the fifty-year period leading up to the Peloponnesian War, and on an extensive, particularly carefully worked-out account of its causes and the outward events that triggered it, between which Thucydides is at pains to distinguish. Books two to four deal with the events of ten years of the war up to the peace of 421, and book five with the connections between the two wars, which are interpreted by Thucydides as a single continuous historical process. Books six and seven deal with the Sicilian expedition up to the disastrous defeat of the Athenian army in 413, and book eight, which is cut short in mid-sentence, gives an account up to the coup of the oligarchs in 411.

The extant work is hence a truncated one whose various parts are moreover in different stages of completion, as is highlighted by the author's own remarks as to his overall plan. His use of speeches in recounting the results of his historical analysis in part two of book one, which deals with the period immediately prior to the outbreak of war, as well as in books six and seven on the Sicilian events, thus corresponds exactly to the methodological principles he laid down. Books five and eight are almost completely lacking such speeches, although there are occasional verbatim citations from documents, which are incompatible with his narrative style. Thus, whereas the former passages evince a narrative quality that is sustained to the very last nuance, the latter are marked by a scarcely discernible system of arrangement.

These discrepancies have led to various attempts to explain how they came

165

about, chief among them being that of Edward Schwartz (1919). He asserts that after 421 BC Thucydides first wrote a history of what was known as the Archidamian War. When hostilities were resumed, he argues, it became clear to Thucydides that this was a continuation of the same conflict, so that by the time of the fall of Athens in 404 at the latest he decided to recount the entire war period as a single entity. This, however, necessitated a substantial rewriting of the first part, now extant in the form of books one to four, a task which Thucydides was unable to complete, like his account of the final years of the war. However, neither this hypothesis nor subsequent attempts to explain the structure of the work in terms of a single overall plan that was never modified have been able to resolve all discrepancies. There is a 'Thucydidean question' as well as a 'Homeric question'. Nevertheless, this detracts nothing from appreciation of Thucydides' scholarly and literary achievements.

The basis of all historiographical endeavour is reliable chronology. This posed special difficulties for Greek historians, since every city had its own way of reckoning the calendar, based on some eponymous official, with the respective New Year depending on the local festival calendar. Thucydides' time saw the first attempts to correlate these various local calendar systems by means of the publication of extremely lengthy and well-documented eponymic lists. Hippias, for example, drew up a list of Olympic winners, and Hellanicus one for the Argive priestesses of Hera. Thucydides devised a way of precisely dating two events – the Theban attack on Plataea in 431 and the peace of 421 BC – by means of multiple eponymic dating involving Spartan ephors, Athenian archons and Argive priestesses. Moreover, he dated all events on the basis of his enumeration of the years of the war itself, further subdividing them into one longer campaign period (summer) and a shorter hiatus (winter). This system conforms to Thucydides' oft-repeated call for 'accuracy' and for distinguishing between the long-term and immediate causes of the war, the careful delineation of military operations, analysis of the various motives behind military and political decisions, and the sources of information on which they were based, as well as the detailed description, without losing sight of essentials, of the social conditions that influenced political events. Thucydides adopted this ideal of accuracy from contemporary natural science, and particularly from medicine, as is clearly evinced by his application of numerous terms and models of thought from these disciplines to his analysis of historical events. His well-known description of the plague of 430–428 BC, which claimed the life of Pericles, shows how conversant Thucydides must have been with specialist medical literature. It would not look out of place in a Hippocratic treatise, aside from its use of Attic vocabulary.

At times Thucydides steps beyond the self-imposed bounds of his historiography. He thus recounts a memorial oration by Pericles in honour of the fallen of the second year of the war – not exactly the most eventful – in which the speaker expounds on the nature of the Athenian state, as well as the motives behind its political, economic and above all cultural activities. These are seen from the perspective of the historian, insofar as he is able to eliminate the passing manifestations of everyday political life. One is left in no doubt even for a moment that Thucydides does not confuse this view with historical reality. Likewise, he does not fall prey to a straightforward identification with the unreservedly positive interpretation of Classical Athens which he puts, not without ulterior purpose, in the mouth of this statesman, who contributed more than any other to the flowering of this city, as described above.

Book one shows the reader the negative aspects of this view, as outlined by envoys from Corinth, which is in danger of being oppressed by the greater might of Athens, and hence seeking to bring Sparta to launch an attack against it. Athenian entrepreneurial zeal is thus depicted here as restlessness and insatiability, its openness to innovation as fickleness, and its pride in cultivation and cultural achievements as presumption and arrogance.

Both here and elsewhere, Thucydides seeks to make clear that while one and the same phenomenon can quite justifiably be evaluated from contradictory historical perspectives the historian is not justified in becoming entrenched in any single one of them. This view accords with the composition of a famous passage inserted by Thucydides prior to his description of a horrendous event that was none the less of little significance in terms of the overall course of history. In 416 BC the supreme power of Athens called on the small island town of Melos to join the Attic confederation. The people of Melos, however, insisted on their right to neutrality, whereupon the Athenians occupied the island and forced them to join the Attic alliance, having first killed the male citizens and taken the women and children as slaves. Thucydides has politicians of both camps conduct a dialogue which analyses with a sang-froid that borders on academic detachment the basic issues underlying this episode, whose atrocious character is revealed by the subsequent account. The Athenians thus argue that political expediency takes precedence over all other considerations, and that the citizens of Melos must thus accept the right of the mightier party in the given situation. The citizens of Melos, on the other hand, appeal to justice, law and convention. The Athenian line of argument displays an affinity to Sophistic theories on the natural right of might, as set forth in the first book of Plato's *Republic* and the *Gorgias*. Thucydides' presentation of the essence of historical events using this kind of dialectic method would probably be impossible to understand were it not for the Sophistic art of debate. It would be incorrect, however, to deduce on the basis of the Melian dialogue that he sought either to validate the Sophistic doctrine of the right of might, or alternatively to expose the unscrupulousness of Athenian imperialism.

The historical insight demonstrated in the account of this episode shows that specific political decisions only tend to pay heed to justice and convention when the latter are adequately backed up by power. By the same token, if, as in this case, the more powerful of two sides asserts itself at the expense of a weaker opponent, it thereby sets a precedent that can turn against it when the situation changes. Athens came to learn this lesson, not only in the final conflict of 404 BC, but even prior to that during the Sicilian venture, which is depicted by Thucydides with particular vividness. Both in the Melian dialogue and in general, Thucydides' aim is to show the laws at work behind historical events. His own moral judgement concerning this episode is not left in doubt for a moment, but the fact that both points of view are expressed so dispassionately in the dispute between Melos and Athens demonstrates his desire for historical objectivity.

Thucydides' entire work is punctuated with passages of varying length giving his insights into human modes of conduct. Sometimes these take the form of explanatory asides pertaining to a causal relationship asserted by the author, and sometimes they take stock of a described episode. Occasionally these passages crystallise into discourses on human nature that are almost detached from the narrative context, such as when Thucydides recounts the changes in moral values that followed the prolonged exceptional situation prevailing in isolated Athens, or the effects of persistent internal discord on the population of Corfu (Corcyra).

Thucydides' interest in the laws governing human behaviour, in turn closely linked with the principles of contemporary natural science and medicine, is qualified by a certain reluctance to pass judgement on outstanding individuals. It was not his conviction that great individuals make history. Despite his aspiration towards objectivity, he does undeniably on occasion betray his personal involvement in the life and work of some men, such as the unfortunate Nicias, Brasidas the Spartan, or Antiphon the oligarch. Only once, in the case of Cleon, does he allow his antipathy to surface fully. By the same token, however, on only two occasions did he undertake to evaluate the historical significance of an individual – a fact which lends them even greater weight. Thus, in the introductory book, outside the narrative proper, there is a brief characterisation of Themistocles, and he appends to his account of the death of Pericles an assessment of this statesman whose influence helped to make Athens great, and whose death set the seal on the ultimate defeat of Athens even on the very threshold of war.

Thucydides' diction is exceptionally convoluted, and scarcely translatable. The reason for this is that the wherewithal of literary prose available at that time was an inadequate medium for expressing his subtle thought processes, analyses and factual interrelationships with ease. This is further complicated by his constant endeavour to find a semantically and syntactically suitable expression for every combination of ideas and nuance of his thought processes, so as to reproduce them with linguistic precision – all without becoming long-winded. This frequently gives rise to turns of phrase that stretch or even exceed the bounds of the linguistically acceptable. Typical of his style, for example, is the copious use of anacoluthons. Although

Thucydides was clearly familiar with Gorgianic stylistic devices, even using them occasionally, they never shaped his style. He only used them when his subject-matter made it appropriate for him to do so. In later times, Thucydides' struggles with a still immature literary language were misconstrued as mannerisms, and his dryness as delightfully old-fashioned; hence it was enthusiastically imitated, both in Greek and Latin. None of his imitators, however, was ever able to reproduce the unsurpassed concentration of his narrative style, which left no loopholes.

The language Thucydides used was Attic, albeit peppered with innumerable Ionic words and forms. His high degree of conversance with contemporary natural science, the findings of which were published exclusively in Ionic, is revealed in his vocabulary at every turn. Indeed, his entire terminology derives from this field, and even those terms he coins himself comply with the conventions of literary Ionic. He was the source of no small number of abstract terms that were later to find their way into common usage. Here, as in his rigorous rationality, he showed his intellectual affinity to the Sophists, although none of the latter ever achieved such a precise knowledge of human nature as revealed in history.

Some authors already touched on above (see p. 87) either before or in Thucydides' time wrote historical works or descriptive accounts of foreign countries and peoples including historical tradition. To these may be added the earliest western Greek historiographers, who compiled the first accounts of the ancient history of southern Italy and Sicily and the Greek cities that were founded there. Unfortunately, these works are nowadays only extant in the form of a few fragments, including that of Antiochus of Syracuse. The modern picture of early historiography thus remains shaped by those two works which even in the judgement of antiquity towered above all the rest.

Part III

CLASSICAL LITERATURE OF THE FOURTH CENTURY BC

11

SOCRATES AND
SOCRATIC THOUGHT

In general and literary history alike, the fourth century BC stands out clearly as an era with a character all its own. The demise of Athens in 404 left Greece with an unstable system and a succession of short-lived power groups, none of which (e.g. Sparta or Thebes) was able to hold its position for long or prevent other cities (Athens or Corinth) from rising to power in their turn. The beneficiaries of this political vacuum were the Persian Empire and other states on the periphery of the Greek-speaking world, where enterprising monarchs set up new kinds of territorial state, disregarding political notions of the classical *polis*, but drawing on the rational administrative and military achievements of the Greek city-state.

These rulers included the tyrant Dionysius of Syracuse, who was able for a brief period to unite the Italian Sicilian region settled by Greeks, the Pherae dynasty which built up a modern state out of the backward agrarian region of Thessaly, and indigenous dynasties on Cyprus and Caria in Asia Minor where modern states loosely dependent on the Persian Empire were likewise set up with the aid of Greek experts.

Pre-eminent among these states was Macedonia, which rose in the course of the fourth century BC to great-power status under a long-Hellenised royal house, taking the Greek mini-states into its thrall on the battlefield of Chaeronea in 338 BC and, sustained by a Greekspeaking world now united under an iron rule, went on to conquer the entire Orient and open it up to the Greek language and civilisation for a full millennium. Greek history in its own right, and the fourth century BC as a historical era, thus extend to the Battle of Chaeronea, or at most to the Alexandrian campaign of conquest.

The apparent weakness of the ancient Greek states in this period was reflected in social and political unrest. Hardly any other era witnessed so many revolutions. Part of the population was constantly in exile in a neighbouring state, waiting for a fresh coup attempt. The roots of this outward powerlessness and internal strife lay in the fact that the prevailing political ideas and institutions and social agenda were out of step with the economic potential of the age. Despite the dismal picture painted by its history at government level, this was in fact an era of steady economic expansion. It saw, for example, rapid recovery from the economic setbacks of repeated warfare, Athens being particularly sorely tried in this respect. Given the poverty of the country in terms of natural resources, the credit for this goes both to the trading and commercial enterprise of the inhabitants, and above all to the fact that they had learned how to combat economic problems with extensive organisational and fiscal policy measures.

The most reliable indicator of this steadily rising prosperity in the teeth of political catastrophe was an enormous population explosion, which on the other hand compelled Greece to offload its surplus population onto surrounding countries, given its own limited territory. The core of the Persian Empire's troops, for example, who were able to make one more lasting impression on Greek history in this period, was made up in the fourth century of Greek mercenaries. Similarly, Greek technical experts, ministers, physicians, bankers, mariners, cooks and dancers were to be found all over the known world. The rapid establishment of smoothly functioning state institutions throughout all the territories of the Persian Empire in the aftermath of the Alexandrian campaign would be inexplicable without this preceding Greek penetration of the east.

It came hard to the Greeks to reconcile themselves to the discrepancy between their potential for wielding power and their calamitous political situation. The reflection revolving around this experience shaped the development of philosophy, historiography, educational theory, political publicity and economic literature more than any other single factor. On the other hand, disenchantment with the institutions of the *polis* was one of the reasons why the dramatic literature that continued to be produced in quantity as part of the Attic state cult was no longer accepted as a legitimate expression of crucial issues, and hence ceased to be represented by works of high calibre. In addition to this, the late fifth century BC onwards saw increasing attempts to solve as many problems as possible by rational means, resulting in prose becoming the suitable vehicle for discursive thought.

The reading public grew ever larger, the book trade and publishing institutions took on established forms, and even political speeches, always intended to address topical situations in particular towns, became widespread reading material on account of their formal or conceptual attributes. The focal point of intellectual life, which became increasingly homogeneous throughout Greece, being experienced similarly by the government official of Philip of Macedon and the personal physician or strategist of the Persian king, was Athens. Attic prevailed as the generally understood literary language, while Athenian philosophical or literary and rhetorical institutions of education provided the world with intellectuals.

In the fourth century BC this central position of Athens in intellectual life was still matched by its strong position in trade and credit transactions, which was successfully maintained into the Hellenistic era on account of its magnanimous dealings with the metics (locally resident foreigners).

Socrates lived on the threshold of this new era. Although his legacy lacks even one surviving written line, his work more than that of any other shaped the written documented intellectual life of the fourth century. Almost all his life was lived in the fifth century BC. Born in 470 BC, he was condemned to death and executed in 399 for alleged *asebia* – infraction of religious and hence political loyalty to the Athenian cult community. Of middle-class origin, he none the less had close contacts among both aristocratic and wealthy metic families in the city. He fulfilled his citizen's duties both as a good soldier and as an official with rotating periods of service, likewise living the normal life of an Athenian citizen, in which the earning of one's living played a much smaller role than in modern times. Like many of his open-minded contemporaries, he became familiar with the theses of natural philosophy. It seems to have been the appearance of the first Sophists, however, that first inspired him to intellectual work of his own. It was in particular their claim that the virtues of the citizen were teachable that led him to ask what these virtues in fact consisted of. In innumerable discussions he sought to investigate the simplest concepts and ideas that shaped human conduct: the process led him time and time again to conclude that both discussion partners were in a state of non-knowing, a conclusion he took with the utmost seriousness. This inquiry into ideas and concepts thus became for him at the same time a form of self-examination, on the assumption that virtue is based on insight rather than on good will or something akin to it, and that no one wittingly acts wrongly. Socrates was firmly convinced of these premises, already long in accordance with prevailing views among the Greeks. What was new was his perception of this insight into general ignorance as an incentive for constant re-examination, and his understanding of lifelong questioning and searching as the principle underlying moral growth.

Unlike the Sophists, Socrates did not seek to resolve the absence of reliable knowledge by seeking refuge in so-called sound common sense or plausible-sounding opinions shared by all people of good will. For him the question of how to live correctly called for stringently demonstrable conclusions, even if they contradicted all generally accepted opinion.

The realisation that this urge towards an incessant search for insight into the nature of justice, friendship and all other moral concepts, which on the one hand could only be made by the uncompromising use of reason, but must ultimately nevertheless be of an irrational nature, is revealed by Socrates himself in his references to his *daimonion*, a divine inner voice that constantly warned him against making wrong decisions, yet which had never restrained him from such action.

How great the impact of Socrates was in his own lifetime is difficult to judge. He undoubtedly fascinated numerous young people from distinguished social and intellectual circles. By all accounts the 'gadfly', as Socrates styled himself on account of his incessant awkward questions, will have been regarded as an 'original', famous in his city, and welcome fodder for comedies. Whereas, however, democratic society was prepared to tolerate him while it was still intact, the restored post-403 BC democracy proved more touchy, taking offence at his unconventional disputes that left no social values unchallenged, and accusing him of *asebia* (impiety). His temporary affiliation with gifted but doubtful personalities from political life, such as Alcibiades and some young aristocrats from the notorious Thirty of 404 BC, may have been an additional aggravating factor. Once sentenced, Socrates disdained to evade his penalty through the openly offered opportunity to escape from prison. He held to the view that a citizen was not justified in flouting a legally passed sentence even if it was objectively unjust, since this would be an infringement of the legal system in and whereby he lived.

The posthumous impact of the life he led and sealed in this manner was enormous, however. It marked the first demonstration that virtue did not consist of achievement and success, but in the moral stature of life as a whole, shaped by the conscientious exercise of reason. Later doxography occasionally designated Socrates as the father of philosophical ethics. This is certainly false inasmuch as Democritus and other philosophers, both before and independently of Socrates, focused on ethical problems in their thought. It is correct, however, insofar as Socrates was the first both to understand philosophy as the *magistra vitae*, and to live his own life accordingly. This precedence of ethics, for the sake of which all philosophy is pursued, was to remain binding for the entire philosophical tradition of antiquity, and also for wide spheres of Occidental philosophy.

Since the primary aim was to gain insight into one's own state of unknowing and the necessity for constant further inquiry, analysis aimed at the acquisition of knowledge and self-knowledge was always conducted through discussion rather than through instructive lecturing. Since, moreover, the Socratic pursuit of philosophy could not be divorced from everyday life like other forms of activity, the community of philosophers thus also became a practical living one.

Following the death of Socrates, therefore, a number of schools sprang up led by people who had had contact with him and now sought to keep up the momentum he had initiated for living a moral life. Naturally, institutional schools of this kind needed positive doctrines over and above Socrates' own 'art of verification'. Socratic philosophers drew these elements from various sources. In Megara, a neighbouring city of Athens, Euclid founded a school that was to flourish for over a century and whose later representatives were to make their names mainly in the discipline of logic (Diodorus Cronus, Stilpon). This school built on Eleatic doctrines. Phaedon, known as the eponymous figure in one of Plato's Dialogues, founded a school in Elis that was later moved by his successor Menedemus to Eretria on the island of Euboea. After extensive travels, another follower of Socrates by the name of Aristippus founded a school in his native city of Cyrene. The problem of desire was central to its teaching, and the school soon splintered in many directions (Anniceris, Theodorus the Atheist, etc.).

In Athens itself, Antisthenes, a pupil of Gorgias, continued the Socratic educational tradition, on the one hand through his efforts to unite the method of Socratic discussion with the Sophistic art of argumentation, and on the other by propounding inurement to physical deprivation and asceticism as a practical road to virtue.

Antisthenes' teaching laid the foundations for the so-called Cynic School, which derived its name from Diogenes the 'Dog', a unique figure famous in Athens life around the middle of the century. He lived a life of extreme frugality and resolute contempt for all convention, had no home, regarded himself as a 'citizen of the world' and saw it as his task to reveal to people with 'doglike' brazenness the haze of prejudices and imaginary needs and requirements in which they lived.

A body of anecdote and legend rapidly grew up around the personality of Diogenes, but his followers, Crates, Monimus, Metrocles and others, are historically documented figures. They roamed the country as beggars with rucksacks and shabby cloaks, preaching ascetic frugality and life in harmony with the laws of nature. They acted as spiritual advisers seeking to bring people to inner independence which is found in action based on sound judgement, unconcerned by the opinion of the world around them, and is a good Socratic legacy. Their model was Heracles, recast in the mould of the ascetic able to overcome the world.

Some of the above Socratic philosophers, such as most Cynics, followed the example of their master by restricting themselves to oral instruction. Crates, however, a man of outstanding literary gifts, clothed his derision of social institutions and philosophical doctrines in amusing parodies of great poetry such as tragedies, some passages of which have survived in the form of quotations. Most such philosophers nevertheless also sought to disseminate their teaching in written form – not surprisingly in a society so accustomed to the written word. They still based this literary form on their recollection of Socrates' oral one, however, thereby instigating a rich tradition of literary dialogues. Although Plato was probably the first to make full use of this form to reproduce complicated discussions, its literary and creative potential, for example in characterisation, generating tension and so on, was also developed by other Socratic literature.

Practically none of this has survived, aside from relics of dialogues by Aeschines, a pupil of Socrates. Credit for the fact that it is still possible to form a relatively accurate picture of Socratic literature goes less to Plato, who generally made only veiled reference to the literary sources he used, than to the prolific and completely extant works of Xenophon of Athens, even though the latter cannot properly be classified as a Socratic philosopher.

The young Xenophon enjoyed only brief contact with Socrates. In 401 BC he joined an army of mercenaries mustered by the Persian Prince Cyrus, who sought thereby to topple his brother Artaxerxes from the throne. Although victorious at the Battle of Cunaxa in Mesopotamia, he himself was killed, and Artaxerxes lured the officers of the Greek mercenaries into his camp, where he had them killed. With some other resolute men, Xenophon then took over command, leading this small Greek fighting force of 10,000 safely through the Persian Empire to the Bosphorus. Xenophon subsequently reappeared as an officer serving a king of Thrace, and later the Spartan strategist Agesilaus, who was campaigning in western Anatolia against the Persians, who were allied with Athens. Xenophon thereby incurred exile from Athens, but was compensated for this by the Spartans, who conferred on him an estate near Olympia. He lived there for several decades as landowner, horse-breeder and writer, until the Eleans sent him into exile for being a Spartan partisan. By this time, however, Athens had made peace with Sparta. His sentence of exile was revoked, and two of his sons served in the Athenian army. It seems that Xenophon himself did not return to Athens for long, however, instead ending his days in Corinth.

Just as Xenophon's military career manifests many features typical of his day, so too his prolific and versatile written works represent a cross-section of the literary scene at that time, despite being by no means of outstanding merit. We shall be returning to Xenophon again later (see below, pp. 215ff.). The survival of his works is owed to the literary taste of the early Imperial period, when his style was admired for its simplicity and lucidity. Remarkably, the fact that his Attic was not pure, on account of his prolonged absence from Athens, was not held against him.

Of his Socratic works, his four-book *Memorabilia* is the most important. This contains a loose sequence of numerous dialogue scenes in which Socrates engages in discussion with specifically named friends and pupils, Sophists, philosophers, politicians, artisans and hetaeras. These dialogue sections are interspersed with Xenophon's own explanatory and apologetic comments, especially in the first book, which opens with a cogent refutation of Polycrates. Soon after the trial of 399 BC, this Sophist had sought to justify the sentence on Socrates with a fictive prosecution address; this provoked a spate of literary responses.

Xenophon's dialogue scenes depict Socrates as a homely, shrewd, quick-witted man well-versed in all disciplines, always ready with the appropriate practical and moral advice for community life. Although often appealingly and skilfully composed, full of urbane repartee, they invariably lack both inner and outer drama.

By the appearance of Olof Gigon's (1953, 1956) major commentary on the *Memorabilia* at the latest, it was clear that the question as to whether Xenophon's or Plato's completely different depiction of Socrates was the correct one was inappropriately posed. Xenophon's contact with Socrates was brief, and his books written many years later, after an eventful military career. The *Memorabilia* are thus not personal memoirs at all, but rather an embellished compilation based on an already existing and extensive literature of Socratic dialogues. Xenophon's relationship with Socrates as a historical figure was thus quite different from that of Plato. One can at least note with satisfaction that they are in agreement concerning the few factual details they give about Socrates' biography.

Xenophon thus passed on a picture of the Socratic literature of his day as it influenced a broad reading public. The colourlessness of his depiction of Socrates derives from his use of multiple sources, which he evaluated with the intention of presenting him in the best possible light, and yet without any philosophical commitment of his own. The combination of these different facets of Socrates derived from various schools produces the image of a benign know-all.

Xenophon also wrote a fictional *Apology of Socrates* and a dialogue entitled *Oeconomicus*, in which Socrates presents his tenets for the correct running of a household. This work is a key source of modern knowledge about prevailing ideas at that time about the family, marriage, child-rearing and so on. His finest Socratic work from the literary viewpoint is his *Symposium*, which was clearly expressly written as a rival to Plato's dialogue of the same name.

12

PLATO, ARISTOTLE AND THEIR SCHOOLS

It is difficult to give an adequate assessment of Plato in a history of literature. An exposition of his enduring importance in the history of both Greek and western thought, and indeed in the whole of European civilisation, would entail a close analysis of his philosophy, which would extend far beyond the scope of this book. On the other hand, some of Plato's Dialogues rank among the most consummate literary compositions ever written in Greek. Their literary merits, however, lie in the way they are able to reproduce extremely subtle lines of thought completely and without any loose ends in a dramatically composed discussion between clearly portrayed partners. With Plato, therefore, it is not possible to separate the philosopher from the writer, even allowing for the fact that in his later Dialogues literary form occasionally took a back seat to content, whereas in his earlier ones his delight in playing with his literary medium, for example with parodies of diverse styles, results in virtuoso formulations that are by no means essential to their philosophical content.

Something is known of Plato on account of the marked interest in the circumstances of the master's life shown from the very beginning of his school and which led to handed-down and subsequently compiled information finding its way into various branches of literature. By the same token, a tendency towards biographical legend also soon set in. Documents of biographical interest include one text that was until recently, and to some extent still is, regarded as a true autobiographical account. The corpus of Platonic works was not compiled in its present form until the first century AD from what were undoubtedly authentic Dialogues and a number of assorted writings of the Platonic tradition dating from between the fourth and first centuries BC. These writings included a collection of thirteen letters alleged to be by Plato, most of which were nevertheless regarded as inauthentic even in antiquity. The seventh letter contains a review by the elderly Plato of his life, and details concerning his oral teaching. There is still disagreement among Plato scholars as to the authenticity of this letter. If not authentic, it originates in all probability from the first generation of his pupils, so that the information conveyed in it should be taken seriously. Spurious works of this kind are a frequent occurrence in philosophical literature especially, and should not necessarily be regarded as 'forgeries' in the modern sense of the term. Authors convinced that they were conveying the content of a doctrinal tradition correctly in fact felt justified, or even obliged, to publish their work under the name of the originator of a tradition who had sometimes died generations earlier. Expressly polemical debates within or between traditional schools, on the other hand, were generally published under individual names.

In terms of his origins in a socially distinguished family, Plato seemed predestined for a political career, and in terms of his gifts for one as a poet (see below, pp. 227–8). Influenced by the life and death of his teacher, he became neither. His contact with Socrates convinced him of the necessity of constantly seeking for knowledge with a view to improving the substance of his life, while the condemnation of Socrates showed him the futility of seeking to improve the existing Attic state. Plato made three separate journeys to the court of the tyrant of Syracuse, each time under different pretexts, but evidently always in the hope of contributing to establishing a political system based on moral principles. This hope seemed justified by his acquaintance with Dion, who was related to the ruling house, and, prior to Plato's second journey, by the accession to the throne of Dionysius, who did indeed show an inclination towards philosophy and also invited other Socratic philosophers to his court. All these hopes were to be dashed, however, the enduring benefit of these journeys to the west lying chiefly in Plato's close contacts with the Pythagoreans, and most particularly with their current leading proponent, Archytas of Tarentum.

Plato's impact as a forger of new tradition grew out of the school he founded in 387 BC, having used his own resources to acquire a plot of land, buildings and a library at the shrine to a local hero by the name of Academus (hence the term academy) at the gates into Athens. It was here that Plato taught and carried out his scholarly research until his death in 348 BC, aged around 80. The nucleus of his large number of pupils instantly established a scholarly tradition that was to extend until the Emperor Justinian abolished philosophy schools in AD 527. Other pupils worked outside Athens, sometimes as advisers to Greek or pro-Greek dynasties. The greatest of these, Aristotle, having been a member of the Academy for twenty years, founded his own school, the first of its kind based on the Platonic model, which was followed by others in the fourth and third centuries BC.

Plato taught orally: unlike proponents of what was then modern education, he saw the sole appropriate vehicle for philosophical teaching not in the set textbook, but in flexible discussion in which account had to be given for every step in the learning process. Plato's *Phaedrus* contains direct assertions of the inadequacy of the written text for philosophical inquiry on the grounds that the text was 'unable to defend itself' once it had passed out of the author's hands. Recent attempts to reconstruct Plato's oral teaching method and to demonstrate it as the quintessence of his philosophy have none the less failed to produce convincing results, even though they have led to valuable insights into relevant references, such as accounts of a lecture entitled 'On the Nature of the Good'. The basis for such reconstruction consists essentially in references to the establishment of a permanent teaching building, which occurred in the first two generations of the Platonic school. This dogmatics was taken up again by Platonists of the first century BC and continued to be developed until the Neoplatonic era in late antiquity, so that relevant sources are often separated from Plato's own lifetime by centuries.

From the very outset doctrines concerning the principles of this dogmatics displayed marked influences from Pythagorean thought, which had been studied by the elderly Plato himself. They are so schematic and scholastic in character, however, that it is difficult to imagine them being presented as a theme for oral instruction in the kind of open discussion encountered in Plato's writings. The reader must therefore first accept that Plato's own philosophy is only to be found in his own extant works. As Ernst Heitsch (1987) has shown, however, Plato's assertions about the written word can quite easily be understood in terms of the oral and written forms being applied to their respectively appropriate targets and themes. It need not then be asserted that he spent a lifetime contradicting himself with his own prolific corpus of writing.

Plato's works adhere to the form of Socratic dialogue even when treating themes for which other forms would undoubtedly have been better suited. Moreover, with few exceptions, Socrates himself is the main speaker in these Dialogues. At first glance, therefore, it seems that Plato is doing no more than conveying the teachings of his master. Aristotle, however, who was always most conscientious about going into the history of any problem he dealt with, showed that this was not the case. To Socrates he attributes only a few specific lines of thought and doctrines, which are encountered in some of Plato's Dialogues, while in others being modified, expanded further or even contradicted. There is clearly a great deal in Plato's work that had little or nothing at all to do with Socrates. Some of his dialogue scenes are precisely located with regard to time, place and the persons involved, such as the situation presented in the *Symposium*. Some make no pretence at all to historical credibility, such as when he has Socrates debate with the much older Parmenides, who is highly unlikely ever to have been in Athens.

These disparities clearly show that Plato's tendency to stand in the shadow of his teacher requires more precise explanation. It needs firstly to be borne in mind that the Socratic dialogue had already fully established itself as a literary form, thus placing Plato within an existing tradition. His approach is equally, however, an expression of the profound gratitude felt by one of the very few truly great and original thinkers for the man whose example had set him on the road to philosophical inquiry. He thus attributed to Socrates everything that he had to say, seeking to perpetuate his influence in the form of dialogue, through the medium of literature.

Plato's various Dialogues evince substantial differences with regard to the problems they treat, the theses they put forward, the methods they follow, the use of plain and unintentional vocabulary, their terminology, and lastly in terms of literary composition. One sometimes encounters highly dramatic dialogue scenes worked out to the last detail, and sometimes no more than a dialogue framework for more or less coherent statements. Over a century of work on all these differences has resulted in a suggested chronology of the Dialogues, and hence a picture of the development of Plato himself as both philosopher and writer. There is still some disagreement over details, however. Even the authenticity of some Dialogues remains to be definitively established, although their main characteristics may now be regarded as defined.

They begin with a group of Dialogues which are unquestionably similar to the inquiries formerly conducted by Socrates in order to clarify the meaning of specific concepts within the sphere of ethics – such as the nature of courage (*Laches*), piety (*Euthyphron*), friendship (*Lysis*) or prudence (*Charmides*). These discussions generally end inconclusively, the dialogue partners unable to find an adequate definition. What they do gain, however, is the state of Socratic ignorance, in which all attempts at definition, regardless of whether they derive from vulgar tradition or are ad hoc proposals, are assessed in terms of their consequences and implications and shown to be inadequate. This reveals to the inquiring partners an abundance of different viewpoints and circumstances which would otherwise remain concealed, constituting an essential component of knowledge, which Socrates held to be the essence of virtue. It is thus the path to the unachieved goal that gives such inquiry its merit. The aim is to grasp the essence of piety (or courage or justice) itself, which is present in all pious deeds and persons without being identical with any of these empirical quantities.

This early group of Dialogues also includes two that are of an eminently Socratic character, but which do not take the form of inconclusive dialogues aimed at definition. These are the *Apology*, a fictional defence speech made by Socrates to his judges, and the *Crito*, a short Dialogue following his sentencing in which he refuses to entertain the idea of escape suggested to him. Taken together, these constitute something of a summing up of the life and death of Socrates, and contain some indisputably authentic biographical detail. At the same time, however, they are also documents of Platonic philosophy, using the example of Socrates to demonstrate the never-ending search for sound rational knowledge as the principle underlying the virtuous life.

The next group in this chronology differs from the above in that although they occasionally also contain an attempt to define a concept, most Dialogues are characterised by a highly ingenious and often startling combination of several discussion themes, each complex in itself. Most of the themes are drawn from contemporary philosophy and Sophistic thought. Socrates appears as a self-assured dialogue partner for the latter's proponents, who are well able to defend their doctrines with valid arguments. The structure of these Dialogues thus tends to be adroit and complex, almost entirely dispensing with purely one-to-one discussion, and displaying vitality in the way scenes are developed, as well as a heightened feel for drama in their characterisation of the persons involved.

This group includes the *Gorgias*, which deals with the problem of moral norms going beyond the context of the natural urge towards self-assertion and obtaining the object of desire – i.e. the old Sophistic theme of nature versus convention – together with the question of the nature of rhetoric; the *Protagoras*, which links the question of the teachability of virtue with traditional themes from Sophistic thought, such as the doctrine of the rise of culture and the moral interpretation of poets; the *Cratylus*, which sheds light with enormous wit on the various approaches to language theory prevalent at that time, reducing this complex of problems to the elements by which it is still recognised today, and the *Meno*, which undertakes a comprehensive analysis of the relationship between virtue and rational knowledge – in the process of which it first points out the significance of mathematics in this context.

Many passages in the early Dialogues already evince modes of thought and argument that certainly have no connection with Socrates, but to which the core of Platonic teaching and tradition may be traced. Pure justice, piety or beauty, by virtue of whose indwelling presence a particular encountered phenomenon is perceived to possess any of these qualities, are accessible through the mind only, not through the senses. On the other hand, the fact that the soul is capable through thought of recognising the pious, the just or the beautiful as such in the individual objects possessed by them, but imperfectly, or even in their absence from certain objects, leads to the assumption that in making this recognition the soul is recalling something which was present to it directly in a non-material world, prior to its current existence which is bound to the material world. What thought recognises here, however, is that which gives its distinguishing characteristics to the world of sensory perception.

It is important to grasp that this early stage of the Platonic doctrine of ideas grew out of inquiry into concepts of moral importance. The principles of moral action, applied in specific judgements as to what is just or unjust, are seen as lying both outside human convention and beyond the scope of experience of human nature, in a realm to which the human soul originally belongs, and which is hence only accessible to pure, undisrupted spiritual activity. Knowledge, which according to ancient Greek tradition was equated with moral virtue, thus also pertained to this realm. Socratic searching and questioning is thus none other than the endeavour by the soul to return to that realm and restore cognition of its prevailing conditions. The relative merit of something is thus measured by the degree to which it either furthers or hinders the activity proper to the soul – not by whether it is in agreement with a particular convention, or a natural urge experienced through the senses. It is thus better to suffer injustice than to commit it, while harm done by one person to another is unjust even when it is in retribution for a previous wrong, since it also entails harm to one's own soul.

In this way, moral norms acquired a new binding nature together with their new ontological foundations. The contradiction between unchanging nature and the laws of social life based on changing conventions – first broached by Sophistic thought – seemed to have been resolved.

The deepening of Socrates' moral speculation outlined here was based on religious premises that Plato seems to have adopted from the Pythagorean tradition, chiefly those of the pre-existence and immortality of the soul. This has far-reaching repercussions apart from notions of morality, creating at the same time an enormous confidence in the potential of rational speculation by placing that which had always constituted the greatest stumbling-block to the free activity of the mind, the confusion of contradictory experience derived from the world of sensory perception, on a level of secondary importance. In this way, Plato's re-establishment and expansion of Socratic rationalism opened up a scarcely quantifiable and wholly new dimension for all philo-sophical and scholarly posterity in terms of the potential for the application of methodical reasoning.

Significantly, Plato's early writings also point to the paramount importance of mathematics to this philosophy, since insight into mathematical laws was seen as taking place independently of experience connected with objects perceived by the senses. Mathematical proof thus also constituted a model of how the soul recognised something that had been present in its previous existence but had been obscured by the world of the senses.

The complete elaboration of the doctrine of ideas, so named after the term *eidos* or *idea* used by Plato to denote intelligible, genuine archetypes, took place in the four major Dialogues of his middle period: the *Symposium*, the *Phaedo*, the *Republic* and the *Phaedrus*. The *Symposium* may unreservedly be described as Plato's most consummate literary work. Six men of diverse character, meeting at a feast in the home of Agathon, the dramatic poet, on the occasion of his first contest victory (which historically occurred in 416 BC), each give a ceremonial address on a single theme: love. Each of them contains, albeit in diverse guises and adapted to suit the situation of the dialogue, philosophical, medical and other opinions on the nature of Eros deriving from the pre-Platonic era, each also being composed in a different prose style, drawn from what was available at the time. Socrates is the last to expound on this theme, with the aid of the doctrine of ideals. He defines Eros as the urge to find perfect and hence enduring beauty – a desire inherent to the human soul, even in its bodily existence. Eros creates the desire for physical beauty with the purpose of procreating a new being whose existence prolongs the limited lifetime of the procreator, at the same time, however, urging the soul to 'beget' moral virtue in the individual and society through the acquisition of knowledge. This produces a series of stages in human growth which cause people first to seek physical, then spiritual beauty in the Other, thereby leading them to find beauty in institutions and laws, and lastly to absolute and eternal beauty through the medium of the highest 'love of wisdom' (philosophy). The Dialogue concludes with the unexpected intrusion of a *komos*, a group of exuberant revellers. Alcibiades, their leader, depicts in a eulogy how this series of stages is revealed in the nature and work of Socrates.

In one major respect, the *Symposium* has shaped theological linguistic usage to this day. In Greek the word *daimon* denoted any divine being when referring to his or her power and force, whereas the word *theos* served as more of an objective designation for deity, devoid of any connotation of experienced power. Plato termed Eros, the human urge for perfection beyond the boundaries of the self, a *daimon* in the sense of a supernatural being mediating between man and the divine. This carried on the traditional usage, which used this term to denote any supernatural force whose effect could be felt without it being possible to name it. Plato's use of the term, however, at the same time makes this usage more precise in the manner described.

The vitality of the *Symposium* contrasts with the earnestness of the *Phaedo*, which seeks to demonstrate the immortality of the soul in a diverse series of broadly drawn lines of argument, set in the context of a simple account of the last hours of Socrates. As in the first part of the *Symposium*, the doctrines and views addressed, refuted and modified by Socrates in this Dialogue derive from earlier philosophical tradition, most particularly Pythagorean, which developed a clearly defined doctrine of the immortality and reincarnation of the soul. This position is represented by two major participants in the Dialogue. The *Phaedo* became the classical work of philosophy understood as the *ars moriendi*. Death brings the philosopher liberation from the constraints of the service to which he is called in this world – to act as a sentry. The soul is to return to the home that it has never ceased methodically to recall in its bodily existence; it is now able to live on in an unalloyed state of pure existence instead of being constrained by the sensory impressions of the constant cycle of growth and decay.

The monumental scheme of the *Republic* is nowadays regarded as Plato's magnum opus. The first of its ten books, with its opening dialogue on justice, still poses an unsolved problem. Although thematically appropriate, this preliminary exploration is historically and compositionally out of step with the other nine books, being more akin to an aporetic definition dialogue of Plato's early period. The main body of the text expounds on the ideal form of state organisation and its institutions, particularly those concerned with educating the class responsible for running them. It draws on all aspects of the Platonic doctrine of ideas or forms – the conception of another, non-material world accessible only to thought, to which our own world of sensory perception, bound to matter, is related inasmuch as it consists of imperfect reflections of perfect ideal archetypes. Since, he argues, the human soul properly belongs in the intelligible sphere, being only temporarily present in

186

the empirical world, correct insight into the nature of the soul also makes knowledge of the higher realm of being accessible. In order to understand the soul, however, one must examine the human social order that is shaped by the forces at work in the soul, since the individual only matures spiritually by belonging to the *polis*.

Plato thus explains the structure of the human soul in terms of three components of progressively increasing importance (desire, courage and intellect), which are duplicated in a similar structuring of society into three estates (pertaining to sustenance, defence and education). The best possible conditions or modes of conduct (virtues) for the various components of the soul and their corresponding estates are prudence, courage, insight and justice, a fourth virtue that relates to all parts of the soul and all three estates.

There are marked parallels between cognisance and being, whose lower sphere, that of becoming, is given life by the sun, and is in turn subdivided into two planes – representations, and living beings and objects respectively. Superior to this realm is a likewise dual sphere of unchanging being, accessible only to thought, in which the prevailing force bestowing life and order is the idea of the Good, and which is made up of mathematical entities and ideas.

This total of four planes of being is matched by four levels of cognisance. The lower sphere pertains to the imaginative faculty, which is made possible by sunlight and is subdivided into conjecture and conviction. The higher pertains to a form of thought characterised by reasoning of a dual nature, the superior form of which bears the name of dialectic. This designation reflects Plato's view of the dialogue-like nature of every act of cognisance, also put forward with a different emphasis in his *Symposium*.

Many of the institutions recommended by Plato for his ideal state arise directly out of his ontological premisses. When, for example, he goes against all Greek tradition by rejecting poetry as an educational medium, this is supported by the assertion that the poet creates only representations of representations, thereby distracting the soul from knowledge of higher levels of existence. Other facets, such as his consistent elimination of all democratic features, can also be justified in ontological terms, but probably derive ultimately from his aristocratic credo. In the wake of disenchantment with radicalised Athenian democracy, this view was shared by many of his contemporaries, thereby showing the earlier Spartan constitution in a new light.

Plato clearly demarcates the point where an assertion reaches the limits of what is accessible through rational and dialectical argumentation. The Platonic order of existence, bound up as it is with the doctrine of the transmigration of souls, suggests a deterministic understanding of human behaviour, although the Socratic legacy Plato had taken up was rendered valueless without the assumption of freedom of choice. Plato supplies a solution to this problem at the end of the whole work in a myth invented by himself. This outlines a grandiose picture of what the soul encounters after death, of the judgement passed on it and of its preparation to enter a new body. Concerning the latter,

Plato stresses that the soul chooses its own lot in life for its bodily existence. He thus gives an affirmative answer to the question of moral choice, while nevertheless removing it to a plane that is closed to rational verification.

Plato also wrote myths, like the one about Er, son of Armenius, for other contexts. The *Gorgias* thus concludes with a grandiose description of the judgement of the dead in the underworld that incorporates motifs from the Orphic tradition. These passages number among the finest pieces of narrative prose in the Greek literary legacy. Myths requiring interpretation, and on themes that cannot be traced back to a discursive line of thought, need to be distinguished from similes, which are often likewise composed with great linguistic skill, but which are invariably intended to illustrate a reproducible line of thought. The best-known of these is the cave allegory in the *Republic*, which depicts the step-by-step ascent to knowledge.

The *Phaedrus* excels for one magnificently elaborated allegory characterising the human soul as a chariot harnessed to unevenly matched horses. Its skilfully composed scenery and its assumption of the doctrine of ideas, to some extent made formally explicit, place this Dialogue in Plato's middle phase, although it has some features in common with his later works.

Up to the *Republic* the Dialogues reveal a steady growth and enrichment in Plato's philosophy, which, although veering far from its Socratic origins, never necessitates an express revision or refutation of previously reached positions. The monumental construction of the *Republic* preserves all previous drafts of partial schemes, even allowing for substantial modifications. The works that came after the *Republic* give if anything an even stronger impression of a scholar constantly re-examining innumerable details of his monumental design in terms of their possible consequences. He is similarly constantly at pains to take into account fresh approaches and material from observation, not infrequently leading to conclusions that contradict his earlier scheme, and ultimately even reassessing problems long since dealt with, again resulting in fresh conclusions.

The biographical details behind this work by the now elderly Plato are not known. It may be assumed, however, that his unabated appetite for posing fresh questions was not unconnected with the presence of numerous productive and original thinkers among the students of the Academy, who included Eudoxus the mathematician and Aristotle.

With some exceptions, Plato's later works dating from his old age are marked by a decline in the meticulous linguistic and stylistic care of their composition, though of course there are exceptions to this. Dialogues lose their drama, dialogue scenes often being no more than outlined; insights are increasingly conveyed in the form of ready-made discourses, and no longer arise out of dialogue – a trend already discernible in parts of the *Republic*. Sentence structure becomes more cumbersome, and the diction generally falls short of the charm and fluidity of the portrayal of discussion characteristic of the early and middle periods. Plato's predilection for the oral mode, including expressions of courtesy or irony as well as the conventional idioms of everyday speech, had initially gone so far as even to avoid many of the seminal terms laid down in the terminology of his philosophy, not infrequently leading to major interpretative difficulties. In his late writings, the scholarly and philosophical terminology becomes increasingly fixed. A reliable indication of this is the increasing incidence of Ionic loan words, adopted from specialist terminology, or foreign words coined according to its rules.

The *Phaedrus* deals among other things with a problem that seemed to have been definitively resolved in the *Gorgias*: the pedagogical importance of rhetoric, formerly classified by Plato as a pseudo-art concerned solely with appearances. The *Phaedrus* revises this conclusion to the extent of asserting that certain aims in rhetorical training call for knowledge that relates to being, thereby salvaging the discipline as a whole from condemnation. These aims revolve around the laws governing the line of argument leading to demonstration of probability, and the knowledge of the human soul required by the orator in order to influence it. (A treatment of these two problem areas also forms the main substance of Aristotle's *Rhetoric*.)

The *Philebus* likewise readdresses and reanswers the question of the importance of desire for the best possible human state, eudaemonia, already dealt with in the *Gorgias*. Plato's reawakened interest in this theme may be attributable to the contemporary presence of Eudemus of Rhodes among his body of students (see below, p. 201). The *Theaetetus*, whose eponymous hero was one of the pre-eminent mathematicians of his day, deals with the relationship between perception, cognition and knowledge, involving a comprehensive analysis of both earlier (Heraclitus, Protagoras) and contemporary (Aristippus, Antisthenes) doctrines. Although reminiscent of early Platonic writings, on closer examination it goes further than they do.

Three Dialogues, the *Parmenides*, the *Sophistes* and the *Politicus*, examine in their respective specialist fields all the difficulties arising out of the application of Eleatic ontology and logic to the doctrine of forms. One particularly knotty problem proved to be that of how to picture the participation of specific objects in the empirical world in the eternal forms to which they owe their existence. The Eleatic tradition, going back to Parmenides, initially taught a clear distinction between being on the one hand, and growth and decay on the other, classifying the latter with sensory perception, the former with thought, in terms of cognitive theory. In the Dialogue bearing his name Parmenides thus features as an instructive discussion partner of the young Socrates. This prosopographic fiction, as well as the substantial limitations placed on the doctrine of ideas in the work, indicate that Plato never regarded his philosophy as complete.

The *Timaeus*, probably the last work in the corpus completed by Plato, was regarded as his magnum opus in later antiquity. It became an early subject for commentary and later for numerous translations into Latin, the first by Cicero. The Dialogue contains a comprehensive cosmology in the form of a creation myth, taking the doctrine of ideas as its basis, also making use of the theories of Democritus, but being predominantly conceived in terms of Pythagorean speculation on numbers and proportions. In this way, even the title figure in the only loosely composed discussion appears as a Pythagorean. The rationally comprehensible order of creation, capable of being expressed in numerical quantities, is seen as suggesting its character as a spiritual entity. The cosmology in the *Timaeus* is systematically explained in all its aspects, including a comprehensive anthropology encompassing even medical details. This makes the work convincing evidence of the energy with which Plato applied himself in his later years to an investigation of the empirical world – just as, in another way, are also his efforts at classification in the 'Eleatic' Dialogues, and those passages in his *Laws* concerned with the history of law.

Efforts to place the *Timaeus* within Plato's works as a whole have given rise to considerable controversy. The cosmology it puts forward presumes a doctrine of ideas, with no consideration of any of the objections dealt with in the 'Eleatic' Dialogues, and yet linguistic and literary criteria suggest that it should be placed after them. Solutions proposed by recent research tend either towards ascribing the *Timaeus* an early date, or towards the assumption that Plato's aim here was to expound on Pythagorean theory rather than his own views. This latter suggestion nevertheless goes against Aristotle's reading of the work, and indeed against the whole tradition of the Platonic school. It might be concluded from Plato's presentation of his cosmology in mythical form, as a piece of fictional prose, that he regarded this theme as one which could not be dealt with comprehensively in the form of discursive argument – like the problem in the *Gorgias* of the metaphysical basis of justice in the order of creation, or that of human freedom of choice in the *Republic*. In this case, his use of an ontological model that was obsolete in certain aspects, although nevertheless still valid overall, would not have been unacceptable.

The *Timaeus* is cast as a continuation of the *Republic*, and is in turn continued by the *Critias*, an incomplete Dialogue intended to deal with the theme of human prehistory. The extant work contains the famous myth of the ancient state of Atlantis, lost in the sea without trace. This myth is narrated with such mastery that despite Plato's unmistakable indication that it is a fictional account the search for traces of the lost continent continues to this day.

The twelve-book *Laws* constitutes Plato's lengthiest work, but it is not certain that all of it is from his pen. The text as a whole lacks a clear compositional concept. Its numerous separate analyses deal with all questions regarding practicable state organisation. It emerges as a second-best to what is set out in the *Republic*, however, since although the overall ontological aims of the latter make its practical political suggestions of highly relative value, there is no doubting Plato's interest in practical politics and the ordering of community life. In this respect, he was a typical representative of the educated class in his native city, viewing the state and constitution first and foremost as instruments for the education of its citizens – a conviction already voiced in the *Gorgias*. Plato's later works, such as the *Politicus*, focused primarily on the best possible qualifications for a statesman and the most effective laws. The work which derived its title from the latter theme offers an exhaustive discussion of its various historical, legal, theological, moral, pedagogical and psychological aspects, occasionally veering substantially from earlier Platonic doctrines. The *Laws* has an addendum, the *Epinomis*, attributed by ancient scholars to Philip of Opus, one of Plato's pupils. With its Pythagorean propensity for mathematical speculation and cosmologically based piety, it forms part of the late Platonic philosophy also to be found in the *Timaeus*, which may have shaped oral teaching in the Academy and certainly shaped the first eighty years of scholarly tradition after the death of Plato.

The full wealth of Plato's life work may be illustrated by examining the impact of its sundry aspects and motifs on the various branches of philosophical tradition, often in widely separated historical periods. We shall be dealing in due course with Aristotle's own elaboration of Platonic philosophy.

The initial period in the Platonic scholarly tradition in the strict sense of the term, beginning with Plato's nephew Speusippus's time as head of the Academy, and carried on by Xenocrates, Polemon, Crates and Crantor, who died in 270 BC, witnessed the crystallisation of a rigid body of dogma based on the *Timaeus* and select passages from the middle and late works. Some application of Plato's later oral teaching style will also have been involved. These early Academics ultimately furthered scholarship through their constantly renewed attempts to master and order empirical reality by means of the principles of classification provided by this system, despite both their departure from inquiry as such, and the fact that their speculation was largely governed by religious concerns. Crantor, the last in this group, also became the father of an enduring special tradition in popular philosophy as the author of a famous work of condolence.

The next period, which lasted about 150 years, saw a decrease in attempts to establish fixed dogma, and the concomitant development of a methodical scepticism with which to draw on the *ars nesciendi* of Socrates. The dogmatically fixed theories of the new schools, the Epicureans and the Stoics (see below, p. 235), were contested with a steady stream of fresh arguments, as was the validity of results from various disciplines, not least the practices of astrology and divination acknowledged by the Stoics, which were shown to be deceptive. The first representative of this 'middle' Academy was Arcesilaus, and its most renowned Carneades, whose pupil Hanno, Cleitomachus (in Greek) of Carthage, taught up to the threshold of the first century BC.

In the first century the Academy reverted to a closed dogmatic system, based on Plato's later theories and the work of his first successors. This shift occurred against the backdrop of a rising classicist movement, reflected in philosophy in a restriction to the major works of the fifth and fourth centuries as the sole sources of knowledge. Seneca expressed this in terms of philosophy threatening to become philology (see below, p. 194). The transition to this new phase is associated with the names of Philo of Larissa and Antiochus of Ascalon, tutor of Cicero. Antiochus adopted into this dogmatic system whole areas of Stoic doctrine that were quite alien to the school, particularly in psychology and ethics. This syncretism, to which centuries of debate surrounding Hellenistic philosophy led, became the hallmark of philosophy in the Imperial age, alongside a tendency to expect all insight to come from correct interpretation of Classical authors.

The chief focus of this Platonically derived philosophy was on cognition of transcendent being as the true reality, and the human soul poised between the empirical and transcendental spheres. This philosophy was to culminate in Neoplatonism, which contributed to Christian dogma, thus making Platonic thought the basis of intellectual life in western civilisation.

As regards the literary merits of Plato's works, it may be said that he commanded a superlative mastery of all available varieties of prose, ranging from urbane conversation, in which 'perhaps' actually means 'definitely' and to which all pomposity is anathema, to elaborate ostentatious diction formulated according to all the rules of the art. This is apparent from many passages in his works in which he avails himself of diverse forms, sometimes in earnest, sometimes with irony and parody. Over and above this, however, his commitment to inquiry, theology and ethics enabled him to expand the potential for a highly artistic discourse that could be distinguished from everyday speech by its use of metaphors and figures of speech, tone and rhythm – hitherto the privilege of poetry. By that period, poetic vehicles seem to have become hackneyed through overuse, or to have become all too ready to hand, therefore being regarded by Plato as unsuitable for expounding on the religious and moral consequences of philosophical inquiry with the necessary gravity. Plato's myths and similes, as well as many of his dialogue passages, are true prose poems, serving similar ends with respect to educational psychology as does, for example, fifth-century tragedy.

The rivalry between artistic prose and poetry as vehicles for educational psychology has already been touched on in connection with Gorgias (pp. 149ff.). Whereas the latter, however, based his work on reflection on the potential for educational psychology of prose presentation, thereby arriving at a strict regulation of artistic prose, Plato's philosophical process of cognition called for an appropriate linguistic form on account of its religious and pedagogical implications. The rivalry between what were to become the two major forces to be reckoned with in education, philosophy and rhetoric (see below, p. 283), can thus be traced back from its very beginnings to a clearly discernible controversy as to principles, even with regard to the correct choice of linguistic medium.

Plato's literary virtuosity is inseparable from his reflection on the nature of literature, as evinced by numerous passages from dialogues of various dates. The *Ion*, an early Dialogue, thus deals with the difficult relationship in all art between inspiration and craftsmanship; Plato's observations on the concept of beauty in the *Symposium* and the *Phaedrus* laid the ontological foundations, in the context of his doctrine of ideas, for an understanding of the work of art and how it comes about, while those passages of the *Republic* and the *Laws* concerned with literature and music expound on the moral and pedagogical aspects of art. Although not in a self-contained form, Plato's theory of art, as set out in many separate discussions, follows on from earlier observations on the subject, accessible chiefly in the work of Aristophanes (see above, p. 138). From the fourth century, the theory of art remained an inseparable part of literary life. From that time onwards there was no more 'naive' writing in Greece, since writers or poets could not credibly carry out their aims without making theoretical efforts concerning the conditions and laws which governed writing. Prose and poetry were thus henceforth accompanied by a steadily growing body of literary theory. Similarly, the interaction between practice and the theory from which literary criticism drew its criteria as it gradually established itself also became a new topic within literary history.

It is virtually impossible to give an accurate assessment of the other out-standing fourth-century philosopher in the context of a literary history. Aristotle's many works, aimed at a broad readership, and hence composed in literary, often dialogue form, have survived solely in quotations by later authors and in an account of the constitution of the state of Athens that came to light with a papyrus find. Our picture of Aristotle the writer, who was accorded high praise by no less than Cicero, is thus highly sketchy. Only occasionally do passages of his scholarly works, composed without literary ambitions, such as the end of his *Nicomachean Ethics*, give some idea of his mastery of language.

His *Protrepticus*, an admonition addressed to a Cypriot ruler, exerted a particularly powerful impact. In Socratic–Platonic style, it advocates the study of philosophy as the sole discipline capable of providing a sound moral basis for all political activity, especially that of rulers. The vigour of this philo-sophical protreptic can largely be explained in terms of the sense of rivalry felt by philosophers, and the perceived threat to their position, vis à vis institu-tions for rhetorical training, which claimed equal authority.

Cicero incorporated Aristotle's *Protrepticus* into his own *Hortensius* – the work that inspired Augustine to study philosophy. Few unequivocally verbatim fragments are now extant, but the *Protrepticus* written by Iamblichus the Neoplatonist (fourth century AD) permits some reconstruction of the main lines of thought in Aristotle's original.

The situation is much the same with other exoteric writings by Aristotle composed in literary form for a broad readership: it is possible to work out some idea of their content, but the compositional structure from which the scholarly world for centuries derived its notions of Aristotle as a writer has been irrevocably lost.

The surviving corpus of Aristotle's written works comprises a collection of lecture manuscripts or transcripts, originally used only for teaching purposes and not published in book form. This was used in the first century BC as a basis for books compiled using the texts themselves with later additions, explanatory notes, a combination of various lectures on a single theme, and rough passages comprising key-words – clearly recognisable as working papers. This is obvious, for example, from the work known today as the *Metaphysics* – an umbrella title for a compilation of separate but sometimes mutually related and overlapping lectures on specific themes in ontology – for which Aristotle coined the term 'first philosophy'. During the editing process these separate papers were compiled into a book of thirteen papyrus scrolls and assigned a place after Aristotle's lectures on natural theory (*Physics*), likewise collated in book form. It is from this that the later term 'metaphysics' derives, meaning simply 'after the treatises on physics'.

Of the three works on ethics in the extant collection, the *Eudemian* and *Nicomachean Ethics* precisely reflect both the consonant and divergent features one would expect from the theoretical development of Aristotle's thought in his middle and later life. The third, however, known as the *Magna Moralia*, contains in addition to wholly Aristotelian sections some passages that presume specific theories of Theophrastus, Aristotle's successor as head of the school. In other cases, such as the *Problems*, which is a collection of discourses on diverse subjects, mainly natural science, the process of collating material continued until well into the Hellenistic period. Even after the first completed editions of these instructional works, however, up to the first century AD pieces continued to be added to the collection, of which some are of a literary character, such as *De Mundo*. The way in which these instructional works were collated and edited stems from the fact that from the first century BC onwards the great thinkers of the fourth century BC were increasingly seen as classic authors, the doctrines of later scholars being backed by exegesis of their works. The same century similarly saw the beginning of a long spate of commentaries on Plato and Aristotle of which many examples are extant, mostly dating from late antiquity. (A parallel phenomenon is also observable in the purely literary sphere, in which fourth-century Attic prose literature likewise came to set the norms for language and style in the first century BC.) The credit for collating, classifying and advancement of Aristotle's instructional works, as well as for perpetuating the biography of the school's founder, is attributed mainly to the Peripatetic scholar Andronicus (approx. 70 BC).

Aristotle came from the colonial town of Stagira in southern Macedonia. He spent twenty years as the pupil and companion of Plato at the Academy, going on to teach and study among groups of Plato's friends, first at Assos in Asia Minor, at the court of a semi-independent dynasty in the Persian Empire, and then on the island of Lesbos, the birthplace of his closest friend and successor Theophrastus. Later he was invited to the Macedonian court to tutor the young Alexander. In 334 BC, having completed this assignment, he returned to Athens, where he founded his own school at the sanctuary of Apollo Lykios (*Lykeion*: hence the term 'lyceum'), sometimes known as the Peripatus on account of its covered walks. When Athens made a renewed attempt to shake off Macedonian suzerainty on receiving news of Alexander's death, Aristotle's close ties with Macedonia compelled him to leave the city. He died the following year in 322 BC at Chalcis in Euboea.

As Werner Jaeger (1948) in particular has shown, in the second half of his life Aristotle's thought took off in directions that veered considerably from the Platonic views he had started out with. He thus resolved, or rather dispensed with, the problem posed by Platonic dualism – how to envisage the involvement of the world of the senses in transcendent intelligible being – through the concept of three different modes of being, coexisting in a state of constant transition in an undivided world. The sole essence of being was thus seen as being transformed from a state of pure potentiality into actuality, as forming principles took control of unformed matter, and from there into complete fulfilment of being known as entelechy (perfection). This metaphysics opened up entirely new paths for the organised comprehension of the empirical world, and continues to exert an impact to this day. Similarly, Aristotle developed dialectics or logic as a philosophical discipline in its own right from Plato's art of methodical discourse, also adding observations of his own to Plato's basic approaches to shape ethics and other disciplines with characters and methods of their own. In ethics, for example, he was able to answer the age-old question as to the origins of morally meaningful modes of conduct by reordering in a new mutual relationship the factors used to explain this phenomenon since the rise of Sophistic thought – natural predisposition, practice or habit, and intellectual training. In Aristotle's view, people did not habitually act courageously after having acquired courage as a morally laudable trait. He rather saw this mode of conduct as arising out of practice, on the basis of predisposition, through a sequence of individual acts of courage, each deliberate in the sense of being guided by the use of reason in the given situation. The deliberateness of these individual acts, as well as the tendency arising out of them always to act bravely, is subject to a moral value judgement which bravery as a natural inclination, for example, tends to shun.

Aristotle made a clear distinction between the practical function of reason, as exercised here, and its theoretical function, which enabled people to perceive generally valid truths rather than equip them for action. In this and other of his theories he incorporated both philosophical approaches from Sophistic thought and the received wisdom current in everyday speech. Unlike Plato, who had disdained the 'opinion of the many', he sought to establish a meaningful relationship between the results of methodical inquiry and generally held views, which he took up time and again as a starting point for inquiry. First and foremost, he took pains to convey all the results of his inquiries in plain, matter-of-fact terminology, always coining specialist terms with intelligible origins in everyday usage. Another mark of the new scholarly approach manifested in Aristotle's work was his constant effort to trace and convey the history behind his treatment of a problem before beginning the actual account of his inquiry, thus elucidating the starting point of his own work.

The sheer scope of subject-matter studied and written about by Aristotle, his colleagues and his successors in the first two generations of the school was prodigious. Together with his pupils, he wrote no less than a hundred monographs on the constitutions and constitutional history of Greek states alone. It was on this empirical basis that he elaborated his sweeping vision of state theory, which survives in his *Politics*. Aristotle also systematised in several works the entire zoological knowledge of his time, Theophrastus doing the same for botany, including material purposely collected by scholars of the Peripatus on the Alexandrian campaign. Aristotle organised and collated all the then available instructional works on rhetoric; Theophrastus wrote the first work on the study of religion; Aristoxenus of Tarentum wrote on the theory of music and the Pythagorean tradition; Dicaearchus collected a vast body of material dealing with various topics concerned with sociology or cultural history; Meno worked on medical literature; Straton studied mechanics, astronomy and physics, and other Peripatetics worked in other fields.

Apart from the above-mentioned works, Aristotle himself also wrote on psychology, physics, ethics, politics, literary theory and meteorology, invariably evaluating an extensive body of material from observation as well as previous scholarly inquiry, and likewise managing to systematise all this through a solidly worked out method of inquiry. These achievements, as well as his co-ordination of the work of numerous colleagues, give Aristotle every right to be regarded as the founder of modern scholarship.

Two special works by Aristotle merit closer examination in a history of literature, even though in fact they created no more fresh potential for prose literature than his other scholarly publications. In the *Phaedrus*, Plato had defined the possible subjects of scholarly, i.e. demonstrable, knowledge, as distinct from rhetoric, which dealt with plausible opinion. Aristotle took this scheme a stage further in his *Rhetoric*, which combines treatises on the various forms the demonstration of probability can take, and on the laws governing the reactions of the psyche that can be evoked through speech, with a discussion of the diverse problems of diction as a craft – here going beyond his Platonic inspiration.

As always, Aristotle starts out from the simple givens of the theme under discussion. One of the textbooks on rhetoric housed in his school, perhaps by Anaximenes of Lampsacus, an older contemporary of his, was mistakenly taken for his own, and hence handed down among his writings. It provides a fairly solid notion of the previous specialist work available for his evaluation. Textbooks, or technai, such as the one by Anaximenes, dealt with the art of presenting evidence and how to structure an address – mostly legal speeches, since here was the greatest need for instruction with a sound theoretical basis. Public and ceremonial addresses (see above, pp. 151f.) were nevertheless by then already established as categories of rhetoric in their own right.

Aristotle retained this focus on the legal speech, simply because it afforded him the broadest scope for clarifying the phenomenon theoretically. Earlier textbooks on rhetoric laid down rules derived from practice and systematised according to didactic principles. The fact that of the surviving legal addresses so few actually adhere to the principles laid down by theory is partly attributable to the fact that theory was subordinate to practice, and partly to the understandable growth of a systematic didactic tradition in its own right in this field. Although, therefore, this tradition shaped the character of rhetorical training, in practice speakers were free to dispense with its rules if the need arose.

Although making use of the systematics it had devised, Aristotle went beyond this didactic tradition in his *Rhetoric*. True to the Platonic approach, he dealt with rhetoric by inquiring time and again into the nature of all phenomena which the discipline of rhetorical didactics merely took note of and established normative rules for. Aristotle, for example, discovered a distinction in linguistic form between texts intended for passive reading and texts intended to be read aloud. He derived this from a definition of the extent to which the mimetic function or representation of reality was fulfilled by the text itself or by its being read aloud. This insight established a criterion of literary theory that was applicable far beyond the narrow confines of rhetoric.

The same applies to the relationships established by Aristotle between the evocative or persuasive power of artistic utterance and empirical psychology on the one hand, and logic on the other. Aristotle's inquiries enriched rhetoric with new fixed concepts of diverse applicability, thereby winning a permanent place for this discipline in most of the major Hellenistic philosophical systems. Philosophical rhetoric none the less provided a steady stream of new concepts and categories for an increasingly rich body of literary criticism focused on prose, continuing to exert an enduring impact on prose literature until well into the Imperial period.

Aristotle's *Rhetoric* contains one chapter dealing briefly with the teaching of style – a theme which to the modern reader would seem to merit the lion's share. His inquiries uncovered some basic rhythmic and syntactic morphology in stylised prose locution, as distinct from everyday speech. It was Theophrastus, however, who subsequently published a comprehensive catalogue of all the elements distinguishing artistic from unstylised prose, and it was from this work that the later variously modified theory of the attributes of utterance derives. A descriptive classification of the conceivable morphology of artistic prose – whether grand, ordinary or simple in style – likewise first seems to have been elaborated by scholars of the early Peripatus. The value of the philosophical study of this theme lies in the fact that it pioneered fixed linguistic criteria for defining prose style. This enabled linguistic stylisation to be taught in a new way that was no longer dependent on the imitation of set-pieces recognised as models (see above, p. 152).

Other Peripatetics of the same generation, for example Hieronymus of Rhodes and Demetrius of Phalerum, also engaged in the study of rhetoric. The Peripatus steadily provided a whole range of literary genres, with a theory that in turn affected literary practice. Theophrastus, for example, and one younger Peripatetic, Praxiphanes, elaborated theories for historiography to which a number of not insignificant third- and second-century historians adhered. Of the earliest examples of literary biography, only Plutarch's life histories, written around 100 AD, are known today. All the indications they give concerning, for example, the rules of the art that were followed would nevertheless seem to suggest an early Peripatetic theory of biography. This is borne out by the books on Solon and Themistocles attributed to Phaenias of Eresus, a Peripatetic born around 375 BC, which should at all events be construed as historical biographies.

Key elements of such theories were taken from ethics. Historical events and the careers of individuals were interpreted as examples of correct or false conduct, and then placed within a scheme of ethical typology for which Aristotle himself had collated a wealth of material in his own ethical work. It was by pursuing this approach that Aristoxenus derived his model for the ideal philosophical life from the legends surrounding the life of Pythagoras, that Dicaearchus and Theophrastus quarrelled over the moral superiority of a life devoted to action or contemplation, and that Clearchus and other Peripatetics analysed normal and abnormal modes of behaviour on the strength of a rich body of historical material. The result was a vast literature primarily intended for the purposes of ethical instruction, but whose subject-matter was also of interest to historians, ancient scholars and storytellers. It thus found a variety of uses in literary tradition both as a source of material and as a basis for literary syllabuses. One of the few surviving works from this field is the *Characters*, in which Theophrastus uses witty depictions of situations to classify typical modes of behaviour arising out of dominant traits in human nature. 'Character' here is thus not at all understood as the individual peculiarities of a personality, which always contains many, often conflicting, characteristics, but as the manifestations of a specific natural attribute of the psyche or moral nature, perhaps particularly conspicuous in one person, such as superstition or garrulousness. Theophrastus' *Characters* thus provides illustrative material for the literature on the virtues and vices that was equally abundant in the Peripatetic tradition.

The rich interaction that unfolded between narrative literary genres and descriptive ethics will be clear from the above. A treatise on the theory of style written by one Demetrius around 100 BC, however, shows that the Peripatus developed its theories for other genres, for example the literary letter, on quite a different basis.

The most important work on literary criticism among Aristotle's writings is his *Poetics*, of which unfortunately only the first book, dealing with epic poetry and tragedy, has survived. Some details of the second book, devoted mainly to comedy, are available from late grammatical treatises, which drew partly on Peripatetic sources.

The theory of poetry put forward by Aristotle in the work does not constitute a completely fresh approach. The brilliant observations of Gorgias, as well as the works of Democritus, have already been touched on above, and Plato also expressed his views on various aspects of the composition and effect of poetry. His estimation of the value of poetry for the educational process proved a particular debating point.

Prior to his *Poetics*, Aristotle wrote a dialogue: *On Poets*. (His *Rhetoric* was similarly preceded by *Gryllus*, a stylised literary dialogue named after an occasional orator.) Another lost work bore the title *Homeric Problems*, which may perhaps be taken as evidence of Aristotle's involvement in the debate surrounding the dating, authenticity, composition and merits of Homeric poetry that arose out of the Sophistic interpretation of this poet, an involvement further confirmed by the stories about Democritus and the late Sophists Zoilus and Alcidamas.

Correctly estimating the value of these documents as sources for literary history, Aristotle published the records of drama performances, known as the didascalia, and the winners' lists of some musical contests, which were kept in the Athenian archive. The material of this kind that he provided was eagerly used by Hellenistic philologists, and hence to some extent survived in Byzantine scholastic commentaries of late antiquity.

According to his *Poetics*, Aristotle regarded tragedy, about whose origins he discovered important information, as the most advanced form of poetry, on the grounds that it combined the attributes of narrative and lyric poetry with the potential for mimesis (representation) in both dialogue and extra-lingual form. Obviously he based his theory on observations of tragedy in his own day, and on the understanding of fifth-century tragedy prevalent at that time. He thus virtually ignores dance and music, which were a substantial component of stage plays for fifth-century audiences, concentrating on defining the character of tragedy in purely literary categories, related to the language of dramaturgy. (Significantly, in Aristotle's time there were already dramas intended purely for reading purposes.) This enabled him to focus entirely on an analysis of the typical tragic plot, and hence to explain the effects of tragic poetry from the features of successful drama which he ascertained in the process.

Aristotle formulated the results of this analysis in terms that have dominated normative poetics since the Renaissance, whether the theories later elaborated on its basis were accepted or not. He thus expounds on the dramatic importance of peripeteia, a necessary component of the tragic plot which transforms misfortune into fortune, or vice versa, for the main protagonists.

Peripeteia is often identical with anagnorisis, when the hero perceives the true nature or identity of a person, a false assessment of whom has thus far governed his actions.

Aristotle likewise discerned that in a good dramatic plot that grips the audience fortune and misfortune should not be dealt out according to a simplistic scheme of reward and punishment. He also specifically states that neither the virtuous hero nor the arch-villain can arouse the sympathies of the audience in fortune or misfortune, since their characters are beyond our experience. The human failings which Aristotle regards as the driving motor and complicating factor in the unfolding of the dramatic plot are thus in his view not at all to be understood as moral lapses, but simply as inexpedient acts arising out of an incorrect assessment of the situation – a characteristic of all human beings.

In one famous passage, Aristotle asserts that poetry differs from historiography not in its use of verse, but by being 'more philosophical'. Unlike historiography, poetry describes events which are liable to occur again and again according to the laws of necessity or probability, and which hence command a general validity lacking in the unique circumstances that make up history. It will be clear from this definition why Aristotle was not prepared to accept coincidence as an element in a good tragic plot. (Later theoreticians, including Theophrastus, did not share this view, however.)

These brief remarks reveal that Aristotle was not concerned with what was later defined as 'the tragic'. For him, as the opening lines of his famous definition read, tragedy was the representation of a serious plot leading towards a goal. It was the very fact that Aristotle refrained from theological or moral definitions of classical tragedy, and defined myth purely as plot, which enabled his structural analysis of the dramas he examined to arrive at such illuminating and, for the European drama tradition, widely applicable results, despite what in the eyes of the literary historian was his far from exhaustive description of the character of Classical tragedy.

Plato's verdict on all poetry made it necessary to reach a more detailed understanding of poetic writing in terms of its psycho-educational effects. Aristotle achieved this in the case of tragedy, attributing the empirically demonstrable enjoyment of audiences to 'catharsis'. In his time, the latter was a specialist medical term denoting the excretion of excess or harmful substances from the body. He saw tragedy as first arousing and then resolving fear and sympathy in the soul of the spectator, thereby bringing about a pleasurable experience of liberation. (It is not advisable to use other translated terms than these, current since Lessing's time, for these two emotions. Aristotle was probably obliged by the then available medical theory to couch these emotions, including their remarkable duality, in such terms. Since, however, the details of this medical theory are no longer known, the precise meaning of its terminology has been lost.) The catharsis theory, however, implicitly refuted Plato's conviction that poetry was dangerous.

Aristotle's pupils eagerly continued this study of poetry. This is borne out by works on tragedy and other poetry genres, monographs on special problems such as the use of the chorus in drama, and lastly by works on specific poets. These include works by Aristoxenus the music theoretician, by the versatile Heraclides Ponticus, by Theophrastus, and by Chamaeleon, who wrote monographs on nearly all the major poets.

Later, such studies were also cultivated outside schools of philosophy, at the great libraries. The poetic interests of grammarians employed in libraries, however, were more philological, historical and critical than theoretical in the Aristotelian sense, and were sometimes even straightforwardly moral and pedagogical. The *Ars poetica* by Horace, the second surviving work of ancient poetics, which exerted an impact far beyond antiquity, represents a summary of post-Aristotelian developments. Horace's work includes ideas going back to the great scholar Eratosthenes (see below, p. 297), while the moral and pedagogical effects of poetry are clearly less important to him. His immediate source for the *Ars poetica* seems to have been the poetics of Neoptolemus of Parium, dating from the second or first century BC.

The unity between philosophy and scholarly inquiry that had shaped the large-scale work of the Aristotelian school soon disintegrated. The Peripatetic Demetrius of Phalerum contributed much that was of value to a number of disciplines. He was also one of the right-hand men behind the Macedonian throne, ruling Athens shrewdly and with moderation for ten years. He was forced into exile in 307 BC when Demetrius son of Antigonus seized control of the city. He found refuge with King Ptolemy I of Egypt, and may have had something to do with the founding by the latter's successor, Ptolemy Philadelphus, of the famous *mouseion* (museum), a scholarly institution in Alexandria. It was here in the course of the third and second centuries BC that such disciplines as physics, geography and philology reached their greatest ever flowering, their results often not being surpassed until the nineteenth century. The scholarly work carried out there was a direct continuation of that of the Peripatus, as may be deduced from the convention whereby all scholars in the employ of the museum held the title of 'philosopher', although all engaged in specialist disciplines of which philosophy proper was only one. Aristotle had expressly subsumed all forms of methodical scholarly inquiry after truth under the heading of philosophy, and his school adhered to this term for some considerable time.

Alexandrian scholars could naturally also draw on other fourth-century achievements, since Aristotle had by no means held a monopoly on scholarship. Even Eudoxus of Cnidus cannot be assigned to any particular scholarly tradition, although he worked at Plato's Academy for a time. He elaborated some original theories on ethics which are referred to by Plato in his *Philebus*, and might be regarded as the most productive mathematician, astronomer and geographer of his time. Traditional medical institutions – Cos and Cnidus in the east, and Metapontum and Locri in the west – continued to produce able physicians. We might mention here Praxagoras of Cos in connection with his extensive written work, of which only fragments are extant.

Even during the Hellenistic period, Athens continued to be the main centre for philosophy, although this discipline took on a new, non-Platonic, non-Aristotelian character in the major systems constructed around 300 BC.

As far as literary presentation of the results of scholarly inquiry is concerned, the work of the Peripatus in the fourth century BC brought about the definitive victory of Attic and the later common language that derived from it. Even eminent physicians now abandoned the use of Ionic associated with the Hippocratic tradition – first Diocles of Carystus in Euboea, who had close ties with the Peripatus. Extracts from his works have survived in a fourth-century AD compilation by Oribasius, personal physician to the Emperor Julian. The fact that not only the philosophical (in the narrower sense of the term) works of Democritus have been lost, but also his major writings on natural science, may perhaps also be attributed to this change in the language of scholarship.

13

RHETORIC

As shown above, by the end of the fifth century BC oratory was increasingly featuring in public life in the form of a learnable technique, side by side with the theory of rhetoric, which was cultivated for didactic purposes. The moral, pedagogical and political implications of this trend involved philosophy, whose approach to rhetoric has already been examined above in Chapter 12 on Plato and Aristotle. By around 400 BC a man who wrote speeches for others and taught the principles of the art of rhetoric was very much part of the Athenian scene, publishing not only authentic speeches, but also model fictitious ones. This presupposes the existence of a reading public with a taste for such works and the capacity to appreciate their technical prowess. The ancient custom of reading everything aloud helps to explain why the distinction between a real speech and a contrived literary piece was less clear-cut then than it is now. However, the dominant role of the speech composed for performance as a subject for literary theory may be explained by the need for a theoretical assessment and didactic accommodation of the prose genre, which first arose out of the importance of oration for public life.

In Plato's *Phaedrus* Lysias, born in the mid-fifth century BC as the son of a wealthy metic from Syracuse named Cephalus, represents the new educational force. Later too he was honoured as one of the classic Attic orators. He was to acquire citizenship in Thurii in Lower Italy, but was forced into exile in 412 as a pro-Athenian, thereafter living on the strength of his political credit as a privileged metic in Athens. He became wealthy as a manufacturer, but as a fervent democrat had to face periodic danger and exile.

Lysias' fame derives from his authorship of legal speeches and his teaching of rhetoric. No less than 425 speeches attributed to him were read in antiquity, of which 230 were regarded as genuine. The large number of inauthentic ones should not cause surprise. Since nothing like all legal and political speeches were published by their authors, after the death of famous orators searches tended to be undertaken in the legal and other records of both state and private archives to find their unpublished works. Not infrequently the speeches of other authors came to light and were included in collections published as the work of famous names. This need not be attributed to deliberate deception.

The thirty-one extant speeches of the Lysian corpus also contain a number of inauthentic speeches of diverse origins.

In post-Classical antiquity, Lysias came to be regarded as a master of straightforward style. In fact he developed his faculties most conspicuously where his aim was to give a graphic account of a particular aspect of Athenian everyday life, rendering plausible the course of events on which the legal claim of a party was based through the clarity and straightforwardness of his narrative. The ceremonial address composed by Lysias for Greeks assembled at the 396 BC Olympic games sets out his democratic creed, but is ineffectual by comparison.

In the first speech of the corpus, Lysias masterfully passes off a highly dubious incident as entirely in accordance with the law. He achieves this largely through minute depiction of detail and by sustaining an innocuous, guileless-sounding tone suited to the speaker, which lends credibility to his account. According to Attic law, a husband was permitted to go unpunished for killing an adulterer caught *in flagrante delicto* with his wife. In this particular case, however, the defendant had obviously lured his wife's seducer back into his house and killed him with the assistance of neighbours, making what would have been regarded under the law as permissible manslaughter into premeditated murder. The plea elaborated by Lysias necessitated bringing all possible means into play to create a powerful impression of the trustworthy inoffensiveness of the defendant, and blandly passing off the events concerned as a case of the legally permissible manslaughter of an adulterer caught *in flagrante delicto*. Lysias achieves this effect partly by having the defendant himself give an apparently naively laborious and meticulous account of the attendant circumstances, which are a welcome source of insight for cultural historians into the private life of the day, but contribute next to nothing to the legal assessment of events. His legal speech pursues the goal of presenting the events as manslaughter by means of urgent allusions to the moral justification of the law permitting the killing of an adulterer caught *in flagrante delicto*. The jury will undoubtedly have concurred with this, while perhaps forgetting in the process that the key issue in this case was whether or not this particular law applied.

Even in antiquity, Lysias was applauded for his consummate ability to convey through his wording the thoughts and reactions of those for whom his speeches were written. The ethos he thereby invoked by no means had to concur with the true character of the speaker. Instead, it offered, as it were, a character sketch drawn up with an eye to obtaining the favour of the judge and increasing the credibility of the presentation – without, of course, slipping into the improbable. Typically for the tradition of legal speeches, in accomplishing this difficult task Lysias refrains from imitating the everyday idiom of his various clients. The diction of his speeches is homogeneous, and consistently clear and decorous. Its transparency appears to conceal no depths or shallows, the presentation of both the persons speaking and those being described deriving almost invariably from the arrangement of facts being related. This may be one of the reasons why such petitions continued to be read as great literature for centuries to come – long after their legal implications or factual substance had ceased to be of interest.

Paradoxically, the linguistic finesse that grew out of this theoretically categorised art of the legal speech was partly the outcome of an extremely crude judicial system, in which the democratic institution of the jury court was used, or rather misused, to resolve any and every political or social dispute in a way inconceivable to us. Judges were thus more inclined to interpret controversial cases in terms of so-called common sense or sentiment than to reduce issues to their juristic essence in terms of abstract notions of law. This is particularly clearly illustrated by the most amusing speech in the Lysian corpus, which forms the defence by an invalid against an action brought by a kind neighbour disputing his state pension on the grounds of the invalid's alleged assets and fitness for work. Lysias seeks to soften the judge by making him laugh with a blend of impudence, servility and clowning. He nevertheless achieves this for the most part with audacious arguments, rather than with impertinent or vulgar expressions. The fact raised in the action, that the defendant could frequently afford the hiring charge for a mount, is thus presented as proof of the gravity of his physical disability, and conversely the fact that no one called on him to carry out responsible duties or occupy senior public office as proof of his destitution.

Lysias wrote one particularly famous speech in which a man defended himself against the charge of having felled on his land an olive tree that had been cultivated from an offshoot of a tree planted by the goddess Athena on the Acropolis. (Such sacred olive trees existed throughout Attica, protected by sacral law, and not infrequently also interfered with the use of the land.) With immense virtuosity the speech employs intricate proofs to demonstrate the non-existence of the offence, i.e. that there had never been an olive tree on this tract of land. This speech helps towards an understanding of how the affinity between the rhetorical demonstration of probability and logic was one of the reasons why Plato and Aristotle included rhetoric in the discipline of philosophical reflection.

Whereas in Plato's *Phaedrus* Socrates summarily dismisses the work of Lysias for falling short of true scholarship, he dubs Isocrates, some ten years his junior, the future exponent of a 'more philosophical' rhetoric. This assertion by the already ageing Plato may for a number of reasons be construed as tongue-in-cheek, since his school was an open rival of that of Isocrates. Nevertheless there can be no doubt that Isocrates' school was the first to raise the art of oratory to a major force to be reckoned with in education, to hold its own beside philosophy for centuries to come.

Isocrates died at the age of 98, shortly after the Battle of Chaeronea (338 BC) had definitively put an end to Greece's independence. At the age of 82 he published a greatly expanded version of a fictitious legal speech designed in defence against a petition to exchange assets. (Attic law made provision for the option of shifting onto a fellow citizen the burden of special taxes on the individual, such as the arming of a war ship, by offering him an exchange of assets.) From the published edition of this speech, Isocrates created the first autobiography accessible to us. Since, moreover, his *Against the Sophists* is also extant, in which he outlines his educational plan, opposed to philosophy and old-style rhetoric, for the founding of his school shortly before 380 BC, information about his plans and successes is very precise.

Isocrates was born into a respectable but impoverished Athenian family, and at first earned his living as a logographer – an author of legal speeches, of which some not very original examples which have survived. Isocrates later came to despise this kind of work, taking considerable pains to cover over the traces of his earlier life wherever possible, leading Aristotle to make a sardonic comment. Details are no longer available as to how he acquired his knowledge of Gorgianic theories. Clearly, however, his concerted efforts to make his reinterpreted rhetoric into a vehicle for inculcating virtue into citizens and statesmen would have been unthinkable without Gorgias, while his epoch-making establishment of new norms in prose style similarly marked a consistent continuation of the latter's pioneering work (see below, p. 208).

Isocrates elaborates his educational strategy in his *Against the Sophists* and in the introduction to a set-piece for oratory exercises, the *Encomium of Helen*. For him, certain knowledge was not the province of humankind, or if so could only be achieved in the form of futile hairsplitting, as demonstrated by the studies of the philosophers, whom Isocrates calls 'Sophists', acknowledging these only as propaedeutics for training the mind. The crucial thing for him was the cultivation of plausible, morally defensible opinions on major issues, as well as being able to make these opinions comprehensible to one's fellow men at the appropriate moment, and thus never be lost for good advice to precede one's own and others' decisions. For Isocrates, good advice did not lose its value in the chance event of the chosen course of action failing as a result of factors outside human control.

Correct opinions were held to be handed down with tradition and confirmed by the judgement of all reasonable people. That is why Isocrates' school avidly collected and reformulated aphorisms from popular tradition. The ability to communicate through speech, however, had to be painstakingly learned and practised. In Isocrates' view, the Socratic technique of conversation was inadequate for this purpose, as was the technique for composing legal speeches put forward in the standard handbooks by Theodectes, Anaximenes, Euenus and others, or even the art of extempore speech on chosen themes, as put forward in the surviving work of Alcidamas. Isocrates set greater store by a command of language down to the minutest detail, and its proper adaptation to the subject-matter being communicated. The speech should not only be comprehensible, but should also compel and convince the hearer or reader with its perfect, self-contained form – a very Gorgianic concept.

This strategy made Isocrates the forefather of a western educational tradition in which the effort to cultivate the spoken or written word shaped the educational process. This tradition was to experience a number of historical high points, such as in the humanist period in the fifteenth and sixteenth centuries, and was to hold its own in constant rivalry with philosophical and scientific educational ideals aimed at achieving the cognition of indubitable truths, rather than the cultivation of the possibilities of communication, as the road to educating the individual. It was in the rivalry between the Isocratean and Platonic and Aristotelian schools that this contrast first came to light – the rivals themselves being fully cognisant of its significance.

Although Plato and Aristotle after him refrained from direct involvement in the Athenian political scene, they made serious efforts to exert an influence on political life with their philosophical education, both through their contacts with potentates in various parts of the Greek-speaking world and by sending their pupils as advisers to people in positions of power. The philosopher as political adviser was to be a recurring figure in the centuries that followed. Isocrates, who claimed the title of philosophy for his educational strategy, also competed with the Academy and Peripatus in this field. He enjoyed friendly relations with a Cypriot dynastic family, writing an encomium (an artistic tribute to the virtues of a ruler) of the newly deceased Prince Euagoras, as well as a princely code and scheme of government for his young successor Nicocles: works with which he created two new literary genres. In the above-mentioned legal speech for the exchange of assets case, he reports with legitimate pride the heroic feats of his pupil Timotheus, who indeed proved both the most successful and the most personable military strategist and diplomat in the chequered annals of fourth-century BC Athens.

Besides all this, throughout his long life Isocrates also marked the fortunes of Athens through the advice imparted in his publicist writings. He harnessed all the decorative and stylistic features of traditional public and ceremonial speeches into political literature – pamphlets and brochures intended for reading.

The first major work of this kind is his *Panegyricus*, a testimony to both Athenian and pan-Hellenic patriotism. Isocrates' political goal was the unification of the Hellenic states, with Sparta as the leading land power and Athens the leading maritime power. The purpose of this unification was national war against the Persian Empire with the aim of liberating the Anatolian Greeks, who since 386 BC had again been subject to the Persian emperor. Accordingly, glorious recollections of the Persian Wars formed the ideological foundation of his scheme. There is one new element in this image of ancient heroic Athens, however. Isocrates also sees his native city as an educational centre for all Greeks, and is prepared to accept anyone as a fellow citizen who has had the benefit of an Attic education, in particular its linguistic and rhetorical disciplines.

Isocrates held to his vision of Greek unification despite rapidly shifting power relations, and regardless of whether adjuring the Athenians to exercise political restraint, as in his *On the Peace* following the break-up of the second maritime alliance, or advising them to seek more vigorous, co-ordinated activity with Sparta, as in his *Plataicus* and *Archidamus*, written during the brief period of Theban hegemony. In his latter years, however, he regarded a strong monarchy as the sole possible means of bringing about unification, seeing potential monarchs first in the tyrant Jason of Pherae in Thessaly, and then, correctly as it turned out, in Philip of Macedon. In 346 BC he sent an open letter to Philip to this effect. His last major work, a general praise of Athens, presenting itself as a festival speech at the Panathenaea, but also intended for reading, was composed at the age of 97. A lengthy digression, on the three basic constitutional forms and how to balance them to achieve the ideal state system, reveals once again that reflection on the state and its possible formal organisation was not the privilege of the philosopher, but a theme in which a politically deeply disenchanted general public was passionately interested.

Isocrates was the creator of Classical period form. By pragmatically applying Gorgian figures (see above, p. 150) to complex syntactical structures he made possible the differentiated arrangement and precise presentation of main and sub-themes within complex statements by means of their rhythmical and associated grammatical structure. This rigorously theme-related rhythmical structuring supported the main threads of the text, exerting an instructive effect on the minds of audiences or readers by rendering the conclusion of a clausal structure predictable at a relatively early point, and hence almost inevitably imposing on them the author's line of reasoning.

Again in line with Gorgias' objectives, Isocrates additionally adopted into prose from poetry the device of avoiding hiatus, i.e. disallowing a collision of vocals in the final and initial sounds of two consecutive words. Even Aristotle was unable in his own literary works to disregard this convention established by his rival. As has already been mentioned above, with his encomium and princely code Isocrates created new genres in literary prose and provided them with compositional rules that were to survive into the era of Baroque literature. The same applies to the letter genre, which he probably also raised to the status of a literary form. He similarly made diverse efforts to formulate moral aphorisms, which on account of their congruence of form and theme were particularly well-suited to his educational strategy. He himself said that he regarded himself in this respect as successor to the ancient gnomic poets. It is thus no coincidence that a work known as an *Admonition of Demonicus*, a lengthy collection of prose aphorisms on moral themes probably compiled in the fourth century BC, came to be included among his works. Confidence in the correctness of moral insights from the vulgar tradition, and the belief that these only needed to be rephrased in memorable form, likewise continued to distinguish later rhetoric-oriented from philosophy-oriented education, the latter in contrast pursuing the never-ending acquisition of fresh knowledge. These two approaches are expounded in exemplary fashion in Aristotle's *Protrepticus* for Themison and Isocrates' princely code for Nicocles.

Isocrates' impact was enormous. By consistently transposing the rules for live oration to literature intended for reading, as well as enriching the latter by some new genres, he showed how any kind of stylised prose could be composed according to exclusively rhetorical categories, and no less important-antly evaluated with them. What for the modern reader constitutes the obscure 'rhetorical' character of all Greek prose literature from the fourth century onwards is rooted in the work of Isocrates. Rhetoric, raised by Isocrates to the status of an educational institution, is responsible for the astounding fact that the extant assortment of Greek prose literature owes its survival only peri-pherally to its content, that an enormous amount of extremely valuable literature was lost because highly specific stylistic features in the relevant works were not appreciated at the time, and that the entire body of ancient scholars measured the merits of historiographical achievements almost exclusively by their compositional and stylistic qualities – an idea quite alien to us now.

By the time of Isocrates' death, Athens had definitively been relegated to small-town status by international standards – whereas its eminence in intellectual circles was upheld as much by Isocrates as the philosophy schools. By the fourth century BC the scholar had to be able to speak and write in the offices of the Macedonian king or at the court of a potentate in Asia Minor – as taught by Isocrates. The number of his former pupils to be found in various branches of literature (we shall be encountering two of them as historiographers) was so vast that the Alexandrian scholar Hermippus wrote a book about them.

Although the cultured prose of the Hellenistic era underwent a gradual initial deviation from the stylistic ideals of Isocrates, the character of his established norms remained undisputed. The classicism of the first century BC was to return to these ideals, elaborating a model for good and 'pure' expression that has continued to shape even modern written Greek. The remaining orators whose work extended into the later fourth century BC were all men engaged in legal or political life. Among them was Isaeus, a metic like Lysias, whose extant speeches are of no particular literary merit, but are of interest to the legal historian on account of the complex cases of inheritance they deal with. His pupil Demosthenes, born in 384 BC, was the greatest of all Attic orators. He won his spurs as a young man recently come of age in a series of actions taken against his guardians, who had squandered or misappropriated a considerable proportion of his substantial family assets, including a shield manufactory. Two of these legal speeches have survived, the authenticity of a third is disputed. The Corpus Demosthenicum includes no less than thirty-three legal speeches of a purely private, although not necessarily private law, character. Only fifteen at most can be genuine, the rest deriving from the archives of firms and families later known to have employed Demosthenes from time to time, so that remarkable speeches dating from that period were published under his name. The difficulties that obtained in correctly ascribing the authorship of such speeches are illustrated by the fact that Demosthenes prepared the petitions for both parties in one series of court actions among the issue of one of the wealthiest Attic bankers, initially involving the disputing of a will, then the division of the inheritance, and finally a case of perjury. This group even contains one speech in which Demosthenes himself comes under attack. The issues dealt with in the legal speeches range from brawling to swindling, and provide an invaluable source of information about the private and commercial life of Athens at that time.

In 355 BC, by which time Athens had again completely recovered from the break-up of the second maritime alliance, Demosthenes made his political debut as the supporter of a moderate statesman who had contributed to the financial recovery of Athens. In the years that followed he was to exert a growing influence on the course of Athenian politics, both at public meetings and as a diplomat. By the run-up to the final struggle of 338 BC he was undisputed leader not only in Athens, but in all of Hellas, of those unwilling to bow to the suzerainty of Macedon.

This is not the place to attempt an assessment of the historical significance of Demosthenes. History was to vindicate the view of those of his opponents who saw recognition of Macedonian hegemony as the sole means of achieving Greek unity. And yet no student of those events could withhold admiration for the patriotic zeal with which Demosthenes sought to preserve his state, the custodian of proud traditions and the embodiment of high civilisation, from dependence on a semi-barbaric monarchy. The tools of the political campaign in which Demosthenes became involved were anything but noble, while bribery, intrigue and calumny of political opponents were daily fare. One should not be precipitate in passing moral judgement here, however. The public nature of political life generally in Athenian democracy brought all such incidents mercilessly to light, whereas the corruption and intrigue that flourished – and still do flourish – in the cabinets, offices and ministries of other historical epochs as often as not went unrecorded.

It was in his political career that Demosthenes developed his unique oratorical gifts. A key weapon, widely used in political campaigns, was the harassment of political opponents because of the real or alleged illegality of measures enforced, or even only proposed, by them in jury courts, which were all too open to persuasion by political argument. Both prosecution and defence speeches by Demosthenes for trials with a political background have survived.

The Corpus Demosthenicum also contains a series of memoranda intended for reading, such as the speech *On the Symmories*, which proposed a more equitable distribution of tax liabilities. Lastly, there are numerous speeches where it is difficult to ascertain whether or not the texts were first delivered orally and then published as contributions for discussion by the council, or at the people's assembly, where most major political decisions were taken. They may have been intended as pamphlets or memoranda. However, the literary forms of journalism developed by Isocrates derived from live oratory.

Despite the rigorous literary character, down to the last detail, of all the works penned by Demosthenes, they remain highly personal documents to a far greater degree than the speeches of Isocrates. They allow the reader to follow almost uninterruptedly the succession of plans and decisions, tactical manoeuvres and political ideas of Demosthenes the statesman. More than this, however, they document a positively demonic temperament, each phrase bearing the utterly unmistakable stamp of its author. This cannot be said of his early legal speeches.

Demosthenes had at his command the whole gamut of cultured prose of his day, and yet did not apply it with the strict adherence to rules that so often makes Isocrates' speeches dull reading; instead, he fully subordinated the rules to his intentions. This enabled him to achieve a precise alignment between the frame of mind underlying his discourse on the one hand, and his sentence structure, line of thought, rhythm and tone on the other. This is particularly clear from the way major sections of Demosthenes' speeches are unmistakably arranged for rhythmic effect, and yet defy classification into a metrical scheme. No other prose author ever found such convincing ways of expressing indignation and contempt, admonition and reassurance, edification and horror, or derision and indictment; and yet Demosthenes used a relatively limited vocabulary which excluded both vulgar and poetic terminology alike. His matching of the expression to suit the atmosphere and subject-matter of his discourse was thus accomplished by almost exclusively syntactic, rhythmic and tonal means, the wealth of which defies all attempts at classification according to a theoretical system of rules. This applies both to his politically motivated legal speeches, such as those against Androtion or Leptines, and to his political speeches – the most famous of which are his Olynthiac and Philippic speeches dealing with the culminating conflict between Philip of Macedon and Athens.

The people of Athens did not abandon their spokesman after the defeat of 338 BC. In 336 one otherwise obscure Ctesiphon ordered that Demosthenes be decorated with a wreath – the equivalent of the conferring of an order – for his services in the defence of Athens. At this, Demosthenes' long-time opponent Aeschines brought a court action against Ctesiphon for alleged infringement of the law. The case did not come up for trial until 330 BC: both speeches are extant. Demosthenes' speech in defence of Ctesiphon is a brilliant testimony to his own political activities, and is arguably the most ingenious and thrilling piece of extant rhetorical literature from the ancient era. Ctesiphon was acquitted by such an overwhelming majority that Aeschines failed to obtain even the number of jury votes necessary under Attic law to avoid being charged himself in the event of the defendant being acquitted. He went into exile to Rhodes, where he died in 314 BC.

The death of Alexander enticed Greek patriots into a renewed attempt to break the Macedonian yoke by force of arms. Once again, Demosthenes found himself the leading figure in Athens, despite having become embroiled only shortly before in an ugly corruption affair in which his long-time fellow combatant Hyperides had opposed him. The hopes of the rebels were dashed on the battlefield at Crannon in Boeotia in 322 BC. Demosthenes was compelled to flee Athens, finally taking his own life at the temple to Poseidon on the island of Calauria, beset by Macedonian myrmidons.

Demosthenes and Aeschines crossed swords repeatedly in the period between 350 and 330 BC. Both were members of the delegation sent to negotiate peace between Philip and Athens in 346. Immediately on their return, Demosthenes brought an action against his adversary, alleging that he had been bribed by Philip and betrayed the interests of Athens. Both speeches from the trial in 343, in which Aeschines was acquitted, are extant. Aeschines' defence speech reveals a not inconsiderable talent, but his creative genius and inventive powers were no match for the gifts of Demosthenes.

Demosthenes' younger fellow combatant Hyperides, who also died a violent death in connection with the events of 322 BC, has been retrieved for posterity with speeches recorded on a papyrus find. His private legal speeches rightly enjoyed wide renown. Like those of Lysias, they are a model of ethopoeia – character portrayal. With visible relish, Hyperides has his clients enact realistic comic scenes from their lower-middle-class milieu. However, his skills are overstretched when his theme calls for a touch of pathos, such as in a funeral oration for the fallen of a military campaign. Hyperides' style is far more lax than that of any other fourth-century orator. His style represents an early form of Koine, the Hellenistic lingua franca based on the Attic dialect that combined various elements and became the common language of Greek civilisation as the Greeks advanced in the east.

Two other orators are of minor importance compared to the above-mentioned. One is Dinarchus, by whom there is a surviving prosecution speech against Demosthenes relating to the corruption affair surrounding Harpalus, the absconded finance minister of Alexander the Great. The other is Lycurgus, a man above moral reproach, descended from the most ancient Attic nobility, who restored domestic and above all economic stability to Athens after the events of 338 BC. He also made his mark by establishing the authoritative texts of the three great tragic poets. There is an extant prosecution speech by him against one Leocrates, who emigrated from his native city shortly before 338 BC prompted by forebodings about the future, later returning, however, and resuming exercise of his rights as a citizen as if nothing had happened. The petition is somewhat ponderous, but sincere and dignified – of more interest for its content than its form.

Of course there were many more orators in fourth-century Athens than have been dealt with here – Demades, famous for his wit, Hegesippus of Sunium, a partisan, and Demochares, a nephew of the great Demosthenes, and many others whose activity extended well into the third century BC. The fact that none of them are read today is the result of the fixed canon of ten outstanding orators created by scholars of the late Hellenistic period, along with the ten lyric poets, three tragic poets and three exponents of old comedy. These literary canons were important for the first century BC theory of style, which in turn contributed to the rise of Atticism – the alignment of all literary prose language with the norms of fourth-century BC Attic. There are thus exhaustive extant analyses of the styles of all orators, as well as valuable historical studies of their works, penned by Dionysius of Halicarnassus, who lived at the time of Augustus and was one of the leading lights of the Atticist movement. A papyrus in the Berlin collection contains fragments of an ancient scholarly commentary on Demosthenes written at roughly the same time by the Alexandrian scholar Didymus. The lexicon of Harpocration, which expounds on the significance to linguistic and antiquarian studies of less well-known expressions occurring in the works of the ten canonical orators, dates from the second century AD.

The establishment of a canon of great Attic orators was not without its justification. As a result of Athens being responsible for its own foreign policy, the final phase in its radically democratic public life was astonishingly intense. This in turn gave rise to a desire to exploit all the teachable potential of prose – to such an extent and with such enormous success that all contributions to public life, from trial speeches to a memorandum on public finance, had to meet the highest linguistic and stylistic standards to achieve the desired effect. There were of course still legal and ceremonial public speeches in the third and later centuries, in both Athens and elsewhere. To excel in this art was a bolster to one's reputation and social status.

Nevertheless, for the *polis* the loss of freedom in Athenian foreign policy resulted in a loss of seriousness in public life, as its erstwhile liberty lapsed into the machinery of municipal self-government. The *polis* thereby forfeited the one thing that had been able to arouse the moral and emotional commitment of citizens, without which its eloquence rang hollow. A similar process occurred in Rome during the transition between the republic and the principate, as correctly demonstrated by none less than Tacitus in his *Dialogue on Orators*. Eloquence as an art, i.e. the desire to make prose above all effective, thus retreated from political life into the schoolroom and to literature – the spheres where Isocrates had already established a rearguard position for it, and where it was able to hold its own until the eighteenth century.

The Hellenistic and Imperial periods produced some famous teachers of rhetoric and a wealth of new rhetorical methods. Literature became so saturated with rhetoric that for centuries to come a major part of higher education consisted of the schoolroom performance by students of addresses for fictitious court actions or public meetings, followed by their critical analysis by teachers (ancient tradition holds that this teaching method was introduced by the Peripatetic Demetrius). Criticism of rhetoric as the dominant force in education and literature has persisted throughout all post-Classical ages. This bears witness to the tenacious view that literary rhetoric – the stylisation of reading texts according to rules conceived for oral performance – is essentially a contradiction in itself. It was this same view that gave rise to the tendency to look on evidence of the fourth-century art of live oratory as unmatchable monuments to the command of language.

14

ENTERTAINMENT
LITERATURE, FACTUAL
LITERATURE AND
HISTORIOGRAPHY

Isocrates would not have been able to exert such far-reaching effects with his rhetorical education strategy had broad sections of the fourth-century public, and by no means only in Athens, not been steeped in the written word. This pertained first and foremost to the judicature, administration, commerce, banking, journalism, education and scholarship, but is also apparent from the way more and more people put their pens to paper whenever they felt they had something important to communicate.

The typical exponent of this entirely modern approach to writing, which was to become increasingly widespread in the ensuing centuries, is Xenophon, already mentioned above as the principal witness to non-Platonic Socratic literature (see above, pp. 177ff.). First on his Scillus estate in the region of Elis, then from 370 BC to the mid-fourth century in Corinth, Xenophon plied his craft without being motivated by any particular creative design or profound commitment to the themes he wrote about. From the literary history viewpoint, his Socratica must also be categorised in the same way, since he contributed nothing original to philosophical discussion.

His most impressive work is his *Anabasis*, which deals in seven books with the most important event of his life, the campaign of Cyrus and the home journey of the Greek mercenaries without their commanders across the enemy territory of the Persian Empire. The strength of the book lies in its vivid description of situations and events to which the author was an observant eye-witness. It also provides insight into the mentality of mercenaries, an important social class in the fourth century BC, including their professional pride and their awkward social status in periods when their services were not called for.

Xenophon avidly followed political discussion in Hellas throughout his life. Shortly after 355 BC the final work in his prolific succession of publications was an astute account of fiscal and tax policy with special reference to the Athenian context. Another book dating from his last decade is about the Spartan political system. This was not a work of ancient history, but intended as a contribution to the contemporary discussion of political theory. The chaotic and disappointing political state of affairs in the fourth century BC prompted proposals for political reform throughout the Greek-speaking world. The constitution of the Spartan state, preserved like a fossil from the seventh and sixth centuries BC, represented a blueprint for the ideal state in the minds of many people at that time, especially men of essentially aristocratic attitudes. This accounts for the emergence of an intense preoccupation with the anachronistic Spartan political system at about the time when its hard-won political hegemony of 404 BC was receding over the horizon, never to return. Plato's *Republic* likewise displays many features of the Laconism that was prevalent at the time.

Most people's hopes for an improvement and stabilisation of the political situation were pinned on the monarchy, however, as is clear from Isocrates' later journalism. Xenophon's writings also reflect this. His *Hieron* is a fictitious discussion between the great Sicilian tyrant of the early fifth century BC and the shrewd poet Simonides concerning what is required of a good monarch – a princely code in the form of a dialogue. The work known as the *Cyropaedia* gives a portrayal of the ideal ruler in the form of a biographical legend. Despite its compositional shortcomings, it was influential for princely code literature in both antiquity and the early modern era, largely on account of its diversity of content, which was ever able to attract readers craving fresh knowledge. The book relates the youth, rise to power and wise government of the elder Cyrus, founder of the Persian Empire. It also evaluates Persian traditions already familiar in sixth- and fifth-century Greece, and knowledge then current among the Greek public concerning the rise and nature of the Persian Empire – enriching the whole using countless characters and episodes with the inventiveness of the romance or novel. The reader is thus presented with a biography of Cyrus containing some historically verified events, some related by ancient legend, and some simply invented. These are not intended to be read for the sake of historical instruction, however, but rather to reveal how a just ruler should be brought up, how he should treat friends, foes, soldiers, advisers and subjects, why he should defend the rule of law, but on the other hand also mitigate that defence with magnanimity and clemency, and so on.

The fact that Xenophon sets this entirely exemplary tale in the Orient responded to a predilection of his day that was also to be found in the early Academy, such as with the author of the *Epinomis* or Heraclides Ponticus, and which heralded a long tradition of enthusiasm for the Orient as a fountainhead of ancient wisdom. The justification for many passages in the book, however, lies not in any didactic intention on the part of the author, but quite simply in their wartime adventure or tragic erotic themes. These episodes and their narrative craft help to increase understanding of how adventure and romantic fiction developed into separate genres in the following epoch of Greek literature.

In the aftermath of the Peloponnesian War, which had demonstrated all too clearly the precariousness of the Greek socio-political system, both monarchs and towering individual personalities in general increasingly captured the imagination of the reading public. In the part of his works discussed above, Xenophon demonstrated his reverence for the memory of Socrates. He also dedicated an encomium to the other man who had made a deep impression on him – the Spartan general Agesilaus under whose command he had served for a number of years. There is a clear affinity between this and the Euagoras encomium by Isocrates which permits us to assume a formal crystallisation of this literary genre before the middle of the century. The work does not attempt a full life history, but a key phase of it in which the subject's qualities are enumerated and illustrated with appropriate episodes from his life, framed with accounts of his youth and death.

Xenophon may additionally be ranked among the large number of specialist authors of his day. One small booklet by him contains complete instructions for training a race-horse, another the regulations for a cavalry officer – in the hands of the professional fourth-century military, warfare developed into an increasingly differentiated art. Tactics, strategy, artillery and weapons techniques were all increasingly dealt with in textbooks.

A little younger than Xenophon was the author Aeneas, perhaps Aeneas of Stymphalus in Arcadia, the politician and commander who wrote the first comprehensive military textbook, of which the section on urban siege strategy has survived. A somewhat older author was the Athenian General Iphicrates, who at the turn of the century had divested the Spartan phalanx of its reputed invincibility by deploying innovative infantry tactics, later describing this new military arm in a now lost treatise.

Xenophon's above-mentioned (p. 179) *Oeconomicus* is also factual literature, despite being styled as a Socratic dialogue. Economic questions, including the household and family as well as the broader context of *polis* or territorial state administration, came under more frequent theoretical discussion from the fourth century BC onwards, most notably in the Aristotelian school, from which some economic dissertations are extant.

Xenophon's minor works survived by virtue of their straightforward, clear, if not flawlessly Attic language, which found favour into the Byzantine era. This similarly benefited the inauthentic works that had found their way into the Xenophonic corpus, including a most instructive treatise on hunting with hounds.

The lengthiest work in the Xenophonic legacy is his *Hellenica*, a Greek history intended as a continuation of the unfinished historical work by Thucydides, and bringing the account up to 362 BC with varying degrees of thoroughness. One will search in vain here for the sweeping historical perspective, or even simply the narrative skill of Herodotus, and even more so for the penetrating anthropological reflection on events treated for their exemplary value that makes Thucydides' account so gripping. Aside from the occasional oversight, however, Xenophon's *Hellenica* is a respectable piece of historiography, clearly and engagingly presented, in which the author is at pains to achieve an objective assessment of events and understand the main actors on the historical stage. With his first-hand expertise, he outstrips even Thucydides in his analysis of military matters.

Xenophon's historiography is not even remotely influenced by historiographical theories dating from the second half of the fourth century which so thoroughly spoiled this branch of Greek literature. Only a handful of authors, among them Polybius, were able to resist the tempting clichés offered by such theories, according to which the task of the historian was either to demonstrate his stylistic prowess by handling difficult subject-matter, or to move and instruct the reader like a tragic poet. Much is often made of the alleged lack among the Greeks of a sense for human historicity – an assertion which can be refuted as nonsensical simply by recalling that prior to Herodotus and Thucydides there was no historiography in the modern sense of the term. It is true, however, that as a consequence of these theories historiography deviated from its true vocation by submitting to literary rules that paid no heed to the communication and presentation of historical facts. In the ensuing centuries the sense of history, as well as the methods used for relating past events, were largely cultivated outside historiography as such – in the study of local traditions and state and religious institutions, chronology and other subjects. It was in these particular spheres of antiquarian scholarship that Hellenism achieved so much.

Along with Xenophon's *Hellenica*, the virtues of a historiography still untainted by literary theories were also shared by another work written around the same time, a fragment of which came to light in 1909 with a papyrus find. It gives an account of the years 396 and 395 BC. The author, whose identity has not been firmly established, despite a number of possible names suggested by tradition, is superior to Xenophon in terms of his historiographical insight and breadth of vision, although not in fluency of expression. He could not be compared with Thucydides, however.

Seeking to continue in the vein of Herodotus, Ctesias the Cnidian wrote his books, in which he tried to take up the Herodotean tradition, approximately concurrently with Xenophon. He spent a considerable time in the east as personal physician to the Persian emperor, thus finding himself on the opposite side to Xenophon at the Battle of Cunaxa in 401 BC. His *Persica*, later continued by one Dino, are a twenty-three-volume treatment of the entire history of the Near East from its legendary beginnings up to 398 BC. A book of excerpts compiled by Photius the Patriarch (ninth century AD) contains an extract from the abridged version compiled in the first century AD, but does not give a particularly favourable impression of the merits of this much-read work. Plutarch's biography of the Persian emperor Artaxerxes, based largely on Ctesias, gives a truer picture of the tenor of the final section, which deals with events he had witnessed personally. There is good reason to admire the virtuosity with which he captures the oppressive atmosphere at the court of an Oriental despot.

Ctesias also wrote geographical works, including a *periplus*, i.e. the already outmoded literary form describing continental coastlines, and a book on India from which Photius preserved quite a lengthy extract. By Ctesias' time northwest India had long been outside the federation of Persian Imperial states, so that his access to reliable information about it was far more limited than that of Hecataeus – and through him of Herodotus – a century earlier. Ctesias' India is thus a land of fable, teeming with the most exciting phenomena. The traditional reputation for the fabulous associated with India that persisted into the Middle Ages thus had its beginnings with Ctesias, aside from a few shades of it in the work of Herodotus. He does nevertheless have some reliable information about India, since commercial and diplomatic contacts between it and the Persian Empire persisted. As has been ascertained from a recent papyrus find, the deliberate continuance of old Ionian historiography, indistinguishable from geography and ethnography, did not prevent Ctesias from writing in Attic. This shows the validity of Attic usage at that time. Placing themselves in the Herodotean tradition, Agathocles of Cyzicus, when writing his local history in the third century BC, and Arrian, when writing his geography of India in the second century AD, likewise readopted Herodotus' Ionic idiom.

The Indian fable-mongering of Ctesias should be distinguished from the incipient mendacious storytelling that also made its appearance in the fourth century BC, associated with the name of Antiphanes of Berge, inventor of the tale of the frozen notes, among others. Some idea about this genre of entertainment literature, which was cultivated throughout the Hellenistic era, is provided by some writings by Lucian of Samosata in Syria (second century AD). He had his heroes travel to a moon made of white cheese, for instance. Two other popular genres of the Hellenistic and Imperial periods, the travelogue and travel romance, were closely related to this type of mendacious storytelling.

Literature 'about the implausible' was of a different character, seeking to offer rational interpretations for myths to prove them either true or probable – presenting Cerberus, for example, as an unusually large dog once sighted in a cave known as the 'entrance to the underworld'. The incipient signs of this genre were to be found in the works of early Ionian logographers, such as Hecataeus. The first extant separate work of the genre is by an author named Palaephatus, of whom nothing further is known.

Finally, there was a third type of fabulous literature which compiled and elucidated remarkable facts and phenomena, largely from the natural world, also containing an element of sound scientific interest. This genre was cultivated by Peripatetic authors among others, so that one of the extant collections, mostly of late date, bears the name of Aristotle (see below, pp. 298f.).

Both the fourth-century authors who made the most lasting impact on the development of historiography came from the school of Isocrates. They applied to this genre the latter's principles of literary rhetoric, thereby making it the principal form of eloquence besides legal, political and ceremonial speeches. It was for this reason that the ambition of the historiographer was henceforth no longer mainly directed at communicating the results of historical inquiry, but rather at something which could only be assessed in terms of formal categories.

The major role played by Ephorus of Cyme in developing the educational strategy of the Isocratic school is documented by a work on the rules of literary style which unfortunately has not survived. It is the earliest treatment of this theme in the rhetorical tradition, which was otherwise stylistically limited to the principle of imitating recognised models. (Significantly, the Classical treatment of this theme goes back to Theophrastus – an exponent of philosophical reflection on the problems of rhetoric: see above, p. 197).

Ephorus achieved fame with a monumental historical work on which he worked for several decades with the intention of encompassing the entire mythical and historical tradition. Parts of it are available today in various fragments, and via a historiographical compilation by Diodorus of Sicily dating from the time of Augustus, large sections of which follow Ephorus' original work.

Ephorus' sense of history was limited. Although his pursuit of truth was clearly sincere, his work contains no original, historically revealing standpoint for his account of events. His trite, rationalistic interpretations of myth, of which a few examples have survived, patently represent a step backwards compared to the sound observations on mythical tradition offered by Herodotus and Thucydides. If one lastly adds to all this the fact that ancient stylistic judgement unanimously attests to the particularly balanced formulation of his thoughts, which by all accounts were hardly original, it is difficult to mourn the loss of this work too much. It would most likely have made very dull reading.

Theopompus of Chios was of quite a different mettle. In a long life extending beyond the death of Alexander he travelled widely, also being forced to take the bitter pill of exile on more than one occasion for his resolute defence of the Macedonian cause. At first he worked as a 'rhetor', i.e. a publicist in the manner of the Isocratic school, writing encomiums of rulers, political pamphlets and the like. He also wrote three historical works, the first of which was only an abridged version of the work of Herodotus. Of the other two, however, so many fragments are extant that they give some idea of the character of their author. Like Xenophon, he follows on from Thucydides in his *Hellenica*. Theopompus' account, however, concludes with the Battle of Cnidos in 394 BC at which the Athenian general Conon used a Persian fleet to put an end to the short-lived Spartan maritime superiority achieved in the Peloponnesian War.

Theopompus reveals his originality in the *Philippica*, a fifty-eight-volume history of Greece from the succession of Philip II (359 BC) until his death (336). Although this is not a historical biography, Theopompus regarded the

King of Macedon as the central figure in the historical events of the period, thus relating every detail in his contemporary historical account to the person and achievements of Philip. It naturally also reflects the political stance of Theopompus, the publicist character of this historical work being matched by the lively invective in which it is steeped, and in which Theopompus does not shrink from the most dubious kind of scandal-mongering. He held the view that society should be governed by aristocratic families, and politics steered by the strong arm of a monarch. Attic democrats are hence given particularly short shrift, and even Plato is dealt a few side-swipes by this Isocratean. Nevertheless, Theopompus was arguably the first Greek historian with a sense for the historical significance of social conditions, and was able to describe the latter with skill. It is also possible to appreciate the quality of some of the ethnographic and geographical digressions included in his work. Overall, however, he lacked the qualities required in a great historian, possessing neither the patience for profound reflection on the subject-matter in hand, nor the desire to set his own political and personal prejudices aside for the sake of truthfulness. Judging from extant samples, however, this magnum opus must have made fairly amusing reading.

The ordering of all events around a central historical figure in the manner first undertaken as a historiographical principle by Theopompus was to prove particularly appropriate in the epoch which immediately followed him, that of Alexander the Great. Of the numerous historians of Alexander still accessible today most were already writing from the perspective of a world fundamentally changed by his campaign. Two, however, belong more to the fourth century BC in company with Theopompus. One is Anaximenes of Lampsacus, already encountered above as the author of a textbook on rhetoric (see p. 196), who also wrote a number of historical works. The other is Callisthenes, nephew and long-time colleague of Aristotle, at whose school he studied scholarly chronology. Callisthenes took part in the great Oriental campaign of Alexander as court historian charged with the task of putting the latter's exploits in the correct light for an educated Greek readership. The King grew suspicious of him, however, and had him executed in 327 BC.

Among other historical and geographical works he wrote an account of Alexander's exploits. Although only a few fragments have survived, it seems to have enjoyed a certain fame, since the popular romantic tale of Alexander's exploits, of which many versions in numerous languages were current for centuries in west and east alike, was attributed to Callisthenes. There is some evidence to suggest that one kind of historiography that first made its emphatic appearance only in the following century, and which saw its task in arousing emotions in the manner of tragedy, had its precursor in Callisthenes.

Many other fourth-century historians are known from records or fragments. The only notable one for the purposes of this account is Philistus of Syracuse, because he may be regarded as the leading exponent of a branch of western Greek and Sicilian historiography dating back to the fifth century BC (see p. 169). Its approach lived on in many later continuations of his work, the third century producing another major author – Timaeus of Tauromenium (see below, pp. 294–5). In antiquity Philistus was renowned for his reliability, and much that is to be found on the early history of the western Greek world in the above-mentioned works of Diodorus and the biographies of Plutarch can directly or indirectly be traced back to him.

Works of research into local ancient history began to appear in the fifth century (Charon of Lampsacus), and became more copious in the fourth century. These are not part of historiography proper in the sense meant by ancient theory. Ephorus too wrote a history of his home town which, like his book *On Discoveries*, is always clearly distinguished from his historiography. Athens was of course the home of the richest tradition of this kind – one far more in accordance with scholarly standards than all the historiography of the fourth and third centuries put together. A succession of scholars known as Attidographers began with Hellanicus of Lesbos, a contemporary of Thucydides, proceeding via Clidemus to its high point in the Isocratean Androtion, who is also familiar to posterity as a political opponent of Demosthenes. The full significance of this scholarly tradition, which lasted into the third century and was drawn on by historians, antiquarians and grammarians alike, was not appreciated until the research of Felix Jacoby (1949). One remarkable feature is that some older exponents of this literature who were active in the fourth century BC presented their works in literary style. This also applies to Aristotle's characterisation of the Athenian constitution, for which he used the same sources as the Attidographers, but not to Philochorus (third century BC), the most erudite of them; the technique probably dates back to the great influence of Isocrates.

Not all these books contained comprehensive accounts of Attic antiquities, however. There were also factual documents, such as works giving chronological lists of government officials, monographs on the festivals of the calendar year and their associated customs, collections of laws and public decrees, descriptions of public works and other monuments, and editions of documents and legal records.

A major proportion of these scholarly studies were clearly connected with the Peripatus, and later with the library at Alexandria. Demetrius of Phalerum, for example, compiled a list of Athenian archons, and Phaenias of Eresus of all traditions relating to the assassinations of tyrants, while Ister, a pupil of Callimachus in Alexandria, collected all monographs on Attica.

Of local historians and antiquarians of the fourth century BC who worked outside Athens only Herodorus of Megara is noteworthy for our purposes here, since what is known of him is indicative of the local patriotism that motivated this kind of scholarly endeavour. Among other things he worked on mythical traditions, consulting textual variants in the Homeric poems texts to this end.

15

POETRY

In terms of the quantity of original works, fourth-century poetry could not remotely compete with prose. It should nevertheless be pointed out that this quantity was comparable with that of the previous century, which even at the time was acknowledged as the high point of dramatic poetry. The great Dionysus festivals of the Attic calendar continued to witness many theatrical celebrations all the year round, the competition by no means solely between repeat performances. New theatres were moreover sprouting up all over the Greek-speaking world. No Greek town could be without one. Although theatres were also used for public meetings, judicial hearings and similar public affairs, they do indicate a need for textbooks for dramatic performances that was widespread far beyond the confines of Athens.

Only one complete example of a fourth-century tragedy has survived. *Rhesus* is based on an episode from the *Iliad* and is ascribed to Euripides. The dramaturgy certainly bears his stamp, with the role of the chorus waning and a division into acts already discernible. It remains to be seen whether the manifest effort of the poet to evoke mood or atmosphere before all else, even at the expense of a consistent and unified plot, may be regarded as the hallmark of fourth-century tragedy, or merely attributed to this particular theme. The episode from the Trojan War it depicts is devoid of heroic traits, but its nocturnal setting offers the tragic poet ample opportunity for the effective creation of mood.

Further information about fourth-century tragedy is available from Aristotle's *Poetics* and chance surviving fragments and titles. The evaluation of tragedies according to purely literary criteria, for example, shows that the trend towards writing dramas for reading purposes only arose directly out of changes in stage drama technique. This is further borne out by increasing evidence in dramatic poetry of adherence to the rules of literary rhetoric.

Records of the singular tragic poetry of the tyrant Dionysius I of Syracuse, albeit a one-time winner at a drama contest in Athens, give a picture of playful variations on tragic language and scene technique that were by that time confined to the category of literature, and only loosely connected with stage practice. The same sources reveal, moreover, that historical events were being used as drama themes. There is even a record of this for a satyr play – Python's *Agen*, a treatment of the scandal surrounding the absconded finance minister Harpalus, written and performed at the military camp of Alexander.

The picture for comedy is somewhat more complete. Ancient philologists distinguished between old comedy, which died out in the wake of the Peloponnesian War, 'middle' comedy which lasted until the time of Alexander, and the New Comedy of the age now known as the Hellenistic period.

In the library at Alexandria middle comedy was represented by the works of several dozen poets, comprising several hundred plays. All that remains today are a few names (such as Antiphanes, Eubulus, Epicrates or Alexis), a few short fragments and various second-hand accounts. However, quite a reliable picture of the development of comic art in the fourth century can be deduced from the last two extant dramas of Aristophanes, which are no longer classifiable as old comedy, either on the strength of the date they were written, or in terms of their character. The *Ecclesiazusae*, performed in 392 BC, has women stealing men's clothing, fastening on false beards and gathering in the public assembly at the crack of dawn in order to seize political power and introduce a new, strictly communist social order. One noteworthy feature about the swift action of the play is that its satirical wit is not aimed primarily at topical political affairs. Aside from occasional side-swipes at personalities or events from Athenian life in the manner of old comedy, the play as a whole takes as its real target the numerous theories about state and society that were current at that time.

Plutus, performed in 388 BC, is even further removed from contemporary political and social life. Despite the opposition of Penia, goddess of poverty, who points out the fatal consequences of such an act on human virtue, an aged peasant sets about curing the blindness of the god of wealth, who distributes his gifts arbitrarily. A loosely composed group of concluding scenes exemplifies the results for humankind of the cure of Plutus, carried out in the temple of Asclepius.

Compared to typical fifth-century comedies, with their accumulation of traditional scenes, these two manifest a more unified plot. There is only minimal involvement by the chorus, whose songs are asides which do not affect the plot. The subdued role of topical political themes is clearly related to the diminished self-confidence of Athenian society with its restored democracy – no longer as sure of its might as it had been in the days of the Athenian Empire, and hence less tolerant of the unbridled criticism characteristic of old comedy.

This brought not only disadvantages to comic poets: dispensing with consistent topicality in a play as often as not made it easier for them to be more consistent with the storyline. Traditional formal components of comedy that had never hitherto been successfully incorporated into a coherent stage plot were moreover left out.

Even fourth-century comedy was not entirely devoid of political and social satire, however. This is apparent from a number of surviving titles and some fragments deriding the refined mannerisms and dialectic hairsplitting of Plato's pupils. Other fragments poke fun at the then prevalent ascetic begging life-style of nomadic Pythagoras followers, known as Pythagoreans. The comic poet Eubulus wrote one comedy whose eponymous hero was Dionysus I of Syracuse. Despite his entirely topical mockery of the womanising and literary ambitions of the tyrant, however, the Athens-based poet was not putting his political head on the block here. (If one is to believe much-embellished anecdotal tradition, on the other hand, the lyric poet Philoxenus (see above, p. 129) seems to have incurred persecution and imprisonment for his un-disguised attack on the tyrant of Sicily in his invented tale describing the love of the ugly Cyclops Polyphemus for the lovely nymph Galatea.)

There was one other respect in which comedy became progressively tamer compared with the standard set by the late plays of Aristophanes. There was a general disappearance of the ribaldry once probably sanctioned by rural fertility cults and later the exclusive province of comedy in the fifth century BC. This ribaldry was now obliged to give way to urban respectability.

New themes appearing in the fourth century included mythical travesties, which had been typical of episodes in ancient comedy but not for entire dramas, and topics from middle-class private life with stock-in-trade characters such as the strict father, the alluring hetaera, the spendthrift son, etc. The latter comic type came to dominate the third phase, New Comedy. Another noteworthy aspect of middle comedy was a predilection for frequent changes of metre in spoken scenes, perhaps by way of compensating for the abeyance of choral songs.

One scarcely answerable question is whether middle comedy adopted wholesale the dramatic technique of late tragedy, most especially Euripidean, thereby giving rise to the comic play later encountered in fully-fledged form in New Comedy – which in turn gave rise to the modern European comic play tradition, by way of Latin comedy. Attempts have been made to draw conclusions in this regard from some plays by the Roman poet Plautus (see below, p. 250), who can undoubtedly be assumed to have drawn models from middle comedy. Since, however, Plautus and Terence generally imitated originals from the New Comedy era it cannot be ruled out that New Comedy techniques retained some degree of influence even when these authors exceptionally drew play themes from the middle period. Latin comedies were adaptations, not translations. This obliges us to be content with the observation that the rich comedy playwriting of the middle period – undoubtedly also intended for performance outside Athens – must have had the benefit of an unbroken but changing tradition of dramatic poetry that continued to enrich itself in diverse ways, although its finest fruits were not to ripen until the Hellenistic period.

The later flowering of ceremonial lyric poetry connected with the New

Music has already been touched on above (p. 128), and persisted well into the fourth century BC. Urban cult festivals throughout the Greek-speaking world sustained an ongoing need for choral song that was met partly by old texts, albeit often adapted to new performing practice, and partly by newly composed works. However, a number of hymns which have survived in the form of inscriptions reveal that their literary merits hardly ever rose above the provincial.

The fourth century also ushered in a modest renaissance of the art of epic poetry. A few verses have survived from an epic poem on the Persian Wars written shortly before 400 BC by Choerilus of Samos, who laments the irretrievable loss of the ancient epic art. The same period also witnessed the first appearance of epic parodies in music contest programmes. A certain Hegemon, mentioned among others by Aristotle, won an Athenian contest in 415 with his *Gigantomachia*, which parodies the high epic style. Other poets from the genre are documented well into the third century BC. There had been some signs of the parodying of the heroic epos even in the Archaic period, such as in the work of Hipponax, Xenophanes or in the anonymous poem *Margites*. What was new here was the rise of this as a genus in its own right, and its institutional encouragement. The *Batrachomyomachia*, an anonymous work probably dating from the third century BC, derives its literary impact, which was to persist into the modern era, from the way it employs all the devices of the high epic style to narrate the story of a war between mice and frogs. Later sources inform us that other parodists such as Euboeus and Boethus sang of heroic contests between thieves, bath attendants and shoemakers. Substantial fragments also survive of the gastronomical poetry of Matron of Pitane and Archestratus of Syracuse, which parody the didactic poetry of Hesiod rather than the heroic epos of the Homeric tradition.

Undoubtedly there is no need for undue lamentation over the loss of most of these texts. However, as Robert Schröter (1967, 8f.) has recently shown, the historical significance of this *poesis ludibunda*, whose effects are still discernible in the work of Horace, should not be underestimated. The general availability of epic forms that is evident from their use in the philosophical polemic of Crates (see above, p. 177) and Timon (p. 246) created the distance from the venerable conventions of the ancient epos without which the artistic refinement of revived epic poetry in the Hellenistic period would have been unthinkable.

The renaissance of epic poetry began in the fourth century BC. At Colophon in Asia Minor, Antimachus wrote a *Thebais*, an epic poem on a thoroughly traditional 'Homeric' theme, even capturing the attention of Plato. This revival of the genre derived from scholarly work. Together with the roughly contemporary Antidorus of Cyme, Antimachus was among the first philologists to seek a scholarly understanding of Homeric poetry, and published editions, glossaries and specialist studies. By imitating ancient epic features uncovered by this scholarly expertise, Antimachus then proceeded to make the genre palatable again to a connoisseur reading public. This explanation is borne out by the fact that in the third century, when this kind of scholarly poetry was coming into its full flower, Antimachus' poetry was the object of lively discussion, and obviously regarded as the starting point of a new poetic tradition. The same applies to his elegies, which followed on from Mimnermus and were collected together by him in a volume named after his lover *Lyde*.

The most remarkable figure among the fourth-century poets was a girl named Erinna, who lived on the small island of Telos near Rhodes and died at the age of 19. Aside from a few epigrams of disputed authenticity, only a single hexametric poem by her of some 300 verses was read in antiquity. A coherent fragment of this, comprising some twenty verses, has recently been retrieved through a papyrus find. Some information about the content of the poem, entitled *Distaff*, is provided by an epigram by Asclepiades in praise of the poetess. It laments the death of a playmate called Baucis, who has recently left the island as a bride, and recalls scenes from their childhood together. The few extant verses evoke a tenderness and deep feeling scarcely encountered in Greek poetry since Sappho. Another of its outstanding features is the formal rigour with which the simple, colloquially phrased language is made to conform to the hexameter without detracting at all from the personal, warm tone of the poem. The formal perfection of Hellenistic verse technique seems to be heralded in this not particularly virtuoso poem. It defies classification within any known genre. Its theme is something one would expect to find in an elegy.

One genre which must be assumed to have had a rich, if for the most part sub-literary, output throughout the century is that of epigrams. There was a constant need for epigrams for dedications, gravestones and other purposes. Where they found favour, they were sooner or later collected into books, such as the texts ascribed to Simonides. There was no definable distinction between the longer epigram, composed of several distichs (hexameters and penta-meters), and the short elegy, comprising only a few distichs. Like the scholion, the short elegy, performed to a flute accompaniment, had been an established form of public promotion at feasts even in the late Archaic period. Examples of the genre were compiled into anthologies such as the book of Theognis. It should come as no surprise, therefore, that in the mid-fourth century BC Theocritus of Chios used epigrams to polemicise against various literary and political opponents. One of his derisive epigrams, in the form of a gravestone inscription and directed at Aristotle, has survived.

The great flowering of artistic, literary epigrammatic poetry was not to occur until the Hellenistic period, but epigrams were ascribed to fourth-century authors that had undoubtedly never been inscribed on stone. The best-known anthology of this kind consists of thirty-three epigrams ascribed to Plato. It is unusually difficult, if not impossible, either to demonstrate or disprove the authenticity of all the pieces with any certainty, although many of them undoubtedly are inauthentic. One of them, composed on the death of

Plato's friend Dion, but certainly not intended for a gravestone, is one of the most impressive works of the epigrammatic art. In only three distichs it contrasts the hieratic rigour of an official evaluation side by side with an utterly personal declaration of deep love for the deceased. One would gladly ascribe these verses to Plato.

Part IV

HELLENISTIC LITERATURE

16

HELLENISM AND ITS
PHILOSOPHY

The Alexandrian campaign probably changed the world more than any other single event in ancient history. Admittedly, Alexander did not have time to expand westwards from the empire he built out of the conquered Persian Empire and the half of the Greek-speaking world that was under his rule. Indeed, the Empire only outlived its creator by a few years. Nevertheless, in the hands of energetic generals from Alexander's army the territory he conquered became a number of substantial territorial states, hereditary monarchies, with government, finance and the military set up according to what were then modern, rational fourth-century BC principles.

The founding of countless new towns, begun by Alexander and carried on by his successors, was even more significant, absorbing active soldiers, veterans and above all immigrants from overpopulated Hellas. These towns became a focus for Hellenisation throughout the Orient, as well as forming the true basis for Greek rule from Asia Minor to Afghanistan. Like the towns of the mother country, they had their public assemblies and their elected officials, their community cults and calendars, their legislation and reckoning of the years, as well as their theatres, *gymnasia*, temples and baths. With few exceptions (e.g. Rhodes or Heraclea on the Pontus), throughout the Hellenistic age neither the old nor the new towns were *de facto* sovereign, or if so only temporarily (e.g. the member towns of the Achaean alliance). They did enjoy a considerable degree of domestic autonomy in matters such as finance and justice, however. Along with belonging to one of the monarchies, and their feeling of cultural superiority in a non-Greek environment, this helped to foster a civic sense that found expression both in impressive achievements by their citizens, and in a rich social life. The army and civil services of the monarchies likewise recruited from the urban Greek population, particularly its upper classes.

The indigenous populations and rural areas were completely uninvolved in this civilisation on which the dynasties rested. Similarly, very few urban centres with an Oriental culture (Jerusalem, Edessa) were able to assert themselves and retrieve a measure of their former importance. As far as the former circumstance is concerned, adaptation to Greek urban culture was the only way for individuals or communities of Oriental origin to achieve social recognition. Even in places such as Egypt where they did not live in towns, the Greeks were 'those of the *gymnasium*', i.e. people who read Homer and practised athletics, holding firm to the social and cultural traditions of ancient Greece. A case in point was the thoroughgoing, not entirely peaceful restoration of Judaism, ushered in just as numerous noble families in Jerusalem were resigning themselves to this 'gymnasial' lifestyle, thereby almost turning Jerusalem into a Greek *polis*.

The broad upper classes of burgeoning towns pursued the culture of Hellenism and of the Imperial Roman period that followed it. It was owing to this bourgeoisie that interest in the literary tradition of the Greeks was sustained throughout this whole period, that literary writing was not interrupted, and that both public and private life alike continued to be shaped by the spirit of a humane ethics bearing the stamp of philosophy.

What made it possible for the Greeks to pursue this rapid cultural and above all economic expansion of the Orient under the protection of the constellation of powers established by the Diadochi, Alexander's successors, was an idea that had been taking an increasing hold during the preceding century – namely that the unprejudiced exercise of reason was in every respect more efficacious than adherence to traditional rules of conduct sanctioned by religion or some other authority. The practical manifestation of this was visible in the rapid emergence of large-scale production, trade and finance organisations, in technical innovations made in administration and warfare, and in the huge strides made in the natural sciences, the findings of the third century BC often not being matched again until the nineteenth century AD. There emerged, in short, a scientific and technical apparatus along quite modern lines that was later essentially still at the command of the Roman Empire, although not being further developed by it. (The dwindling capacity to maintain these achievements that was discernible in the third century AD denotes among other things the transition to the Middle Ages.) Another result of the Greek 'Enlightenment' of the late fifth and fourth centuries BC, however, was that in the wake of the Alexandrian campaign individuals began as never before to seek their fortunes on the strength of their own abilities within the scope of the new economic milieu. They turned their backs on what had been, as in all archaic social forms, the previously unquestioned matrix for personal growth – the social life of the community into which they had been born. It may come as no surprise that service in the army or governments of the great monarchs attracted applicants from all over the Greek-speaking world, like the worldwide catchment area of great centres of learning and education. What should be emphasised here, however, is that artisans from Argos or Miletus, peasants from Attica or Phocis, and merchants from Corinth or Syracuse were making new lives for themselves in a Greek city in Syria or Persia, while their nephews or neighbours were doing the same on the Nile.

This freedom of movement in a vast outside world of which people living at the time were fully aware called for completely new social and religious modes of conduct. The associations people joined and the cult community to which they paid their devotions by choice gained precedence over blood ties. Loyalty towards those to whom one felt bound by a common education, religion or profession became at least as important, if not more so, than the bonds between fellow citizens or members of the same tribe or clan. Concomitant with the habit of organising outward life along rational lines was the effort to resolve moral problems equally rationally. This explains the wide influence of philosophy. There was a widely acknowledged truth that individuals fashioned their own destiny, and yet in the attempt to organise their lives independently could still be hopelessly shipwrecked by unforeseen circumstances. This led to a new concept of the nature of fate which manifested itself, in contrast to the highly developed rationality marking the outward organisation of life, in the irrational pursuit of salvation and certainty by such means as astrology and mystery religions. In addition, astrology owed much of the power it wielded for centuries over the minds of many to a rigorous systematisation of its methods which took place in the second century BC with the aid of Greek astronomy in Egypt.

Another detail surprises the present-day observer of what appears in many respects to have been a modern Hellenistic civilisation with markedly rationalist features. This was the ubiquitous cult veneration not only of deceased rulers – there was a precedent for this in the Greek hero cult, a form of the cult of the dead – but of the living sovereign. Numerous attempts have been made to account for this: the model of the ancient Egyptian monarchy, the necessity to provide subjects from widely differing cult traditions with a religious foundation for their loyalty to the state system, the precarious relationship between what were in principle autonomous Greek towns and the superior power of kings, which could be made more politically acceptable by cloaking it in religion. The deep impression left by both the person and career of Alexander undoubtedly made the Greeks more receptive to the charisma of an individual ruler, as well as providing an up-to-date mani-festation of ancient Greek ideas on the possibility of transcending the boundary between men and gods by means of superlative feats.

Philosophers' notions of the ideal ruler centred on the figure of Heracles, who was granted a place among the gods for his lifelong exertions for the benefit of humankind. Official ideology, on the other hand, stressed the charismatic character of rulers, taking Dionysus, the enigmatic conqueror of the world, as its model. Common to both versions was a cosmic aspect and an implicit claim to world rule that was typical of this kind of monarchy, the eternal order of the universe being seen as brought about by the just ruler in the form of justice among people. Not least, this reference to universal order legitimated rule. The fact that people remained cognisant of the humanity of the king even in the midst of their religious rites is indicative of a major distinction between kings and other cult figures. There is substantial evidence documenting how people prayed to the gods for the well-being of the ruler, but no evidence of sacrifices or petitions made to one god for the well-being of another. The religious legitimation of political rule common to all pre-modern cultures of the world was thus present in Hellenism, and moreover in a particularly effective form that was later adopted and elaborated further by the Emperors of Rome. The cult veneration of the ruler, to which no one could take direct exception in the context of a polytheistic tradition, was to provide the main spur to conflict with the state and the surrounding culture, first for the Jews in the Maccabean revolt, and later for Christians in the Roman Empire.

This brief outline may suffice to indicate the far-reaching changes to Greek society that occurred in the aftermath of the Alexandrian campaign. It is misleading to obscure the epoch-making character of this event, as has recently been the case in historical scholarship, by setting the date for the rise of Hellenism in the mid-fourth century BC simply because the intellectual preconditions, and in some cases the early forms of new phenomena, were in place prior to Alexander.

The outward history of Hellenism falls into three periods roughly co-inciding with the centuries, and likewise matched by three distinct periods in scholarship and literature. In the third century BC no power outside the Hellenistic state system was able to exert any discernible influence on the destinies of the civilised nations of the Mediterranean world. (The Seleucid kings were in friendly contact with the great Mauryan Empire of India.) This century witnessed both the high point of Greek scholarship in almost every field and the final flowering of Greek poetry.

In the second century the Romans made their influence powerfully felt all over the eastern Mediterranean. Parallel with this, the Parthian state was establishing itself, first in Iran and then in Mesopotamia. Despite an overtly friendly stance towards the Greeks, it covertly supported all anti-Greek influences in the Orient, while the Romans, notwithstanding their ruthless demolition of the political and economic foundations of the Greek state, were in fact themselves coming increasingly under the sway of Greek civilisation. The Parthians furthermore isolated the easternmost of the Greek states in distant Afghanistan, whose expansion into India entailed repercussions in geographical terms, but hardly any for political conditions throughout the rest of the Greek-speaking world. The intellectual life of the second century BC was dominated by the achievements of historiography, literary criticism and the exact sciences.

The first century BC saw the complete annexation of the Greek east by the Romans, who had already been bequeathed a substantial territory in Anatolia by the last ruler of Pergamum in 133 BC. The subsequent incorporation of Egypt following the Battle of Actium in 31 BC terminated the independence of the last, economically most powerful and culturally richest of the Greek states. The Romans similarly succeeded in securing the Euphrates border against the Parthians, thereby perpetuating Greek cultural domination of Syria and Egypt for more than half a millennium, and of Asia Minor for a full millennium. The structure of the Roman Empire thus became bilingual, with the Greek-speaking half rapidly superseding the Latin-speaking half in economic and cultural importance. The dissolution of the Hellenistic system of states in the first century BC, accompanied as it was by constant warfare, curbed progress in scholarship and literature. Aside from the versatile Posidonius it produced no author of any great significance.

This trend in intellectual life did not apply to philosophy, however, which produced achievements of considerable originality in all three periods. Around 300 BC two schools were founded in Athens that provide evidence of a redefinition of philosophical objectives. The ground for this had already been prepared by the small Socratic schools of the fourth century, but here it appeared in a new form. Zeno of Citium in Cyprus and Epicurus of Athens elaborated the first closed systems in philosophy. In these, a systematic theory for the correct utilisation of the means for interpersonal communication, and a not necessarily detailed but exhaustive explanation of the principles of nature, formed the basis for ascertaining human nature and modes of conduct. Compliance with these principles guaranteed a life of perfect happiness (eudaemonia). These philosophies were thus concerned not with a continuing inquiry after truth, but with a watertight scientific basis for rational ethics. The conventional triad of the philosophical disciplines – logic (usually named otherwise in Hellenism), physics or metaphysics, and ethics – has its roots here, where philosophy was pursued solely to obtain a practicable ethics. Like the Cynics, the early Stoics and Epicureans regarded scholarly research for its own sake or in order to expand the body of knowledge as a total waste of time. The reason why philosophical inquiry continued at all in the Hellenistic age (including the crystallisation of new philosophical disciplines and the pursuit of specialist sciences, sometimes within philosophy schools) lies in the constant disputes between numerous schools concerning each and every detail of their teaching, which compelled them to examine and develop their dogmas in relation to one another. Arguments drawn from scientific inquiry could not be omitted in these disputes.

This new brand of philosophy thus sought no more than to teach the individual how to live correctly. It was unconcerned with reforming either the state or society. People with an accurate knowledge of the individual and his or her role in the cosmos, and able to draw from it the necessary conclusions for their own moral actions regardless of the vicissitudes of fortune and the conflicting opinions of their fellows, seemed best able to cope with the new historical milieu. In fulfilling their own social obligations, a necessity stressed by all philosophical theories, people were first and foremost furthering their own happiness. As beings equipped with reason, they were free agents in all circumstances provided they followed only their own correct understanding. In the view of this new anthropology, the social side of human nature no longer required the traditional order of the *polis* in order to unfold fully, as Aristotle had still taught. The sage, in the sense of the model conceived of in Hellenistic philosophy, could find the fellowship called for by his nature anywhere in the world.

Moral theories of this kind made philosophy the dominant force in Hellenistic education. It became customary among the middle classes to devote a period of one's higher education to philosophy, frequently in the form of a trip to study at Athens. Professional philosophers enjoyed high esteem as tutors, confidants and advisers to the courts of kings, as well as in urban life. When Athens had to negotiate with the Roman Senate in 155 BC, it was the heads of the Academic, Peripatetic and Stoic schools who were sent to Rome as emissaries.

So great was the direct and indirect influence of philosophical ethics that traces of it are found not only everywhere in literature but also in many records of public life. The theories of specific schools differed widely, but inasmuch as philosophy in general was popularised it was the features they held in common that tended to be stressed. This trend was of some social moment. As a consequence of their ready grasp of matters pertaining to philosophy-based ethics, and the literary taste cultivated by an education in rhetoric, the intellectuals of that time felt at home anywhere in the world. Wherever exponents of certain schools or trends within these disciplines were to be found it was possible to establish local groups or circles of friends, so providing a social base for individuals in a greatly expanded world. The same function was served in the Hellenistic age by the increasingly widespread mystery religions, which had local communities scattered all over the civilised world. This was particularly the case with the Hellenised cult of the Egyptian goddess Isis.

The history of Hellenistic philosophy and its schools can only be given here in the broadest outlines. The son of an Athenian family, Epicurus was born on Samos in 341 BC. He taught first in northern Greece, then at a school in Athens known as the Garden after the piece of land he acquired for it. There is evidence of his acquaintance with followers of the Academic and Peripatetic schools, but the major inspiration for the elaboration of his system came from Nausiphanes of Teos, an adherent of the school of Democritus that was still active in some places in northern Greece (Anaxarchus of Abdera, etc.), quite independently of the Attic tradition. It was from this school that Epicurus adopted elements of a rigorously materialistic interpretation of the world. According to this, an infinite number of indivisible and variously formed atoms fall into the empty void, occasionally deviating from a vertical path and thus colliding with others, joining with them and thus bringing about the changing atomic agglutinations that go to make up the phenomena of nature. The entire natural mechanism was thus seen as being explained by random atomic processes. There was no providence, no purpose to the natural mechanism, nothing resembling a divine will, and no existence independent of matter.

Epicurus expressly rejected a differentiation and elaboration of this basic conception by means of inquiry into nature. It sufficed him as the foundation for his ethics, particularly since the theory of cognition that went with it entailed no further complications. All perceptions were seen as being true, while the truth of concepts devised on the strength of present and past perceptions, and of the opinions associated with those concepts, was determined by fresh perceptions, or, where opinions related to what was desirable to strive after, by bodily sensations of pleasure or aversion.

Since, it was argued, a human being consisted solely of atoms, including the soul, he or she completely disintegrated into the various component parts after death. There was thus no reason for concern with any hereafter. There were gods, i.e. perfect beings, but they lived apart from the world of humans, since any concern with the people's doings or the natural mechanism would detract from their perfect happiness. It would be impious to regard the gods as imperfect.

Freed by this theory from the fear of both death and the gods, people could now organise their lives wholly according to the requirements of nature, which manifest themselves clearly in sensations of pleasure and aversion. The goal of all effort thus became a state of continual, unchanging pleasure. In order to achieve this state the sage was obliged to put up with an aversion here and there, e.g. physical effort, in exchange for obtaining the higher pleasure of peace of mind. Similarly, despite the sensations of aversion thereby entailed he would comply with social conventions in order to avoid the greater aversion he might incur along with social sanctions against him. In this way the radical hedonism and individualism of Epicurean teaching led directly to practical instructions for a moderate lifestyle in keeping with the dictates of convention.

There was one point, however, on which Epicurus conspicuously diverged from middle-class tradition. He held that the sage should not take part in politics, but lead an unobtrusive secluded life in the select company of people of like mind. This alone could guarantee him peace of mind. Epicureans felt a strong bond with their circle of friends. The charisma emanated by the personality of Epicurus himself persisted until the demise of his school in the second century AD in the almost conventicle-like communal life of the Epicurean circle. There were serious efforts to further moral progress by means of mutual assistance, including for example the earliest confessional technique. Significantly, the word 'conscience', which derives from the Greek via the Latin translated loan word *conscientia*, first acquired its terminological meaning with the Epicureans.

The zeal with which the Epicureans strove after moral improvement seems to contrast oddly with their mechanistic, materialistic world view, but is likewise traceable to their teaching. The divergence of some atoms from their vertical downward path through empty space is left without an adequate explanation, despite being essential for the creative process. So too human freedom of choice is taken as a necessary precondition for morality, despite being scarcely compatible with a psychology that explains all spiritual phenomena as arising out of random atomic ones. Even later Epicurean theory continued to leave unexplained the cosmic freedom of choice of atoms and the moral freedom of choice of people.

In contrast with the Academy, Peripatus and Stoa (see p. 239), the Epicurean tradition did not undergo any substantial dogmatic changes. Late Epicurean philosophical studies are known today from the works of Philodemus (first century BC), preserved on papyrus scrolls from the ruins of Herculaneum, from Cicero's accounts, from a Latin didactic poem by Lucretius, and from a lengthy wall inscription by the Epicurean Diogenes of Oenoanda (second century AD). These do not differ significantly from what can be reconstructed of Epicurus' system using fragments of his own prolific literary output.

Again in contrast with other philosophical schools, Epicureanism remained largely indifferent, even hostile, to scholarly inquiry. Genuine contributions to research by Epicurus and some later Epicureans were made only in logic, known as canonics in the school's own terminology, and mathematics. Epicureans likewise rejected rhetoric, the other major educational force in the Hellenistic age, and did not seek to incorporate this element of civilisation into their own system, unlike all other schools. As a consequence of this they deliberately favoured an ordinary vernacular style, limiting the literary merits of all Epicurean writings, beginning with those of the founder and including numerous treatises intended for a broader reading public. It remained for the Roman author Lucretius to compose a fine poetic work preaching the Epicurean theory of peace of mind.

Epicurus' teaching, which promised the individual peace and liberty, found its adherents in Rome, most especially during the civil wars of the first century AD. Both Virgil and Cassius, one of those who assassinated Caesar, were Epicureans for a time. Whenever external circumstances stabilised, however, public opinion tended to be less favourably disposed towards the Epicureans on account of their recommended withdrawal from public life. In these conditions the Epicurean theory of pleasure provided a welcome pretext for incorrectly discrediting the ethics of the school as libertine. From the first century BC onwards intellectuals felt a growing need to root their views on life and the world in a religious basis. In this context Epicurean theology, which denied any link between men and the gods, was denounced as 'godlessness'. Despite this highly unfavourable background for the preservation of Epicurean literature and theory, surviving fragments and letters by Epicurus still give an impressive picture of his philosophical seriousness and knowledge of the human heart. They also help to explain the persuasive power of a philosophy that derived in no small measure from his own personality.

The history of the Stoa, the other school of the Hellenistic age, took quite a different course. Zeno, from Citium in Cyprus, founded a school in Athens whose lectures had to be held in a public building – a colonnade (*stoa*) at the marketplace – since as a foreigner he was not permitted to purchase property. Initially he adhered to the Cynics, and Cynic principles such as inurement, and inner and outer detachment of the individual from the standards of society, continued to feature heavily in Stoic ethics into late antiquity. Zeno's earliest known writings, including the outline of a communist ideal state, were entirely in the Cynic tradition. He seems at some point to have taken exception to the Cynics' lack of respectability. At all events the Stoa came to deny its Cynic beginnings and to regard the system elaborated by Zeno as a legitimate continuation of Socratic philosophical thought – which is un-doubtedly true of certain of its aspects.

After Zeno's death, a number of his pupils carried on teaching in highly divergent ways in the Stoa, which never had such a fixed organisational structure as the Epicurean school or the Academy. The most important of these teachers were Ariston of the island of Chios and Cleanthes of Assos in Asia Minor. At the same time Arcesilaus, an astute scholar trained in mathematics – under whose headship the Academy departed from its tra-ditional dogmatism to develop a type of methodical scepticism (see above, p. 191) – began to submit Zeno's philosophical system to penetrating criticism. This might have dealt the death blow to the Stoa, since its initial reluctance to engage in scholarly inquiry made it difficult for the Stoics to fend off such attacks. The Stoa nevertheless found its champion in the shape of Chrysippus, a scholar from the Cilician town of Soli, who was later venerated as its second founder. In a dumbfounding total of books, now alas irretrievably lost aside from a few quotations, Chrysippus modified the Zenonian system, strength-ening it on all sides with intelligent arguments, and establishing a relationship with all scholarly disciplines. Although no additional theories were produced by the Stoa until the second century AD Chrysippus' doctrinal system was associated until the end of antiquity with the notion of Stoic orthodoxy. This is apparent, for example, from Diogenes Laertius' second-century AD bio-graphies of the philosophers – the key source for modern knowledge of the ancient history of philosophy – which are arranged according to school traditions and combine a life history of each major philosopher with a summary of the theory concerned. The seventh volume, dealing with the Stoa, gives an account of the theory of Chrysippus' pupil Diogenes of Seleucia on the Tigris.

The orthodox Stoic system likewise offered, this time without recourse to a theory of atoms, a materialistic explanation of the world that excluded the possibility of non-corporeal existence. It defined the most important sub-stance, however, as an infinitely fine pneuma that permeated all things as a life-giving force, manifesting itself to the senses as warmth and fire, and con-centrated in its most complete and pure form in the stars. Pneuma was at the same time regarded as the sustainer of reason (*logos*). The mathematically predictable movements of the stars most clearly demonstrated the rationality and plan behind all natural phenomena. Man was able to recognise and understand this, himself consisting of a high proportion of pneuma that made it possible for him to think. In the animal kingdom the level of pneumatic substance sufficed for sensation, in the plant kingdom for nutrition and reproduction, and in inanimate objects only for the achievement of a specific form. Inasmuch as the whole universe was permeated by pneuma it was thus also divine. Since, moreover, human beings had always had a share in pneuma, the ideas of all religions and myths manifested a veiled insight into the nature of the cosmos – made clear when correctly interpreted (i.e. in the form of allegory). In the Stoic view divination and astrology, dismissed by Epicureans and Sceptics as nonsense, were easily explained and rationalised as an expression of the link between pneumatic substances in the world and in the human soul.

The cosmic process was seen as unfolding according to a sound and rational plan in which even apparent evils such as natural catastrophes served a positive purpose. Strict predetermination (*heimarmene*) was at the same time a benevolent providence (*pronoia*) that equipped all creatures with the means for self-preservation and self-realisation. All natural phenomena, including apparent evils and catastrophes, were thus seen as fulfilling a meaningful function to a positive end. *Heimarmene* meant the best possible order for the world. It was assumed that after some millennia the course of cosmic events would have produced a strong concentration of pneuma, this in turn causing the world to burn up in a huge cosmic fire. This would bring one cycle in the world's history to an end, but initiate another creative cycle in its wake.

The place and role of man in the world was seen as shaped by the fact that he was a reasoning being provided with a substantial quantity of cosmic reason. Since all beings strove for the highest possible degree of self-realisation (an Aristotelian idea), man thus strove after the unfettered exercise of reason. This found expression in the capacity for judgement (thought) and communication with other reasoning beings (speech), so that human growth or self-realisation (*oikeiosis*) invariably affected both the individual and society alike. Growth to the perfect state of 'sage', the empirically unfathomable state of the exemplary man, was achieved when all actions derived without exception from correct discernment, and were hence virtuous.

The Stoics rooted their ethical concepts in a richly elaborated psychology. Following on logically from Socratic intellectualism but unlike the Academics and Peripatetics, the Stoics taught that spiritual processes, in so far as they were of moral significance, were invariably of a rational nature. Apparently irrational emotional states such as fear, desire, pleasure and pain, called by the Stoics states of affect or pathological changes in the spiritual life, were not thought to derive from independently existing irrational capacities of the soul. They stemmed from an act of judgement that wrongly attributed a positive or negative value to its notion of some detail of the environment, hence triggering an incorrect stimulus to action. Apathy, a state devoid of affect, was thus regarded as the most desirable condition for the human soul.

People were regarded as being inherently equipped with the capacity to make correct assessments of environmental phenomena at any time. This was borne out by the fundamental moral principles common to all nations which reflected the positive initial condition of man. Similarly, 'the philosophy of the barbarians', the wisdom handed down among exotic peoples such as the brahmins of India or Egyptian priests, was a residue from the natural primeval wisdom of humankind. As civilisation grew, however, a tradition of distorted judgements and values had formed and gained influence over every individual from birth. The empirical individual must thus first learn that there is only one good, namely the exercise of reason, which includes all virtues, and one evil, namely its obstruction or depravation, which is identical with the sum of all vices, as expressed in action based on affect. What philosophical speculation or general opinion might regard as good or evil – poverty and wealth, fame and notoriety, health and disease – was only of relative value (*adiaphoron*), and did not affect the human state of eudaemonia, which depended solely on the presence of the one (moral and intellectual) good, and operated in one's life according to natural principles.

The ruthless intellectualism of Stoic ethics, which regarded all spontaneous human reactions with suspicion, and the irreconcilable contradiction between conventional and Stoic views, led to a kind of rigorism that was often expressed in highly paradoxical forms. Stoics sought to accommodate their basic theories, derided by their opponents as ivory-towered, to the everyday contingencies of the person striving after moral growth by presenting as a supplement a comprehensive casuistry of decency (the theory of obligation) whose precepts did not lead directly to virtue as such, but were intended to prepare the ground for its intellectual acquisition.

In one respect both Stoic and Epicurean theory remained inconsistent. Their insistent appeal for the tireless pursuit of the acquisition and exercise of discernment, interpreted as virtue, could easily be refuted on the grounds that the conscious decisions of human beings were completely irrelevant in a context of the total and ideal determination of all that occurred. The Stoics responded to this objection by asserting that moral decisions made on the basis of correct discernment always coincided with what *heimarmene* had preordained, thus in fact simply signifying acquiescence to a cosmic order governed by fate. The happiness that derived from a morally sound life thus consisted of consciously thinking and acting in harmony with nature. However, living in harmony with nature also brought freedom, since the experience of being compelled to do something against one's will only arose when it opposed the order of nature without being able to prevail. Chrysippus illustrated this with a drastic example. The foolish dog was dragged howling behind the cart to which it was tied, while the clever dog trotted contentedly behind. In order to uphold the concept of human responsibility in a context of universal determination (*heimarmene*), the Stoa devised its own theory of causality, illustrated by Chrysippus with the example of the barrel. The barrel needed a push from outside in order to start rolling. This corresponded to the chain of causal events in fate, which man had no power to influence. The way the barrel rolled downhill depended on its characteristics. This corresponded to the inner state of man, which formed the basis of the actions, set in motion by the external cause, for which he bore the moral responsibility. To draw another analogy from the moral exhortations of the Stoics, the role attributed to one on the stage of the world theatre by fate was less important than how well one played it.

No philosophy exerted such an influence on general moral concepts throughout of the Hellenistic age as the Stoic school. These included the earnestness of moral responsibility and pastoral concern arising out of its rigorism, the notion of equal status and of a fraternal bond among all human beings (based on the theory of pneuma), and most particularly the liberty of man, rooted solely in a sound spiritual state. Man could not be ejected from full possession of eudaemonia by destitution or disease, contempt or malevolence. Indeed it befitted him as an autonomous being to put an end to his own life after a conscientious examination of circumstances.

All these ideas had a particularly strong appeal for men of action working in the interests of public welfare. The Stoic Persaeus served at the court of Antigonus Gonatas of Macedon, Sphaerus inspired the reform ideas of Cleomenes in Sparta, and Blossius the plan of Tiberius Gracchus in Rome. Notions of justice and equity deriving from Stoic theories of natural justice manifested themselves in the legislation of the Hellenistic states, and from the first century BC onwards among Roman jurists. As long as the Stoic school tradition persisted, its proponents sought to influence public life through their writings on monarchy, legislation and government.

The impact of Stoic philosophy on public life and general moral opinion matched the zeal with which it immersed itself in virtually all spheres of intellectual life. Many scholars of the age commended the Stoic world view, such as the great philologist, geographer and astronomer Eratosthenes in the third century, or the antiquarian and historian Apollodorus in the second century. As a result, Stoic-oriented approaches inevitably tended to shape scholarly inquiry. Speculation on *logos* led Stoics to reflect on the nature of language, giving rise to a highly subtle philosophy of language whose concepts were adopted in Latin and continue to serve to this day as categories of traditional grammar. Challenging Epicureans in the discipline of logic, the Stoics elaborated a logic of statements whose significance, like that of Aristotelian syllogistics, has only recently been rediscovered. Like Aristotle, albeit in a different way, they related logic to rhetoric, giving rise to a Stoic theory of rhetoric that helped the Romans to validate their creative literature. The Stoics' conviction that ancient poetry exhibited traces of a primeval human faculty for discernment bestowed by nature led them to elaborate a complex method of allegorical interpretation that first made itself felt in Homeric, and later in Judaeo-Christian biblical exegesis. The Stoic approach to nature was ultimately to find expression in discrete medical, ethnographic, meteorological and astronomical theories, which in turn stimulated further scholarly inquiry.

Panaetius led the Stoa along new paths. He was born around 180 BC into a noble family on Rhodes which, although allied with Rome, was then still completely independent. During a prolonged stay in Rome he found the homes of the senatorial aristocracy open to him. These social contacts brought the very first influences of the Greek philosophical spirit to some of the leading lights of the Roman upper class. Panaetius had studied in Athens under Antipater of Tarsus and Diogenes of Seleucia, the two most outstanding of Chrysippus' many pupils. However, the philosophy that Panaetius himself later taught during an Athenian career lasting into the next century bore some quite unorthodox traits. He abandoned rigid intellectualism, for example, by distinguishing between practical and theoretical intelligence, and acknowledging the independent existence of irrational emotional drives that needed to be governed and channelled by reason. Leaving to one side complex Stoic theory concerning the conduct of the perfect sage, he concentrated on the theory of obligation that was intended to assist the everyday activities of the person in his private and, above all, public life. These and other modifications to Stoic theory may be understood as arising out of adoptions from Plato and Aristotle, whom Panaetius venerated more than the founder of his own school, and whose philosophies were familiar to him not only from his own reading, but also from the discussions of his tutors with Carneades the Academic and Critolaus the Peripatetic. Panaetius' philosophy moreover emphatically went against the middle-class professorial spirit of Stoic orthodoxy. The first aristocrat and man of the world among the Stoics, he gravitated towards Plato's literary elegance and away from Chrysippus' amorphously structured erudition. It is no coincidence that the Roman consular Cicero was attracted by both the form and content of Panaetius' writings. Panaetius' magnum opus, his theory of obligation, formed the basis for Cicero's own work *De officiis*, which was to exert a lasting influence on Christian moral theology in a reworked version by the Church Father Ambrose of Milan.

Panaetius' fresh approach was further elaborated in all directions by his brilliant pupil Posidonius – another man of the world. Born in the Syrian town of Apamea, he travelled widely after his studies in Athens, later settling in Rhodes, where for a time he occupied the highest office of state. Cicero and Pompey were among those who attended the offshoot of the Stoa he founded there. In a later chapter (see below, p. 298) we shall be dealing with Posidonius' great achievements as historiographer, geographer and ethnographer – achievements inextricably linked with his philosophy.

243

Posidonius amplified the Stoic cosmology into an entirely new system, taking into account innumerable biological, meteorological, climatological, geological and astronomical observations, mostly of his own, which reveal him to be a natural scientist akin to Aristotle. In this way the schematic materialism of traditional Stoic physics faded almost entirely into the background behind his description of the forces responsible for the constant process of change in nature. As Karl Reinhardt (1928) has shown, of all ancient philosophers Posidonius perhaps came closest to the modern concept of evolution.

Posidonius, for whom, as for all Stoics, ethics was the cornerstone of philosophy, provided the discipline with a completely new psychological foundation – in constant polemic with Chrysippus' rigorous rationalism. Like Panaetius before him, he adopted from the Aristotelian and Platonic traditions the idea of the intrinsic value of irrational emotional drives. He then combined this with penetrating observations on the behaviour of children and animals to elaborate such modern-sounding psychological conceptions as the idea that man was the only creature characterised by permanently fragile mental equilibrium. His comprehensive theory of the rise of human culture proceeds in equally unconventional fashion, incorporating some Epicurean elements along the way, and explaining the rise of the human species in terms of the dearth of its natural resources, in other words its minimal chances for survival. His system of ethics, so far little researched, marked the first deliberate combination of a non-philosophical propaedeutics with philosophical doctrine.

The Stoa did not follow the lead of Posidonius, however. Hecaton, Panaetius' other outstanding pupil, soon set a return course to the orthodoxy that was to dominate the school's work throughout the Imperial period. Echoes of Posidonius' work are thus much more discernible among Platonists of the Imperial period, whose dogmatics largely operated with Stoic elements. His teaching offered numerous starting points for a spiritual reinterpretation along Platonist lines of the Stoic concepts of *logos* and pneuma, originally part of a materialistic interpretation of the cosmos. The philosophical syncretism that arose out of this encounter proved eminently suitable for philosophical formulation of religious ideas, and manifested itself at every turn during the Imperial period. Documentary evidence of this syncretism cannot always be unequivocally traced back to Posidonius, however, since sizeable fragments survive only from his geographical works. Nevertheless a sufficient number of passages referring to the specific theories of Posidonius in Cicero, Seneca, Plutarch and other authors do permit a reconstruction of at least the broad outlines of his system.

As the Hellenistic age drew to a close the Stoa, like the Peripatus (see above, p. 196), evinced a greater interest in the history of doctrines. Stratocles, a pupil of Panaetius, wrote the first book on the subject. He was followed by Apollonius of Tyre with a compilation of biographies and bibliographies of the

Stoics, and by Arius Didymus, a Stoic close to Augustus who wrote a comparative account of the schools' dogmas. Substantial extracts have survived.

All four major schools of the Hellenistic age – the Academy, Peripatus, Stoa and Garden – can make equal claim to represent its official philosophy. As has already been mentioned above (pp. 177ff.), some minor Socratic schools also survived into the period. By the same token, there must also have been Pythagoreans throughout the entire Hellenistic age. Admittedly, surviving records of earnest scholarly inquiry on the part of a school established by Philolaus in the fifth century BC and taken to the Greek homeland by numerous Pythagoreans (see above, p. 143) discontinue shortly after the time of Plato, who maintained friendly contacts with the Pythagorean Archytas of Tarentum. An inventory of the Pythagorean tradition, which was moved from Tarentum, the old Pythagorean centre, by Aristoxenus, a pupil of Aristotle, bears all the hallmarks of retrospection. Late fourth-century reports merely mention somewhat disreputable 'Pythagoreans' who roamed the countryside as preachers. There is then a gap until first-century BC reports of a Pythagorean school tradition which enjoyed close ties with the Academy and which was later to acquire some importance in connection with the newly emerging Neoplatonism.

No complex within Greek literature is thus so difficult to assess and classify as the heritage of Pythagoreanism. Some of the fragments and two completely extant works are under the name of Pythagoras himself, some in those of his legendary pupils (e.g. Ocellus of Lucania), while others are attributed to tangible literary persons (Archytas, Philolaus, or Timaeus from Plato's Dialogue of the same name). Research by W. Burkert (1971) and H. Thesleff (1971) show that in all probability a considerable proportion of these works date from the third and second centuries BC. This proves that the literary tradition of Pythagoreanism was never broken even though its social background is now obscure. Specific philosophical theories propounded by this literature stem in the case of cosmology from Academic, and in the case of ethics mostly from Peripatetic sources, the entirety none the less being steeped in the mysticism of a doctrine of salvation. It is not clear whether numerical speculation is part of the Pythagorean legacy or derives from the early Academy, which was highly receptive to the Pythagorean tradition. The texts bear witness to an interest in themes concerned with social ethics – an area for which Hellenistic philosophy in general evinced little concern – such as the status of women, children's education, and political theory. Another remarkable feature distinguishing Pythagorean literature of the Hellenistic age almost entirely from the conventions of the age is the fact that it was written in a simulated Doric. This, together with the fictitious authors' names, was clearly intended in deference to the early Pythagorean tradition of Lower Italy, which had been partially settled by Dorians. It was inconsistent with the historical facts, however. Indisputably authentic fragments of the earliest known Pythagorean writings, by Philolaus, dating from the fifth century BC, were in fact written in Ionic, the customary idiom for the philosophy and scholarly inquiry in which Pythagorean sects were at that time involving themselves as a result of the work of Philolaus.

One more school tradition remains to be mentioned: that of the Sceptics. Scepticism, understood as the striving after the most accurate possible criteria of probability in the conviction that humans are incapable of achieving irrefutable knowledge, had already existed among some Sophists. Democritus' theory of cognition also runs along similar lines. A separate school named after this endeavour, however, was founded by Pyrrho of Elis – who followed Stilpon of Megara in the Socratic tradition – after serving as a soldier in the Alexandrian campaign. Pyrrho taught the methodical refutation of claims to certain knowledge made within and outside philosophy. It was primarily the philosophical disciplines of logic and theory of cognition that drew lasting benefit from the work of the Sceptic school. Pyrrho's original aim, however, had been an ethical one. Enhancing the critical faculty was intended to inculcate apathy in a person, i.e. complete independence from changing sensory impressions and environmental influences. The Stoics had also defined the perfect human moral state as that of apathy – freedom from all intrusions by the emotional life, which they attributed to incorrect intellectual judgements. Whereas Stoic apathy had been based on correct discernment and certain knowledge, however, Sceptic apathy was rooted in the certain refutation of all knowledge. Nevertheless, in both cases the aim was for the individual to achieve an unassailable state with which to face his or her environment – a state that Epicureans also claimed to teach as ataraxia (tranquillity).

Although Pyrrho left no written legacy his teaching was carried on by a number of his pupils, notably Timon of Phlius in the Peloponnese. Timon wrote a three-volume satirical poem on the philosophy schools and their dogmatically fixed theories. Several fragments of this have survived, showing it to be in the literary tradition of Xenophanes' *Silloi* (see above, p. 81). An outline of his teaching preserved in a very late text seems to suggest that the poem also contains a systematic exposition of the Sceptic method.

The Sceptic school tradition seems to have splintered immediately after the first generation, from which some names are still known, including that of Nausiphanes, who came from a Democritan school and tutored Epicurus for a time, thus representing a marriage of the Democritan and Sceptic traditions.

Under the headship of Arcesilaus the Academy commandeered the Sceptic methods, which proved to be a cogent weapon primarily in the struggle against the dogmatism of the Stoa, and were to dominate the Academy for a century and a half. The fact that present-day knowledge of this area derives largely from indirect sources makes it difficult to ascertain which achievements in Sceptic logic and theory of cognition are attributable to the Sceptic school itself and which to the Academy. The Sceptic school tradition was revived again by Aenesidemus of Alexandria with express reference to Pyrrho in the first half of the first century BC, parallel with the lapse of the Academy into dogmatism. This tradition was to continue until the third century AD. Extant works by the physician Sextus, a member of the so-called Empiricist school, date from its final phase, and represent arguably the most valuable source material on post-Classical philosophy available today, expounding at length on the methods of late Scepticism and providing highly useful insights into its previous history.

Some familiarity with the philosophy of the epoch is indispensable for an understanding of Hellenistic literature. As has been shown, philosophy was understood to be a generally accessible, rationally conceived theory of nature from which postulates of individual morality could be deduced. Virtually all intellectuals of the period had philosophical connections of some kind, and many overtly professed the doctrines of specific schools. It should thus come as no surprise in non-philosophical texts to encounter such characteristic school dogmas as the Peripatetic division of moral resources into psychological, bodily and exterior, the Stoic classification of the four fundamental emotional states, or the Platonic tripartite division of the human soul. The biographies by Antigonus of Carystus (third century BC), from which substantial passages have survived in a compilation by Diogenes Laertius (around 200 AD), reveal how philosophy and philosophers were viewed by the educated public. Antigonus was a man of catholic intellectual interests. His works include, for example, a book on painting, but betray no trace of a particular philosophical commitment. This did not prevent him, however, from writing a lengthy volume comprising portraits of all the major philosophers teaching in Athens at the time. He took these seriously as tutors in the art of living, also viewing both their characters and lifestyles with a critical eye.

Hellenistic philosophy did not significantly enrich the storehouse of literary forms. Aside from the philosophical letter of condolence (see above, p. 191), it produced only two new genres, which developed in the Cynic tradition (see above, p. 177). This tradition remained entirely unproductive in terms of philosophical speculation, being carried on solely by mendicant popular and itinerant preachers.

Recent research has labelled one of these two genres with the misnomer of 'diatribe': the term 'homily' would be more appropriate. It imitates the earthy humour and edifying purpose of an instructive address given at the marketplace by itinerant spiritual advisers on practical ethical questions. The presentation is shaped largely by the expressed, unexpressed or pre-empted objections of the listener, producing a lively diction often akin to that of conversation. The irreverent approach of the Cynics, and their tendency to reduce *ad absurdum* all the foolish pretensions of people in the civilised world, find expression in a vulgar bluntness of vocabulary and in drastic metaphors, analogies and anecdotes.

Bion of Borysthenes (a Greek town on the northern coast of the Black Sea) lived for a time at the court of Antigonus Gonatas, King of Macedon (around 270 BC), and was regarded as a classic author of this both entertaining and edifying literature. Extant reports and fragments reveal him to have been a versatile and cultured man of letters. Despite evincing distinctly philosophical interests, however, he cannot be ranked with the Cynic tradition. Lengthy fragments from the sermons of the roughly contemporary Teles that have survived in the Florilegium of Bishop John of Stoboi (fifth century AD) on the other hand clearly propound Cynic doctrines.

The 'diatribe' was later employed by other philosophers either for expounding on practical moral questions for a broader readership or when the instruction of a philosophy school was intended not for future professional philosophers but to provide a general education. The best-known examples of such advisory texts issue from the pen of the Stoic Epictetus (around 100 AD). The Christian sermon was influenced from the very outset by this popular philosophical literary form. Apart from the works of Seneca (first century AD), who employed the genre with the utmost finesse, it was via this route that the diatribe found its way into European literature.

The Cynic Menippus of Gadara in Syria (around 250 BC), who found himself in Thebes in his latter years, succeeded in enriching the simple form of the Cynic sermon. By shifting its purpose from moral injunction to straightforward derision and satire he created both greater scope for literary invention, and expanded the potential for his portrayals. He ruthlessly derided Academicians and Epicureans alike as well as poking fun at traditional religion with witty invented myths. His short prose pieces, which are either interspersed with dialogues or entirely in dialogue form, also contained passages in verse. Menippus may have been inspired to use this technique by the treatment of philosophical advisory themes in iambic and other poetry forms at that time by such poets as Phoenix of Colophon and Cercidas (see below, p. 261). Only a handful of fragments have survived from Menippus' prolific writings. However, a clear enough idea of this new literary genre that emerged in the early Hellenistic age is provided by what remains both of Menippean satires by the Roman author Varro (first century BC) and more especially by the works of the Syrian Lucian of Samosata (second century AD), who closely adhered to Menippus' style and choice of themes. Here too the impact of the genre extends far into European literature, again with key mediating roles played by Roman authors such as Seneca and Petronius.

17

DRAMATIC POETRY

The theatrical practice that grew up in Athens began to spread throughout the Greek-speaking world from the fourth century BC onwards. No town in the Hellenistic-Roman age was without a theatre house, which could nevertheless serve a variety of purposes. Performances of Classical tragedies on the theatrical days of each town's respective festival calendar will mostly have involved only select parts such as the arias, songs or isolated scenes with newly composed melodies. It could be assumed that audiences would be familiar with the content of this dramatic literature. Educated people had read tragedies at school, and may have possessed a copy of Euripides or a mythological handbook in their private libraries. The man in the street was for his part surrounded by mythical representations at the marketplace and in every public building. Professional actors, whose associations or guilds enjoyed a legal status recognised across state frontiers, vied to perform these dramas. The nature of the theatre scene at the time can be deduced from honorary inscriptions dedicated to successful actors.

Obviously Athens with its long-standing theatrical tradition continued to be the leading centre for the performing arts. Inscriptions dating from the first century BC show that newly written tragedies were also performed. The prolific output of 'New Comedy', a trend that lasted until the end of the third century BC, was almost entirely restricted to Athens. Nevertheless in newly founded Alexandria the second Ptolemaic king of Egypt prepared the ground for a renaissance of tragedy writing with his generous sponsorship of all arts and sciences. He established drama contests and invited poets to Egypt from among whom seven were later selected to form a tragic *pleias*. It is no longer known how many of those whose names have been handed down wrote dramas for reading solely – a practice that appeared in the fourth century BC and became integral to literary education throughout the Hellenistic-Roman age. Seneca's tragedies are the sole complete extant examples of this genre. In addition to these some 269 extant verses of a tragedy have survived by chance in the work of a Christian author. Composed by a Hellenised Jew by the name of Ezekiel, probably in the late second century

BC, they deal with the exodus of the children of Israel from Egypt (see below, p. 308), and document just how widespread drama for reading was.

When in the third and second centuries BC the Romans began to write and perform stage works they clearly focused on the dramas of Euripides. These thus came to dominate performing practice in the Hellenistic age, with the exception of the *fabula praetexta* that dealt with contemporary historical themes and may have been modelled on Hellenistic tragedy. Some titles which may be construed as having contemporary historical themes are documented for the fourth and third centuries BC besides those of the customary tragedies on mythical themes. The best-known tragic poets of the third century, Alexander the Aetolian, Lycophron and Philicus, also wrote in other genres. Since these tragedies have been lost aside from a handful of lines, it is no longer possible to evaluate their merit. Sixteen lines of a tragedy dating from this period were retrieved some years ago with a papyrus find. Dealing with the story of Gyges, King of the Lydians, and drawing heavily on Herodotus, they may be assumed to date from the Hellenistic age.

Of far greater significance is the last flowering of Attic comedy, known as New Comedy according to the classification scheme of librarians at Alexandria, whose stock included the works of at least sixty-four poets of this group. Aside from a sizeable number of titles and authors' names in the grammatical literature, until a few decades ago all that remained of this rich legacy – still to some extent accessible to an educated fifth- and sixth-century readership in the form of 'school and home' editions – was a handful of isolated lines or line groups. These had survived as citations by later authors, either in the form of aphorisms, or on account of their linguistic or thematic peculiarities. It was nevertheless still possible to form some idea of the structure of plays, since the nineteen surviving comedies of Plautus (late third century BC) and the six by Terence (second century BC) were all without exception imitations of Greek originals, the source sometimes even being expressly named in the prologue. Some of their plays, however, acquired a certain independent status, either as a result of contamination from several models, or through additional material or substantial rewriting.

Deeper insight into the art of New Comedy came with a spate of papyrus finds from the beginning of this century onwards that retrieved a number of plays by the leading New Comedy poet (ranked in the Hellenistic-Roman age even above Aristophanes). Some of these have survived complete, others only as lengthy passages. The writing career of Menander, who completed his military service as an Athenian ephebe in the same year as Epicurus, extended from around 320 BC to the first decade of the third century: some of his plays contain references to events from this period. He is rightly regarded as the classic New Comedy author, in whose works all the hallmarks of the genre come to full flower. The underlying tone of these plays was cheerful and relaxed without being comic in the burlesque sense. Apart from a few mythical travesties, they are set in the milieu of well-to-do middle-class families and deal with incidents and intrigue. The derision of real-life personalities from Athenian public life that had permeated all earlier comedy had by this time almost completely disappeared, as had ribaldry, which now only issued occasionally from the mouth of a slave.

The structure and enactment of the plot conformed to the rules of Euripidean dramaturgy, the devices and accomplishments of which had partly been elaborated in the context of mythical themes presented without their heroic lustre, thus rendering them easily transferable to middle-class comedy plots. Their strict division into acts went beyond Euripides, although not always adhering to the five-act structure regarded as canonical by Horace and later commentators. The chorus was by now completely removed from the action. Its appearance as an interlude ballet as documented in a few surviving plays is so peripheral that it is merely noted in the script without even giving the lyrics of the choral song. The intricate plot tends to arise out of a complex setting that is generally set forth in a lengthy prologue quite apart from the action itself. The prologue is often spoken by deities, such as Pan, the patron of the rural setting, in which the comedy is set, or Air, because she is everywhere and all-knowing, or Agnoia, Ignorance, the cause of all the entanglements of the play. This prologue technique also derives from Euripidean tragedy.

In terms of the European stagecraft tradition, therefore, New Comedy and its Latin imitations fall between Euripides and the sixteenth-century comic play. Old comedy, which shared with New Comedy the basis of being performed in qualifications for participation in the Athenian festival calendar, was only loosely related to its successor by the mediating form of middle comedy, whose distinguishing characteristics are hard to discover.

Through a number of papyrus finds almost three-quarters of the verse text have survived of *Epitrepontes – Court of Arbitration*, a comedy in Menander's mature style. Charisius, a young Athenian, has married Pamphila, a middle-class girl. Soon after their wedding he is obliged to go away on business. On his return he is informed by his slave Onesimus that Pamphila has given birth to and exposed a child (in those days the exposure of children was a widespread custom and not frowned upon, hence a frequent motif for comedies). Greatly disappointed, Charisius moves into the home of his friend Chairestratus and hires the hetaera Habrotonon. As the audience later discovers, however, he has nothing to do with her – thus revealing his unabated love for Pamphila – while outwardly living the life of a bachelor belonging to the Athenian *jeunesse dorée*. Anxious about his daughter (and her dowry), Pamphila's father Smicrines sets off for the city. He is stopped on the way by two slaves, Daos the shepherd and Syriscus the charcoal-burner. Daos has discovered an exposed baby and handed it over to Syriscus at the latter's request to bring it up. However, he has kept for himself the items found with the child and by which it might one day be recognised. Asked by them both to arbitrate, Smicrines decides in favour of giving the items to

Syriscus. As the latter is rummaging through them, Charisius' slave Onesimus arrives and recognises a ring that his master has lost. Although he succeeds in retrieving it, he is reluctant to approach his master with a new revelation, and discusses the matter with Habrotonon. It turns out that Charisius lost the ring while attacking a girl in a drunken stupor at a nocturnal Tauropolian festival – an incident of which Habrotonon is also aware. The foundling is thus very probably Charisius' child. Habrotonon summarily takes the ring and the child, and confronts him, posing as the raped girl to test him. Deeply ashamed, Charisius realises that he has done wrong. When Smicrines hears of it, however, he believes himself justified in taking his daughter away from such a husband, although she wants to stand by him. The full story emerges in conversation after the long-suffering Pamphila is sought out by the kind Habrotonon: none other than Pamphila herself was the girl attacked by Charisius in his nocturnal drunkenness. The foundling is thus the child of the married couple. Nothing further stands in the way of a reconciliation, now that Charisius is overwhelmed with remorse and gratitude.

This intricate, somewhat far-fetched plot has scope for many stage effects, of which Menander nevertheless avails himself with the utmost tact. Its capacity to involve the audience or reader, and seem more than a mere extraordinary occurrence, lies in his psychological enhancement of the events. The cast is ostensibly composed of easily recognisable comic types: the stingy old man, the feckless young man of good family, the sly slave from a city household and the awkward one from the country, the merry hetaera, etc. On closer examination, however, the action acquires its dramatic tension from the very way the main protagonists behave contrary to clichéed expectations. Habrotonon's warmheartedness and helpfulness are injurious to her profession, while Charisius, who unbeknown to himself remains devoted to his wife, learns full acceptance of his moral responsibility, thereby ·becoming worthy of his wife's love. In another play, *The Shorn Girl*, the main male character, a soldier who ought to be a red-necked lout according to comic convention, reveals the tenderness and passion of his feelings. In *Misoumenos* (*The Man She Hated*), another soldier attains love and marriage with a slave he has bought – who of course turns out to be freeborn – and declares his feelings for her with devotion, patience and respect. These and other episodes reveal the warm humanity with which Menander lent lifelike credibility to the essentially stilted plots supplied by contemporary stage convention, for all their ingenious entanglements and abundant situation comedy.

Dyskolos (*The Misanthropist*), a comedy written in Menander's youth, has survived complete on a papyrus. Its early date is apparent from the relatively large amount of burlesque elements and certain deficiencies of composition, although it remains a good example of another kind of psychological emphasis for which Menander was famous. The main character of the play is an elderly misanthrope who regards the amenities of urban civilisation as pernicious, and lives on the fruits of his own labours on a small country estate, avoiding all social connections in order to avoid obligation to anyone. The plot, which does not need to be examined in detail here, derives from this extreme false attitude on the part of the old misanthrope, which is shown up for what it is through the device of a contrasting character, a kindly and optimistic old man, and then reduced *ad absurdum* by the outcome of the play. (Menander may have drawn in this comedy on anecdotes connected with Timon the Misanthrope, a real-life Athenian character, which have been revived and adapted again and again in many branches of literature up to the modern era.)

Such character studies as these, the sincerity with which Menander classified his characters by their moral qualities rather than their social origins, and the way they exemplify what is best in humanity, enabling them to rise in mutual kindness above the unpredictable vicissitudes of fate – *tyche* – have caused commentators to ask whether he was directly influenced by philosophical ethics. All attempts to correlate his comedies with the moral typology of the Peripatus or other distinct philosophical doctrines, however, have simply led to the conclusion that philosophical ethics and the morality manifested in Menander's comedies represent two different fruits from the same tree – the urban civilisation of Attica. A dependent relationship as such cannot be proved, as it is little surprise to find a line revealing an author's conversance with contemporary philosophical theories. It should not be overlooked, however, that Menander's ethical reflection goes far deeper at times than that of the philosophers of his day. Menander's view, for example, that married couples should bear moral responsibility together in mutual love, and that a lapse on the part of the husband should be judged in the same way as that of a wife, was quite beyond the horizon of philosophy. When asked whether the sage should marry, philosophers replied affirmatively along with Theo-phrastus – provided he could find a beautiful, virtuous and well-off wife from a good family who would not distract him from his work. It was not until the late Stoa era that reflection on love, marriage and the family began to slacken the grip of traditional individualism on philosophical ethics, which had hitherto only inquired after individual moral growth.

Menander's humanity, expressed not least in his affectionate depictions of the most varied human types with all their strengths and weaknesses, represents the fruit of a rich civilisation whose tradition had attained a high level of social awareness. It reached its fullest flower just as Athens was lapsing into the status of a provincial town lying for a time leeward of big-power politics. It was only by virtue of its social culture and philosophy schools that Athens remained a centre of refined living until the very end of antiquity, despite this provincial backwater status.

Attic urbanity shaped Menander's finely nuanced ordering of scenes, and even more so his language. With apparently complete effortlessness he casts into traditional dramatic spoken verse a conversational style furnished with countless little turns of phrase to suit both the peculiarities of the dramatic situation and the character and social rank of the speaker. A small example pointed out by W. H. Friedrich (1953, p. 25) is when, in the quarrel between the two country-born slaves over the items found with the exposed baby (see above, pp. 251–2) Syriscus says that they 'belong baby', rather than 'the things belong to the baby'. This respects the familiar, simple form of expression whereby a person or object for which one has affection tends to be denoted with a proper name-type word rather than with an appellative. Despite such differentiations when representing usage, however, Menander almost invariably avoided placing crude and vulgar expressions in the mouths of slaves or cooks. The unity of urban decorum and ease is thus always preserved in his diction. It says something for the literary taste of the great Caesar that he used the term 'semi-Menander' to describe the comic poet Terence, who has been held up as a model of elegant and decorous language in the literary traditions of Rome and the Occident alike.

Of the remaining poets in the group, Philemon of Syracuse, who was made a citizen of Athens in 300 BC at the age of 50, was regarded by ancient literary critics as coming closest artistically to Menander, who was twenty years his junior. Their generation also included Diphilus of Sinope on the Black Sea, who worked in Athens but died in Smyrna. His dramatic technique has been examined in detail by W. H. Friedrich. It differs from that of Menander chiefly in a certain blunting of dramatic emphases and its greater complexity of plot. Plautus was fond of imitating the plays of Diphilus. Two other comic poets of the same period both bore the name of Apollodorus. One came from Carystus on Euboea, the other from Gela in Sicily. In contrast with these Demophilus, now known only via Plautus, and Posidippus of Cassandria in Macedon, the two last poets of the New Comedy known by name, decidedly belong in the third century BC.

As the writing of new plays abated, revivals also helped to fill the gaps for planned comedy performances in Athens. Menander acquired a dominant position similar to that of Euripides among the tragic poets. Numerous extant announcements testify to repeat performances of his plays in Athens. Over and above this, however, he also acquired classic status, his works continuing to find readers among educated families.

Tragedies and comedies never sank to the level of mere spectacle, however, but continued to maintain a relatively high literary standard. They were thus not designed to answer the requirements met in the modern era by variety theatre, film and television. Mime was the form of sub-literary dramatic entertainment prevalent in the Hellenistic-Roman age. This term covers a wide variety of performances which, it should be recalled, dominated the countless theatres of the entire civilised world. They included show-type dancing displays, either by solo performers or groups and to a musical accompaniment without words; songs performed by solo performers with mimetic extravagance; short verse narratives with dialogue interludes performed by the speaker in various voice registers and accompanied by mime, and lastly short plays, mostly in prose, involving massive casts and spectacular, amusing or erotic motifs from tragedy, comedy or narrative literature – exactly, in fact, like modern entertainment films.

The first mime form mentioned above, also known as pantomime, does not concern us here. The third form we shall be discussing in more detail, since it found its way into higher literature. Two examples of the solo song with mime accompaniment are known from the Hellenistic age. One is a paraclausithyron, the touching lament of a rejected girl at the door of her former lover, and has been preserved on papyrus. The other is a song sung by a hetaera in conversation with a lover who has been locked out. This has survived on a second-century BC inscription in Marissa in Palestine. Some names of poets who wrote songs of this kind have also survived. Surprisingly enough, they include the tragic poet Alexander of Aetolia, but more notably Sotades, whose poetry was notorious for its lasciviousness. Documentary evidence of complete theatre plays in mime does not appear until several substantial papyrus fragments dating from the Imperial period, but archaeological evidence suggests that this form of entertainment for city audiences was already practised in the early Hellenistic age. Women performed in all forms of mime, and moreover without masks, whereas in tragedy and comedy tradition dictated that all roles be played by masked male actors.

18

CALLIMACHUS AND LYRIC POETRY

The founding and expansion of the museum at Alexandria by the first two Ptolemies heralded a new epoch for scholarly disciplines. Its achievements will be dealt with below (see pp. 281ff.). Magnificent library facilities boasting fine collections, research amenities and, not least, well-remunerated professorial chairs whose incumbents enjoyed high esteem both in society at large and at court (the library superintendent was usually tutor to the crown prince) constituted ideal conditions for a rich flowering of scholarship, and to a certain extent poetry.

The systematic collation, ordering and cataloguing of the entire treasury of Greek poetry was entrusted to scholars of whom most were poets themselves. They had recourse to poetic tradition in a way hitherto unknown, enabling them to select, imitate or modify elements of both form and content of which they had the broadest possible understanding. In their colleagues they furthermore had a readership, albeit of limited numbers, able to appraise and savour a poetry that presupposed an intellectual and comprehensive literary education. It is easy to understand how this circle, its lifestyle presumably influenced by its connections with the brilliant Ptolemaic court, brought the formal attributes of poetry to the peak of perfection. Thus, in its final flower, Greek poetry acquired an esoteric character marked by a consummate craftsmanship that placed heavy demands on the literary and antiquarian education of poet and reader alike.

The best-known and in many respects the most important proponent of this new poetry was Callimachus, who was born in the ancient North African Greek city of Cyrene. He came to Alexandria as a young scholar on the threshold of the third century BC, first eking out a living as a schoolmaster, then being brought to the attention of Ptolemy II and appointed as librarian to the museum, although in fact he never became superintendent. Callimachus' scholarly career was almost unimaginably prolific, extending beyond the mid-third century. In some 120 volumes (i.e. papyrus scrolls) he catalogued the entire stock of the library at Alexandria, as well as writing countless specialist monographs on antiquarian themes such as the names of nations in literature, contests, foundation myths, miraculous stories, foreign customs, the names of months and many others.

Callimachus' poetry needs to be understood against the background of this huge scholarly output. Of his poetry, only one compilation of hymns to the gods has survived in full, written with a single exception in heroic hexameters. The hexametric hymn, of which the most ornate examples comprise several hundred verses, invokes a specific deity, recounts his or her feats (aretalogy), and usually concludes with a prayer for support and blessing. It is an ancient form of authentic cult poetry intended for oral performance. Despite their literary transmission, the so-called *Homeric Hymns* are entirely in keeping with this character. Callimachus mastered this form purely for its literary potential, availing himself of the fixed formulas of the cult tradition in order to compose poetry which met the requirement for artistic homogeneity. He achieves this with startling combinations of the most diverse narrative elements drawn from little-known antiquarian themes, blended with a filigree of literary citations and borrowings, allusions to contemporary events from life at court, and witty jibes. This highly heterogeneous blend thus embraced a wealth of detail that was only accessible to a readership of connoisseurs. These characteristic features of Callimachus' hymnic poetry are particularly well illustrated with the example of his hymn to Zeus, the first in the anthology.

Following traditional prayer custom, the poet opens with a series of invocations of Zeus, since the deity must be invoked by as many of his names as possible in order to be sure of including the one to which he is most favourably disposed. This immediately poses the learned Callimachus with a problem, however: should he make his plea to Zeus from Mount Ida on Crete or from Lycaeum in Arcadia? Both were held by different traditions to have been the birthplace of Zeus. A solution to the problem is nevertheless found: 'The Cretans have always been liars.' This is a quotation from an early Archaic epigrammatic poem, and is further bolstered by Callimachus with the archaeological argument that in Crete there is even a grave of Zeus (a cult site, dating from pre-Greek times, of a god who died and rose from the dead and whom the Greeks later took to be Zeus). Since, however, Zeus and the Olympian gods were known to immortal, the Cretan tradition had to be refuted. Callimachus goes on to narrate how Rhea gives birth to Zeus in the mountainous wilderness of Arcadia, how the earth goddess has a spring rise from the ground to facilitate his care, the child then being taken to Crete and suckled by the she-goat Amalthaea, cared for by the nymph Neda, and protected by the noisy weapon dance of the Corybants from an attack by his father Cronus. In this way a sequence of terse allusions suffices to provide a wealth of detail from mythical history. The scholarly character of what is imparted is enhanced not so much by the reference to so many little-known names as by an enumeration of modern topographical detail such as did not in fact exist at that time in Arcadia. The superior level of knowledge used by the scholar to compile his account of events in the myth thus at the same time forms the basis for his ironic, amused approach to the events themselves.

The account thus revolves around how Zeus grew up, which brings the poet to another problem. Is Homer correct in recounting how power over the earth, sea and underworld was distributed equally among the brothers Zeus, Poseidon and Hades? Or is Hesiod's version correct whereby Poseidon and Hades willingly accepted the superior power of Zeus and obtained their domains from him? Callimachus emphatically concludes that the latter is the correct interpretation. This conclusion has rightly been seen as alluding to a dynastic dispute in the house of Ptolemy. The subsequent verses likewise go on to describe in spirited terms the status of the earthly king as a replica of the rulership of Zeus. Here too the author bases his account on Hesiod, who described kings as the descendants of Zeus, and possibly also on Homer's description of the sceptre of King Agamemnon, given by Zeus to one of his forefathers and handed down from father to son as a symbol of rule ever since. Following this homage to the king the poem concludes with the customary prayer for blessing and wealth familiar from the *Homeric Hymns*. By playing with traditional vocabulary the poet is able to make an up-to-date point here. He prays for *arete* and wealth, since he would not care to have one without the other. The wit of this passage does not become fully apparent solely by pointing out that it may represent a veiled request by the penniless poet to his royal patron. In archaic language, *arete* signified the privileged position and hereditary virtue of nobles, as manifest in visible success. The full substance of the prayer is thus revealed in the terms of the ancient tradition. By Callimachus' time *arete* had long signified a moral virtue entirely separate from outward circumstances. By expressly praying for both *arete* and wealth, Callimachus was taking a stand on a much-disputed topical issue within philosophy with which all intellectuals were familiar – namely, whether *arete* was sufficient to attain full eudaemonia, or whether the outward appurtenances of fortune were also necessary. Callimachus thus shows himself to be the man of the world and courtier that he is, naturally opposed to the rigorism of the Stoics and in favour of the moderate views of the Peripatetics.

The artistic character of this thoroughly playful poetry manifests itself not only through analysis of its content, but most of all through examination of the verse and style. Like other poets of his day, Callimachus subjected the hexameter to a range of euphonic rules that were quite alien to ancient heroic poetry. This formal rigour of verse is matched by a highly meticulous treatment of language. The wealth of literary allusion aimed at in these poems of course entirely precluded the poet from simply utilising the formal style of ancient epic. Moreover, the abundance of rare names and allusions to little-known myths that had never been treated in epic form inevitably led to new words and combinations continuously being formed within the convention of heroic style. This notwithstanding, Callimachus did occasionally deliberately revive an ancient epic formula – albeit usually imbuing it with slight variations and a fresh emphasis – thereby assigning himself a place in the epic stylistic tradition on the strength of his position as a learned authority.

There was thus a massive erudition behind all these verse narratives that constituted the sole source of subject-matter to be expected in each and every poem at that time, and which was seen to justify the poetic attempt. This erudition was both accommodated and mitigated by the extreme formal rigour to be found in the verse and wording, and by the witty elegance of the narrative method used.

The fifth hymn is also worth noting as it does not adhere to the hymnic prayer form, being composed in elegiac distichs rather than hexameters. Like other hymns by Callimachus it has a narrator, who describes the ancient Argive cult custom of the annual bathing of the temple image of Athena. He also encourages the female temple attendants in their work. What gives this poem its charm as it unfolds is the difficulty in distinguishing the goddess from her image. The reader is clearly intended to be reminded of the bathing goddess herself during the account of the bathing of her cult image, since we are also given the story of how Teiresias was punished for accidentally catching sight of her at her bath.

The fifth and sixth hymns are composed in a style peppered with numerous Dorisms. There are other early examples of this dialectal enhancement of the hexametric or even dactylic verse customarily associated with Homeric style, such as in a processional poem by Sappho, or local epigrammatic poetry. Hellenistic poets eagerly seized on its potential for variation, thereby ushering in a new tradition for a separate genre of hexametric poetry in non-Homeric style.

Like the rest of Callimachus' poetry his hymns were avidly read in the ensuing centuries, and soon became the object of philological interpretation. Egyptian papyrus finds have thus brought to light not only numerous fragments of texts themselves, but also substantial relics of commentaries and prose paraphrases of more demanding poems.

Callimachus was not the sole exponent of Hellenistic hymnic poetry. An equally famous and fine example of hexametric hymn poetry is available in the form of a full quotation of a hymn to Zeus by Cleanthes, the second leader of the Stoa. Here, however, the name Zeus is used to evoke not the highest of the Olympian gods, but the Stoics' universal law, at work in the life-giving substance of *logos*. This makes the poem both the earliest and most impressive evidence of pantheistic piety inspired by a philosophical doctrine, expressed in willing submission to a fate understood as a benign and benevolent providence. This hymn by Cleanthes shows that the hexametric hymn was still fully acknowledged as a form of true cult poetry, as is borne out by a number of hexametric hymns preserved on inscriptions praising the feats of Isis and other deities. The most famous of these are a poem to Sarapis by

Maiistas of Delos and a hymn to Isis from the island of Andros, both dating from the third century BC.

There are also examples of narrative hymns to deities composed in iambic trimeters. There can be no doubt as to the cult nature of such texts, most of which derive from inscriptions from temple precincts. In the case of anonymous hymns preserved on papyrus it is more difficult to decide whether they were cultic or purely literary texts – such as fragments of a third-century BC narrative hymn to Demeter composed in elegiac distichs.

Much the same applies to relics of sung hymnic poetry or poetry in song verse. A good dozen hymns to various gods have come to light in the form of inscriptions found during the excavation of Greek shrines. These are genuine purpose-written liturgical poems, composed in what compared to great choral lyric poetry are simple strophes made up of well-known types of song verse, generally of very limited literary merit. Sometimes the name of the poet is mentioned on the stone, and in a few cases even a musical annotation is included. These documents from Epidaurus, Athens, Delphi and other sites span a period from the fourth century BC, to which the hymns by Isyllus may be dated, up to the first century BC. Sometimes a much earlier text seems to have been adapted to the performance practice of the Hellenistic age and preserved on an inscription.

Quite a number of papyri indicate that the anapaest (∪∪–) was a favoured metre for song poetry throughout the Hellenistic age. Both literary and epigraphic evidence documents the increasing employment of all these various forms of cult poetry for the veneration of kings and military leaders.

Cultic song poetry also served the scholar-poets of the Hellenistic age as a model for creative literature, although the latter was probably mostly intended for spoken rather than sung performance. It became fashionable during this period to employ specific types of song verse and verse combinations in the composition of spoken poetry. There was little to stand in the way of this trend, since musical performance practice was constantly changing anyway.

Most types of Greek verse are still known today by the names they were given by grammarians of the Hellenistic or Imperial periods – the grammatical classification of verse proved both meaningful and necessary as soon as text and music became separate. Many of these names (Asclepiads, Phalaecians, etc.) refer to the poet who in the view of grammarians either first or most aptly used the verse type, or who made use of it for spoken verse.

A good example of the literary imitation and adaptation of cultic song poetry is a hymn to Demeter by Philicus of Corcyra (Corfu), who also made a name for himself as a tragedian at the court of Ptolemy II. The most valuable treatise on metre in the Greek language, written by one Hephaestion in the second century AD, used one line from this poem as an example of the metre. A papyrus find some years ago retrieved a further fifteen lines.

Dealing with an episode from the Demeter myth, the poem is narrated in a very lively style, and contains direct speech. Remarkably, it is in Attic rather than one of the poetic idioms. The sole metre used throughout is extremely difficult to manage on account of the distribution of long and short syllables it calls for, thus compelling us to view the entire work primarily as a showcase for verse technique. Callimachus also wrote a number of quite lengthy hymn-like poems using rarer forms of lyric metre. Fragments of these have survived mainly in the collections of examples in later treatises on metre. Melinno, a now otherwise unknown female poet of the second or first century BC, is the author of a hymn to Rome in pure Sapphic strophes that was also probably intended for oral performance, and should therefore be treated as a piece of literature. It has survived all this time by chance in a late antique anthology. Cercidas of Megalopolis in Arcadia, whose dates almost certainly fall in the third century BC, executed his popular philosophical advisory texts not in iambic metre like other Hellenistic authors (see pp. 264–5), but in various types of song verse. Substantial extracts of this somewhat earthy poetry, undoubtedly meant to be spoken aloud and read, and written in a style enhanced with Dorisms, have survived partly on papyrus and partly in the late antique anthology of Stobaeus.

This spoken verse poetry in song verse metres produced no outstanding achievements, if the circumstances in which it has come down to us are anything to go by (so few of Callimachus' scant lyric works have survived that they do not permit a reliable assessment of their merits). Its historical significance derives from the fact that these forms of Hellenistic and Archaic lyric poetry were adopted into the Latin by Catullus and Horace, whose own works are of the highest literary merit, thereby ensuring them an established place in the European literary tradition. All the distinguishing technical characteristics of Hellenistic practice are to be found in the works of these two Roman poets – such as the stricter regulation of quantities in what was by then spoken song verse, and the display of poetic skill in technical showcase poems, such as Catullus' poem on Attis.

Callimachus' poetic magnum opus was a four-volume collection of separate verse narratives in elegiac metre. It is entitled *Aetia* (*Causes*), containing myths recounted in explanation of existing names, cults or customs. A substantial number of papyrus finds have been compiled by Rudolf Pfeiffer into a commendable edition entitled *Callimachus* (1949–53) providing both fragments of text and relics of ancient exegesis. This has permitted scholars to form a relatively reliable picture of the style and structure of a work previously only documented by scant notices and short fragments.

The prologue explicitly states that the publication of the whole work took place in his old age. Some elegies seem to have been written and published much earlier, however, since Apollonius Rhodius refers to passages from them in his heroic poetry. The prologue, whose statements are supplemented by two extant epigrams and the conclusion of the second hymn, adopts a position against opponents of the poet, who are presented in the guise of *Telchines*, malevolent goblins. It provides some insight into the controversies surrounding literature and literary theory that must inevitably have existed in such a poetry hothouse. Callimachus commended not the grand-scale heroic poem in the Homeric tradition, which, like the Euphrates, inevitably swept a great deal of sludge along in its wake, but the short poem, which he likened to a modest but clear spring. It is now no longer clear exactly where the lines were drawn between the two sides of this particular controversy. One ancient commentary gives the two epigrammatic poets Asclepiades and Posidippus as masters of the short form and yet as opponents of Callimachus, while irrefutable evidence of what one would expect on the other hand to be a dispute between Callimachus and Apollonius Rhodius, author of a major epic poem about the Argonauts, has not been forthcoming. Callimachus further- more also wrote a treatise on poetry theory that opposed the Peripatetic Praxiphanes, while totally concurring with one of the conclusions of Aris- totelian poetics in preferring on principle the succinct adaptation of an episode to the extensive epic account. What is certain, however, is that Callimachus' preference for the short form of verse narrative placed him within an already existing tradition whose original exponent was held to be Philetas of Cos. The latter was of the same generation as Alexander, spending his final years in Alexandria at the court of Ptolemy I. Like Callimachus, he was also a philologist, publishing a collection of rare words (glosses). Virtually nothing has survived of Philetas' poetry aside from some indication of his titles, but reports by Callimachus and the Roman elegists regarded his work without doubt as an authoritative influence on Hellenistic elegies and short epic poetry (to be discussed below).

Assuming present-day information to be correct, the themes of this narrative poetry were drawn from mythology. Mythical traditions and, what comes to the same thing, historical and anecdotal ones, provided poets with episodes which were then adapted into poems of moderate length, focusing on pathetic, spectacular, witty and above all erotic elements that were either already present or potentially to be construed from them. There is no evidence to suggest that Hellenistic elegists wrote about their own love experiences. Roman elegiac poets of the Augustan period (Tibullus, Pro- pertius) may well have derived this distinguishing feature of their poetry from Hellenistic models in epigrammatic poetry, which of course is formally very close to the elegy.

The grammarian Athenaeus (second century AD) has preserved an elegy by Hermesianax, who was traditionally held to have been a pupil of Philetas. The poem contains an account, reminiscent of Hesiodic catalogue poetry, of the mostly legendary romantic experiences of great poets and philosophers. Elegies and elegy fragments by Phanocles, Alexander of Aetolia (also a well- known tragedian) and other less well-known poets of the period have been preserved in a similar way. To these may be added various papyrus fragments, whose numbers have continued to increase up to the most recent times. These texts evince immense variations in both style and narrative method – ranging from sentimental display to distanced description. Like its precursor, the Archaic elegy, the Hellenistic elegy was inextricably linked with the epic stylistic tradition, although the publicist element found in Solon, Tyrtaeus or Theognis was foreign to it.

Callimachus' *Aetia* may be regarded as the classic work of the genre, excelling both for its profusion of some of the least-known mythographical subject-matter, and an unsurpassedly evocative, deadly accurate, and not infrequently ironic and witty expressional mode, of which the extant fragments provide abundant evidence. At the very end of the collection was a poem in which the elderly but gallant court poet paid charming homage to his young queen. Shortly after his marriage to the Cyrenian Princess Berenice, Ptolemy III had left to fight in the war against the Seleucid Empire. The queen had consecrated a lock of her hair for the safe return of her husband, but soon afterwards the votive gift had mysteriously disappeared from the temple. At this Conon, director of the observatory at Alexandria, declared that he had discovered a new constellation – none other than Berenice's lock of hair removed to the heavens. In the poem Callimachus has the lock of hair-turned-constellation narrate its fate. In a delightfully intricate sequence of ideas incorporating motifs from little-known antiquarian and astronomical learning, all contrived to lead the reader to view the whole affair with mildly amused ironic detachment, the lock of hair bitterly laments having had to leave its place on the head of such a gracious queen, avowing that its relocation and new imperishable status among the stars are but poor compensation for the loss. The only extant complete version of the poem's full hundred lines is in a translation by Catullus dating from the first century BC. Its merits can nevertheless now be better appreciated since more than a quarter of the original has been retrieved with papyrus finds.

Closely related to the narrative elegy was the short epic poem, which was extremely popular in the Hellenistic age. Almost all the elegists mentioned in the preceding account also wrote short epic poems (epyllia). These did not differ from elegies either in subject-matter or in length. Occasional differences are discernible only in the narrative method, and may be attributed to the use of different types of verse. The emphatic caesura following each distich, which consisted of a hexameter and a pentameter, understandably had its effect on the flow of the narrative.

In this sphere too a work by Callimachus may be regarded as the most representative and influential in the Graeco-Latin tradition. It bore the title *Hecale* and dealt with various episodes from the mythical complex concerning the Attic national hero Theseus – his arrival in Athens and subduing of the bull at Marathon. The heroic deeds presented in the traditional version nevertheless constitute no more than a background framework for the narrative. Callimachus gives a detailed description of the sojourn of the tired hero with Hecale, an old woman who has seen better days and who now

263

offers Theseus sincere and solicitous hospitality. Various details from this homely idyllic scene were later incorporated by the Roman poet Ovid in his verse narrative on Philemon and Baucis, thereby ensuring Callimachus' *Hecale* an enduring influence into the most recent times. Aside from a couple of literary fragments, only some forty verses of *Hecale* have survived in the form of a passage carved on a wooden tablet now located in Vienna. The content of the epyllion nevertheless survives in adaptations found in late mythographical handbooks.

Short epic poems were written by authors including Simias or Simmias of Rhodes, Hermesianax and the great scholar Eratosthenes, whose *Erigone* can be reconstructed from Greek and Latin adaptations. The latter work described the introduction of viniculture to Attica by the god Dionysus. Put into literary form by Eratosthenes, this was a relatively less familiar local myth that was supposed to provide the mythical explanation for the beginning of tragic poetry.

Euphorion, another man who excelled in short epic poetry, was already regarded by ancient literary critics as a typical representative of a form whose verse technique, language and narrative method gave it a degree of rarefied artifice that went beyond the style typified by Callimachus. First-century BC poets known as the Neoterics who endeavoured to translate highly cultured Hellenistic poetry into Latin were significantly labelled *cantores Euphorionis* by their opponents, who represented a Roman tradition going back to Ennius. Since a find of some fairly lengthy papyrus fragments, comprising ten to fifteen consecutive lines, has helped put scholars on the right track with regard to the innovations associated with him, the most reliable picture of Euphorion's epic poetry is to be gained from Latin adapations such as *Ciris*, once falsely attributed to Virgil. One of the remarkable and characteristic features of his late style, for example, is his habit at key points in the narrative of giving an exhaustive account of what did not happen but might have happened, while offering only a terse indication of what really did happen that contrasts with this lengthy account. Like Callimachus, Euphorion was a *poeta doctus* (scholar poet) who sought to surprise his readers with the least-known versions of myths, discovered by scholarly inquiry.

The true flowering of epyllic and elegiac poetry fell entirely within the third century BC, but the existence of such poetry is also documented for the second and first centuries. In 73 BC Parthenius of Nicaea – author of an anthology on transformation myths entitled *Metamorphoses* – arrived in Rome as a prisoner-of-war. Although he was not the sole channel for Hellenistic poetry, the account of his life reveals how Catullus, Helvius Cinna, Valerius Cato, Virgil and other first-century BC Romans began to draw directly on Hellenistic poetry. This in turn legitimates the use of poetry by Catullus or the young Virgil for reconstructing our picture of Hellenistic poetry.

The Hellenistic age also witnessed the retrieval and cultivation of the iambus (see above, pp. 38ff.), a genre that had last witnessed great exponents in the Archaic period, but had by all accounts lived on in the popular tradition throughout the intervening centuries. Substantial papyrus relics have survived of Callimachus' twelve volumes of iambic poetry, including both verse passages and the lengthy prose paraphrases used by ancient grammarians for the exegesis of poetry texts. The proem invokes old Hipponax as the originator of the genre. Callimachus has him summon the Alexandrian literati and tell them the story of the cup of Bathycles, which was sent round from one of the Seven Sages to another because it was intended for the best. This was a pointed jibe at the envious relations that prevailed among the assiduous literati of the court and metropolis. Other iambic poems clothe similar witty moral advice as animal fables, while others contain more or less familiar anecdotes.

The metre varies: besides limping iambics in which, counter to the flow of the verse, the penultimate syllable is a long instead of the expected short one, there are also normal and truncated trimeters, as well as joined pairs of verses with different forms. As in hexametric poetry the verse structure evinces a masterly rigour of form that seems at first glance to clash with the nonchalant narrative method, but is in fact supremely suited to it.

One of the most remarkable poems to have survived from the ancient period is composed in iambic trimeters. Lycophron of Chalcis was already well-known in the time of Ptolemy II as a grammarian, learned connoisseur of old comedy, and author of tragedies and satyr plays (see above, p. 249). Totally couched in riddles as a result of its use of indirect and metaphorical expression, his poem presents the herald's message concerning Cassandra's prophecy on the occasion of the recognition of Paris, as narrated in the *Cypria*, adapted into a tragedy by Euripides. The prophecy, of course, mainly concerns the Trojan War, but part of it extends into the time of the poet and also concerns the west, i.e. Sicily and Italy. There is even a reference to Rome, which was starting to rise to power in the third century. Even in antiquity an understanding of the text must have entailed a substantial body of commentary. Difficulties arose not only in connection with its language, but also from the sheer quantity of scholarly material this poetry incorporated.

19

APOLLONIUS RHODIUS
AND EPIC POETRY

It was not only the short forms of narrative poetry which enjoyed a revival in the Hellenistic age. Major heroic poetry in the Homeric tradition, derided by Callimachus for its epic uncouthness, also underwent a revival, drawing on efforts to that end by Antimachus (see above, p. 226). The classic Hellenistic epic poet was Apollonius Rhodius, who was superintendent of the library at Alexandria after the Homeric philologist Zenodotus and before the geographer Eratosthenes – i.e. shortly before the mid-third century BC. Traditionally held to have been a pupil of Callimachus, Apollonius is said to have subsequently fallen out with him. Callimachus' fundamental rejection, expressed in no uncertain terms, of the kind of major epic poetry that Apollonius sought to write, is in any event well-documented.

Apollonius' four-book epic, the *Argonautica*, deals with the myth of the Argonauts – the story of Jason and his companions, the outward voyage to bring back the wonderful Golden Fleece from the distant land of King Aeetes, and of his relationship with the sorceress Medea, who helps him to obtain the Fleece and returns to Hellas with him. The theme represents one of the most ancient Greek seafaring tales, having evolved along with Greek commercial exploitation of the Black Sea. The ancient Argonaut epic of the oral tradition, vestiges of which have been uncovered by W. Meuli (1921) in the *Odyssey*, was long-forgotten by Apollonius' time, although the content of the myth will still have been widely familiar from adaptations into lyric and dramatic poetry, as well as the visual arts. It cannot be ruled out either that an epic poem on the Argonauts dating from the late Imperial period, which relates the myth from the perspective of Orphic theology, had Hellenistic or even pre-Hellenistic precursors in the literature of the sect, which believed in an afterlife.

Apollonius' narrative of events from the outward voyage up to the return of the Argo, the ship built by Jason, is entirely in the Homeric vein. Despite the dramatic emphasis evoked by innumerable episodes, allusions to other mythical complexes, catalogue passages such as his enumeration of Jason's companions, and its many similes, the plot retains all the variety of the ancient epic poem that probably goes to make up its charm. Moreover, as in Homer's

266

version, the plot unfolds on two levels, the divine and the human, the events of the latter being determined by those of the former. In the ancient epic, however, this duality represented an all-embracing view of creation, whereas in Apollonius it has become no more than a literary technique – the 'divine apparatus' with which epic poets of the Hellenistic-Roman tradition were obliged to work, until the convention was discarded by Lucan under highly specific circumstances quite unrelated to literature.

In keeping with the ancient epic legacy, Apollonius' work also appealed to the Muses, who inspired the poet with their account of the events of earlier times. In the days of ancient epic poetry this convention had signified a reference to authorities that for poet and audience alike prevailed over all individual opinion or knowledge. In extant Homeric poetry the invocation of the Muses thus occurs not only at the beginning of the narrative as a whole, but also prior to his account of particularly memorable episodes, even though this serves no discernible function in terms of compositional technique. Apollonius' epic thus opens with a prayer to Apollo, chief among the Muses, while a Muse, mentioned by name on the first occasion, is invoked at the start of the third and fourth books – the second book forms a compositional whole with the first, and does not require an introduction. The conclusion of the epic, on the other hand, consists of a prayer-like invocation of those heroes descended from the gods whose deeds have just been sung by the poet. Here again, a literary convention once rooted in everyday reality has become a purely literary device.

Other elements of Apollonius' poetic craftsmanship deviate considerably from the Homeric tradition, however. The purposefulness of his plot, achieved by a rigorous division and accentuation of its themes, goes far beyond Homer's achievement in his two epic poems at the beginning of large-scale coherent composition, but without in any way curbing either the proliferation or the autonomy of detail. Particularly in the third book, for example, Apollonius succeeds in dissolving a plot that is perceived by the reader as entirely homogeneous into several distinct strands, which divide up and rejoin at crucial points. This represents a fundamentally different approach to the secondary appending of several originally separate plots to what was, at least by the standards of Hellenistic technique, the straightforward compositional plan of the *Odyssey* (see above, p. 18).

Another innovative feature compared to the Homeric narrative method, albeit one for which the ground had been prepared in a long literary tradition, is the poet's concern to depict what is going on in the minds of his heroes. The essential character of Homer's heroes manifested itself in their deeds, and left no room for loose ends. They lived in a one-dimensional world in which any unexpected decisions could quickly be ascribed to the essentially predictable intervention of a god in a specific context. Although very early attempts to explain the psychological motives of Homeric heroes certainly did not conform to the intentions of the old epic poets themselves, they were far from being illegitimate, since mythical characters had acquired a degree of individuality at their hands that required psychological explanation by the time of late Attic drama or the nascent discipline of philosophy. Apollonius' psychological epic must thus have conformed completely with the expectations of his contemporaries. Classical evidence of this aspect of his poetry is to be found in the third book. This depicts the inner torment of Medea, torn between her growing love for Jason and her devotion to her father and king. Set beside the power with which this psychological study is created, the clumsy explanation in the Homeric manner for Medea's love seems like a conventional motif devoid of intrinsic poetic merit – to facilitate Jason's theft of the Fleece, his patrons Athena and Hera persuade the goddess Aphrodite to send Eros to Colchis and incline the heart of the king's daughter to favour the stranger. It will be clear from this that the Homeric and psychological motifs do not form a coherent whole.

One further 'modern' feature of the epic craft of Apollonius may be mentioned here. Book four narrates the return of the Argonauts with their prize. During the voyage they are pursued by several groups of ships from Colchis, which set out along various routes. This allows the poet to combine the geography of ancient mythology, which was based on this myth of a journey to the ends of the earth, with up-to-date knowledge and theories about the shape of the earth. He even has his heroes sail up the Danube and the Rhone – an attractive added touch for the scholarly tastes of the Hellenistic readership.

For the modern reader, whose notions of the Greek epic have been shaped primarily by Homeric poetry, the language of Apollonius represents the least satisfactory aspect of a poetic craftsmanship that is otherwise impressive and highly perceptive. The fascinatingly discrete world presented by Homer's poems, each in its own way, is largely evoked through the discreteness of the storehouse of set formulas the heroic tradition used in compliance with the strict rules of oral poetry. Clearly the point at which the *Iliad* and *Odyssey* were composed marks a stage in literary development by which formulas from the smallest component parts of heroic narrative were becoming no more than models used by the respective poets in order to create expressions drawn from both old and new component words. The price paid for this new technique, which arose with the advent of the written word – and which by Apollonius' time had long been the sole dominant one – was the loss of that experience of a storehouse of formulas, gathered slowly and painstakingly through a constantly repeated process of trial and error. The epic poet's complete freedom to select old and new words at will could just as easily result in bad taste as in thrilling phrases. Inevitably, therefore, the monumental unity of diction that had been the hallmark of oral or sub-oral poetry became a thing of the past.

The fact that this shortcoming in the craft of Apollonius was not passed on to Classical Roman epic poetry, despite the latter's continued dependence on

Hellenistic models, is easily explained. In Latin the style of epic language was rooted from the very outset in a written literature, and thus in the absence of an unattainable model of highly advanced oral epic poetry.

Although the revival of the major epos in early Hellenistic art theory was not without its opponents, papyrus finds have confirmed that Apollonius was avidly read in the centuries that followed. Grammarians similarly soon took to epic poetry, and substantial relics of their commentaries have survived in Byzantine manuscripts. These notes include authors' names and the titles of numerous epics on mythical heroic themes that must have been written either at the same time as Apollonius' *Argonautica* or directly after it.

Marching into an Indian city, Alexander and his army are reputed to have been convinced that they had come upon the Nysa mentioned in the Dionysus myth – the place where the god spent his youth and from where he launched his victorious progress through the world. Even before then the location of the city had been assumed to be in some exotic country, usually Oriental. Subsequent to this experience, Alexander appears to have regarded himself as successor to Dionysus – a god who from then on was to play, besides Heracles, a key role in the ideology of rulers and ruler cults of Hellenism, especially for the Ptolemaic kings. Both were seen as deities who had demonstrated their power throughout the world, acting as benevolent forces who freed people from affliction and bestowed on them the blessings of a civilised way of life. The names of several authors of epics on Dionysus, evidently inspired by the new topicality of the Dionysus tradition, are known from the early Hellenistic age. Although nothing survives of their work, it may reasonably be assumed that they were the first to manifest a new motif in the Dionysus myth that was soon to become the dominant one. A monumental epic on Dionysus by Nonnus comprising forty-eight books is extant from the period around 400 AD, besides relics from other epics on Dionysus dating from the Imperial period. All of these poems contain vivid depictions of the Indian episode in Dionysus' progress through the world. Since the Hellenistic age the visual arts had favoured portraying the god riding in a chariot drawn by elephants. It is not certain what other conclusions about Hellenistic Dionysus poetry may be inferred from late antique epic poetry, however.

The Hellenistic age likewise witnessed a rich burgeoning of the historical epic, which had first appeared in the fifth century BC (see above, p. 21). The chief exponent of this genre was Rhianus from the small Cretan town of Bene, who most probably lived in the mid-third century BC. Only minute fragments, mostly geographical names, have survived of his numerous epics dealing with the early history of Greek provinces such as Thessaly and Messenia. It may nevertheless be assumed that anecdotes and semi-legendary tales from early Greek history, to be found in Imperial prose works such as the Greek geography by Pausanias, occasionally owe their character to Rhianus or other Hellenistic exponents of the historical epic (Rhianus also wrote an epic about Heracles, as well as collating an edition of Homer). However, this no longer accessible historical poetry must have exerted a particularly powerful influence on Roman epic poets, who showed a marked proclivity for historical subjects from the very beginnings with Naevius and Ennius right up to Lucan and Silius Italicus. It is known that Alexander the Great, Antiochus I and other Hellenistic rulers employed court poets to record their deeds for posterity in epic form, while Cicero wrote an epic on the events of his consular year.

The final offshoot of the epic tradition to be mentioned here as flowering afresh in the Hellenistic age is the didactic poem, whose first exponent was Hesiod. The most celebrated Hellenistic didactic poet was undoubtedly Aratus of Soli in Asia Minor. An epic poem entitled *Phaenomena* comprising some 1,200 hexameters is the sole extant example of an immense body of astronomical didactic poetry. It was painstakingly commented on, and translated into Latin by Cicero, Germanicus Caesar, and one Avienus in the fourth century AD.

Aratus lived for a time at the court of King Antigonus Gonatas of Macedon, which places him in the second third of the third century BC, as is borne out by repeated evidence of his inclination towards Stoic philosophy. The poem gives a detailed description of the astronomical system of Eudoxus, but without any actual specialist background knowledge, so that his presentation of the more complex theories remains quite inadequate, as was pointed out even at the time by ancient commentators conversant with astronomy. Clearly, however, the poem was never intended as a serious contribution to astronomical literature. Its artistic objective was most probably to present this inflexible subject-matter and its subtle terminology in a seamless verse form with an aesthetically pleasing compositional framework. Significantly, Aratus drew only occasionally on the rich treasury of celestial myths which might have eased the ordering and narration of his theme, and which was in any case a not infrequent subject for poetry in the Hellenistic age (see above, p. 262). His primary concern was to accomplish his aesthetic objectives. Only where his Stoic belief in universal reason, made visible in the regularity of the cosmic process, comes into play, is Aratus inspired to create poetic formulations and inventions that go beyond these poetic objectives. The second half of the epic is concerned not with the stars but with weather – again employing a specialist source from a sphere with which Aratus was not conversant.

There had been didactic poetry in the pre-Hellenistic era. Euenus of Paros had set rhetorical rules to verse, and Menecrates of Ephesus had written an epic poem on bee-keeping, quite apart from comic didactic epic parodies. Nevertheless didactic poetry with the artistic objectives exemplified by Aratus may be regarded as something typical of the Hellenistic age, and the rich proliferation it went on to enjoy on Roman soil in the work of Virgil and Manilius was likewise a direct continuation of Hellenistic mastery of the didactic art. This evolution included epic poems on bee-keeping, geographical problems, snakes and birds, medicinal prescriptions set to verse, and catalogue-like presentations of widely familiar myths in a rich variety of versions, such as all metamorphosis myths after the manner of Ovid, all myths containing pederastic motifs, or all celestial myths. In this type of poetry, as in the mythological handbook, myth became a subject for antiquarian instruction.

The boundaries of this poetic genre were fluid. A geographical didactic poem entitled *On Rivers* is known, composed in elegiac distichs like Ovid's *Fasti*, while the hexametrical description of the earth by Dionysius the *periegete* (guide) (second century AD) is in the Hellenistic tradition.

The most prolific poet in the didactic sphere as a whole was Nicander, to whom epic didactic poetry on varying themes has been attributed. Although biographical accounts and the sheer volume of documented epic poems point unequivocally to the existence of several poets by the same name, it may be assumed that two didactic poems comprising a hundred and 650 verses respectively that are still read today were written by Nicander of Colophon in Asia Minor, who lived in the mid-second century BC and enjoyed links with the last Attalid rulers of Pergamum.

The longer of these two poems, *Theriaca*, deals with the treatment of bites by poisonous animals, the other, the *Alexipharmaca*, with the treatment of food poisoning. As with Aratus' works, these are based on scholarly medical texts, the content of which is used by Nicander in a vain attempt to give it an engaging poetic form. Only against the background of this tedious and artificial (in the negative sense of the term) poetry can one fully appreciate the magnificent achievement of Virgil's monumental yet graceful poem on agriculture – given that he had no option but to continue in the Hellenistic tradition of the genre.

20

THEOCRITUS AND BUCOLIC POETRY

For inventiveness, taste and technical skill only one poet of the Hellenistic age was a match for Callimachus – Theocritus of Syracuse. Of the same generation as Callimachus, Theocritus was nevertheless already an acknowledged, even renowned poet on his arrival in Alexandria, then the literary capital of the world. He had launched his poetic career on his native island of Sicily. In Hieron II, under whose auspices the state of Syracuse attained a new golden age, he found the royal patron without whom the highly cultured poetry of the day would have been unable to flourish. Some poems by Theocritus also indicate a protracted period of residence on the island of Cos off the south-west coast of Asia Minor, where he must have established close contacts with social groups who were interested in literature. It is no longer known when and under what circumstances this occurred, but links between Alexandria and Cos had always been very close, the island having been for some considerable time part of the Ptolemies' sphere of interest.

Although comprising no more than a slender volume and representing several different genres, the sole extant collection of poems by Theocritus (which furthermore includes several inauthentic and doubtful pieces) has had a more powerful literary impact than the work of any other Alexandrian poet.

Many of the poems represent genres already discussed above in previous chapters. Number 22, for example, is a typical short epic poem dealing with a mythical episode that is also treated in detail in Apollonius' epic poem on the Argonauts. The Argonauts land on the shores of the land of the wild Bebryces, whose King Amycus challenges all strangers to a boxing contest. Polydeuces, one of the two Dioscuri, accepts the challenge and defeats the barbarian. This scene, which is enlivened by a dialogue in stichomythia between the boxers, as well as being furnished with every conceivable device of miniature portrayal, prompts comparison with the corresponding passage in the work by Apollonius Rhodius. However, despite manifold similarities it has not yet been possible to demonstrate definitively either a dependent relationship or which of the two was written first – a fact which bears out the astonishing homogeneity of the epic narrative style in the period, regardless of distinctions between the merits and styles of individuals.

Theocritus wrote the Dioscuri epyllion in the conventional but highly refined dialect of the epic genre. In the finest short epic poem of his that has survived, this idiom is peppered with Dorisms. In this way a language kept alive by literary tradition, although never in fact spoken, was made one degree more artificial with this addition of a new ingredient. The poem tells of how the baby Heracles is sleeping peacefully with his half-brother Iphicles in a shield made up as a cot, when two huge snakes sent by Hera creep into the room. Terrified, Iphicles cries for help, but by the time their mother Alcmene has hurried to their side the young Heracles has already strangled the snakes with his bare hands. This theme fully reflected the taste of the period, which was the first to discover in psychology the specific behaviour of the child, as well as the charm of the child's body in the visual arts. In this respect Theocritus' verse narrative, with its abundance of humour and affectionate phrasing, may be regarded as a classic work of the Hellenistic age. Rather than parodying the myth by transposing it into a child-like, family milieu, he succeeds in making it consummately human (Number 24).

Two encomiums to Hieron of Syracuse (Number 16) and Ptolemy Philadelphus (Number 17), incorporating elements of the hexametric hymn to a god into the context of court poetry, are likewise composed in an epic dialect peppered with Dorisms. An epithalamium (hexametric wedding song dedicated to Helen), however, is enhanced with Aeolisms, perhaps by way of alluding to similar poems by Sappho.

Among Theocritus' most original poetry are the second and fifteenth idylls, which most exquisitely transform the sub-literary poetry of mime into literary form (see above, pp. 254–5.). The first of the two is styled as a monologue by a girl abandoned by her lover. Aided by her maidservant, she seeks to win back his love by means of an intricate and sinister nocturnal magical rite. Repetition of the magic formula in hexameters arranged in strophe-like groups evokes the progression of the magic rite as clearly as it does the details of the simple everyday love story and the inner state of the girl, who is torn between rage, despair and her longing for love. This poem has little in common with a mime by Sophron about a sorceress (see above, p. 142) with which Theocritus will undoubtedly have been familiar, part of which has been retrieved through a papyrus find.

The other mime is presented as a dialogue: Gorgo, a Syracusan woman who has settled in Alexandria, visits her friend Praxinoa in a far-flung suburb of the city. After they have been chatting for a while about their husbands, Praxinoa hands her baby over to the care of a slave and does herself up, setting off back into town with her friend in the direction of the royal palace, where a valuable picture carpet is being exhibited on the occasion of an Adonis festival. On the way they are caught up in the crowds, admire the horses in the royal stables, exchange words with various passers-by, and admire the picture until a blind female singer captures their attention with her rendition of a hymn to Adonis that evidently explains the content of the picture scene they are looking at. The charm of the poem lies in its vivid reconstruction of a scene from everyday life that could be confirmed in every detail by contemporaries. The style is far removed from the epic tradition, not only on account of its conspicuously Doric colouring – as, incidentally in the *Pharmaceutria* – but also and chiefly in its highly skilful adaptation of colloquial words and idioms to the metre used.

It is no longer clear whether Theocritus' mime poems, including Number 14, were intended for oral performance or purely reading purposes. A major papyrus find has retrieved several mime poems by the poet Herodas of Cos, who may have been slightly younger than Theocritus. His poetry is earthier than that of Theocritus, and written in limping iambics rather than hexameters. We read of a procuress seeking to persuade a young grass widow into an extramarital escapade, a mother having her naughty son beaten by his teacher in the schoolroom, and two women, who have come to the temple of Asclepius on Cos to offer a sacrifice, admiring the statues and pictures on display there. The cruder effects of Herodas' poetry are more easily brought out in mime performance – probably by a solo performer rather than an ensemble, since his poems are very short. The purport of Theocritus' more subtle poetry, on the other hand, only reveals itself with careful and informed reading, making it unlikely that he wrote for the stage.

The most powerful of Theocritus' work within the poetic tradition is his pastoral poetry, for which the term 'eidyllion' was coined in the ancient era, by which time its original meaning was obscure. This term was then later applied to the entire collection (initially the term bore no relation at all to the modern notion of idyll).

Pastoral poetry should probably also be viewed as a variation of the mime genre. Here, the skill of the poet consists in his use of the demanding hexameter, generally reserved for high poetry, to give shape to subject-matter drawn from the lowest social milieu. Using allusions to archaic mores that were certainly still current among the herdsmen of the Sicilian mountains in those days, local non-heroic myths (some of which had already provided Stesichorus of Himera with literary themes), as well as the kind of wishful thinking a rarefied, thoroughgoing urban civilisation is apt to cherish about the simple country life, Theocritus created a poetic world of such a distinct character that it was to endure for millennia alongside other worlds of poetic invention. Herdsmen hold a singing contest in the midday sun around a stone-pine for a prize of a goat kid or a carved wooden cup. They sing of how the handsome herdsman Daphnis died of love – evidently an ancient local myth – or the love of the Cyclops Polyphemus for the nymph Galatea. They serenade their sweethearts while another herdsman minds their flocks, or bicker and tease one another about their romantic escapades.

The dialogue stylisation of most pastoral poetry, as well as its frequently graphic and earthy representation of certain aspects of country life, all make it part of the mime tradition. One poem is steeped in this atmosphere created by the poet, whose first-person narrative must undoubtedly be understood to indicate the poet himself behind the main character Simichidas. Its auto-biographical content could not, however, be conveyed fully on account of the transposition of the whole into a world of bucolic fantasy. Poem Number 7 tells of how Simichidas and two friends set out from the town of Cos for the estate of a mutual friend, where they are to join in celebrating the harvest festival of the Thalysia, and how they meet a goatherd on the way with whom Simichidas engages in a poetry contest. This poem is one of the finest in the whole collection, although its beauty can only be appreciated in its depth of atmosphere and the well-balanced tranquillity of its phrasing. The full scope of those literary circumstances which must certainly be assumed to have formed the background to names and allusions, and which gave the poem its purport, is no longer accessible to the modern reader.

This part of Theocritus' poetry is composed in rigidly structured hexameters, not, however, in epic dialect but in a fairly pure Doric, in which ancient grammarians could already discern local Sicilian idioms. This was likewise clearly an artificial dialect containing no small number of non-Doric elements from the purely literary tradition. There can be no doubt, however, that this newly created literary language was intended to evoke the isolated world of Sicilian herdsmen.

The inauthentic pastoral poems in the Theocritus collection, combined with the fact that two poets, Moschus of Syracuse (second century BC) and Bion of Smyrna (around 100 BC), were viewed as Theocritus' successors by grammatical and manuscript traditions, provide a remarkable example of reception history. While there is nothing to suggest that Theocritus was seeking to create a new genre with his pastoral poetry, posterity nevertheless embraced this part of his work as if he had, coining the term 'bucolic' for the new genre. There are in fact no complete extant bucolic poems by either of the two above-named poets. The most important extant piece by Moschus is an engaging epyllion about the abduction of Europa by Zeus, who has taken the form of a bull. Its *pièce de résistance* is a description of the golden basket carried by Europa. The most interesting poem by Bion is a lament for Adonis, representing as it does the first incorporation of motifs of Oriental piety into high Hellenistic poetry. The impressive verses of an epitaph to the same Bion, however, probably written by a pupil or friend, celebrates the deceased as the successor to the bucolic poetry of Theocritus.

The Roman Virgil was to be the great reviver of bucolic poetry. His imitation of Theocritus extended even to word-for-word translations of whole lines. He nevertheless imbued this adopted traditional material with fresh substance and potential effects, firstly by doing away with the realism of Theocritus, relocating his herdsmen in a new landscape of poetic invention, Arcadia, and secondly by making pastoral poetry a vehicle for the most earnest reflection on the needs and aspirations of his own age. Virgil's

Eclogues alone confirmed a literary continuity that joined Theocritus with the pastoral poetry of the Renaissance and Baroque.

One more curiosity may be mentioned here as a genre whose most important specimens were handed down together with those of the bucolic poets. Known as *technopaignia*, these were poems of varying content in which the face of the text formed the image of an axe, shepherd's pipe or some other such artefact. Simias of Rhodes (see above, p. 264), who was also a grammarian, seems to have been among the first to cultivate this unusual technique, in which verse types belonging to the same class but of different lengths were used to create graphic effects. This genre came into great favour in the Baroque era. Its beginnings in the Hellenistic age, however, are only of importance to the literary historian insofar as they indicate just how deeply rooted in the written word the craft of poetry must have been if even the text face became the object of poetic invention – and furthermore in an age when reading written texts aloud was still the norm.

21

THE EPIGRAM

No other genre in Greek literature enjoyed such a long or uninterrupted tradition as the epigram, spanning a period from the seventh century BC until well into the Byzantine age. The reason for this continuity lies chiefly in the persistent demand throughout this period for verse inscriptions for graves, votive offerings, public tributes, buildings and so on. Epigrammatic poetry was thus never faced with the need to reconquer its particular niche, and indeed was constantly able to draw fresh inspiration from sub-literary inscription work.

The boundary between genuine and literary epigrammatic poetry is difficult to locate precisely. Even prominent poets composed inscriptions, and well-composed stone epigrams likewise found their way into literary epigram anthologies, or were published in books by their authors themselves.

An outline has already been given above (pp. 227ff.) of how the epigram came to be a freely available literary form. This process was largely complete by the fourth century BC, so that the burgeoning of the literary epigram in the early Hellenistic age, and then again in the first century BC, was in essence no more than a continuation, or at most the occasional elaboration, of a potential that had already been tapped in the fourth century BC.

We are eminently well supplied as regards the epigram tradition. The famous Codex Palatinus 23 that arrived in Heidelberg in the sixteenth century was donated by Maximilian of Bavaria in 1623 to Pope Gregory XV. It was carried off as booty to Paris by Napoleon, but most of it was returned to Heidelberg in 1815. The Codex Palatinus comprises an anthology of several thousand epigrams collated and edited around 980 AD, ordered according to subject groups, and originally composed by poets whose dates fall between the fourth century BC and the sixth century AD.

Byzantine epigram anthologies (there are or were others besides the *Anthologia Palatina*) revived a tradition dating back to the *Stephanos*, or *Garland*, of Meleager of Gadara (around 70 BC), and extending through an anthology also entitled *Stephanos* or *Garland* by Philippus of Salonika (around AD 40), to Agathias (sixth century AD). All these authors were prolific epigrammatists who were anxious to preserve the legacy of previous work, therefore deliberately and successfully seeking to perpetuate the tradition of the genre. All the anthologies, whose introductory poems have survived in the *Anthologia Palatina*, thus incorporated their respective predecessors either complete or in their main substance, probably ordering the epigrams, according to thematic groups such as devotional epigrams, grave epigrams, erotic epigrams and so on. This distinguished them from earlier anthologies simply comprising epigrams by a single author, such as Simonides, Plato or Leonidas.

The emancipation of the epigram from inscriptional use and its rise to become a creative art form in and after the fourth century brought it into contact with various other poetry genres. It thus began to manifest both an increasingly accomplished use of dialogue under the influence of mime and comedy, and skilful descriptions of objects, influenced by epic ecphrasis.

The epigram had always been closely linked with the elegy in ways that extended considerably beyond their use of the same metre. The short elegy, which could embrace a wide variety of remarks at a banquet, was an equally ancient and widespread form of poetry that differed in no way from lengthier epigrams comprising several distichs. It is no wonder that drinking and love themes, as well as all manner of personal, political and literary issues, became subjects for the literary epigram, particularly where the purport was of a polemic character, since the demand for terse, to-the-point wording that was intrinsic to the form made it well-suited to invective and derision. In this way the literary epigram gradually cast its nets over the full gamut of everyday and intellectual life. There are epigrams about actors, paintings, philosophical doctrines, bath sponges, water-pipes, hetaeras and countless other themes.

The magnitude of extant epigram material furthermore permits the recreation of a fairly accurate picture of the various schools and trends according to which epigram writing of the Hellenistic age can be classified. Within the Greek homeland a number of places had an epigrammatic tradition that enjoyed a flowering between the final decade of the fourth century and the mid-third century BC. This tradition is represented by both male and female poets, such as Phalaecus of Phocis, Mnasalces of Sicyon, Moero of Byzantium, Nossis of Locri, Anyte of Tegea and others. Those of their poems preserved in the *Anthologia Palatina* (*AP*) are certainly partly genuine epigrams, i.e. composed for an inscription, although all of them were probably also published in books. The high literary standards demanded of the epigram are demonstrated by one written by Nossis, which is stylised as her own grave inscription, but may have been intended to conclude the collection of her poems (*AP* 7, 718). She asks the traveller passing by her grave to go to Mytilene and proclaim the fame of the poetess of Locri in the land of Sappho. Anyte's poetry contains some later famous, emotional grave inscriptions for domestic pets. These reveal a depth of feeling for nature that was rare even in the Hellenistic age.

All the above-mentioned poets wrote in a language in which traditional epic vocabulary was enhanced by elements drawn from the Doric of north-western Greece, thereby obscuring its epic origins. The distinctiveness of epigrammatic poetry in the Greek homeland did not of course rule out borrowings of motifs and points from other schools, as some delightful examples by Mnasalces demonstrate. He parodies, for example, an epigram by Asclepiades in which Virtue sits lamenting over the grave of Ajax, having been deceived by a ruse in the events surrounding his death (poems like this can well be imagined as annotations to pictures). By altering only a few words, Mnasalces contrives a speech in which Virtue laments having been subordinated to pleasure in Epicurean philosophy.

Mainland Greek epigrammatic poetry experienced a late flowering just as the Spartans and Aetolians were taking their final stand against the Macedonian monarchy at the end of the third century BC, immediately prior to the establishment of Roman rule in Greece. Epigrams by Alcaeus of Messene and Dioscurides resounded with the last applause of Hellenic, and most particularly Spartan valour that signified more than mere historical reminiscence. Even in the heyday of the Imperial period these epigrams were read as a testimony to the military fame of the ancient Greeks. There is also a clear thematic correlation between this poetry and the ancient elegy.

A good number of poets of varying origins number among a group of Alexandrians, none of whose writing extended substantially beyond the mid-third century, but in some cases had already begun by the end of the fourth century BC. Besides Callimachus and Theocritus, both of whom wrote outstanding epigrams and may be regarded as late exponents of the golden age of the Alexandrian epigram, Asclepiades of Samos was the oldest and most famous of a group that could also boast his no less prominent younger contemporary Posidippus of Pella. The chief merit of Alexandrian epigrammatic poetry lay in its masterly advances in precision of expression, thus allowing even quite complex themes to be accommodated with the terseness characteristic of the genre. At times one has the impression that obscure, humdrum, pointless or exacting themes have been deliberately chosen to demonstrate the poet's stylistic prowess. Callimachus, for example, achieved a considerable feat by containing in epigram form the entire complex story of the origin of the nautilus using the device of one such creature that has been dedicated in the shrine to Aphrodite at Zephyrion (5).

Epigrammatic poetry did not confine itself to displays of virtuosity, however. The same Callimachus wrote an epigram on learning of the death of his friend Heraclitus of Halicarnassus. It tells of deep emotion, evoking the long evenings they spent in conversation (2). One solitary epigram is extant by this same Heraclitus (*AP* 7, 465) – a grave inscription composed in literary Doric for a young woman who died in childbirth. The first two distichs give a desolate description of the fresh grave mound with its withered wreaths, while in the second half the dead woman herself speaks simply of her life and death: 'I gave life to twins. One I left with my husband as a comfort for his old age, the other I took with me to remind me of him.'

The leading exponent of western Greek epigrammatic poetry was Leonidas of Tarentum, the only major epigram poet whose work was restricted solely to this genre. Leonidas died shortly before the middle of the third century BC, having lived an unsettled itinerant life that had taken him for a while to the court of King Pyrrhus of Epirus, who is occasionally referred to in his poetry. Notwithstanding individual differences of style, the ideal in epigrammatic and other forms for Alexandrian poets was balance and precision. Parallel with them, Leonidas lent poetic expression an opulence and elaborateness that at times bordered on the baroque. His themes ranged from the fictitious dedication of fishing tackle through itinerant Cynic philosophers to descriptions of pictures and statues, grave inscriptions composed as a dialogue between the deceased and the visitor to his grave, and opinions on the theory of literature and art. Some of his poems are reminiscent of the bucolic atmosphere of Theocritus' poetry, taking the reader into the world of herdsmen and peasants. Aside from the customary dactylic distich, Leonidas occasionally used iambic verse in his epigrams. Like the majority of Alexandrian epigrammatic poetry, some of his work was composed in Homeric Greek, some in the Doric dialect.

A second, if much less impressive flowering of Hellenistic epigrammatic poetry occurred towards the end of the second century BC, virtually all the exponents of which were of Syrian origin. The oldest of them was Antipater of Sidon. He was followed by Meleager of Gadara (already mentioned above as editor of the first comprehensive anthology of epigrams), and Philodemus, also of Gadara, an Epicurean philosopher who taught in Naples and whose pupils around 40 BC included the poet Virgil. Part of his philosophical works survived on charred papyrus scrolls from the buried Herculaneum.

Meleager and Philodemus arguably achieved the ultimate mastery of the epigram form. Philodemus achieved the feat of an epigram in dialogue style in which the partners communicate using only single words and phrases. Many of the motifs encountered throughout the epigram tradition likewise attained their creative apotheosis in the work of Meleager or Philodemus. In neither case is the poetic substance exactly remarkable. Many of Philodemus' poems are marked by a lasciviousness that compares most unfavourably with the unconstrained and yet never lewd tone in which Asclepiades and other early Hellenistic poets dealt with erotic themes.

Crinagoras of Mytilene, a supporter of the house of Augustus, ushered in a new era in the epigram tradition that reflected in this sphere of arts the altered international conditions brought about in art and elsewhere by the incorporation of Egypt into the Roman Empire.

22

SPECIALIST PROSE AND RHETORIC

Writing was an exceptionally popular pursuit in the Hellenistic age, and given that the written word by then dominated legal, political, economic and private life, the illiterate were effectively social outsiders. The levels of knowledge in all spheres of science, technology, craftsmanship, finance and military science were set down in specialist textbooks, and scholarly discussion was similarly conducted in book publications. Research and education alike were linked with major libraries. The analogy with present-day conditions falls short only in the absence of periodicals in the Hellenistic age. Aside from this, however, the lack of a printing industry should not be seen as too much of a handicap. Large copying workshops in which armies of scribes reproduced texts from dictation, combined with a well-organised book retailing trade, ensured a dissemination of the written word that was unparalleled in the days of medieval Latin prior to the invention of printing.

Aside from a handful of mathematical (Archimedes, Apollonius of Perge, Euclid), mechanical (Philo), astronomical (Hypsicles, Geminus) and grammatical (Dionysius Thrax) works, nothing original has survived of the vast body of Hellenistic scientific and technical literature. In science the modern book always tends to supplant its predecessors. This does not matter as long as inquiry in the relevant field continues to make advances, but in the Imperial Roman period this was unfortunately not the case, as the level of erudition was then declining in virtually all spheres. As a result, the incomparably higher standard of Hellenistic, especially early Hellenistic, inquiry is poorly documented in the much better-preserved scientific literature of the Imperial Roman period. This makes it difficult to piece together, for example, a picture of the achievements of the Alexandrian physicians Herophilus and Erasistratus (third century BC), who in addition to other anatomical findings also discovered the structure of the nervous system. Similarly, the closed medical systems of the Pneumaticists, Methodists and Empirics (second/first centuries BC) are nowadays only understood in the broadest outlines and from fragments. Other findings, such as the discovery of the revolution of the earth about the sun by Aristarchus of Samos (third century BC), or the astronomical calculations of Hipparchus (end of the second century BC), are fairly well-documented in the work of Ptolemy (second century AD) and elsewhere. Grammar is the best-represented discipline, where Byzantine scholiastic commentaries on specific authors, and late handbooks and lexicons, have preserved so much information about ancient scholarly literature that it is still possible to form a clear picture of the great Alexandrian philologists Zenodotus (third century BC), Aristophanes of Byzantium, and Aristarchus of Samothrace (second century BC), or about the allegorical Homeric exegesis and stylistic theory of the Stoic Crates and his flourishing school at Pergamum, the grammatical systematics of adherents of Dionysius Thrax, and the treatment of specialist questions concerning grammar and antiquities by a large number of famous philologists who are still known by name.

Hardly any epoch in the history of philology in the broadest sense of the term – i.e. the interpretation of literary texts in terms of language and style, antiquarianism and history, textual criticism and editorial technique – has witnessed so many breakthroughs as the Hellenistic age. Most complexes of questions and later methods found in this discipline were anticipated then. The same era witnessed the first attempts at a comprehensive description of language, based on the language theory of the Stoics. The terminology coined at that time, and translated into Latin in the first century AD, still dominates grammars today.

A striking aspect of this rich development in the linguistic and literary disciplines – both of which were termed 'grammar' in antiquity – is the fact that it never took account of any language other than Greek. Many Greeks in those days lived in non-Greek-speaking communities, and there is sufficient evidence to confirm the use of foreign languages by Greeks in everyday situations such as trade, commerce and diplomacy. Philology, however, arose out of the desire to keep the Greek literary heritage pure and accessible in just such foreign environments. Hellenistic linguistic and literary disciplines were in this sense born of a classicism to which the idea of learning a foreign language for any other than practical purposes, for self-improvement, or to enrich one's own culture, was quite alien.

Only in exceptional instances is the disappearance of Hellenistic scientific literature a loss for literary history in the strict sense of the term. The days of forging new paths in prose expression and literary composition as part of the attempt to present the results of scholarly inquiry were long gone. Since the fourth century BC had enriched Greek civilisation with a wealth of learnable techniques in prose expression the presentation of demanding material was at the command of many educated people. Scholarly prose had definitively separated from literary prose, while in the latter progress could only be expected in an artistic creativity focused on the mode of presentation. By this stage, however, this sphere could no longer afford to ignore discussion of literary theory. In a handful of cases, such as in the geographical works of Eratosthenes (third century BC) and Posidonius (second/first centuries BC), this creative purpose coincided with genuine scholarly information, making it regrettable that only lengthy summaries of these works have survived, rather than the originals.

If on this basis, therefore, most Hellenistic scholarly prose can be omitted from the history of literature, its former existence must still be borne in mind, since any scholarly subject-matter stored in it was potentially significant and beneficial educational material in literary terms. A good idea of the range of this literature, which extended from agriculture to painting, and from cult history to mineralogy, is provided by the endless index of sources contained in the natural history by the elder Pliny (first century AD), which represents a mammoth uncritical compilation drawn from every possible branch of science.

Despite this burgeoning of scholarly inquiry in all spheres, and the volume of scientific output, all higher education in that epoch had either a philosophical or a literary and rhetorical character, so that science as a medium of education in its own right was excluded. In the former case the object of education lay in a stable moral approach to life which, although necessitating a grounding in verified elements of learning did not perceive the constant acquisition of knowledge as the path to building a moral life. In the latter case the aim was to acquire the largest possible number of the finest tools for linguistic communication, as the prerequisite for civilised communal life – with knowledge serving at best as material on which to test those tools. In both cases science, at least within the education system, was relegated to a propaedeutic role.

In terms of its wide influence, rhetorical education was undoubtedly the dominant type in the Hellenistic age and the Imperial period, shaping the character and future of all prose literature. Almost every prose work whose author aspired to literary status was judged entirely, or at least predominantly, from the stylistic and rhetorical viewpoint rather than for its content (we shall have to pay attention to this point, particularly when considering historiography).

The almost total loss to posterity of Hellenistic creative prose was the result of a radical change in literary taste in the second half of the first century BC. Since authors of the third to first centuries BC ceased to be models for style, any interest in continuing to read them was the exception to the rule. The literary and rhetorical education of post-Classical antiquity was exclusively form- rather than content-oriented. Isocrates' educational strategy had prevailed across the board.

Rhetorical education pertained to the last of the three levels of the educational process, besides or as an alternative to philosophy. It began in elementary school, where pupils learnt reading, writing and arithmetic, then continuing in instruction that provided the basis for a number of mathematically and grammatically oriented disciplines, as well as a thorough reading of Classical poetry. This is the reason, for example, why all intellectuals can be assumed to have had an extensive knowledge of mythology.

The rhetorical education that followed was in the hands of professional teachers, who had schools in towns throughout the Hellenistic world. It was carried out as if all their pupils were would-be orators, that is by means of an unremitting declamation of fictitious legal or public speeches, which had both to be composed in compliance with the rules of currently held rhetorical theory, and modelled on acknowledged stylistic paradigms. There was additional drilling, *inter alia*, in letter-writing and descriptive prose, the paraphrasing of poetic texts, and the adaptation of historical episodes. In keeping with the educational strategy of the Isocratic school, therefore, a substantial proportion of literature, particularly historiography, was taught under the aegis of rhetoric, acquiring the justification for its existence from its attributes as a stylistic model. It may be assumed that one important consequence of such an education was that the intellectuals of that time excelled in their ability both to draft prose according to artistic rules and to assess its quality.

There was no lack of opportunity for the practical application of rhetoric in Hellenistic urban life – in court, for example, where proficient solicitors could make their name and build careers for themselves. What this rhetorical craftsmanship lacked, however, was the incentive to discuss key issues in the public assemblies of sovereign individual states. Anyone ambitious to become one of the power elite aimed to join the armed forces or civil service of a great monarchy – institutions where leadership and expertise were in greater demand than oratorical gifts.

Significantly, therefore, the finest hour of Hellenistic rhetoric – whose educational objective was divorced from reality in the Greek climate – came in conjunction with Roman subjugation of the east. From the second century BC onwards there was a steady flow of Greek culture towards Rome, and soon not even the aristocrat in public life could afford to ignore it. In this way eloquence, the decisive weapon in political encounters either in court or the Senate, came under Greek influence, and well-to-do Romans began to seek an education in the famous rhetoric schools of the east – on Rhodes, in Miletus or Smyrna. Alternatively, they engaged orators as private tutors, who then often established independent schools in Rome and Italy. The names of most Greek oratory tutors are known from Cicero's *Brutus*, a history of Roman eloquence from the third to first centuries BC. They included Apollonius Molon of Rhodes, from whom both Cicero and Caesar received part of their rhetorical education. The brief flowering of Roman eloquence during the closing years of the republic is thus explained by the rise of highly developed Hellenistic rhetorical technique to become a sought-after weapon with a variety of applications in an intense politico-social encounter.

The sole surviving Hellenistic hand- and textbook on rhetoric is in Latin – an anonymous work dating from the first half of the first century BC and dedicated to one Herennius. It comprises part of a rhetoric course for schools as laid down everywhere in textbook form from the fourth century BC onwards. In parts, the system of the work reveals the influence of philosophical distinctions. This derives from the fact that some philosophy schools, notably the Peripatetics and Stoics, followed Aristotle's example by including rhetoric as one of the range of topics suitable for philosophical teaching, hence bringing about a certain feedback effect on the rhetorical teaching tradition. Most modifications to rhetorical theory, however, took place within the teaching tradition itself. Noteworthy in this regard is the name of Hermagoras of Temnos (second century BC) – perhaps the most outstanding systematist in all ancient rhetoric. An adequate notion of his influence can be gained from numerous fragments and references in treatises of the Imperial period.

Perhaps the greatest achievement of all in the philosophical study of rhetoric was its consideration of linguistic and stylistic phenomena first initiated by Aristotle and Theophrastus (see above, pp. 195ff.), and the link thereby established between rhetoric and grammar or philology. The sole surviving work of philosophical rhetoric dating from the Hellenistic age is devoted to this thematic sphere – the short work *On Style* by Demetrius the Peripatetic dating from the late second or first century BC.

Within the rhetorical teaching tradition proper it was largely possible to dispense with a theoretical consideration of linguistic and stylistic details, since students were invariably dealing with their own mother tongue. New stylistic fashions were thus created from the analysis of earlier models, and gained wide currency by means of straightforward imitation. The relationship between language, diction and grammar in rhetorical theory postulated by philosophical treatments only regained its practical significance in Rome. A desire to apply Greek rhetoric to Latin called for interest of quite a different order in a theoretical consideration of linguistic phenomena in creative prose since Latin, unlike Greek, still lacked suitable earlier stylistic models. Cicero introduced to Rome what was then the most up-to-date system of philosophical rhetoric, as taught by the Academicians Philo and Antiochus. Cicero's opponents Brutus and Calvus for their part declared the grammatical regulation of Latin to be a prerequisite for all rhetoric.

There are only very sketchy extant reports of shifting stylistic fashions instigated by teachers of rhetoric between the third and first centuries BC. However, the schools of towns in Asia Minor must have been particularly influential, since from the first century BC onwards Hellenistic creative prose, by then no longer current, was occasionally denigrated as 'Asiatic'. In general it may be asserted that Hellenistic rhetoric teachers saw themselves faced with the task of either somehow modifying or superseding the Classical periodic style developed in the Isocratean school. There was nowhere else for this style, with its strict symmetry, to go. For all its beauty, unremitting imitation of this form had yielded nothing but paralysing tedium. There was thus a recourse to pre-Isocratean manners of speech, with a sequence of short, staccato sentences or clauses replacing the wellrounded system of symmetrically arranged clauses that corresponded both logically and rhythmically. Alternatively there was an attempt to put Isocrates and the Classical prose of Athens in the shade by trying to make the diction more interesting and attractive, *inter alia* by means of audacious metaphors, neologisms, borrowings from poetry, or expressions that stretched grammatical potential to the limit – sometimes retaining the periodic form, sometimes not. Additionally there were attempts to regulate prose rhythm by agreeing on a number of syllable sequences for sentence and clause endings, marked by a fixed rhythm of quantities that characteristically differed from customary poetic metres. When this clause technique was applied to a style that worked with short clauses, the rhythm took over virtually the entire text, as in a poem. When it occurred in conjunction with periodic style and long clauses, however, the latter had to be particularly carefully co-ordinated in length and arrangement, since otherwise they failed to be discerned.

Clearly the potential combinations of stylistic elements enumerated above could give rise to any number of stylistic trends. Modern documentary evidence of these, however, is very scant. Aside from a few fairly late citations in rhetorical and historiographical texts the most important modern source of information about Hellenistic prose style is a series of public inscriptions composed by professional rhetors commissioned by monarchs or communities. Of particular importance are some verbose inscriptions for Antiochus of Commagene, a half-Greek minor Syrian king of the first century BC whose rhetors commanded all the gimmicks of a diction that was as subtle as it was in bad taste.

As documentary evidence attests, the period as a whole was not devoid of classicising impulses towards a deliberate return to fourth-century Attic prose. Details of how this discussion unfolded are no longer available, however. The degree of present-day uncertainty may be illustrated by the following instance. The famous orator Hegesias of Magnesia (third century BC), held by later authorities to be the most notable representative of 'Asiatic' bad taste – and the few extant fragments by him appear to confirm this assessment – regarded himself as an imitator of Lysias, whose diction was the most austere and unadorned of all Attic orators.

Although Classical Attic prose undoubtedly retained its role as stylistic model throughout the entire Hellenistic age, Hellenistic prose never lost touch with the colloquial idiom. Attic idiosyncrasies in vocabulary, morphology and phonetics had permeated written usage far further afield than Attica itself as a result of the authority of Attic as a language of literature. These were now replaced by equivalent vocabulary and morphology from Koine, the standard language that was gradually permeating local dialects everywhere and in turn incorporating into itself elements of divers origin. Whereas, therefore, all poetry genres had from the very outset been connected with artificial languages that bore no relationship to spoken language, creative prose retained its links with the colloquial idiom.

At the end of the epoch this all changed as part of a radical literary reform movement that advocated a return to Attic authors of the fourth century BC, not only at the higher stylistic level, but even in elements of linguistic usage. The first Atticists taught mostly in the west, since by the first century BC Rome had become the leading centre of Greek intellectual life. They demanded no more and no less than that any author writing a literary or any other kind of text transcending prosaic themes should henceforth do so in a dead language. This necessitated, for example, mastering the many forms and complex use of the optative, the third Greek mood besides the indicative and the subjunctive. Attic, along with some other dialects, had retained this into the fourth century BC, as a consequence of which its use still occurred among Attic orators. The standard Hellenistic language, on the other hand, had never had an optative mood, so that in the first century BC it was customary neither in prose literature nor in everyday speech.

The Atticists achieved a sweeping success with their objective. By the first century AD every single prose author possessing any literary ambitions was at pains to reproduce correct Classical Attic usage – although this could never of course be fully achieved. More than this, however, Attic came to dominate in elementary education, as well as becoming *the* written language. Official documents and private letters, of which thousands have been preserved in Egypt, show a steady increase in the use of the optative from the first to the second century AD, accompanied by a decrease in illiteracy. Since large-scale Greek settlement of Egypt did not begin until after the Alexandrian campaign, there was probably never an optative in the spoken Greek of that country apart from in idiomatic expressions.

The Atticist reaction of the first century BC was accompanied by a separation of written Greek from the colloquial language that persisted throughout the entire Byzantine age and up to the present day. Spoken Greek as a vernacular has developed organically through the centuries to the present stage of modern Greek, also undergoing new dialectic differentiations. The so-called pure language, which was initially required for literary purposes only, but very soon needed to be mastered for all written usage, was left largely untouched by this process, being modified solely in response to changing literary fashions.

Obviously writers were unable to free themselves from their own language so entirely as not to make mistakes in their use of the Archaic written language. Those mistakes now make it possible to date texts. Scholars, however, often achieved an astonishingly assured command of a spoken form that in the Imperial period was as remote as Middle High German seems to a modern German, or classical Latin to an Italian.

The complete works of one early Atticist theoretician have survived – Dionysius of Halicarnassus who lived in the time of Augustus and wrote a number of monographs on specific Attic orators as well as on specialist problems in rhetoric (he also wrote an early history of Rome). His contemporary Caecilius, a Jew who lived at Kale Acte in Sicily, was the author of a lexicon that could be used as an aid to mastering the obsolete idiom – the first in a long line of similar aids extending into the Byzantine Middle Ages. These give the 'Greek', i.e. contemporary words used in the spoken language, beside Attic words with the same meaning, documented as having been used by Classical authors of the fifth and fourth centuries BC.

Lexicons of ancient Greek dialects, including Attic, had already been compiled by Alexandrian grammarians in the third and second centuries BC to aid the exegesis of poetry – by the above-mentioned (p. 282) Aristophanes of Byzantium, for example. However, any idea of influencing the prose style of their own time, such as prompted the compilation of lexicons from the period of Atticist reaction onwards, had been far from their thoughts. Nevertheless, the rapid success of Atticism can partly be explained by the degree to which Alexandrian scholars had made the language of Classical literature accessible, thereby smoothing the path for theoreticians and teachers of the new stylistic trend.

The rapid success of Atticism – the consequences of which are by no means expended in modern Greek, despite its very rich vernacular literature – should not be understood as a process confined to literature alone, even though a principle that had always been upheld in poetry initially asserted itself in creative prose only. It was no accident that this total departure from the creative prose tradition fostered hitherto, and the recourse to the language and literature of an admired bygone age, occurred precisely as Egypt, along with the last independent relic of the world of Greek states, was falling under the dominion of the Romans. This brought to an end the protracted death throes of an entire civilisation, allowing everyone to look forward to a fresh start after the distress of the previous century, now that peace had finally been achieved within the Empire. Subsequent civilising and literary achievements within the Greek-speaking world henceforth constituted one half of a two-language Imperial culture that deliberately assimilated the classical historical heritage of Greece.

23

HISTORIOGRAPHY AND GEOGRAPHY

The rich historiographical output of the fourth century continued unabated in the Hellenistic age. Apart from the *Histories* of Polybius, the original works have been lost, but the content and character of many can be reconstructed on the basis of the major compilation by Diodorus during the time of Augustus, the biographies of Plutarch (around 100 AD), and later historical sources who used Hellenistic authors. To these may be added occasional word-for-word citations, which appear mostly in the form of samples of style or references in later texts.

The major events of Alexander's rule understandably attracted many historiographers (see above, pp. 221f.), although unfortunately none of any real note. After Alexander's death Ptolemy, later the first Greek king of Egypt, and Nearchus of Crete, Alexander's admiral of the fleet, published both valuable and reliable accounts of events in which they had been involved in their positions of high command. Neither of them possessed any literary talent, however. Some idea of their works is provided by Arrian of Bithynia (second century AD). A book by Onesicritus, a Cynic philosopher who took part in the campaign as a helmsman, is of quite a different order. Fairly lengthy fragments, some of which have survived in various places, show that he viewed Alexander's exploits from the perspective of his philosophy. Onesicritus is the original source for numerous tales showing Alexander debating with Indian brahmins and yogis, gymnosophists, who for their part speak and act like dyed-in-the-wool Cynics and as if learned in ancient philosophical tradition. In histories by Clitarchus and Aristobulus, which are known to us mainly through their reflections in Roman authors, the exploits of Alexander are amplified, bringing them into the realm of the miraculous and marvellous. Although both authors had taken part in the campaign, Aristobulus was already a very old man when he wrote his book, and used an already considerably embellished literature on Alexander. Clitarchus was for his part regarded as a notorious liar even in antiquity. It is only one step from him to the Alexander legend that was already mushrooming in the Hellenistic age, although a complete version of it is only extant from the second or third century AD. Traces of it are discernible considerably earlier, most particularly in a rich anecdotal tradition and an apocryphal body of letters (see below, p. 302).

More important than these and other Alexander historians was Hieronymus of Cardia, the historiographer of the wars of succession who experienced events at first hand as private secretary to Eumenes, one of the generals who fought over Alexander's succession. His work is accessible nowadays chiefly through Plutarch's biography of Eumenes.

Duris of Samos, a pupil of Theophrastus the Peripatetic, and Phylarchus of Naucratis or Athens, who lived towards the end of the third century BC, were the leading exponents of so-called tragic historiography (see above, p. 221), which sought to achieve through historiographical means the educational psychology effects ascribed to tragedy by Peripatetic theory. In addition to a history of the Sicilian tyrant Agathocles (around 300 BC), Duris, who also made his mark as the author of works on painting, Homer, Sophocles, tragedy and legislation, wrote a comprehensive account of the period from 350 to 290 BC, only a very small part of which he had lived through himself. Aside from other works, Phylarchus wrote a history of the period 260–220 BC. Duris appears mainly in the work of Diodorus, Phylarchus in Plutarch's lives of the Spartan reformers Agis and Cleomenes. Both sought to arouse the emotions of their readers by depicting heart-warming, horrific or poignant scenes and, judging from relics and reflections, they did succeed in writing some stirring passages. Polybius nevertheless censures Phylarchus for neglecting historicity in his pursuit of this tragic effect. However justified such censure may be, it misses the point, since this kind of historiography was not at all concerned with historicity: its very precisely defined goals related to literary and educational psychology effects.

All the many dynasties of the Hellenistic age had their historiographers, as did specific great events and outstanding personalities. Timaeus (see below, pp. 294–5) thus described the wars of Pyrrhus, Philinus of Agrigentum in Sicily the First Punic War, and Sosylus and Silenus the exploits of Hannibal. This kind of historiography was of course also a tool for political propaganda. Thus in the third century BC Roman notables also took up their pens for the first time, and described contemporary events in Greek, putting the Roman cause and their own policies into a favourable light, and addressing intellectuals of the Greek-speaking world and members of their own class.

The first Greek to reach a true understanding of the Roman state was Polybius of Arcadia. Rising to the rank of allied military leader within the Achaean alliance, the last political structure within the Greek homeland, he was taken off to Rome and kept as a hostage along with other prominent Greeks in 166 BC, remaining there for seventeen years. At the house of Aemilius Paullus he became tutor and friend to Scipio Aemilianus, the first great philhellene and truly educated man among the Roman nobility. Following a brief stay in his native Greece, Polybius accompanied Scipio throughout the whole campaign leading to the destruction of Carthage in 146 BC, also undertaking further expeditions along the African coast. His latter years were spent back in Greece in strenuous efforts to utilise his good relations with the Roman aristocracy to alleviate the untold suffering brought on his country by the Roman conquest. He died at the age of 82 after falling from a horse.

Polybius' magnum opus was a comprehensive history of the period 220–168 BC taking in the entire civilised world. The first five of the total forty books have survived directly in manuscript form, while substantial parts of the remainder are available through Byzantine excerpt compilations. Its surprising fortune in this respect compared to the rest of Hellenistic prose should not be attributed to the stylistic or literary qualities of the work, but solely to the fact that it represents the most reliable Greek-language account of what was arguably the single most important event in the heroic era of Rome, the Second Punic War. It was during this war, the epoch selected by Polybius, that Rome recovered from a crisis that threatened its very existence, rising to become the undisputed leading power in the civilised world.

Polybius nursed neither stylistic nor rhetorical ambitions. His style is dry and cumbersome, betraying its affinity with the diction used for imparting the results of scientific inquiry or technical advances in the specialist sphere. He ruthlessly takes to task those historians whose works he is obliged to use as sources, but who garble historical facts for the sake of pathetic and dramatic effects, out of obeisance to rhetorical stylistic rules, or simply out of negligence and lack of critical faculty (this in places harsh polemic is a welcome source for filling in gaps in the present-day picture of Hellenistic historiography). Polybius was a hard taskmaster to himself when imparting facts: he never passed on information he had collated without first subjecting it to critical examination. His critical faculty was trained not so much by a scholarly education as by a lifetime of service in politics and warfare, be it in responsible positions or as a privileged observer. Even where his information derives solely from literary sources, his accounts of campaigns or diplomatic negotiations betray the keen eye of an expert.

However, it is neither the accuracy of his presentation and assessment of historical detail nor the breadth of his political horizon (encompassing both the Indian campaign of Antiochus III and the geography of north Africa) that makes Polybius significant as a historian. His chief accomplishment lies in having recognised his chosen historical epoch as the decisive phase in the rise of Rome to the status of ruling power. He revealed to his fellow countrymen on the one hand the causes for the disintegration of their system of states, despite its intrinsic cultural and economic superiority, and to the Romans on the other the reasons for the meteoric rise of their political system. He drew his explanations for the salient features and potency of the Roman state in the first instance from theories of the state within Greek philosophy that will probably have been widely familiar to intellectuals of the day. For Polybius the political constitution of Rome was marked by an unusually fortunate blend of democratic, aristocratic and monarchic elements that was conducive to lasting internal stability, and hence an unimpeded expansion of power. A constitution stressing one aspect alone, he argued, tended to foster corruption, mobilise opposition and, sooner or later, to be replaced by another through revolutionary upheaval. This theory, known as the cycle of constitutions, had been current Greek political theory since Plato. Although a trifle schematic, Polybius' interpretation is understandable, given what petty Greek states had been through in the way of unparalleled judicial and political instability. More than this, however, his keen eye discerned another key factor in Roman political life that recent historical science has been quite slow to acknowledge. In one famous passage Polybius describes the funeral rites in an aristocratic Roman family in which slaves processed behind the deceased bearing the official attire and death masks of his or her ancestors. Polybius rightly interprets this as a demonstration of the continuity on which the strength of the Roman state was based. No Greek *polis* or Oriental monarchy had anything to match the Roman aristocratic families who were unreservedly dedicated to public life through long generations, or their own vitality and seasoned political experience. Roman political life drew its dynamic from communality and competition among these dynastic families.

Polybius coined the designations 'pragmatic historiography' and 'historiography with an account of causes' for his own work, distancing it emphatically from other historiographical agendas conceived from various literary standpoints. His aim was to ascertain, collate and order undisputable facts, interpreting them as documents of political changes for the instruction of future statesmen. His aim was thus not dissimilar to that of Thucydides, except that he was examining not the modes of conduct of human nature in general, but rather the rise and fall of complex institutions of power.

Polybius' work was continued by the great Stoic Posidonius (see above, pp. 243–4), who took the account as far as the 80s BC. Posidonius equated world history even more closely with that of the Roman Empire than Polybius had done. Albeit under different circumstances, he too moved on an equal footing with the Roman aristocrats who ruled the world. Pompey and Cicero were his pupils: he wrote a special account of Pompey's exploits in the Orient, politely declining to do the same for Cicero. However, whereas Polybius had been completely under the sway of the meteoric rise of the Roman state to the status of great power, Posidonius was a witness to the far-reaching reverberations, and indeed process of decay, that set in with the bloody turmoil of a century of civil wars.

If the few extant remains of his work are to be trusted, Posidonius saw historiography in the first instance as an auxiliary discipline to ethics, affording an immense body of illustrative material for understanding human, particularly social, conduct and its consequences. This probably explains why more than any ancient historian before or after him, Posidonius focused on social conditions, for example making a detailed study of the numerous slave rebellions and wars of the late second and early first centuries BC. Despite repeatedly pointing out infringements to justice and human dignity per-petrated by the ruling class in this context, he was staunchly opposed to social and political revolutions. His sympathies were firmly on the side of conservative groups within the senatorial aristocracy, and he vigorously condemned all reformers and innovators, from Tiberius Gracchus to Marius and Cinna. For all its incipient symptoms of decay, he still viewed the stability guaranteed by continuity in the Roman balance of power and property ownership as superior to abrupt upsets to the status quo that opened the way for the incompetent, the irresponsible and the unscrupulous. In one lengthy passage that happens to have survived word for word, Posidonius bitterly derides the short-lived revolutionary social regime set up in Athens during the Mithridatic War by an errant philosopher. Under the terrorist leadership of this adventurer, Athens allied itself with the king of Pontus in a war against the Romans, thereby incurring conquest and plunder by the troops of Sulla.

Posidonius' work, reflections of which appear in Plutarch and Diodorus, must have painted a desolate picture of the impoverished Greek-speaking world, and the omnipotent but deeply corrupt Roman state – particularly since this brilliant stylist had at his command the full gamut of a late and highly subtle use of language that was able to evoke hatred, sympathy, scorn, awe and admiration in his readers.

The last Greek historians of the Hellenistic Age, Timagenes and Theophanes of Mytilene, were completely under the spell of late Roman republican infighting. The versatile work of Nicolaus of Damascus, court historian to Herod of Judaea and biographer of Augustus, takes us across the threshold into another age.

Besides the impressive number of authors representing contemporary historiography who have been discussed so far, there were also hundreds who concentrated on a wide variety of subsidiary and specialist spheres within historiography. Scholarly chronology and the analysis of manifold local lists of officials and calendar systems thus found its compiler in the great philologist and geographer Eratosthenes, who taught in the third century BC at the museum in Alexandria; in Apollodorus of Athens (second century BC), who also came out with a learned commentary on the catalogue of ships in the *Iliad*; and in Castor, a Rome-based slave emancipated by Sulla.

The number of authors who devoted themselves to local history in the broadest sense is incalculable. No town or province was without a histori-ographer in those days. The term 'local historiography' encompassed a wide range of activities, however. One type was the antiquarian study of legal and cultural traditions, festival customs and monuments, using an elaborate method of inquiry that examined everything from inscriptions and archive materials to anecdotes and proper names. This local research reached its high point in Athens in the third century BC with numerous publications by Philochorus (see above, pp. 222f.). Another type comprised comprehensive accounts, compiled from literary sources, of the history of specific cities or provinces, mostly including mythical prehistory. An outstanding exponent of this type was Demetrius of Scepsis in north-western Asia Minor (second century BC).

It is not always easy on the basis of extant reports and fragments to distinguish true local or regional historiography – which was certainly also obliged to meet literary and stylistic criteria – from publications by learned antiquarians with no literary ambitions on the one hand, and entertainment literature on the other, in so far as the latter made use of the findings of scholarly research, like modern popular non-fiction (see p. 299). Many antiquarians and learned men of the third and second centuries are known by name. Ister (see p. 222), a pupil of Callimachus, thus published collected material on the history of Greek regions, as well as monographs on festivals, contests, sacrificial customs and composers, in addition to a compilation of Attic expressions to assist in reading the great poetry of Athens, whose idiom differed not inconsiderably from standard Hellenistic Greek. Hermippus, another pupil of Callimachus (see p. 209) who also worked in Alexandria, wrote books on the Seven Sages (see above, p. 60), as well as legislators and philosophers. Like his contemporary Satyrus (see p. 301), however, he seems to have been more interested in entertaining his readers than in serious inquiry. Polemon of Ilium in Asia Minor, who lived in the second century BC, was a true scholar. He was nicknamed 'Stelokopas' for devouring stone inscriptions like a hungry man would a good meal. Based on his thorough study of inscriptions, monuments and archive materials, he wrote numerous monographs on cities, regions and shrines. His contemporary Sotion likewise wrote solid scholarly studies. He collated traditions about the lives of philosophers, which were cultivated in many places, and classified them by according each one his place within a school tradition, a diadoche (succession). Although undoubtedly useful in the Hellenistic age, this system could only be implemented with some contrivance in the case of pre-Classical philosophy, as is clearly discernible from a collected edition of biographies by Diogenes Laertius (around AD 200). Like other antiquarians and learned men, he labelled Sotion a Peripatetic, although it cannot be demonstrated with any certainty that he was a member of the Aristotelian school. It was the Peripatetics, however, who had longest adhered to the view that all forms of intellectual or scholarly endeavour could be subsumed within philosophy, as this use of the label in the broader sense was intended to indicate.

Timaeus of Tauromenium (modern Taormina) in Sicily merits a special status among local historians. He spent around half of his almost hundred-year life in political exile in Athens, in whose libraries he wrote the sixty-eight volumes of his history of Sicily and Lower Italy, from the beginnings to the outbreak of the First Punic War. The distinctive feature of this historical work, which exerted a demonstrable impact on subsequent authors, is the way it incorporated all available information concerning the geography and history of the western Mediterranean region. The picture of the west he thus created was to prevail in literature until replaced by the version by Posidonius at the time of Augustus.

Expansion of the geographical horizon in the aftermath of the Alexandrian campaign, combined with diverse new contacts brought about through such means as commerce and diplomacy with foreign peoples of widely diverging cultural levels, reawakened the interest in the historical traditions of the world abroad that had once flourished among Herodotus and his predecessors. As early as the early third century BC Berossus the Babylonian and Manetho the Egyptian published histories of their respective countries in Greek, for a Greek readership. The dynastic division of ancient Egyptian history current to this day goes back to Manetho's work. Hecataeus the Abderite, a contemporary of Callimachus, wrote a history and geography of Egypt that is admittedly embellished with romantic elements. Like the Peripatetics Theophrastus and Clearchus before him, he was interested in the Jews, their religion with its written code – which he viewed as 'philosophy' – and the theocratic community in Judaea that was based on it. Other peoples, such as the Ethiopians and the Celtic Galatians, also attracted Greek historiographers in the course of time. A reservoir of such literature was provided in the compilations by one Alexander, called Polyhistor, who lived in Rome in the first half of the first century BC. By various routes, the material he accumulated found its way into Imperial handbooks, some of which have survived.

One first-rate historian described the rise of the power that finished off the eastern outposts of the Greek-speaking world, and held back the Romans for centuries at the frontier formed by the Euphrates. This Apollodorus hailed from Artemita (near present-day Kermanshah), which was founded in the Hellenistic age. Despite having long been part of the Parthian Empire, by his lifetime (around or shortly after 100 BC) Artemita had retained its character as a Greek *polis* under the rule of the pro-Greek early Arsacids. Apollodorus' history of the Parthians, of which unfortunately only sparse fragments are now known from geographies and histories of the Imperial age, also covered the fortunes of the Greek state in distant Bactria (Afghanistan), which had been cut off from the rest of the Hellenistic world since the third century BC, although renewing its expansion towards India in the second century BC. Excavations at Ai Khanum on the (former) Soviet–Afghan border have provided insight into the life of a Bactrian Greek town of the third and second centuries BC. Despite their geographical and political isolation, its inhabitants did not want for cultural contact with the Greek-speaking world. Inscriptions provide evidence of lectures given by an itinerant orator or philosopher, while a library housed specialist literature on philosophy. The style and craftsmanship of public buildings correspond to this cultural level.

There was likewise a remarkable increase in geographical literature during the Hellenistic age. Nearchus, Alexander's admiral, whose fleet had accompanied the army on its return march from India along the coast from the mouth of the Indus to that of the Euphrates, provides in his account of the expedition a detailed description of the regions and peoples they met on the way. It has survived in an adaptation by Arrian (second century AD). Major Hellenistic states, the successors to Alexander's empire, most notably the Seleucid Empire, enjoyed lively diplomatic contacts with the Mauryan Empire in the first third of the third century. Soon after the Alexandrian campaign, its founder Chandragupta – Sandrocottus in the Greek texts – had united the greater part of the Indian subcontinent, expelling the Greeks from the western regions conquered by Alexander. He nevertheless seems to have been well-disposed to Greeks, and an admirer of Alexander. His second successor Ashoka, under whom the Empire reached the limits of its expansion, used Greek as an official language in the administration of his north-western territories, in addition to Aramaic, the lingua franca of the Near East. He boasts in one inscription of having sent Buddhist missionaries to the Greek-speaking world of the Mediterranean. Of a number of legation reports dating from that time the most famous is by a certain Megasthenes, who spent over ten years as envoy to the Mauryan seat at Pataliputra on the central reaches of the Ganges. It contains a detailed description of northern India – its landscape, flora and fauna, its inhabitants and their mores, customs and institutions. Substantial parts of his account have survived in adaptations by later authors. Although Megasthenes had a reputation with ancient scholars for not being strictly truthful, modern Indology has nevertheless been able to confirm many reports on which doubt had been cast, and to reveal many of his errors as simple misunderstandings. Megasthenes' picture of India was to dominate literary tradition up to the sixteenth and seventeenth centuries.

In texts that trace back to Megasthenes, as well as the word definitions of later lexicographers, words crop up from time to time from Sanskrit or an Indian language of the Mauryan era, as do Greek words coined as literal imitations of Indian expressions. This demonstrates that Greek visitors to India must have acquired knowledge of the languages of that country. There is no evidence to suggest, however, that any Greek attempted to use such language skills to gain insight into the rich literature of India, and hence into the intellectual life of the country. The same applies to Egypt, where there was a symbiotic relationship between the indigenous population and the Greeks for centuries, where there was a centre of Greek intellectual life, and most particularly of Greek science, and where many Egyptian families used both languages, or became Hellenised as part of the process of upward mobility. There are only faint traces of Greek interest in gaining knowledge of the indigenous tradition of this country through its language, despite increasing Greek fascination with its religion, particularly from the second century BC onwards, and the marked power of attraction exerted on Greek thought by the wonders of Egypt.

Numerous reports kept the reading public abreast of the results of further expeditions, which became increasingly commonplace after the Alexandrian campaign. As early as the late fourth century BC the intrepid Pytheas of

Massilia (Marseille) circumnavigated Spain and France, sailing as far as Ireland and Scotland, and perhaps even to the northern seaboard of Denmark. Patrocles was commissioned by King Seleucus I to explore regions around the Caspian Sea, Androsthenes the Persian Gulf and the northern coast of Arabia. The first Ptolemaic kings sent expeditions to the Red Sea and Abyssinia, as well as to Central Africa and the northern coast of Africa, led by Timosthenes.

Accounts of all these expeditions were utilised by the versatile Eratosthenes in his geography. He combined the qualities of the accurate scholar with those of the literary training of the poet and philologist. His geography – on which parts of the extant geographical compilation by Strabo (first century AD) are based – thus combines what ancient theory regarded as the most stylistically demanding type of literature – geographical and anthropological descriptions, with the essentially non-literary scientific presentation of his mathematical calculations of position and distance. On account of this disjointedness of genres the criticism made in the second century BC of the pioneering computations of Eratosthenes by the great mathematician and astronomer Hipparchus did not affect the literary impact of his geographical descriptions. The latter can partly be retrieved from the geographical compilation of Strabo of Amaseia, a contemporary of Augustus.

Substantial fragments have survived of a late second-century BC work by Agatharchides of Cnidos on African and Arabian coastal areas of the Red Sea and the north-west Indian Ocean, in the *Library*, a compilation of excerpts by the patriarch Photius (ninth century AD). Although basing himself in part on literary sources, Agatharchides also reported his own experiences. His account excels both for its wealth of observed detail, and above all for the lack of prejudice with which he seeks to arrive at a correct understanding of the customs of the sometimes primitive tribes in those areas. In this respect Hellenistic geographers differed most favourably from European explorers of the nineteenth century, who frequently made arrogant pronouncements about the misunderstood way of life of primitive peoples. The reason for this difference may perhaps be sought in the degree of familiarity with questions of philosophical ethics that was available to all intellectuals of the Hellenistic age. This afforded them the potential for an anthropological understanding of phenomena once encountered, whereas in western Christendom the prescriptions of a religious-based morality were accepted for all too long as natural law, condemning anything that deviated from them.

As in the days of Herodotus, Greek travellers of the Hellenistic age also recognised their own gods in those of foreign countries. Shiva in India and Osiris in Egypt were thus both identified with Dionysus. An additional factor was the Stoic doctrine concerning the natural primeval knowledge of humankind, which prompted a search for correlations between exotic tradition, the 'philosophy of barbarians' (see above, p. 240), and Greek philosophy. This idea played a special role in the encounter between Greek culture and Judaism (see below, pp. 305ff.), and later Christianity.

Both the high point and the end of Hellenistic geography is to be found in the works of Posidonius, who is therefore mentioned again here (see above, pp. 243–4). Posidonius' grand conception – based on a synthesis of Stoic and Aristotelian ideas – of a ubiquitous relationship between cause and effect, as a unified law encompassing all nature, both animate and inanimate, spurred him on to assemble a virtually incalculable body of facts into a single grand portrait of the world. On his extensive travels he studied tides along the Atlantic coast of Spain, volcanic activity in Italy, and baboons in the Atlas Mountains. In the port of Gadeira, modern Cadiz, he inquired after the missing seafarer Eudoxus of Cyzicus, the first to cross the Indian Ocean in the monsoon season, who later attempted to circumnavigate the African continent from Spain. He observed slaves labouring in Spanish mines, caroused with the half-savage henchmen of Gallic chieftains in the heartland of present-day France, and was as interested in their head trophies as he was in the theocratic order of the Jewish community in Palestine.

The wealth of his own observations was reinforced by his catholic knowledge, acquired through scholarly endeavour. Unfortunately here again only reflections have survived of the literary shape Posidonius gave to his knowledge and understanding. Some idea of the charm of the original is nevertheless conveyed by a lengthy section devoted to Spain in Strabo's geography that was perhaps drawn entirely from Posidonius' work – with its picture of the landscape and inhabitants, nature and civilisation, past and contemporary history.

24

ENTERTAINMENT LITERATURE

It is difficult to demarcate the entertainment literature genre within prose with any precision, since the known works pertaining to it frequently differ from scholarly or historical works in aim rather than in content. There was, for example, a rich literature of paradoxographic entertainment, recounting *inter alia* ghost stories, bizarre occurrences and freaks of nature. The same themes were also the subject of entirely serious natural scientific studies, however. The same goes for astrological treatises, dream books and magical texts. Although there is only documentary evidence of these genres from later texts, these were often based on earlier works. The ghost stories told by Phlegon of Tralles (second century AD) on which Goethe's *Bride of Corinth* is modelled, for example, probably go back to a Hellenistic original. A mythography, a compilation of ancient myths of the Greek tradition, similarly appeared both in the context of entertainment literature and in philological and antiquarian scholarship (see above, p. 294). A certain Dionysius, who acquired the odd nickname 'leather arm', wrote his adaptations of Greek myths in the third century BC as novel-like literature of entertainment, rather than to impart essential mythological knowledge as an aid to reading the poets. At the very end of the epoch under consideration came a still extant book by Parthenius that is dedicated to Cornelius Gallus, the first Roman governor of Egypt, a friend of Virgil, and the first poet to write love elegies in Latin. The book contains a compilation of thirty-six erotic myths of a pathetic and tragic character, adapted from a wide variety of literary sources and recommended to Gallus as material for his elegiac poetry.

Numerous accounts of expeditions facilitated an increase in travel and adventure novels, or their emergence as a genre in its own right. Euhemerus, who wrote around 300 BC, in fact used his account of a fantastic journey merely as a vehicle for his theory that the cult of the gods had originated in the veneration paid to prominent rulers after their deaths. However, Iambulus (around 100 BC), of whom we know through a brief reference by Diodorus, probably told the story of a marvellous voyage to an island in the southern Indian Ocean, and from there to India, purely for its own sake.

However, in addition to spectacular accounts of real or imagined journeys to distant lands, there were also literary descriptions dealing with regions and peoples closer to the readers' own realm of experience, such as the exuberant travelogues of Heraclides Criticus, of which substantial fragments have survived. Written around 200 BC, these provide a glimpse of conditions within Greece at that time. Once this literary form joined forces with antiquarian scholarship, the resulting genre was a historical and antiquarian geography, although there is only one extant example of it, dating from as late as the second century AD – the famous *Periegesis* by Pausanias, which in recent times has proved a valuable aid for the archaeological exploration of Greece.

The historical fiction that attached itself to the person of Alexander has already been touched on (see above, p. 289). The first separate version of a novel about the legendary Ninos, King of Assyria, that is not inserted in some other work likewise dates from the Hellenistic age. Of novel fragments that have become known through papyrus finds the earliest invariably seem to document events drawn from historical or pseudo-historical tradition.

From the series of extant Greek romantic novels only the earliest, by Chariton, falls within the final phase of the Hellenistic period, since his language shows no traces of Atticism, even though he makes repeated references to works dating from the Classical age. Chariton similarly sets his romantic plot in a situation described in the historical work of Thucydides at the end of his account of the Sicilian expedition of the Athenians. Romantic novels of this type invariably relate how a young couple distinguished by beauty, virtue and noble origins are separated by untoward circumstances shortly before their wedding, whereupon both are compelled to undergo the most deplorable suffering – being carried off to foreign countries, abused, sold into slavery, or even buried alive – before being reunited after withstanding these trials, both partners remaining chaste all the while.

This storyline shows that the travelogue was among the godfathers present at the birth of this type of novel. Its high pathos and moral rectitude distinguish it from the lascivious short stories of Aristides, known as 'Milesian tales'. A Latin equivalent was produced by Sisenna as early as around 70 BC. Isolated episodes in the novel of Petronius can provide some idea of their character – such as the subsequently often treated story of the young widow of Ephesus who spends the night weeping inconsolably at the grave of her recently dead husband. Hearing her, a soldier who has been assigned to guard the body of a crucified criminal at a nearby place of execution comes over to her and consoles her so vigorously that relatives of the executed criminal are able to steal his body from the cross. To save her new lover from punishment, the widow hands over to him the corpse of the husband she was until recently weeping over, so that he can hang him on the empty cross.

Any attempt to draw distinctions in entertainment literature within the sphere of biographies and memoirs is quite pointless. In the pre-Hellenistic period life histories had existed in the form of encomia, eulogies or tributes to leading public figures (see above, p. 207). Polybius was following in the footsteps of this tradition by writing a life history of Philopoemen, the last statesman of note in the Achaean alliance and his own political mentor. Brief life histories of major poets and prose writers, containing the bare facts and usually based on a fixed compositional plan, were written by philologists engaged in the collation, critical editing and commentary of their works. The biography of the poet was thus part of the scholarly exegesis of his works. As we have seen (p. 198), in philosophical ethics an interest arose in the life history of a man as the realisation of his moral perceptions and principles. The type of the philosophical biography grew up out of this – first within the Peripatus, whose anthropology offered particularly appropriate categories for recording life histories as a moral phenomenon, and then in other schools. The aim, therefore, was to record a life history as a moral phenomenon, with the additional concern of preserving with piety in the context of a philosophical school tradition the memory of the influence exerted by the school's founder and other leading exponents of the philosophy.

It is only natural that these three approaches to biographical writing did not evolve in three entirely separate strands of tradition: the three types continued to influence one another. This makes it impossible to arrive at a clear-cut distribution of the many familiar names of Hellenistic biographers among distinct biographical genres. The only exceptions are occasional supplementary reports facilitating assertions that the author in question was writing either for a readership interested in philosophy, literature or philology, or for a more general readership seeking to be entertained with anecdotes and the like.

In this context, one name may stand for many – that of Satyrus – since a papyrus find has retrieved a major fragment of his life of Euripides. This work was styled as a dialogue, indicating significant literary ambitions, and contains a wealth of information on the character and habits of the poet, which are extrapolated from germane passages in his tragedies, i.e. fabricated without reliable evidence.

Any further conclusions regarding the nature of the art of biography in Hellenism have to be drawn from extant biographies of the Imperial period. Plutarch (around AD 100) wrote moral assessment-type, essentially philosophical portraits of historical figures based on historiographical sources. Diogenes Laertius (around 200 AD) wrote life histories of famous philosophers drawn mainly from earlier biographical material, sometimes also assessing their moral qualities, sometimes merely conveying the facts assembled through scholarly research. There is documentary evidence of catalogues of famous philosophers having been compiled in the Hellenistic age according to the schools to which they belonged, also giving biographical information – particularly in the case of Sotion, who was designated a Peripatetic (see above, p. 294). In addition to these there are extant short life histories of virtually all poets and writers who had ever been the object of grammatical exegesis. These stand in the tradition of Hellenistic literary research, and were not usually definitively revised until late antiquity. Some of them have survived in medieval manuscripts together with the works of the poet, some in lexical form.

Finally, some examples of memoir literature should be mentioned. Aratus, instigator and foremost military leader of the Achaean alliance at the end of the third century BC, wrote an autobiography at quite an advanced age with the aim of writing an apologia for the historical events in which he had played such a key role. Plutarch used this book as a source for his biography of Aratus. Fewer traces remain of an autobiography by King Pyrrhus of Epirus dating from the first half of the third century BC.

As early as the second century BC this literary form was likewise adopted by major Roman authors, and developed further in Latin. Antigonus of Carystus (see above, p. 247), a versatile man of letters whose other works included a book on painting, was also author of a book of reminiscences, containing descriptions of all the teachers of philosophy whom he had either observed or known personally in third-century BC Athens.

Biography and autobiography have less in common than the terms might suggest. No autobiography is capable of accomplishing the prime object of the biographer, which is to record a life as a whole and in its entirety. Autobiography is moreover also subject to various constraints of convention, differing from one culture to another, as to the degree of self-portrayal a society will tolerate. For this reason occasional references by an author to his own experiences in other literary works can often be far more revealing than entire autobiographies.

Another branch of entertainment literature is epistolography. As has been shown above (p. 208), letters became customary as a literary form in the course of the fourth century BC, both within publicity and as part of philosophical school debate. The authenticity that the letter form can evoke indeed led philosophers to use it for putting forward theories and opinions as part of the debate as to correct school dogma, and within a school, traditional details concerning the life of its founder, purported to be of his authorship. The corpus of Plato's letters is a good example of this. With traditional historical or literary figures who had become legendary, the device suggested itself of styling letters written as if by them, amplifying on specific situations in their lives. Fictitious letters were thus penned among others for the tyrant Phalaris, infamous for his brutality, the philosopher Heraclitus, Pythagoras the miracle worker, Diogenes the Cynic, and Socrates. Whole branches of the fictional tradition surrounding Alexander consisted of fabricated correspondences between him, Aristotle and Indian philosophers. Moreover, since training in rhetoric by then included letter-writing, and composition ranked among prescribed stylistic exercises, it should come as no surprise to encounter letter types by hetaeras or exiles. By far the greater proportion of surviving literary letters date from as late as the Imperial period, but there is no doubt that epistolography was already in full flower as a branch of entertainment literature in the Hellenistic age. Although little has survived of Hellenistic entertainment literature, the fact that it existed must be taken sufficiently into account when attempting to gain a picture of the literary life of that era.

25

JEWISH
LITERATURE

Scattered widely across the Hellenistic world, and particularly in capital cities such as Alexandria and Antioch, Ephesus and Corinth, was a sizeable Jewish population whose steady geographical expansion was fostered by the scope of the Hellenistic economic and trading system. In the aftermath of the Alexandrian campaign, as Greek intellectuals came into fairly close contact with Jewish communities for the first time, they perceived their own philosophical conception of God in the strict monotheism of the Old Covenant. Similarly, the Jewish community of Palestine shaped by Mosaic law reminded them of their own ideal of government by philosophers.

An express interest in Jewish tradition is documented even for the early Hellenistic age, for example in the Peripatetics Theophrastus and Clearchus. Megasthenes (see above, p. 296) is reputed to have said that all discoveries made by Greek philosophy could be shown to have been made previously by the Indian gymnosophists (yogis) and the Jews.

Conversely, the Jews very rapidly adapted themselves to the language and customs of the Greek population in Greek or Hellenised towns, including in Egypt, for example, where they had settled in substantial numbers even before Alexander's time, mainly as mercenaries in the Persian army. This process of Hellenisation also embraced Palestine, which with Jerusalem comprised the cultural centre of all Jewry. The country was surrounded by a circle of Greek-founded urban centres whose social, cultural and economic life exerted an irresistible attraction on the Jewish nobility especially. By the third century BC they were reading Homer and practising athletics, opening themselves up to Greek civilisation. This apparently unstoppable process was nevertheless interrupted by the Maccabean revolt that was unleashed by abuses by the Syrian crown in the mid-second century BC. This galvanised anti-Hellenist feelings, leading via a series of bloody wars to the establishment of a Jewish state that was feared for its plundering encroachments, as well as being hostile to foreign languages and mores. It was only with some considerable effort that Pompey managed in the 60s BC to incorporate this community superficially into the order he imposed on the civilised Orient. In the Diaspora, by contrast, the Hellenisation of the Jews continued unabated everywhere. Only in

Mesopotamia, Persia and Arabia – i.e. outside the subsequent boundaries of the Roman Empire – did Jewish communities using a Semitic language (Aramaic) arise, like that in Palestine.

The Greek literature of the Jews began with translations of the Bible. Not even Hellenised Jews became fickle about their religion. On the contrary, they were soon able to attract throngs of proselytes to their ranks. The Greek Old Testament that is read today is based on editorial work carried out by Christian scholars in the third and fourth centuries AD using the techniques of philological criticism on the many texts that were used in the religious services of Jewish communities. The oldest of these no longer extant translations date from as early as the third century BC, and were exact equivalents of the Aramaic translations – paraphrases, or Targums, used by communities in Palestine or Mesopotamia, where Hebrew had by then died out as a colloquial language. This naturally posed a problem concerning the authenticity of texts, and it was doubts of this kind that one piece of Jewish literature written in the second century BC was designed to dispel. This was the pseudo-epigraphic *Aristeas Letter*, which tells how Ptolemy II, in order to complete his library, invited seventy-two scribes from Jerusalem to Alexandria, where they worked in separate rooms on Pentateuch translations which were found to agree word for word. It has long been assumed that this work was carried out in order to assist a certain Greek translation of the Bible to achieve general recognition. The attempt was successful insofar as the Greek Bible bears the name Septuagint to this day on account of this legend. The second half of the fictitious letter contains a depiction of the banquet held by the King for his guests from Jerusalem, at which they answer with appropriate wisdom his questions as to how a true ruler should conduct himself. There is a surprising parallel to this story: a central Indian text tells of dialogues between Buddhist scholars and King Milinda. It was under this name that the memory lived on of Menander, the foremost Greek ruler of Indian territory in the second century BC. It may also be deduced from Greek sources that he, like the great Mauryan ruler Ashoka, encouraged Buddhism. No detail either in the language or the form of the *Aristeas Letter*, aside from its specifically Jewish content, could be regarded as foreign to either the spirit or tradition within Greek literature. The same cannot be said, of course, for the translation of the Old Testament, which not only reproduced foreign literary forms in Greek, but also gave rise to a Greek biblical language permeated with many Semitisms. This idiom became the vehicle for the earliest Christian theology, since Christianity spread chiefly in the synagogue congregations of the Graeco-Roman world, who had long since become linguistically assimilated to their environment and for whom the Greek translation of the Bible was *the* Bible.

The so-called Apocryphal books of the Old Testament – works which all came about after the fourth century BC, and, for various reasons which need not be gone into here, did not find their way into the canon established around AD 100 – have largely come down in Greek versions. Many of them, especially those written in Palestine and Mesopotamia, were originally written in Hebrew or Aramaic, so that the texts extant today are translations. Some, however, were originally written in Greek, which makes them part of the Graeco-Jewish history of literature in the more specific sense. Of the two accounts of the Maccabean revolt and its consequences, for example, the book known as the *First Book of the Maccabees* was undoubtedly the translation of a Hebrew original. The *Second Book of the Maccabees*, however, is a Greek historical account, apart from the epistle from Palestinian to Egyptian Jews at the beginning. The second book describes itself as an extract from a historical work comprising five books by Jason of Cyrene – probably an author who both wrote in Greek and bore a Greek name. There is documentary evidence of a large and influential Jewish community in his north African native city. Both books of the Maccabees should be regarded, notwithstanding certain legendary embellishments, entirely as historical works. They are by and large reliable, if not entirely non-tendentious, accounts of the events of the Maccabean rebellion.

Besides the above, the Apocryphal literature of the Old Testament also includes self-contained historical legends. These should be distinguished from legends, told purely against a historical background, about the fortunes of devout individuals after the manner of the lovely story of Tobit, translated from the Aramaic. Among historical legends concerned with the fortunes of all Jews, or of large Jewish communities in a specific historical situation, the *Book of Judith* is based on a Hebrew original. The book erroneously known as the *Third Book of the Maccabees* describes a persecution of the Jews, and how it is brought to an end by divine intervention, reputed to have been instigated by the Ptolemaic king after the Battle of Raphia in 217 BC. Couched in an ambitious style, it was written in Greek either in the first century BC or perhaps a hundred years later, possibly in Alexandria. One remarkable feature of the book is its many quotations from tragedies by Aeschylus – a poet whose demanding style alone meant that he was less widely read than Euripides at that time. The Jews seem to have been particularly drawn by Aeschylus' concept of the justice of a universal order presided over by Zeus as the supreme god. Among people of Jewish origin whose names crop up in papyrus documents, a disproportionately high number bear the name of Aeschylus – an extremely rare name among the Greek population.

Even in the pre-Hellenistic period the Jews were already familiar with elegantly told historical legends, sometimes in the form of the aetiological history of a cult. The *Book of Esther*, set against the background of the plight of the Jews in the Persian Empire, is a fine example of this. From the third to the first century BC this literary tradition lived on independently of all Greek influence in such writings as the *Book of Daniel*. This was written in the mid-second century BC after the first conflict of Palestinian Jews with Antiochus Epiphanes, the Seleucid King, relocating the story among sixth-century Jews who had been deported to Babylon. These works reflect the complex situation of Jewish individuals and communities in the Diaspora. Both in the Persian Empire and later in the Hellenistic state system, Jews could on the one hand quite easily rise to positions of authority and influence, but on the other were in constant danger of falling victim to anti-Jewish sentiment. These legends thus mostly tell of Jewish communities in deadly peril, followed by a miraculous deliverance and improvement in their standing.

After the Maccabean revolt the risk of anti-Jewish eruptions throughout the Hellenistic world was greatly increased. The linguistic and cultural assimilation of Diaspora Jews to their respective environments was nevertheless unaffected by this event confined to Palestine, nor indeed did the power of the Jewish religion to attract intellectuals in particular suffer appreciably as a result. This situation produced a need for a missionary apologetic literature intended to point out to the Greeks that a complete fulfilment of the ideas of Greek civilisation could be expected within the Jewish tradition. The so-called *Fourth Book of the Maccabees* is a fine example of this literature. This long-winded tract takes an episode from the *Second Book of the Maccabees*, the martyrdom of Eleazar, his seven brothers and their mother, to demonstrate the triumph of judgement over desires and emotions in a state of complete virtue. This example from recent Jewish history is thus used to illustrate a generally familiar concept from Stoic ethics.

The Jewish parts of the *Sibylline Books* are propaganda literature in the trivial sense. Sibylline oracles in hexametric form appeared in Greece as early as the seventh century BC as part of a religious movement encompassing the entire Greek-speaking world (see above, pp. 60ff.) This literary genre became increasingly popular in the Hellenistic age, being employed for political publicity, particularly for promoting oppositional ideas in the major monarchies, and later for anti-Roman propaganda. Other kinds of oracle literature were also used for this purpose. Papyrus finds have thus uncovered several versions of a so-called *Potter's Oracle*, a vehicle for Egyptian resistance to Greek foreign rule that predicted the restoration of the Pharaohs. The Sibylline oracles additionally served as vehicles for religious propaganda, although this is not always easy to separate from the political variety. Theologumena – a hotch-potch of Greek philosophy, traditional cult piety and Oriental concepts that came into their own in the second half of the Hellenistic Age in particular, associated with the formation of new sects – were more memorable because they were in the guise of Sibylline prophecies. The Jews adopted the form, using it to impart their interpretation of history and Messianic expectations for the last days to a Greek readership. The extant corpus of Sibylline prophecies comprises pagan, Jewish and Christian components of widely varying dates. The Jewish prophecies are for the most part in the third and fourth books, and some date from the second to first centuries BC. Readers will be aware of the importance that became attached to Sibylline poetry in the medieval Christian tradition, chiefly through Virgil's fourth

Eclogue. The genre called for a sound command of Homeric style and metre in the poet.

Hexametric Sibylline oracles were not the only form of Greek poetry adopted by the Jews. As early as the second century BC one Ezekiel, of whom no further details are known, wrote a tragedy about the exodus of the people of Israel out of Egypt. Of this, 269 verses have survived in the work of a Christian writer. The elder Philo wrote, probably in the first century BC, a hexametric epic poem on themes drawn from the historical books of the Old Testament. A moral advisory poem that has come down under the name of Phocylides likewise documents the adoption by the Jews of Archaic gnomic poetry forms. Two editions of the *Testament of Orpheus*, similarly in hexametric hymn form, again surviving in works by Christian authors, attest to the fact that even the Orphic revelation, which gained in popularity with the rise of religio-philosophical syncretism in the second half of the Hellenistic age, was adopted by the Jews. It contains a renunciation by the mythical bard, who had become the eponym of a religious movement, of his polytheistic mystical theology, and a confession to his son Musaeus of his conversion to monotheism of the Mosaic variety.

A wealth of Graeco-Jewish prose literature on the Pentateuch adapted, paraphrased and interpreted its content in the spirit of Greek philosophy, science or historical vision. It used an allegorical method of interpretation that had been developed chiefly by the Stoics with the aim of interpreting Greek myths and Homeric texts as testimonies to their natural theories. Fragments of Jewish interpretative literature have survived predominantly in works by Christian authors, who for the most part worked from the extracts of Alexander Polyhistor (see above, p. 295), rather than the originals.

This group of Jewish authors includes among others Aristobulus (around 150 BC), who sought to prove that Greek poets and philosophers derived their wisdom from the Old Testament, as well as attempting an allegorical explanation of the anthropomorphic aspects of the Old Testament conception of God – which must have been a particular stumbling-block to Greek intellectuals. Another author who deserves mentioning is the Egyptian Jew Artapanus (around 80 BC), whose Iranian name is an indication of the far-reaching influence of Iranian culture and religion on post-exilic Judaism. He even traces Egyptian culture, whose great age was well-known to all Greeks, back to Joseph and Moses. In so doing, he was following a tradition established by a Jewish author in the early second century BC who published an ancient Jewish history under the name of Hecataeus of Abdera, known for his book on Egypt (see above, p. 295). A biblical chronological compendium published under the name of Demetrius of Phalerum (around 300 BC) but in fact dating from the second or first century BC is probably more reliable. Fragments by a certain Eupolemus suggest adaptations of biblical stories concerned solely with the wonderful. Some passages of *The Jewish Antiquities* by Flavius Josephus, dating from the late first century AD, which assume such a tradition, show that biblical stories were even restyled into the erotic novelette and adventure novel genres of the Hellenistic age.

Still more fashionable forms of prose literature can be documented among the Jews, such as the fictitious letter, as is borne out not only by the above-mentioned *Aristeas Letter*, but also by two unquestionably Jewish pieces in a forged compilation of letters allegedly by Heraclitus.

Whereas the account has thus far been predominantly concerned with literary forms from the Greek tradition that were adapted to the purposes of Jewish communities, an opposite trend also manifested itself in the imitation in Greek of originally Hebrew and Aramaic literary forms. The predecessor of this was Bible translation, and particularly the Greek imitation of Hebrew poetry and the forms laid down for it in psalms, prophetic revelation and proverbs. A style thus evolved that was independent of the Greek formal tradition, but was used in works originally conceived in Greek. This sometimes makes it difficult to ascertain whether late psalm verse now extant in Greek, such as the *Psalms of Solomon*, was always preceded by a Semitic original or not.

Apocalyptic literature occupies a special place in this context. In the last centuries before Christ, Judaism produced an unusually large number of apocalyptic works describing visions of the last days. Confrontation with the superior might of Greek civilisation erupted in the time of the Maccabeans, and many Jews sought to come to terms with this experience through chiliastic ideas, perhaps originating in Iran, by placing it in the context of human history as a whole. The *Book of Daniel*, which was included in the canon of the Old Testament, is the oldest such apocalypse (see above, p. 306). It interprets history as a sequence of four great empires, and the military engagements between the Seleucid state in Syria and the Ptolemaic kings of Egypt – in which the Romans also became involved, ultimately triggering the Maccabean revolt – as a prelude to the last days. These were to bring the judgement of God on all humankind and establish an everlasting kingdom ruled by his elect. In this way the time-honoured hope for a restoration of the Davidic kingdom acquired a universal historical perspective. Numerous subsequent apocalypses outdid one another in their invention of new metaphors and tales intended to illustrate both the experiences of the visionary and the events of the last days. All were nevertheless united by the conviction that a judgement of humankind, succeeding a period of extreme privation and affliction, would mark the culmination of history, and be followed by a heavenly kingdom of eternal and unchanging justice. Apocalyptic literature and its historical theology, which is still influential to this day, appeared against a background of numerous Jewish sects being formed in the period, and often contain cosmological and moral doctrines that are alien to the Old Testament, deriving from a variety of sources. From the second century AD onwards orthodox rabbis progressively eradicated these doctrines, so that apocalypses have only survived in Christian adaptations in (*inter alia*) Ethiopic, Syriac and Armenian translations. Oriental

Churches in particular evinced a considerable fondness for this literature, of which the originals were almost exclusively written in Hebrew or Aramaic. One of the lengthiest such works is the Apocalypse of Enoch, of which only one version in Ethiopic has survived intact, although it goes back to an Aramaic original. Another version of Enoch's journey though heaven and earth which shows substantial deviations from the Ethiopic version is now extant only in a Church Slavonic translation, which was preceded by a Greek original. It shows that even Greek-speaking Diaspora communities cultivated apocalyptic literature and did not content themselves merely with translation work in the sphere.

Another remarkable book, especially from the literary history standpoint, is the *Wisdom of Solomon*, included in the Old Testament Apocrypha. Naturally Greek Bible translation also included the various compilations of aphorisms (in the case of Jesus ben Sirach something is even known of the time and background of the translation). A number of these were attributed to the wise King Solomon, another, at least its Greek version, to the Attic comic poet Menander, whose authentic aphorisms were read by the Greeks, together with unauthentic ones, in florilegiums.

A typical compilation of aphorisms as a rule contains short, separate maxims, often set to a rhythm, and occasionally grouped together according to theme. A sequence of these could then become the model for a sermon on a particular moral problem – phrased in aphoristic style, but composed in one piece, as is occasionally the case in Jesus ben Sirach. This idiom derived from wisdom literature was used here by the author of the *Wisdom of Solomon* to put forward an expressly Jewish, and yet thoroughly original theology, based broadly speaking on Greek philosophemes. Its pessimistic, ascetic, unworldly dualism shows remarkable similarities to gnosis, which otherwise is hardly accessible to us except in its Christian variety. In its extant form the book was written in Greek, although Hebrew or Aramaic models are likely to have been available for certain short passages. Its date is as much disputed as its place of origin. Both the second and first centuries BC have been put forward, but some linguistic idiosyncrasies would tend to suggest the first century AD. Similarities with the doctrines of Philo of Alexandria, as well as the fact that this international city on the Nile acquired a leading role in the intellectual life of the Jewish Diaspora, have led some to surmise that the *Wisdom* was in fact written there. Recent research inclines more in favour of Syria, however.

The two leading witnesses testifying to Hellenised Judaism, Philo of Alexandria and Flavius Josephus, both fell within the Imperial Roman period. Since Christians were interested in their works, both have survived intact. Philo's writings mark the final and most productive phase in the two-way process of adoptions between Hellenistic philosophy and Jewish tradition. Josephus wrote an ancient history of his people that transposed the biblical account into the style of Greek historiography, as well as an exhaustive account of the war that ended with the destruction of Jerusalem in 70 AD, in which he had been involved.

The bloody confrontations between the Roman state and the Jews, lasting from the war of 68–70 AD through revolts in the Diaspora up to the dreadful Bar-Kochba uprising at the time of Emperor Hadrian, nipped Graeco-Jewish literature in the bud. Aversion intensified on both sides. The Roman state banned conversions to Judaism, also abolishing many of the privileges that Jews had initially enjoyed, while the Jews gradually eradicated from their intellectual life both Greek language and philosophy, the essential features of the civilisation to which they had once so willingly succumbed. The *Septuagint* – by then claimed as their Bible and the foundation for their position by Christian communities who were becoming emancipated from Judaism – was gradually replaced, firstly by the more accurate translations of Aquila, Symmachus and Theodotion, and then completely by the original text. Literature testifying to the two-way adoption of Greek and Old Testament ideas was gradually condemned as heterodox and excluded from doctrinal tradition, which from now on focused entirely on Hebrew and Aramaic literary scholarship emanating from centres in northern Palestine and Meso-potamia. The legacy of Hellenistic Judaism was passed on to the Christian Church, which preserved within its own literary tradition everything that can still be read today of the writings and fragments discussed in this chapter. The assimilation of the Christian Church into the civilisation of the Roman Empire, and the growth of a Christian theology that sought to encompass the evangelical message in the conceptual language of Greek philosophy – processes which have shaped the entire European culture – nevertheless occurred along the self-same lines established by Hellenistic Judaism.

EPILOGUE

This account of Greek literary history concludes with the onset of the Augustan era in the second half of the first century BC. The sphere delineated by Greek language and civilisation, which extended from Sicily to Egypt and Mesopotamia, making its cultural presence felt in places as far apart as India and Spain, was absorbed *en bloc* to become one portion of the Roman Empire. For the first hundred years Imperial Roman culture was dominated more by its Latin component, notably in the literary sphere. It nevertheless retained this bilingual character until the end of antiquity, despite becoming increasingly homogeneous. This process grew out of the profound exhaustion into which the east fell as a result of the protracted death throes of the Hellenistic system of states and the ruthless economic practices of the Roman conquerors. However, by the end of the first century AD this exhaustion had been cured. Braced by its disproportionately greater economic and cultural potential, the east then went on to seize the intellectual, economic and ultimately also political reins within the Roman Empire. Christianity – the new historical force that was to salvage the Roman idea of the state and carry it into the Middle Ages – acquired its distinctive character in the East from Greek philosophy, and from there too it launched its triumphal march.

It follows from this that the Greek literature of the Imperial period – which is not only rich, but has also survived far better than Hellenistic literature – is not Greek literature pure and simple as it had been in previous epochs, but the Greek facet of an Imperial Roman literature written in two cultural languages. The fact that bilingualism was a key feature of Imperial culture precludes a literary historical examination of this epoch from the perspective of one single language. This argument holds good despite the existence of independent literary traditions in both language spheres, and despite the classicism on the Greek side that led everyone involved in literature for centuries to draw their criteria of excellence from pre-Hellenistic writing (see above, pp. 286ff.). The awareness of all people living at that time was shaped by their sense of belonging to a Graeco-Roman *oikumene* (inhabited world), and Greek classicism was an integral part of the civilisation that flourished within that

312

oikumene. The picture of the course of ancient history that held sway into the nineteenth century, and by which humanist tradition continues to be guided to this day, was drawn from the perspective of the Imperial Roman era. In terms of the creation of enduring elements of human civilisation, Greek history ended on the battlefield of Chaeronea, or at the latest with the death of Alexander. From then on attention shifts to the Romans alone and their forward march through the age of Caesar and Augustus, Cicero and Virgil. It was in this age that the Romans not only supplied humankind within both cultural spheres, Greek and Latin alike, with an enduring peaceful order, but also produced the unsurpassable masterpieces of their own literature. The exemplary significance of history for all human civilisation derives from the fact that it contains both a classical Greek and a classical Latin literature – both Homer and Virgil, Demosthenes and Cicero. The essential features of this humanist conception just outlined were already shaping educational aware- ness in the Imperial Roman period. Its basic approach towards Graeco-Latin literature was classicist, except that the set of authors on the Greek side was established somewhat earlier, classical Greek authors being of greater signifi- cance for Latin literature than vice versa.

It was soon acknowledged that the proper task of the historian, faced with a scheme of values stretching so far back and having such deep roots as the humanist tradition, was to assist in reaching a correct assessment of epochs such as these, which do not fit into it. Since the nineteenth century, efforts to reach an appropriate evaluation of the Archaic era, the Hellenistic age, and Late Antiquity have consequently been accepted within classical studies as a matter of course. More than this, however, it is also incumbent on scholars to record and understand, as part of the historical process in which they came about, those values which still form the most powerful driving force behind all inquiry into antiquity, since they themselves were shaped over a long period within Graeco-Roman intellectual life. As in the age of European classicism, this period witnessed an admiration and veneration of literary achievements of the classical era from which, albeit not without some differences and modifi- cations in taste, the criteria for what was beautiful and good were sought. It was no coincidence that the definitive incorporation of Greek culture *en bloc* into the Roman Empire, and the rise of literary Atticism – and with it a new- old Greek written language – occurred at the same time.

In many respects Graeco-Roman literature of the Imperial period bears striking similarities to observations within European humanism at the begin- ning of the modern era, which nevertheless for its part quite often viewed authors of the Imperial period as classic, rather than classicising. Literature of the Imperial period is the most impressive witness to a humane civilisation based largely on reason that succeeded to a degree never since repeated in bringing peace, prosperity and security to the community of nations around the entire Mediterranean. However, precisely this close relationship between literature of the Imperial period and the conditions prevailing in the bilingual

313

empire makes it possible to arrange its two components into exclusive histories of Greek and Latin literature only with major reservations. This book will therefore need to be completed by an account of the bilingual literature of the Imperial Roman era.

BIBLIOGRAPHY

GENERAL

The best English history of Greek literature is *The Cambridge History of Classical Literature, I: Greek Literature*' (Cambridge, 1982–5). Useful accounts of just about every aspect of the classical world, including literature, can be found in *The Oxford History of the Classical World* (Oxford, 1986). A lively shorter literary history is P. Levi, *The Pelican History of Greek Literature* (London, 1985). Another good history is A. Lesky, *A History of Greek Literature*, trans. J. Willis and C. de Heer (London, 1966). Seminal for the Archaic era is H. Fränkel, *Early Greek Poetry and Philosophy*, trans. M. Hadas and J. Willis (Oxford, 1975).

On Greek history see J. B. Bury, *A History of Greece*, rev. R. Meiggs (4th edn, London, 1975); H. Bengtson, *History of Greece from the Beginnings to the Byzantine Era*, trans. and rev. E. F. Bloedow (Ottawa, 1988). A. Andrewes, *Greek Society* (Harmondsworth, 1975), is a good general introduction. On Greek religion, see W. Burkert, *Greek Religion: Archaic and Classical*, trans. J. Raffan (Oxford, 1985). A shorter general study is W. K. C. Guthrie, *The Greeks and their Gods* (London, 1950).

A concise account of ancient philosophy is A. Wedberg, *A History of Philosophy, I: Antiquity and the Middle Ages* (Oxford, 1982). More detailed is W. K. C. Guthrie, *A History of Greek Philosophy* (Cambridge, 1962–81).

For an account of the major myths, see H. J. Rose, *A Handbook of Greek Mythology* (London, 1928; 6th edn, 1958). G. S. Kirks discusses the character of Greek mythology in *The Nature of Greek Myths* (Harmondsworth, 1974).

Introductions to the political and legal thought of the Greeks are: J. W. Jones, *The Law and Legal Theory of the Greeks* (Oxford, 1956); D. M. McDowell, *The Law in Classical Athens* (London, 1978); and V. Ehrenberg, *The Greek State* (Oxford, 1960). An aspect of cultural history particularly important for the history of literature is dealt with by H. I. Marrou, *A History of Education in Antiquity*, trans. G. R. Lamb (New York, 1956). Of great general interest is F. Wehrli, *Hauptrichtungen des griechischen Denkens* (Zurich, 1964).

On metre, see M. L. West, *Greek Metre* (Oxford, 1987). On the history of the Greek language and the growth of its dialects, which appears in a new light since the discovery of Mycenaean Greek from the second millennium, see L. R. Palmer, *The Greek Language* (London, 1980) and C. D. Buck, *The Greek Dialects* (Chicago, 1955).

A comprehensive account of Greek Art is M. Robertson, *A History of Greek Art* (Cambridge, 1975), and a shorter introduction is J. Boardman, *Greek Art* (London, 1985).

On the background to Homer, see A. J. B. Wace and F. H. Stubbings (eds), *A Companion to Homer* (London, 1962) with contributions by critics, linguists, archaeologists and historians, and G. S. Kirk, *The Songs of Homer* (Cambridge, 1962). For an

315

examination of the oral epic tradition, see especially M. Parry, *The Making of Homeric Verse*, ed. A. Parry (Oxford, 1971), with an introduction by the editor that provides an excellent survey of modern Homeric criticism; and A. B. Lord, *The Singer of Tales* (Cambridge, Mass., 1960). A more literary study is J. Griffin's perceptive *Homer on Life and Death* (Oxford, 1980). The same author has written a short introduction to Homer in the 'Past Masters' series (Oxford, 1980). There are several good recent introductions to the *Iliad*: particularly useful are M. Edwards, *Homer: Poet of the Iliad* (Baltimore and London, 1987), and M. Silk, *Homer, the Iliad* (Cambridge, 1987). For a historical interpretation, see M. I. Finley, *The World of Odysseus* (2nd edn, London, 1977).

The standard commentary on the Hymns is by T. W. Allen, W. R. Halliday and G. E. Sikes (Oxford, 1936); the earlier edition of Allen and Sikes (London, 1904) is often superior. There is a detailed commentary on the Hymn to Demeter by N. J. Richardson, *The Homeric Hymn to Demeter* (Oxford, 1974). The best general book is J. S. Clay, *The Politics of Olympus* (Princeton, 1989).

Indispensable for Hesiod are the commentaries of M. L. West on the *Theogony* (Oxford, 1966) and *Works and Days* (Oxford, 1978).

1 THE BEGINNINGS AND THE EARLY EPIC POEM

The most convenient edition of all Homerica, including the Hymns and the most important fragments of the Epic Cycle, is D. Monro and T. W. Allen (eds), *Homeri Opera*, 5 vols (Oxford, 1920). Its edition of the *Odyssey* has nevertheless been surpassed by that of P. von der Mühll (Basle, 1946).

The best English translation is still that of Pope, accessible in *The Twickenham Edition of the Poems of Alexander Pope*, vols 7–10, ed. M. Mack (London, 1967). The most popular modern translations are those of R. Lattimore (Chicago, 1951) which stays very close to the original, and R. Fitzgerald (New York, 1961) which is faster paced and pithier. Prose translations include those by M. Hammond of the *Iliad* (Harmondsworth, 1987) and Walter Shewring of the *Odyssey* (Oxford, 1980). The remains of ancient Homeric exegesis in medieval scholia, particularly extensive for the *Iliad*, are collected in H. Erbse (ed.) *Scholia Graeca in Homeri Iliadem*, 7 vols (Berlin, 1969–88), and W. Dindorf, *Scholia Graeca in Homeri Odysseam* (Oxford, 1855; repr. Amsterdam, 1962).

The most important recent commentaries are G. S. Kirk (ed.), *The Iliad – a Commentary*, 6 vols (Cambridge, 1985–93), and J. B. Hainsworth, A. Heubeck, A. Hoekstra and S. West (eds), *A Commentary on Homer's Odyssey*, 3 vols (Oxford, 1988–92).

Other secondary literature cited: Adam Parry (ed.) *The Making of Homeric Verse: The Collected Papers of Milman Parry* (Oxford, 1971); W. H. Friedrich, *Verwundung und Tod in der Ilias* – Abhandl. Akad. (Göttingen 38, 1956); H. Fränkel, *Dichtung und Philosophie des frühen Griechentums*, (2nd edn, Munich, 1962, 84 ff.); K. Meuli, *Odyssee und Argonautika* (Berlin, 1921); K. Meuli, *Wesen und Herkunft der Fabel* – Schweiz. Archiv F. Volkskunde 50 (1954, 65 ff.).

The fragments are in R. Merkelbach and M. L. West, *Fragmenta Hesiodea* (Oxford, 1967). There is a good survey of Hesiod scholarship in the collection of essays edited by E. Heitsch, *Hesiod* (Darmstadt, 1966). There is a translation by M. L. West (Oxford, 1988).

2 THE EARLIEST NON-EPIC POETRY

Texts of the elegists and iambographers can be found in E. Diehl (ed.), *Anthologia Lyrica Graeca*, 3 vols (3rd edn, Leipzig, 1950–2) and M. L. West (ed.), *Iambi et Elegi*

Graeci (Oxford, 1971–2). The lyric poets apart from Pindar and Bacchylides are in D. L. Page (ed.), *Poetae Melici Graeci* (Oxford, 1968) with more recent fragments in D. L. Page (ed.), *Supplementum Lyricis Graecis* (Oxford, 1974). There is a new edition by M. Davies, *Poetarum Melicorum Graecorum Fragmenta* (Oxford, 1991), of which Volume I has so far appeared containing Alcman, Stesichorus and Ibycus (Oxford, 1991). There is useful commentary on selected poems in D. A. Campbell (ed.), *Greek Lyric Poetry* (2nd edn Bristol, 1981); and see also the commentaries in J. M. Bremer, A. M. Van Erp, Taalman Kip and S. R. Slings, *Some Recently Found Greek Poems* (Leiden, 1987).

The Lesbian poets are in E. Lobel and D. L. Page (eds), *Poetarum Lesbiorum Fragmenta* (Oxford, 1955). There are selected Greek texts with English translations in the *Penguin Book of Greek Verse* ed. C. A. Trypanis (Harmondsworth, 1971) and Greek texts with facing page translations in the Loeb, *Greek Lyric* ed. D. A. Campbell, 4 vols (Harvard, 1981–92). Epigrams are in the OCT *Epigrammata Graeca* ed. D. L. Page (Oxford, 1975). The best account for understanding early Greek lyric poetry is H. Fränkel, *Early Greek Poetry and Philosophy*, trans. M. Haddas and J. Willis (Oxford, 1975). A more recent overview is A. J. Podlecki, *The Early Greek Poets and Their Themes* (Vancouver, 1984). For a socio-historical analysis of Greek lyric poetry, see B. Gentili, *Poetry and its Public in Ancient Greece*, trans. A. T. Cole (Baltimore and London, 1988). Interesting and problematic is H. Koller, *Musik und Dichtung im alten Griechenland* (Berne, 1963).

3 EARLY PROSE

For the so-called logography, see bibliography to Chapter 5. The most useful collection of the texts of early Greek philosophers is still H. Diels and W. Kranz, *Die Fragmente der vorsokratiker*, 2 vols (6th edn, Berlin, 1951–2). The fragments are translated into English in K. Freeman, *Ancilla to the Pre-Socratic Philosophers* (Oxford, 1956). For an introduction to their philosophy, see E. Hussey, *The Presocratics* (London, 1972), and G. S. Kirk, J. E. Raven and M. Schofield, *The Presocratic Philosophers* (Cambridge, 1983), a selection of texts with translation and critical discussion.

Recommended reading for the early history of Pythagoreanism is W. Burkert, *Lore and Science in Ancient Pythagoreanism*, trans. E. L. Minar (Cambridge, Mass., 1972), which is rich in both ideas and material. Counter-trends to the predominantly intellectualist culture of the Greeks, of which philosophy is the most important expression, are dealt with by E. R. Dodds, *The Greeks and the Irrational* (Berkeley and Los Angeles, 1951); see also J. D. P. Bolton, *Aristeas of Proconnesus* (Oxford, 1962).

The text of the Derveni papyrus is in *Zeitschrift für Papyrologie und Epigraphik* 47 (1982). For Orphic poetry, see M. L. West, *The Orphic Poems* (Oxford, 1983). The fullest available collection of texts associated with Aesop is in B. E. Perry (ed.) *Aesopica* (Illinois, 1952). The traditions of the 'seven sages' have been edited by B. Snell, *Leben und Meinungen der Sieben Weisen* (Munich, 1952).

4 LATE ARCHAIC POETRY

The texts are given in the bibliography for Chapter 2 and 3. See also B. Snell and H. Maehler (eds), *Pindari Carmina cum Fragmentis*, 2 vols (Leipzig, 1987). A good English translation is that of F. J. Niesetich, *Pindar's Victory Songs* (Baltimore, 1980). Seminal for Pindar exegesis is U. von Wilamowitz-Moellendorf, *Pindaros* (Berlin, 1922) in spite of the changes since in the interpretation of Pindaric poetry, especially on the basis of G. Bundy, *Studia Pindarica*, 1–2 (Berkeley, 1962). For a good introduction to more recent Pindar research see the contributions to A. Hurst (ed.) 'Pindare' in *Entretiens Foundation Hardt* 31 (Geneva, 1987). Also useful are M. R. Lefkowitz, *The Victory Ode* (Park Ridge NJ, 1976); C. Carey, *A Commentary on Five Odes of Pindar* (New York, 1981) and H. Fränkel, *Early Greek Poetry and Philosophy*, trans. M. Hadas and J. Willis (Oxford, 1975). In this case particularly important remains of ancient interpretation of Pindar are available in A. B. Drachmann, *Scholia Vetera in Pindari Carmina*, 3 vols (Leipzig, 1903–27; repr. Amsterdam, 1964).

5 PHILOSOPHY AND SCIENCE

For literature on Heraclitus and Parmenides, see Chapter 3, and also E. Heitsch (ed.), *Parmenides* (Munich, 1974) with an important introduction. The fragments of all Greek historiography are collected with a detailed commentary in the monumental work of F. Jacoby, *Die Fragmente der griechischen Historiker* (Leiden, 1923–), which should always be referred to with regard to the treatment of later historiography. On the beginnings of historiography, see L. Pearson, *Early Ionian Historians* (Oxford, 1939). On the development of Greek science, see M. R. Cohen and I. E. Drabkin, *A Source Book in Greek Science* (New York, 1948); O. Neugebauer, *The Exact Sciences in Antiquity* (Princeton, NJ, 1952); and the works of G. E. R. Lloyd, *Early Greek Science* (London, 1970), *Greek Science after Aristotle* (London, 1973), and *The Revolution of Wisdom* (Berkeley, 1987). On the beginnings of methodical scientific accounts, see M. Fuhrmann, *Das systematische Lehrbuch* (Göttingen, 1960). For a comprehensive history of geography, see J. Thomson, *History of Ancient Geography* (Cambridge, 1948).

6 AESCHYLUS AND THE BEGINNINGS OF TRAGEDY

An excellent comprehensive introduction to tragedy with an extensive bibliography is A. Lesky, *Greek Tragic Poetry* (Yale, 1983). A livelier book is B. Vickers, *Towards Greek Tragedy* (London, 1973). On the origins of tragedy and the institution of dramatic performance in the Athenian state cult, see three works rich in material by A. W. Pickard-Cambridge: *Dithyramb, Tragedy and Comedy*, 2nd edn, rev. T. B. L. Webster (Oxford, 1962), *The Theatre of Dionysus* (Oxford, 1946), and *The Dramatic Festivals of Athens*, 2nd edn, rev. J. Gould and D. Lewis (Oxford, 1968). Still basic on the language, style and tradition of tragedy is U. von Wilamowitz-Moellendorf, *Euripides: Herakles* (Berlin, 1895; repr. Darmstadt, 1959). The fragments of pre-Aeschylean tragedy are in B. Snell, *Tragicorum Graecorum Fragmenta, I* (Göttingen, 1971); this also contains the remains of the didascaliae, ancient performance records. The best editions of Aeschylus are those of U. von Wilamowitz-Moellendorf (Berlin, 1914) and M. L. West (Stuttgart, 1990). English translations can be found in D. Grene and R. Lattimore (eds), *The Complete Greek Tragedies*, Aeschylus 1–2 (Chicago, 1959–60). Fragments of Aeschylus are in S. Radt, *Tragicorum Graecorum Fragmenta*, Vol. 3 (Göttingen, 1985). A good commentary on the disputed 'Prometheus Bound', see M. Griffith, *Aeschylus' Prometheus Bound* (Cambridge, 1983)). For important inter-pretations of the art of Aeschylus, see K. Reinhardt, *Aischylos als Regisseur und Theologe* (Bern, 1949); F. Solmsen, *Hesiod and Aeschylus* (Ithaca, NY, 1949); O. Taplin, *The Stagecraft of Aeschylus* (Oxford, 1977).

Other works cited: B. Snell, *Aischylos und das Handeln in Drama*, (Leipzig, 1928); Kurt von Fritz, *Antike und moderne Tragödie* (Berlin, 1962).

7 SOPHOCLES AND EURIPIDES

There are editions of Sophocles by R. D. Dawe (Stuttgart, 1975–9) and H. Lloyd-Jones and N. G. Wilson (Oxford, 1990). The fragments are in S. Radt, *Tragicorum Graecorum Fragmenta*, 4 (Göttingen, 1977). Of the numerous commentaries, none of which is of the calibre of Fraenkel's commentary on Aeschylus' *Agamemnon* or Wilamowitz's on Euripides' *Heracles*, the most notable are those of R. C. Jebb (all the plays, Cambridge, 1883 onwards) which are outdated in literary approach but invaluable on linguistic points, and the separate commentary on *Electra* by G. Kaibel (Stuttgart, 1967; 1st edn Leipzig, 1911). English translations in D. Grene and R. Lattimore (eds) *Complete Greek Tragedies*, Sophocles 1–2. An impressive interpretation is K. Reinhardt, *Sophocles* (English translation Oxford, 1978). Also valuable are R. P. Winnington-Ingram, *Sophocles: an Interpretation* (Cambridge, 1980) and B. M. W. Knox, *The Heroic Temper* (Berkeley and Los Angeles, 1964). See also Tycho von Wilamowitz-Moellendorf, *Die dramatische Technik des Sophokles* (Berlin, 1917). Ulrich von Wilamowitz-Moellendorf, *Hermes* (18) 1883.

There is a good edition of Euripides in the (to date) two volumes by J. Diggle (Oxford, 1981, 1984), replacing the edition of G. Murray (Oxford, 1902–9). For the fragments, see A. Nauck, *Tragicorum Graecorum Fragmenta* (Leipzig, 1889; repr. Gottingen, 1964, with a supplement by B. Snell), and papyrus fragments in D. L. Page, *Select Papyrii* III (Literary Papyri, Poetry) (London, 1950). For English translations, see D. Grene and R. Lattimore (eds), *Complete Greek Tragedies* (Chicago, 1959–60). Euripides 1–2. Noteworthy among the numerous commentaries are: E. R. Dodds, *Euripides: Bacchae* (2nd edn, Oxford, 1960); W. S. Barrett, *Euripides: Hippolytus* (Oxford, 1964), and R. Kannicht, *Euripides: Helen* (Heidelberg, 1969).

A good introduction to understanding the poet is A. Rivier, *Essai sur le tragique d'Euripide* (2nd edn, Paris, 1975). Gilbert Murray's classic *Euripides and his Age* (London, 1913) is still worth reading. Some contemporary perspectives on Euripides can be found in A. Powell (ed.), *Euripides, Women and Sexuality* (London, 1990).

Still a seminal work for understanding the 'new' dithyramb is U. von Wilamowitz-Moellendorf, *Timotheos, Die Perser* (Leipzig, 1903). The fragments are in D. T. Sutton, *Dithyrambographi Graeci* (Berlin, 1989).

Other works cited: E. R. Dodds, *The Greeks and the Irrational* (Berkeley, 1966); W. H. Friedrich, *Euripides und Diphilos* (Munich, 1953); A. Lesky, *Die tragische Dichtung der Hellenen*, 3rd edn (Göttingen, 1972); G. Zuntz, *The Political Plays of Euripides*, 2nd edn (Manchester, 1963).

8 OLD COMEDY

The remains of all Attic comedy are collected in T. Kock, *Comicorum Atticorum Frgamenta, 1–3*, (Leipzig, 1880); and texts that have come to light since, in J. Demianczuk, *Supplementum Cornicum* (Cracow, 1912), and A. Austin (ed.), *Comicorum Graecorum Fragmenta in Papyris Reperta* (Berlin, 1973). The remains of non-Attic comedy are in G. Kaibel, *Comicorum Graecorum Fragmenta* I.1 (Berlin, 1889; repr. 1958), together with treatises on comedy by ancient grammarians, and in A. Olivieri, *I frammenti della commedia greca e del mimo nella Sicilia e nella Magna Graecia* 2 vols (2nd edn, Naples, 1947). Of the new edition of comic fragments by C. Austin and R. Kassel, *Poetae Comici Graecae*, volumes 2, 3.2, 4, 5 and 7 are available to date (New York, 1989). The foremost edition of Aristophanes is the Budé of V. Coulon, 5 vols (Paris, 1923 onwards). Of the complete edition of the numerous remains of ancient and medieval interpretation of Aristophanes by D. Holwerda and W. J. W. Koster *et al.* (Amsterdam, 1961 onwards), ten volumes or parts of volumes are so far available, arranged according to seperate comedies. The older scholia are for now most conveniently consulted in F. Dübner, *Scholia in Aristophanem* (Paris, 1899). Translations of Aristophanes take various approaches: the Penguins translations by D. Barrett and A. H. Sommerstein are the most widely available. The best introduction to Aristophanes is K. J. Dover, *Aristophanic Comedy* (London, 1972); the same author has written a good commentary on the *Clouds*, which is of special interest because of its caricature of Socrates (Oxford, 1970).

9 PHILOSOPHY, RHETORIC AND SCIENCE

For literature on Anaxagoras and Democritus see Bibliography to Chapter 3. On the Sophists, see M. Untersteiner, *I Sofisti*, 1–4 (Florence, 1961 onwards), which contains fragments with Italian translation, extensive commentary and a good bibliography; G. B. Kerferd, *The Sophistic Movement* (Cambridge, 1981); J. de Romilly, *Les Sophistes* (Paris, 1988). The remains of pre-Aristotelian rhetorical and stylistic theory are in L. Radermacher, *Artium Scriptores* (Vienna, 1951); for further information, see below on Chapter 13. On the importance of Gorgias, see F. Zucker, *Der Stil des Gorgias nach seiner inneren Form* (Berlin, 1956). There is an English translation, with notes, of the most important texts of ancient literary criticism by D. A. Russell and M. Winterbottom, *Classical Literary Criticism* (Oxford, 1989); and see the *Cambridge History of Literary Criticism, I: Classical Criticism*, ed. G. A. Kennedy, (Cambridge, 1989). There is an edition with commentary of the pseudo-Xenophontic *Constitution of Athens* by H. Frisk (New York, 1976; 1st edn Copenhagen, 1946). There is a good edition of Antiphon by L. Gernet (Budé, Paris, 1954) and of Andocides by G. Dalmeyda (Paris, 1930). The most recent complete edition of the Corpus Hippocraticum is that of E. Littré (with French translation), *Oeuvres complètes d'Hippocrate*, 10 vols (Paris 1839–61). Some older treatises have been edited by J. L. Heiberg in *Corpus Medicorum Graecorum* I.i (Leipzig, 1927). There are English translations of selected works in the Penguin *Hippocratic Writings* ed. G. E. R. Lloyd (London, 1978). Important general works on Hippocratic medicine are W. A. Heidel, *Hippocractic Medicine: Its Spirit and Method* (New York, 1941), and L. Edelstein, *Ancient Medicine* (Baltimore, 1967). Among commentaries on specific Hippocratic works, recommended is A. J. Festaugière, *Hippocrate, l'ancienne médecine* (Paris, 1948), containing a particularly good explanation of the relationship between medicine and later philosophy. For the other sciences, see the bibliography for Chapter 5 and I. L. Heath, *A Manual of Greek Mathematics* (3rd edn, New York, 1963).

10 HERODOTUS AND THUCYDIDES

For good editions of Herodotus, see C. Hude, 2 vols (3rd edn, Oxford, 1927) and E. Legrand, 9 vols (with introduction and French translation, Paris 1932–54). There is a good commentary on the Egyptian book by A. B. Lloyd, *Herodotus: Book 2*, 3 vols (Leiden, 1975–88). There is a new commentary by D. Asheri *et al.*, *Erodoto, le storie* (Rome, 1989), of which vols 1, 2, 3, 8 and 9 have so far appeared; English translation by A. de Selincourt (Harmondsworth, 1954). Still a seminal treatment of Herodotus is F. Jacoby, art. in Pauly-Wissowa, *Realencyclopädie der classischen Altertumswissenschaft*, Suppl. 2 (Stuttgart 1913). A good general book is J. A. S. Evans, *Herodotus* (Boston, Mass., 1982).

Good editions of Thucydides are available by H. Stuart Jones and J. E. Powell, *Historiae*, 2 vols (2nd edn, Oxford, 1942) and O. Luschnat (2nd edn, Leipzig, 1960; still incomplete). The best English translation is that of R. Crawley (London, 1876). There is a detailed commentary in five volumes, begun by A. W. Gomme, and finished by A. Andrewes and K. J. Dover, *An Historical Commentary on Thucydides* (Oxford, 1945–81); and now there is a new commentary by S. Hornblower, of which Vol. 1 has so far appeared, *A Commentary on Thucydides, Books I, II, III* (Oxford, 1991). The foundation of modern Thucydidean research, although specific aspects of it have often been surpassed since, is E. Schwartz, *Das Geschichtswerk des Thukydides* (Bonn, 1919), which triggered a discussion that continues to this day and can scarcely be ignored. More recent notable works include J. de Romilly, *Thucydides and Athenian Imperialism*, trans. P. Thody (Oxford, 1963); G. E. M. de Sainte Croix, *The Origins of the Peloponnesian War* (London, 1972); S. Hornblower, *Thucydides* (London, 1987).

11 SOCRATES AND SOCRATIC THOUGHT

A standard account of Socrates is O. Gigon, *Sokrates* (Bern, 1947). Important recent works include G. Vlastos, *Socrates: Ironist and Philosopher* (Cambridge, 1991); *Socratic Questions*, a collection of essays edited by B. S. Gower and M. C. Stokes (London, 1992). The remains of non-Platonic Socratic literature are in G. Giannantoni, *Socraticorum reliquiae*, 4 vols (Rome, 1983–5); F. Decleva Caizzi (ed.) *Antisthenes* (Turin, 1967). See also D. L. Dudley, *A History of Cynicism* (Hildesheim, 1967; 1st edn London, 1937); K. Döring, *Die Megariker*; E. Marchant (ed.) *Xenophon*, 5 vols (Oxford, 1919); O. Gigon, *Kommentar zum ersten Buch von Xenophons Memorabilien* (Basel, 1953) and *Kommentar zum zweiten Buch von Xenophons Memorabilien* (Basel, 1956). Xenophon's Socratic writings are translated in H. Tredennick, *Xenophon: Memoirs of Socrates and the Symposium* (Harmondsworth, 1970).

12 PLATO, ARISTOTLE AND THEIR SCHOOLS

Plato, ed. J. Burnet, 5 vols (Oxford, 1899–), Vol. 5, contains also inauthentic works, outside the tetralogies of the Corpus Platonicum. All the evidence on Plato's teaching and the content of his oral instruction is collected in K. Gaiser, *Platons ungeschriebene Lehre* (Stuttgart, 1963). On the disputed questions of how extant works relate to Plato's oral teaching, see E. Heitsch, *Platon über die rechte Art zu reden und zu schreiben* (Mainz, 1987). E. Hamilton and H. Cairns (eds), *The Collected Dialogues of Plato* (Princeton, 1973), has good translations of all but a few dubious dialogues. Some important works on Plato are U. von Wilamowitz-Moellendorf, *Platon* (Berlin, 1919); A. E. Taylor, *Plato, the Man and his Work* (London 1960); P. Friedländer, *Plato: an Introduction*, 3 vols, trans. H. Meyerhoff (London, 1958); I. Crombie, *An Examination of Plato's Doctrines*, 2 vols (London, 1963); G. Vlastos, *Platonic Studies* (2nd edn, Princeton, 1981). There are good commentaries on the *Gorgias* by E. R. Dodds (Oxford, 1959) and on the *Symposium* by K. J. Dover (Cambridge, 1980).

The fragments of Plato's first followers are in F. W. A. Mullach, *Fragmenta Philosophorum Graecorum*, vol. 3 (Paris, 1864); L. Taran, *Speusippus of Athens* (Leiden, 1981), and N. Isnardi Parente, *Senocrate e Polemone* (Naples, 1982). On the older Platonic tradition, see H. Flashar (ed.) *Altere Akademie, Aristoteles, Peripatos* (Basle, 1983); vol. 3 of a revised edition of F. Überweg, *Die Philosophie des Altertums*; see also H. Dörrie and M. Baltes, *Der Platonismus in der Antike*, 2 vols (Stuttgart, 1986, 1990). On post-Platonist Socratic literature, see C. W. Müller, *Die Kurzdialoge der Appendix Platonica* (Munich, 1975).

The foundation of modern Aristotle research is the major edition commissioned by the Berlin Academy by I. Bekker (Berlin, 1831–). The best collection of fragments is V. Rose, *Aristotelis Fragmenta* (Leipzig 1886). *The Oxford Translation of Aristotle* revised by J. Barnes (Princeton, 1984) contains translations of the complete extant works. The first attempt to understand Aristotle's intellectual development is W. Jaeger, *Aristotle: Fundamentals of the History of His Development* (Oxford, 1948). An important monograph is I. Düring *Aristoteles* (Heidelberg, 1966). A good general book is G. E. R. Lloyd, *Aristotle: the Growth and Structure of his Thought* (Cambridge, 1968).

Basic for research on Theophrastus is O. Regenbogen, 'Theophrastus', in Pauly-Wissowa, *Realencyclopädie der classischen Altertumswissenschaft*, Suppl. 7 (1940). See also W. W. Fortenbaugh (ed.) *Theophrastus of Eresus: his Life and Work* (New Brunswick, NJ, 1985). The Loeb has a Greek text of the botanical works with facing translation (6 vols).

The remains of Peripatetic philosophy up to the second century BC are collected, with commentary, by F. Wehrli, *Die Schule des Aristoteles*, 9 vols (Basle, 1944); W. Jaeger, *Diokles von Karystos* (Berlin, 1937).

13 RHETORIC

There are editions of Lysias with French translation by L. Gernet and M. Bizos, 2 vols (Paris 1924–6); and of Isocrates by G. Matthieu and E. Bremond, 4 vols (Paris, 1928–62). English translation in the Loebs of Lysias by W. Lam (Harvard, 1930) and Isocrates by G. Norlin, 3 vols (Harvard, 1928–45). For a summarising account, see E. Mikkola, *Isokrates* (Helsinki, 1954) and the excellent account in W. Jaeger, *Paideia* vol. 3, trans. G. Highet (Oxford, 1945). On Lysias, see K. J. Dover, *Lysias and the Corpus Lysiacum* (Berkeley Los Angeles, 1968). On the history of rhetoric, see M. Fuhrmann, *Die Antike Rhetorik* (Munich, 1968), and G. Kennedy, *The Art of Persuasion in Greece* (Princeton, NJ, 1963). For a good account of ancient literary criticism, see D. A. Russell, *Criticism in Antiquity* (Berkeley, 1981). See also the works cited for Chapter 9. Isaeus is available in an edition by T. Thalheim (Leipzig 1903); English translation in the Loeb by E. S. Forster (Harvard, 1927). Demosthenes is edited by S. H. Butcher and W. Rennie, *Demosthenes: Orationes*, 2 vols (Oxford, 1903–). English translation in the Loeb by J. H. Vince, A. T. Murray and N. W. and N. J. De Witt, 7 vols. A useful commentary is C. Carey and R. A. Reid (eds) *Demosthenes: Selected Private Speeches*. A fine general account is W. Jaeger, *Demosthenes: The Origin and Growth of his Policy* (Cambridge, 1938). Aeschines is translated in the Loeb by C. D. Adams (London, 1948); for minor orators see J. O. Burtt, *The Minor Attic Orators* (London, 1954). On the development of rhetorical instruction, see D. A. Russell, *Greek Declamation* (Oxford, 1983).

14 ENTERTAINMENT LITERATURE, FACTUAL LITERATURE AND HISTORIOGRAPHY

All the fragments of historians are in F. Jacoby, *Die Fragmente der griechischen Historike* (Leiden, 1923–). There are Penguin translations of Xenophon's *Hellenica* (*A History of my Times*), trans. R. Warner (Harmondsworth, 1949). For general editions see above on Chapter 11. Still unsurpassed for an account of the beginnings of narrative literature and its forms is E. Schwartz, *Fünf Vorträge über den griechischen Roman* (Berlin, 1943). See also T. Hägg, *The Novel in Antiquity* (Oxford, 1983); F. Jacoby, *Atthis* (Oxford, 1949).

15 POETRY

Texts of middle comedy in works cited for Chapter 8, for fourth–century BC tragedy in B. Snell and R. Kannicht, *Tragicorum Graecorum Fragmenta*, 1–2 (Göttingen, 1971, 1981). See also T. B. L. Webster, *Art and Literature in Fourth Century Athens* (London, 1956), and *Greek Theatre Production* (London, 1956); and K. J. Dover, article 'Comedy' in *Fifty Years of Classical Scholarship* ed. Platnauer (1954). See also B. Wyss (ed.) *Antimachi Colophonii Reliquiae* (Berlin, 1936) with an important introduction; K. Latte, *Erinna* (Göttingen, 1953); R. Schröter, *Poetica* 1 (1967).

16 HELLENISM AND ITS PHILOSOPHY

The classic account of the Hellenistic age is M. Rostovtzeff, *The Social and Economic History of the Hellenistic World*, 3 vols (Oxford, 1941). See also W. W. Tarn and G. T. Griffith, *Hellenistic Civilisation* (3rd edn London, 1952); F. W. Walbank, *The Hellenistic World* (London, 1981). A comprehensive account of the most important cultural centre of the Hellenistic age is P. M. Fraser, *Ptolemaic Alexandria* (Oxford, 1972).

The fragments of older Stoic philosophy are in H. von Arnim (ed.) *Stoicorum Veterum Fragmenta* (Leipzig, 1903–24). For Epicurus, see G. Arrighetti (ed.) *Epicuro–Opere* (Turin, 1973); H. Usener (ed.) *Epicurea* (Leipzig, 1887); also M. van der Straaten, *Panaetii Rhodii Fragmenta* (Leiden, 1952). Fragments of Posidonius are in L. Edelstein and I. G. Kidd, *Posidonius: The Fragments*, 2 vols (Cambridge, 1972–88) (see also K. Reinhardt, *Poseidonios über Ursprung und Entartung* (Heidelberg, 1928)); *Teletis Reliquiae*, ed. O. Hense (Tübingen, 1909). Fragments of Bion of Borysthenes are compiled by J. F. Kindstrand in *Bion of Borysthenes* (Uppsala, 1976).

For an introduction to Hellenistic philosophy see A. A. Long, *Hellenistic Philosophy* (Berkeley 1986). A. A. Long and D. N. Sedley, *The Hellenistic Philosophers* (Cambridge, 1987) contains in vol. 1 translations of the sources with philosophical commentary and in vol. 2 Greek and Latin texts, with notes and bibliography. A seminal account of the history of the Stoa, but also including all Hellenistic philosophy, is M. Pohlenz, *Die Stoa*, 2 vols (Göttingen, 1955–9). See also F. H. Sandbach, *The Stoics* (London, 1979). There is an excellent summary of our knowledge of Epicurean philosophy in W. Schmid, article 'Epikur' in *Reallexikon f. Antike u. Christentum* 5 (1961) 681–819. A shorter account is J. N. Rist, *Epicurus: an Introduction* (Cambridge, 1972). On sceptical philosophy, see F. Decleva Caizzi, *Pirrone: testimanianze* (Naples, 1981), which has testimonia on Pyrrho, with Italian translation and extensive commentary; C. L. Stough, *Greek Scepticism* (Berkeley/Los Angeles, 1969); M. F. Burnyeat (ed.) *The Skeptical Tradition* (Berkeley/Los Angeles, 1983). Texts of Hellenistic Pythagoreans are in H. Thesleff, *The Pythagorean Texts of the Hellenistic Period* (Abo, 1965); and see also the contributions of W. Burkert and H. Thesleff to K. von Fritz (ed.) 'Pseudepigrapha I', *Entretiens Fondation Hardt* 8 (Geneva, 1971).

17 DRAMATIC POETRY

For the remains of Hellenistic tragedy see the bibliography for Chapter 15. The remains of New Comedy are in the collections cited for Chapter 8; A. Körte and A. Thierfelder, (ed.) *Menandri quae supersunt*, 2 vols (Leipzig, 1959); the most important fragments are in the edition of F. H. Sandbach, *Menander: Reliquiae Selectae* (2nd edn Oxford, 1990). See also A. W. Gomme and F. H. Sandbach, *Menander, a Commentary* (Oxford, 1973). Two essential commentaries for understanding the language and art of Menander are those by U. von Wilamowitz-Moellendorf, *Menander: Das Schiedsgericht* (Berlin, 1958), and E. W. Handley, *The Dyskolos of Menander* (London, 1965). A useful introduction is T. B. L. Webster, *Introduction to Menander* (London, 1974); and there are good observations in F. H. Sandbach, *The Comic Theatre of Greece and Rome* (London, 1977). The most accessible translation of Menander is the Penguin by N. Miller (London, 1987).

Other works cited: W. H. Friedrich, *Euripides und Diphilos* (Munich, 1953).

18 CALLIMACHUS AND LYRIC POETRY

Callimachus, ed. R. Pfeiffer, 2 vols (Oxford, 1949–53); the rich annotations give this edition the value of a full commentary. English translation in the Loeb editions of G. Mair (1921) and C. A. Trypanis (1958). See also J. Ferguson, *Callimachus* (Boston, 1980), and P. M. Fraser, *Ptolemaic Alexandria* (Oxford, 1972). Fragments of Hellenistic poetry (excluding Callimachus, Theocritus, Apollonius, Aratus, Lycophron and Herodas) are collected in J. U. Powell, *Collectanea Alexandrina* (Oxford, 1925), and H. Lloyd-Jones and P. Parsons, *Supplementum Hellenisticum* (Berlin, 1983). Herodas, *Mimiambi*, ed. I. A. Cunningham (Oxford, 1971) with commentary; the edition by the same author contains the known fragments of Greek mime. For Lycophron, see the translations in the Loebby A. W. Mair cited above for Callimachus (1921). The substantial remains of ancient commentary on Lycophron are contained in the edition of the *Alexandra* by E. Scheer, 2 vols (Berlin, 1881–1908).

An important contribution to an understanding of Hellenistic poetry is U. von Wilamowitz-Moellendorf, *Hellenistische Dichtung in der Zeit des Kallimachos*, 2 vols (Berlin, 1924). A recent general book is C. O. Hutchinson, *Hellenistic Poetry* (Oxford, 1988); and there is an excellent commentary on selected poems by N. Hopkinson, *A Hellenistic Anthology* (Cambridge 1988).

19 APPOLLONIUS RHODIUS AND EPIC POETRY

Apollonii Rhodii Argonautica, ed. H. Fränkel (Oxford, 1961); translation in the Penguin by E. V. Rieu (Harmondsworth, 1958). For literary discussion, see C. R. Beye, *Epic and Romance in the Argonautica of Apollonius* (Illinois, 1982) and R. L. Hunter, *The Argonautica of Apollonius Rhodius: Literary Studies* (Cambridge, 1993). The most important ancient scholia have been edited by C. Wendel, *Scholia in Theocritum vetera* (Leipzig, 1914; repr. Stuttgart, 1967); *Arati Phaenomena*, ed. E. Maass (Berlin, 1893); *Nicander*, ed. A. S. F. Gow and A. F. Scholfield (Cambridge, 1953), with English translation and detailed commentary.

Other works cited: K. Meuli, *Odyssee und Argonautika* (Berlin, 1921).

20 THEOCRITUS AND BUCOLIC POETRY

Bucolici Graeci, ed. A. S. F. Gow (Oxford, 1952); *Theocritus*, ed. A. S. F. Gow, 2 vols (Cambridge, 1950) with English translation and detailed commentary. On the influence of Theocritus on European pastoral poetry, see T. G. Rosenmeyer, *The Green Cabinet* (Berkely, 1969).

21 THE EPIGRAPH

There is a Loeb text (Greek and English) of the whole Greek Anthology by W. R. Paton (5 vols, 1916–18). There is a text and commentary on the Hellenistic epigrams of the *Anthologia Palatina*, and thus of the *Garland* of Meleager of Gadara included in it, in A. S. F. Gow and D. L. Page, *The Greek Anthology. Hellenistic Epigrams*, 2 vols (Cambridge, 1965). This is supplemented by the same editors' *The Garland of Philip and Some Contemporary Epigrams* (Cambridge, 1968) and *Further Greek Epigrams*, ed. D. L Page (Cambridge, 1981).

22 SPECIALIST PROSE AND RHETORIC

Still indispensable for an understanding of post-Classical prose literature is E. Norden, *Die Antike Kunstprosa* (Leipzig, 1909; repr. Darmstadt, 1958). On the problem of Atticism, see A. Dihle, *Analogie und Attizismus* (Hermes 38, 1957); D. Matthes (ed.) *Hermagoras* (Leipzig, 1962); L. Radermacher (ed.) *Demetrius De Elocutione* (Leipzig, 1901). On Hellenistic science, see bibliographies to Chapters 5 and 9, also H. von Staden, *Herophilos: the Art of Medicine in Early Alexandria* (Cambridge, 1989). A good initial guide to ancient philology, in particular a picture of its role in the preservation and transmission of Greek literature, is provided by R. Pfeiffer, *A History of Classical Scholarship from the Beginnings to the End of the Hellenistic Age* (Oxford, 1968); and L. D. Reynolds and N. G. Wilson, *Scribes and Scholars* (3rd edn, Oxford, 1991).

23 HISTORIOGRAPHY AND GEOGRAPHY

The collections of fragments in F. Jacoby, *Die Fragmente der griechischen Historiker* (Leiden, 1923–) are indispensable; Part Three, unfortunately left without commentary, includes the ethnographers. On specific authors and passages, see L. Pearson, *The Lost Histories of Alexander the Great* (New York, 1960); F. Jacoby, *Atthis* (Oxford, 1949); and E. Schwarts, *Griechische Geschichtsschreiber* (Berlin, 1957). *Polybius*, ed. T. Büttner-Wobst, 5 vols (Leipzig, 1899–); translation in W. R. Paton (ed.) (Loeb, 1922–7); F. W. Walbank, *A Historical Commentary on Polybius*, 1–3 (Oxford, 1957–79). On Polybius' assessment of the Roman state, see K. von Fritz, *The Theory of Mixed Constitution in Antiquity* (New York, 1954). On Posidonius, see bibliography for Chapter 16. For geography and ethnography, see bibliography for Chapter 5, and also H. J. Mette, *Pytheas von Massilia* (Berlin, 1952); D. R. Dicks, *The Geographical Fragments of Hipparchus* (London, 1960) which has the best introduction to mathematical geography in Hellenism. All texts are in C. Müller, *Geographi Graeci Minores*, 3 vols (Paris, 1852). On ethnography, see A. Dihle, *Zur hellenistischen Ethnographie* (Entretiens Fondation Hardt, Geneva, 1961), and A. Zambrini, *Annali della Scuola Normale di Pisa* 12 (Pisa, 1982) and 15 (Pisa, 1985) with the incorporation of Megasthenes in the tradition of Greek ethnography.

24 ENTERTAINMENT LITERATURE

On Greek novels, see N. Holzberg, *Der antike Roman* (Munich, 1986); T. Hägg, *The Novel in Antiquity* (Berkeley, 1983); B. E. Perry, *The Ancient Romances: a Literary-historical Account of their Origins* (Berkeley, 1967). See also R. Merkelbach, *Die Quellen des griechischen Alexanderromans* (Munich, 1954); *Chariton*, ed. W. E. Blake (Oxford, 1938). Fragments of Heraclides are in F. Pfister, *Die Reisebilder des Herakleides Kritikos* (Vienna, 1951). The paradoxographers are in *Rerum naturalium scriptores*, ed. O. Keller, vol. I (Leipzig, 1877). *Parthenius* with English translation in the Loeb by S. Gaselee (London, 1929); with Longus, *Daphnis and Chloe*, trans. G. Thornley, rev. J. M. Edmonds. All of Greek epistolography with Latin translations in

R. Hercher, *Epistolographi Graeci* (Paris, n.d.). A seminal account of memoir literature is G. Misch, *History of Autobiography in Antiquity* (London, 1950). Various aspects of biographical literature are stressed in A. Momigliano, *The Development of Greek Biography* (Cambridge, Mass., 1971); *Second Thoughts on Greek Biography* (Amsterdam, 1971); and A. Dihle, *Die Entstehung der historischen Biographie* (Heidelberg, 1986).

25 JEWISH LITERATURE

The best treatment of the whole topic, with full bibliography, is in the relevant sections of W. D. Davies and Louis Finkelstein (eds), *The Cambridge History of Judaism, 2: The Hellenistic Age* (Cambridge, 1990). A good collection of relevant writings in English translation, with short introductions, is J. H. Charlesworth (ed.) *The Pseudepigrapha of the Old Testament*, 2 vols (Garden City, NY, 1983–5). There is a short introduction to particular works, with extensive bibliography, in O. Eissfeldt, *The Old Testament: An Introduction* (New York and Oxford, 1965). For the historical background, see also M. Hengel, *Judaism and Hellenism* (London, 1974), and *Jews, Greeks and Barbarians* (Philadelphia, 1980).

INDEX

5809306R00189

Printed in Great Britain
by Amazon.co.uk, Ltd.,
Marston Gate.